Peter Norton's
Windows NT™ Tips and Tricks

Peter Norton's

Windows NT™
Tips and Tricks

Peter Norton
and
Peter Kent

RANDOM HOUSE
ELECTRONIC PUBLISHING

New York

Peter Norton's Windows NT Tips and Tricks

Published in the United States by Random House, Inc., New York, and simultaneously in Canada by Random House of Canada, Limited.

Produced and composed by Parker-Fields Typesetters, Ltd.

Manufactured in the United States of America

First Edition

0   9   8   7   6   5   4   3   2   1

ISBN 0-679-79200-7

The author and publisher have used their best efforts in preparing this book, and the programs contained herein. However, the author and publisher make no warranties of any kind, express or implied, with regard to the documentation or programs contained in this book, and specifically disclaim without limitation, any implied warranties of merchantability and fitness for a particular purpose with respect to program listings in the book and/or the techniques described in the book. In no event shall the author or publisher be responsible or liable for any loss of profit or any other commercial damages, including but not limited to special, incidental, consequential or any other damages in connection with or arising out of furnishing, performance, or use of this book or the programs.

Trademarks
A number of entered words in which we have reason to believe trademark, service mark, or other proprietary rights may exist have been designated as such by use of initial capitalization. However, no attempt has been made to designate as trademarks or service marks all personal computer words or terms in which proprietary rights might exist. The inclusion, exclusion or definition of a word or term is not intended to affect, or to express any judgment on, the validity or legal status of any proprietary right which may be claimed in that word or term.

New York   Toronto   London   Sydney   Auckland

Contents

Introduction   xv

1 What Is Windows NT?   1

So What's New About NT?   3
  A Graphical User Interface   4
  Compatibility with Other Operating Systems   5
  Multitasking and Multiprocessing   7
  Reliability   8
  System Security   9
  Portability   9
  Extensibility   10
  NTFS — An Advanced File System   11
  Performance   11
  Integrated Networking   11
The User Interface   13
What Machines Will Run NT?   14

2 Preparing for Windows NT   17

Multiple Operating Systems   17
  Missing Hardware Drivers?   18
  Missing Software Drivers?   19
NTFS vs. FAT vs. HPFS   19
  Which Do You Choose?   21
Where Do You Put NT?   21
MS-DOS and OS/2?   22
Designating an Administrator   23
  Important—Don't Lose Your Password!   23
  Who Does What?   25

What Next? 26
    Hardware Requirements 27

3 Installing and Starting Windows NT 29

Beginning Installation 30
    Starting from Floppies 31
    Starting from a SCSI CD-ROM 31
    Starting from a Network or Non-SCSI CD-ROM Drive 31
Installing NT— First Phase 32
Installing NT— NT Setup Phase 34
    Installing NT from a Network 38
Logging On 39
Leaving NT 41
Starting NT 42
    Warning and Error Messages 43
    The Guest Account — A Trojan Horse 43
    Stop Access to Registry Editor 43
    Modifying Flexboot 44
    Bypassing the Logon Procedure 45
    The Boot Files 45
Future Changes — Using Windows NT Setup 46
    Removing User Profiles 47
Converting File Formats 47
    Removing the Other Operating System 47
    Converting to NTFS 47
    Converting from NTFS to Another Operating System 48
    Removing NT 48
Recovering from Problems 49
    Last Known Good Configuration 49
    Using the Emergency Recovery Disk 50
Reinstalling NT 52

4 Program Manager 53

Creating Program Groups 56
Hidden Applications 56
Ctrl-Alt-Del — Windows NT Security 58
Starting Applications and Multitasking 60
    Starting Applications from Task List 61
Limiting Access to Features 61
Jumping to Program Manager 63
Program Manager's Menu Options 63

5 User Manager 65

Using User Manager 67
    Creating Groups 68
More About Groups 70

Rights vs. Built-in Abilities   71
Creating User Accounts   72
Copying User Accounts   77
Modifying Information and Deleting   77
Forgotten Passwords   79
Assigning Rights to Users   79
Changing Account (Password) Policies   82
Auditing Security Events   84
Assigning Permissions to Files and Directories   85
"Disabling" User Management   85
User Manager's Menu   85

6   Control Panel   87

Fonts   88
Ports   89
Mouse   89
System   89
Virtual Memory   91
Multitasking   92
Date/Time   93
Cursors   94
Sound   95
Services   95
Startup Options   97
A Word About Accounts   98
Devices   99
UPS   100
Testing the UPS   103
Fast Access To Control Panel Dialog Boxes   103

7   File Manager   105

The Menus and Toolbar   105
Customizing the Toolbar   106
Finally, Long File and Directory Names!   108
Viewing File Properties   110
File Manager's Security Options   111
Owning Files and Directories   112
Defining Access Permissions   113
Assigning Permissions   117
A Few Guidelines   119
File and Directory Auditing   120
Deactivating File Access Security   121
Sharing Data on a Network   121
Sharing Directories   121
Checking on File Use   123
Ending Network Sharing   124

Accessing Data on a Network   124
   Disconnecting a Network Drive   126
Associating Document Files   126
A Few More Features   128
File Manager's Menu Options   129

8   Print Manager   133

"Creating" Printers   135
   Printer Details   137
   Changing Job Defaults   139
   Working with Halftones   140
   Printer Settings   142
   Loading the Printer Driver   143
Entering Printer Setup Information   143
Creating Separator Files   144
Working with Forms   146
Printer Security   147
   Setting Permissions   147
   Taking Ownership   148
   Auditing Printing   148
Networking Printers   149
   Connecting to a Printer   149
   Sharing Printers   149
   Using Server Viewer   150
Printing   150
Modifying Printer Profiles   154
The Menu Options   154

9   Command Prompt   157

Command Types   158
The NT Command Set   159
Using the Command Prompt Window   165
   NTFS Limitations   165
   Using Doskey   166
Modifying the Command Prompt Window   172
   Changing Fonts   172
   Display Options and Terminating   173
   Changing Screen Size and Position   174
   Selecting Screen Colors   175
   Changing the Display Mode   175
Creating a Home Directory   176
Creating Different Command Prompt Windows   176
Copying Data Between Windows   176
The Help System   177
Error Messages   178
The Command List   179

OS/2 CONFIG.SYS Commands 188
TCP/IP Utility Commands 188
Command Symbols 189

10 Working with Non-NT Programs 191

Running Windows 3.1 Programs 192
Running MS-DOS Applications 192
The CONFIG.NT Commands 194
Using PIFs (Program Information Files) 194
Defining Custom Startup Files 198
Compatible Timer Hardware Emulation 199
Running OS/2 Programs 200
Modifying the OS/2 Configuration 200
The OS/2 CONFIG.SYS Commands 200
Starting Programs 201
Cutting and Pasting with the Command Prompt Window 202

11 System Configuration 203

System Security 203
The Configuration Structure 204
Configuration Registry Editor 204
HKEY_USERS 206
HKEY_CURRENT_USER 206
HKEY_LOCAL_MACHINE 206
HKEY_CLASSES_ROOT 207
Working with Registry Editor 207
Advanced Operations 209
The Menu Options 210

12 Performance Monitor 213

Starting Performance Monitor 214
Creating a Chart 216
Modifying the Chart 219
Working with Alerts 221
Customizing Alerts 223
The Report Window 224
Recording Data in the Log Window 225
Entering Bookmarks 227
Using Saved Data 228
Splitting Log Files (Relogging) 229
Saving and Reusing Settings 230
Exporting Data 230
Customizing the Window 231
The Menus and Toolbar 232

13 Event Viewer 235

Setting Up Logging 236
    What Will Be Logged? 237
    User Manager 237
    File Manager 238
    Print Manager 239
    ClipBook Viewer 239
    Registry Editor 240
Using Event Viewer 240
Arranging the Data 244
Setting Event Viewer Preferences 245
Saving Data 246
Clearing Logs 247
Logging Another Computer 247
The Menu Options 247

14 Disk Administrator 249

Deleting a Partition 250
Configuring a Disk 250
    Creating a Primary Partition 251
    Creating an Extended Partition 251
    Creating Logical Drives 252
Creating and Extending Volume Sets 252
Creating Stripe Sets 252
Completing Your Changes 253
    Formatting the Disk 253
Assigning Drive Letters 254
Marking a Volume as Active 254
Saving and Restoring Configurations 254
Customizing Disk Administrator 255
Mirror Sets and Windows NT Advanced Server 256
The Menu Options 257

15 Managing Your Network 259

Installing Your Network 260
    Installing Network Software 261
    Modifying Network Search Order 262
    Configuring Software Components 262
    Joining a Domain or Workgroup 263
    Viewing Network Bindings 264
Acting as a Server 265
    Providing System Resources 266
Controlling Server Connections 266
    Viewing Resource Use 268
Using Directory Replication 271
Managing Alerts 273

Managing a Workstation   273
More Network Utilities   274

16   Network Utilities — Mail   275

Setting Up Mail   275
  Adding Mail Terminals   277
  Adding Mail Accounts   278
  Opening Windows NT Mail   278
  Using the Address Book   280
  Sending Messages   281
  Embedding and Attaching Data   284
  Reading and Replying   284
  Organizing Messages   286
  Saving Messages and Attached Data   288
  Creating "Mailing Lists"   291
  Searching for Messages   291
  Printing Messages   292
  Selecting Mail Options   293
  Administering the Post Office   294
  Moving and Renaming the Postoffice   294
Closing Mail   295
The Menu Options   295

17   Network Utilities — Schedule+   299

Starting Schedule+   299
Working with Appointments   300
  The Appointment Dialog Box   301
  Entering Appointments Directly   305
  The Reminder   307
  Deleting Appointments   308
  Recurring Appointments   308
Using the Planner   309
Using the Task List   311
  Using Projects   312
  Recurring Tasks   312
  Selecting the View   313
  Working in the List   313
  Missing Tasks   314
  Assigning Time to Tasks   314
Letting Others Use Your Data   314
  Selecting an Assistant   316
Using Other People's Data   316
Setting up "Resources"   316
Online vs. Offline   317
  Taking Your Data with You   318
Printing Reports   319

Archiving Schedule+ Data 321
Working with Other Scheduling Programs 322
Adjusting Display Colors and Font 323
Setting Default Options 324
Close Schedule+ — But Continue Seeing Reminders 325
The Schedule+ Menu Options 326

18 Network Utilities — Chat and ClipBook Viewer 331

Chat 331
ClipBook Viewer 334
    Copying to and from the ClipBook 335
Sharing Your Data 336
    Connecting to Another ClipBook 337
    OLE and ClipBook 338
    ClipBook Viewer Security 338
    ClipBook's Menu Options and Toolbar 338

19 Tape Backup 341

Preparing the Hardware 342
    Installing the Driver 342
Initializing Backup 343
Backing Up a Hard Drive 344
Restoring Data 350
Tape Utilities 351
Unattended and Automated Backups 352
The Menu Options 354
The Toolbar Buttons 356

20 Neat Stuff — Multimedia and Games 357

CD Player 357
    Playlists 359
    Viewing Information 359
Volume Control 360
Media Player 360
    Playing the Device 361
    Modifying the Scale 362
    Marking Selections 362
    Media Player and OLE 363
    Configuring Media Player 364
    Configuring the Device 365
    The Menu Options 365
Sound Recorder 366
FreeCell 367
QBASIC Games—Gorilla and Nibbles 370

21 Finding More Information 373

What's Inside NT? 373
CompuServe 373
    CompuServe Navigators 375
Microsoft Seminars and Training 376
Microsoft TechNet 376
Installation Questions 376

22 Improving Windows NT 377

Microsoft Windows NT Shareware Contest 377
Control Panel Upgrade—Desktop+ 379
Open a Command Prompt Window—FM Shell 380
File Manager Utilities—FExtend 380
Drag 'n' Drop Utilities— clySmic Software 381
Drag-and-Drop Viewing—File Viewer and LI 382
Exiting Windows NT—WinEXIT 383
Improved Command Prompt— 4DOS 384
Organizing Program Manager Icons—Icon Manager 384
Add Applications To Program Manager 385
Animated Cursors—ANI Make 385
A Software Observatory—Astronomy Lab 386
A Programmer's Editor—M-Edit 386
ASCII Files—Notebook 387
Talking Calculator—RCALC NT 388
Stopwatch, Talking Clock, and Astronomy Clock 388
System Tests—WinTach 389
Messages—While You Were Out 390
Screen Savers—Spooks and Melt 391
Klotz—A Tapcis-Like Game 392
Card Games—Thieves and Kings 392
Word Games—Bog NT and Hangman NT 393
Fractals—FracView NT 394
A Number Puzzle—Puzzle-8 NT 395
Desktop Music—MIDI JukeBox NT 395

Appendix   Applet Updates 397

Calendar 397
ClipBook Viewer (Clipboard in Windows 3.1) 398
Clock 398
Command Prompt (MS-DOS Prompt in Windows 3.1) 398
Control Panel 398
File Manager 398
Help 398
Media Player 401
Notepad 401
Object Packager 401

Paintbrush   401
PIF Editor   402
Print Manager   402
Recorder   402
Sound Recorder   402
Windows Setup   402

Index   403

Introduction

When you first open Windows NT, much of what you'll see will look very much like the Windows you are used to. Microsoft has maintained the general look and feel of Windows 3.1, while adding many features and modifying a few. If this book were to cover NT completely, it would be twice the size, so we've assumed that our readers understand basic Windows concepts—using dialog boxes, buttons, list boxes; sizing and moving windows; opening and closing applications, and so on. We've also avoided subjects that would normally be covered in a Windows 3.1 book. We don't explain how to use Windows Write, Calendar, or the MIDI Mapper, for instance.

Many people using Windows NT are already familiar with Windows 3.1. They've used it for a while, know what they need to know, and now need to learn what's *new* about NT. If you want to get to heart of the matter—to find out about NT-specific features—this is the book for you. Where we discuss File Manager, for instance, we are explaining the features in NT that are not present in Windows 3.1, such as the file- and directory-security system. We won't tell you how to copy and move files, for instance, because NT works in the same way that Windows 3.1 does. This book is not a substitute for a guide to Windows, it's a complement. If you need more information about features common to both Windows 3.1 and NT, take a look at *Peter Norton's User's Guide to Windows 3.1*. And for a quick summary of the changes made to the Windows "applets," see Appendix A.

Windows NT is the most recent entry in the Microsoft Windows "family" of "operating systems." We've used the term "operating systems" in quotation marks because most of the Windows family—Windows 3.1 and earlier versions, and Windows for Workgroups—are not true operating systems. They rely on DOS to provide many of the important features one normally expects from an operating system. Windows NT, however, *is* a true operating system, and an advanced one at that. We'll discuss exactly what that means in Chapter 1.

Windows NT also varies from Windows 3.1 in significant areas, some of which may at first glance be confusing. So here's a quick list of things to watch for:

How do you run the equivalent of autoexec.bat and config.sys files, to load drivers and so on? NT uses CONFIG.NT and AUTOEXEC.NT to configure your DOS environment. See Chapter 10.

Which file format should you use? NT lets you use the DOS FAT (File Allocation Table) system, HPFS (OS/2's High Performance File System), or NTFS (NT File System), but you should decide which you'll use *before* you install NT, and it may not be a simple decision (see Chapter 2). The new NTFS system lets you use 256-character names and assign user-privileges to files and directories, and is required if you want to use NT's file-security system.

How can you protect directories and data? One of NT's most important features is the ability to limit access to specified data files. See Chapter 7.

How can you limit users' access to certain commands and procedures? NT's User Manager lets an Administrator configure each user account, defining what each user may and may not do. Combined with File Manager's security features, this provides a powerful way to control user rights. See Chapter 5.

How do you add and configure printers? The Printers icon is still in the Control Panel, but it just opens an improved Print Manager. Now you'll do virtually all printer-related procedures from there (where, many people felt, they should have been in the first place!). See Chapter 8.

How do you create disk partitions? Windows NT has a graphical system called Disk Administrator which takes over from DOS's FDISK command. You can create and delete partitions, create volume sets and stripe sets, and assign drive letters. See Chapter 14.

Is there a command prompt? Yes, there's a familiar > prompt, which you can use to run DOS, OS/2, Windows 3.1, Windows NT, and POSIX programs. It uses MS-DOS 5.0 and LAN Manager 2.1 commands, and includes some new and enhanced commands. See Chapter 9.

How does NT handle networking? NT has networking capabilities built in—it's intended to be "network independent and network enabled." In other words, it's designed to work with just about any network in wide use today. You'll find several networking utilities that were originally in Windows for Workgroups—Chat, Mail, Schedule+, and ClipBook Viewer (see Chapters 16, 17, and 18). And File Manager has been modified to help you share your files and directories and connect to other systems (see Chapter 7). Control Panel now has three icons that are used to administer networking—Server, Services, and Networks (see Chapter 6).

How do you close Windows NT? There are two ways to "end" a Windows NT session. You can log off NT. This leaves NT running—if your computer is sharing data on a network, other computers will be able to continue working with your computer's files—but disables all features until a user logs back on by entering a valid username and password. You can also Shutdown NT. This logs you off, and then closes NT itself. This is what you will do when you want to turn off your computer or use a different operating system. See Chapter 3.

What other unusual features does this operating system contain? Lots. There's a tape-backup utility; a performance monitor that lets you store information about hundreds of different performance parameters; a UPS (uninterruptible power supply) interface; an "event" viewer that lets you view stored event logs and error messages; an interface for playing audio disks on your CD-ROM drive; and a Volume Control to control your sound board.

Before we start, a quick word about a stylistic shortcut you may be familiar with already, especially if you read our *User's Guide to Windows 3.1*. When we tell you to select a command from a menu, we are going to describe the command in this manner: *menuname|commandname*. We are not going to say "open the File menu and select the Shutdown option." Rather, we will say, "select File|Shutdown."

1

What Is Windows NT?

What is Windows NT? You've probably read that the Microsoft Windows NT operating system is the "portable, secure, 32-bit, preemptive multitasking member of the Microsoft Windows operating system family," or something similar. But what exactly does this mean? Well, let's start at the beginning with another question— what is an operating system?

A computer comprises two main parts: its hardware and its software. The software is the set of instructions that tells the hardware what you want to do, and the hardware simply carries out the software's instructions. But you might also think of the software as having two main functions. First, there's the part of the software that carries out the application itself—the software that manipulates your typed words, makes mathematical calculations, draws pictures, and so on. Then there's software that carries out more mundane tasks: acting as an intermediary, carrying instructions from the application software to the hardware. It arranges for data to be printed on a screen, transmitted through an I/O (Input/Output) port, saved on a hard disk, and so on. This intermediary software understands the language the hardware speaks, the language the software speaks, and, in effect, translates between the two.

It's quite possible to write a program that carries out both these tasks, one that has a real-world function (an application such as a word processor, for instance), and that talks directly to the hardware. That's the way computer software was written in the early days, but it's not very efficient, because it means that every software publisher has to spend enormous effort just to allow the application to talk to the computer hardware.

There's an easier way, of course. Create an *operating system* (OS), one program that can talk to software and hardware. Then write application programs that talk to the operating system. The operating system acts as an intermediary between the application programs and the hardware, translating messages between the two, as shown in Figure 1.1.

1

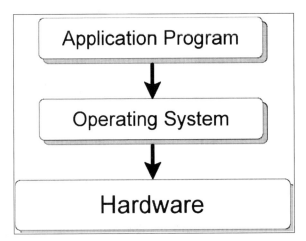

**Figure 1.1 The operating system mediates between
the application software and the hardware**

MS-DOS is the world's most popular operating system. (Perhaps we should say the world's most *used* operating system—we don't want to imply that it's the most loved.) It has provided a set of standards and a software/hardware intermediary that has allowed thousands of software developers to create tens of thousands of programs. Had each program required its own built-in operating system, we would have far fewer programs to choose from, and a more confusing, diverse computing industry.

Of course MS-DOS is not the world's most powerful operating system, and as computers get more powerful its limitations become more obvious. (That's not to say that MS-DOS is a bad operating system, by the way—its limitations were due to a great extent to the limitations of the hardware for which it was originally designed.) It doesn't handle graphics very well. It won't let you run several programs at the same time (DOS now has task switching, which lets you jump from one application to another, but only one application can run at a time). And, perhaps most irksome, it limits file names to a total of 11 characters, making it impossible to create sensible, recognizable names.

A number of programs have been created that try to improve on DOS, to *extend* DOS. Most importantly, Microsoft Windows provided a GUI (a graphical user interface), the ability to multitask applications—to run two or more at the same time—and added improved graphics functions. (To avoid confusion, throughout this book we will refer to Microsoft Windows as Windows 3.1. You may also see it referred to elsewhere as Win16 or 16-bit Windows.) You may have heard Windows 3.1 referred to as an operating system, though strictly speaking it's not, at least not quite. It requires DOS in order to run, so it's really an application program. Other application programs then use it as an intermediary between them and the operating system. However, it can bypass DOS in certain conditions—when writing to the hard disk and printing, for instance—so one might consider it to be almost (but not quite) an operating system (or, perhaps, a co-operating system). Figure 1.2 shows where Windows 3.1 fits into the puzzle.

Windows NT, unlike Windows 3.1, is a true operating system. It is an intermediary between your computer's hardware and your application software, requiring no other operating system between it and the hardware: Good-bye MS-DOS. But Windows NT is much more sophisticated than MS-DOS. The NT in its name refers to *new technology*, and it is.

So What's New About NT?

What, then, makes Windows NT so special? Lets summarize its most important features, and then look at each one in detail. Microsoft set out to design an operating system with the following features:

A graphical user interface

Compatibility with other operating systems

Capability of multitasking and multiprocessing

Reliability

Security

Portability to different hardware "platforms"

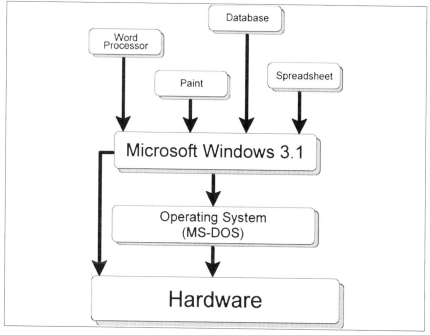

Figure 1.2 Windows 3.1 might be termed a "co-operating" system

Extensibility (upgradeability)

A new, advanced file system

High performance

Integrated networking

A Graphical User Interface

Windows NT is an operating system that uses a "graphical" user interface (a GUI, often pronounced "gooey"). DOS and UNIX, for example, have text-based user interfaces. To carry out procedures you type command names. A GUI, on the other hand, uses graphical "elements" to represent commands—icons, buttons, menu bars, and so on. Instead of typing commands, you can work with these elements—usually using a mouse, though often using keyboard shortcuts—to carry out the various procedures.

For instance, let's say you want to format your hard disk partitions. In DOS you start by typing FDISK at the DOS prompt. You then see a list of options. Pressing the number associated with the option you want displays another list of options. You continue in this manner, typing the option numbers and partition sizes as needed. In Windows NT, FDISK is replaced by a program called Disk Administrator. To start Disk Administrator you will double-click on a small picture of a hard disk. A window opens, and displays a graphical representation (okay, a picture) of your hard disks' partitions. You can select options from the menu bar, and each option drops down a list of more options. Not only can you carry out the procedure for which Disk Administrator was intended—modifying partitions—but you can even adjust the way Disk Administrator appears. You can change the colors and patterns it uses to represent the different types of partitions, for instance. (Disk Administrator actually does more than FDISK. It also allows you to "mirror" disks and create "stripe" sets, for instance. But we're comparing *how* these programs do what they do, not what they actually do.)

In the example we've just looked at, it could be argued that the text-based operating system is more efficient than NT's GUI. You can certainly get to the commands much quicker in DOS than in NT. Indeed many "power users" have great disdain for GUIs, believing text-based systems to be quicker and more powerful. But the battle's over, graphical user interfaces have won, and for some very good reasons. While it's true that in many cases a knowledgeable user working in DOS, for example, can execute commands very quickly, most of us are not power users, and the GUI makes learning new programs and working infrequently with certain programs much easier. It also makes working with graphics inside applications much easier.

Also, while it's true that GUIs are a drag on a system's processor—just displaying all those pictures and colors takes a lot of processing time—the hardware is catching up with the software, and the processing energy spent running the GUI itself is becoming less important. Running Windows 3.1 on a 486 is a totally different experience from running an early version of Windows on a 286, for instance.

In the past, most computer users have worked with text-based operating systems—mainly DOS and UNIX, with the most notable exception being users of the Macintosh's operating system, the most popular GUI operating system to date. Outside the Mac world, GUIs were limited to applications running on text-based operating systems, applications such as Windows. Windows NT simply takes the GUI one step further, replacing the text-based system almost (but not quite) entirely. Although NT is primarily a GUI, its Command Prompt actually lets those of us wedded to the command line carry out a lot of procedures in a text mode.

Compatibility with Other Operating Systems

Windows NT has its own file system, NTFS (NT File System, of course). There are a variety of advantages to this new system, as we shall see in a moment, but NT is also capable of reading files stored under the FAT (File Allocation Table) system used by MS-DOS, HPFS (High Performance File System) used by OS/2, and POSIX (a "Portable Operating System Interface based on UniX"). Windows NT can not only read files created by these operating systems, but also run applications designed for them. Thus you can run Windows NT, Windows 3.1, DOS, OS/2, and even POSIX applications—POSIX may be thought of as the "lowest common denominator in the UNIX world." DEC is using the POSIX subsystem to transfer its X-Windows system to NT machines. (Currently Windows NT runs only OS/2 version 1.x character-based applications on computers with Intel processors, and not at all on RISC-based machines.)

In order to do this, Windows NT uses what are known as *environment subsystems*. At the heart is the *Win32 Subsystem*, which provides the user interface for Windows NT programs. When you run a Windows NT program, it talks to the Win32 Subsystem, which in turn talks with the *NT native services*, code that acts as a gateway to the rest of the operating system. When you want to run an application designed for another operating system, NT automatically opens another subsystem—the OS/2 Subsystem, the *virtual DOS machine* (VDM) Subsystem, or the POSIX subsystem. Windows 3.1 programs (16-bit Windows programs) and DOS programs run in the VDM. You may have heard statements from Microsoft saying that the VDM provides a perfect emulation of a DOS machine. In general this is true, but there's a very important feature lacking in this perfect machine—the VDM cannot get to the hardware. NT won't let any of its subsystems communicate with hardware directly. This may not matter in most cases, but there are cases where it means you simply can't use your software. Don't imagine, for instance, that a perfect copy of a DOS machine means you can use all your usual device drivers in a VDM—you can't, so you won't be able to run peripherals unless you also have an NT driver for that peripheral.

Support for Windows 3.1 programs is excellent, and in most cases you won't be able to see any way in which a Windows 3.1 program runs differently from a Windows NT program (except of course NT's 32-bit programs will be faster). Both types of Windows programs can use OLE (Object Linking and Embedding) and DDE (Dynamic Data Exchange), sharing data from programs of the other type. An NT word processor could import data from a Windows 3.1 spreadsheet, for instance. Windows 3.1 programs will usually run a little slower on NT than they do in Windows 3.1, however, though Microsoft claims they will run within 10% of their normal, Windows 3.1, speed. Incidentally, running Windows 3.1 programs in NT is sometimes referred to in NT-speak as WOW (16-bit Windows On Windows NT).

Each subsystem communicates with the NT native services, but it must also talk to the Win32 Subsystem, which provides video output. Subsystems are not seen or controlled by the user, by the way; it appears that Windows NT runs the programs directly. The situation is summed up in Figure 1.3.

Note What about "backward compatibility"—running NT programs in Windows 3.1? Yes, it can be done. The Win32 Software Development Kit includes "Win32s," a library of DLLs and a virtual device driver that lets NT applications run in 3.1. Companies developing new software will ship the Win32s with their NT programs, so buyers can install them on either type of machine.

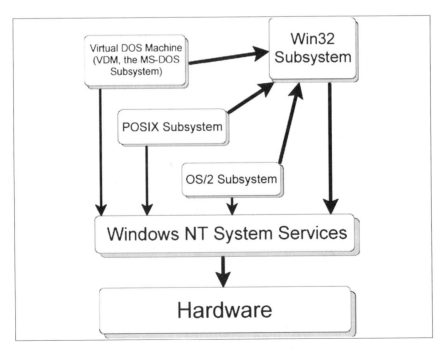

Figure 1.3 NT's environment subsystems run non-NT programs

Multitasking and Multiprocessing

Windows NT is capable of both multitasking and multiprocessing. Multitasking is the ability to share a single processor among several different processes (threads, as they're called in NT). A processor can only execute one thread at a time, so multitasking shares processing time among the various threads. Multitasking is important from the user's point of view, because it allows you to do more than one thing at a time—print a document while you work on another one, search a large database while you use your phone-book program to auto-dial a telephone number, and so on. Even Windows 3.1 can multitask in a simple way. When multitasking is working well it appears that all the processes are occurring at the same time, though actually each process uses the microprocessor for a split second at a time, and then stops while the next process runs. (When multitasking isn't working well, processes slow down drastically, as anyone who's tried multitasking in Windows on a slow computer knows.)

Windows 3.1 uses what is known as *nonpreemptive multitasking*. This is a system in which a thread can use the processor as long as it wants—it must release control of the processor before any other thread can take control. Thus some programs, those not designed to multitask well, can slow others, or even the entire system. Windows NT uses *preemptive* multitasking, a much more efficient system which gives the operating system total control over multitasking. The OS can suspend a thread after a certain amount of time, or even interrupt the thread, if a thread with a higher priority appears. Preemptive multitasking allows NT to control thread execution smoothly, providing higher priority to areas—such as user input—that need it. You'll see that it's easier to continue working in NT, without noticing the application in which you are working slowing down. (Of course, if you are using NT you are probably using a fast machine that also handles multitasking in Windows 3.1 more easily, but still, you'll notice that NT does a better job.)

Windows NT is also a *symmetric multiprocessing* (SMP) operating system, one which can run several threads at the same time if it has access to multiple processors. This won't help most users for a while, as the vast majority of computers are single-processor machines. But multiprocessor machines are available, and will probably become more popular as Windows NT's popularity grows.

A machine capable of *symmetric* multiprocessing can use any available microprocessor for any thread. Unlike *asymmetric* multiprocessors—which run the operating system on one microprocessor and user jobs on others—symmetric microprocessors can run both operating system and user jobs anywhere, on any of the computers available processors.

Furthermore, Windows NT can also multitask and multiprocess at the same time. If it has more threads pending than available microprocessors, it can multitask threads on several processors at once.

These are capabilities that most desktop computers can't use—the 386, 486, or Pentium-based computer sitting in your office won't use symmetric processing. Even some servers with multiple processors don't use symmetric processing—they use asymmetric processing instead.

But machines are in the works which will. Even before NT was released, NCR had demonstrated NT on a RISC (Reduced Instruction Set Computing) 8-processor machine, and Sequent ran it on a 16-processor computer. Low-cost machines that use symmetric processing will soon be available.

Reliability

Microsoft made reliability a key design goal for Windows NT. They wanted the system to act predictably when encountering software and hardware errors, and they wanted it to protect data and programs from damage caused by problems. Windows NT uses *structured exception handling* to respond to errors. An extensive system of exception-handling code, program areas that respond to *exceptions* (errors), was built into NT to watch for exceptions and protect the system, applications, and data whenever a problem arises. NT also uses *termination handlers* to take over from code that has terminated unexpectedly, freeing resources that might otherwise remain locked up.

In addition, NT's file system, NTFS, is designed to recover from disk errors, and to store data in a manner that will allow it to be recovered even if disk errors occur. It uses *transaction logging* to record information about data being copied to a disk. *Checkpoints* are copied into a transaction log every few seconds, so if the system crashes or power is lost, NT can recover the next time it boots. And NT's *Virtual Memory Manager* retains absolute control over memory allocation, limiting programs from getting to memory locations used by other programs. No application can access memory directly, so when one application crashes or tries to use an area of memory that it shouldn't, it won't bring down other programs.

NT uses *desynchronized input queues*. In Windows 3.1 all user input to an application is placed in a single, *synchronized* queue, and each application has to collect the input from the queue. If one application fails to collect the input correctly, or collects input too soon, taking another application's input, *all* applications are affected—the system appears to lock up because none of the programs knows what to do. NT's desynchronized queues make sure this can't happen, because each application has its own queue.

When you use NT you will find that it is clearly much more reliable than Windows 3.1. While Windows 3.1 often crashed—one application would stop all others from working—that doesn't happen in NT. If an application freezes you can usually swap to another, using the Alt-Tab, Alt-Esc, or Ctrl-Esc methods. If you display the Task List dialog box (Ctrl-Esc) you can close the frozen application using the End Task button. In some cases a frozen application might even lock up application switching—the Alt-Tab, Alt-Esc, and Ctrl-Esc methods are not available. But as a last resort you can always press Ctrl-Alt-Del. NT will stop all applications and display a special panel, from which you can view the Task List dialog box and close the offending application.

System Security

Windows NT uses a sophisticated method for providing system security, a procedure that allows NT to comply with the U.S. Government's Class C2 security requirements. An *object manager* is used to control all system resources that need to be shared, protected, named, or displayed to user programs. The user-interface portion of the security code prompts the user to enter a password when logging on. Once the password has been entered, object manager can determine exactly which resources will be available to that user. Unlike many add-on security systems for the PC, there is no way to bypass object manager—it's an integral part of the operating system's code, and it has absolute control over access to system resources.

NT's security features include User Manager, a utility that lets a computer's Administrator assign user rights and deny access to other users, and a File Manager system for allowing and denying access to individual files and directories. However, these File Manager features are only available on NTFS partitions. If you have a computer with some non-NTFS partitions, the files and directories on those partitions cannot be protected.

NT's security features include *discretionary access control* (the resource's owner determines who may use it), *authentication* (a password is required to access resources), *accountability* (NT can log security events, keeping a record of who does what with system resources), and *access control lists* (ACLs—each object is assigned a list of protections when it is created, saying who may use the object and how).

Although these security features might be considered a great strength, many users may find them more of a headache than anything—and some in the industry have even said that the hassle of these security features could even deter people from using NT. Perhaps only 1 or 2% of all users are required to meet C2 security standards, and though many others will want to use the same features, many won't. That's not a problem—if you don't want to use security, you can, in effect, deactivate it and never have to work with it. There's even a shareware program available—Desktop+—which deactivates the logon procedure, so you can open NT as easily as opening Windows 3.1, without having to enter an account name or password. (See Chapter 22 for information about Desktop+.)

Portability

One of the most talked about features of Windows NT is its *portability*. While most users of NT will initially be personal computer users, NT is intended for use on a wide variety of platforms. NT was designed to be easily transferred to machines using 32-bit linear addressing and virtual memory capabilities. The initial release can also be used on workstations with the MIPS R4000 processor.

NT was written mostly in C and C++, programming languages that can be used on many different computers. The code written in assembly language—a nonportable language—was restricted to those areas that required it, such as parts of the program that must communicate with the hardware, and in some areas where it is used to speed processing. Thus, to "port" NT to other platforms, the areas using assembly language must be rewritten—a relatively minor job, as those areas were kept isolated.

In fact NT was designed to isolate all areas of the code that are platform-dependent, areas which must be rewritten in order to run the operating system on a different platform (processor). It uses something called the hardware abstraction level (HAL), a dynamic link library which "liases" between the NT kernel (the code that performs low-level operating system functions) and the hardware. Putting NT on another type of hardware requires that the HAL is modified. So porting to another system means rewriting the few areas that will not run on the other computer, and then recompiling. You can expect to see NT running on a number of other computers very soon.

Extensibility

Windows NT was also designed to be *extensible* (to use NT-speak; upgradeable to most of us). Microsoft wanted to ensure that NT could be quickly adapted to handle new technologies as they became available. They wanted to be able to easily modify NT to interface with new hardware devices, new networks, new software technologies and environments.

NT has a modular structure, in which different processes are carried out by different software modules, acting together through interfaces—new modules can be added easily to accommodate new requirements. Furthermore, system resources are treated as discrete objects—as we saw when we looked at the security system. New objects can be added without affecting existing objects.

Most importantly, NT uses a system by which an *executive*, the core of the operating system, interacts with *protected subsystems*, which provide more advanced operating-system facilities than the executive. Subsystems can be added and modified without making major changes to the executive.

There's much more to Windows NT than we've discussed here. Microsoft sees this as a product that will constantly evolve. Microsoft plans to ship a Japanese version called Windows NT-J within six months of the initial release. That's not a simple matter, as Japanese characters require a double-byte coding system. Windows NT-J will also be available on the NEC 9800-based personal computer, a non-AT-compatible machine. NT's security system is still evolving also, and Microsoft expects NT to be hooked up to bank teller machines, retinal scanners, and fingerprint scanners, and to include other security features such as U.S. Government Class B security and the Kerberos security system. If you are interested in a detailed description of how NT does what it does, and what it's likely to do in the future, see *Inside Windows NT* by Helen Custer.

NTFS—An Advanced File System

As you've already seen, the NTFS (NT file system) makes many of NT's other features possible—security and reliability in particular. It also supports very large disks and files—up to 17 billion gigabytes, surely enough for the next year or two. NTFS also allows long filenames—up to 256 characters, including spaces and many characters not allowed in DOS filenames, and multiple extensions, each one separated by a period. (`This could be a filename.yes.it.really. could.`) To maintain compatibility, though, each file is also automatically provided with a DOS-style filename (an "8.3" name, with eight characters, a period, and three characters in the extension). Then Windows 3.1 applications can use the file, for instance.

Less noticeable to most people will be *Unicode*, developed by Microsoft to make computing truly international. Unicode is a system that can contain up to 65,536 distinct characters, enough, Microsoft claims, for every character in use in every language in the world, including punctuation, mathematical symbols, and "dingbats" (small drawings). This will make translations between languages easier. Transferring documents between computers using different languages will no longer garble the text.

Performance

Last, but by no means least, is performance. Microsoft wanted Windows NT to work very quickly, to run Windows 3.1 and DOS programs as quickly as they would run in Windows 3.1, and to run 32-bit Windows NT programs even faster. (By April of 1993 Microsoft had backed off the "as fast as Windows 3.1" claim a little, and stated that Windows 3.1 applications would run in NT within 10% of their normal speed.) Many users are switching to NT mainly for the performance—CAD (Computer Aided Design) users, for instance, have been looking forward to NT for a couple of years now, hoping that it would handle CAD's processor-intensive workload more effectively.

Microsoft used a variety of techniques to give NT its performance. It included a *local procedure call system* to speed messaging between subsystems, built networking components into the privileged portion, or core, of the operating system, and performance-tested critical components with an eye to increasing speed. And NT's advanced memory management also lets programs access memory quickly and efficiently.

Integrated Networking

Unlike most operating systems—which were developed with a single machine in mind, and have to be adapted with special drivers to link to other computers—NT was designed with networking in mind. If you've ever worked on a **DOS** network you're likely to have run into problems with "conflicts"—cases in which networking software imposed on top of the operating system interferes with your application programs, causing problems with certain features or perhaps even stopping some applications altogether. NT, however, doesn't have these problems because the networking software is an integral part of the operating system.

Certainly you can't simply plug in a network card and expect it to work—there are too many different cards, too many network protocols for that to happen. But NT has networking code ready to run, with a few "gaps" into which you will "plug" the correct software drivers (the code that tells NT how to work with a specific card and a specific protocol). Once these gaps have been plugged, NT can let your computer operate as a *client* or *workstation*—using files, directories, and printers on other computers on the network—and as a *server*—letting other computers use its own files, directories, and printers. You can even run your computer as a workstation and server at the same time.

Windows NT contains a "superset" of Windows for Workgroups features. You can use File Manager to determine which of your files and directories will be available to whom, and what may be done with them—some users will have full access, others will be able to read files but not modify them. You can use Mail to send electronic mail, Chat to "talk" in real time with other network users, Schedule+ to schedule an entire workgroup's appointments. You can share printers, share Clipboard data, and monitor the hardware and software performance of other computers on the network. All this is ready to run in Windows NT. In fact, if you already have a Microsoft Windows for Workgroups network, all you need to do to add an NT workstation to the network is install a network card and install the drivers. Even if you are running NT as an NTFS machine, you can still access files on the other computers, and the other computers can use the files on both your NTFS and FAT disks.

Microsoft aimed to create an operating system that is both "network enabled," one that is well suited to running on a network, and "network independent," one that will run on virtually any network in use today (and, they plan, tomorrow).

Windows NT Advanced Server

At the same time that Microsoft released NT, it also released an "add-on" product, Windows NT Advanced Server. This program provides advanced networking features, such as advanced fault-tolerance capabilities. It gives large organizations a secure and reliable server, providing applications such as database servers access to multiprocessor machines and high-performance processors. It has tools that make network management easy, and provides a "domain," a system by which a user can log onto the network, and then use system resources without logging on each time he wants to use a resource on a different server.

With Advanced Server you can use *file replication* (the automatic copying of files and entire directories between networked computers, so if the data is lost from one computer it is still available on another); *disk mirroring* (writing the same data to two disk drives at the same time, so if one disk drive fails the data can be recovered from the other); *disk duplexing* (like disk mirroring, except that the disks must be on separate controller boards, providing another level of reliability), and *disk striping with parity*, also known as *RAID5* (using partitions on different disk drives to create one "logical" drive—data is written across these stripes, and, thanks to parity checks, if one area fails the logical drive can automatically recover). Windows NT itself has a limited form of disk striping, but not the parity striping used by Windows NT Advanced Server. (This book is about Windows NT itself, and does not cover NT Advanced Server.)

The User Interface

Windows NT is more than simply a programmer's toy. What's in it for you, the user? What can it actually do for you? Here's a rundown of what you'll find in Windows NT:

Password security	Users enter passwords to log onto the machine. Without a password the user cannot access any programs. (If you prefer not to use it, though, the password feature can be disabled in several ways.)
Program Manager	The familiar Program Manager, used to launch programs.
User Manager	A system that allows an Administrator to define what each user may be allowed to do. If several people use a computer, you can give each one different rights, allowing some users to change the system time, for example, but not others.
File security features	Different users can have different file- and directory-access rights. You can ensure that some users cannot get into certain directories or run certain applications, or can only read—but not modify—certain files.
Networking features	Built-in networking features, such as client and server capabilities, the ability to view who is using what resources on your computer, and the ability to define which resources—files, directories, and printers—other users may work with.
Disk Administrator	A disk-management system which lets you create, delete, and modify partitions, set up disk volume sets and disk stripes, assign disk letters, and so on.
Event Logging and Event Viewer	A system that records significant security, system, and application events, and a utility in which you can view an event log.

UPS interface	A built-in interface to a smart UPS (uninterruptible power supply), which can accept signals from the UPS telling it of a power shutdown and informing it of the UPS battery-power level.
Performance Monitor	A utility that displays and records data about system performance, such as disk and processor use.
Tape Backup	A SCSI and QIC-compatible tape-backup utility.
Advanced Printer Control	An enhanced Print Manager, which lets you configure printer drivers in various ways, such as defining printer pools, printing separator pages, and locking drivers at certain times of the day.
NT File System	A new file system that allows long file and directory names, and system security features.

What Machines Will Run NT?

It seems likely that for the first year or two of NT's life it will be installed mostly on IBM-compatible PCs—486-based and Pentium-based computers. But that may not be the way things continue. Before NT was even released the computer press was examining non-Intel-based machines that could run NT, and run it much faster. As the prices of these machines drop, we may see more and more NT installations on real workstations, the sorts of machines that can take advantage of this operating system's New Technology.

The secret is in NT's symmetric multiprocessing and multithreaded multitasking, important features which a PC can't use. Machines such as the NCR Panther (around $10,000), the Wyse 7000i series ($16,000 to $22,000), and RISC (reduced instruction-set computing) machines using the Mips 4000 chip *can* use these features, and do so to great advantage. These machines can run NT two or three times quicker than the fastest PCs. And RISC clone-builders are getting in on the act. DeskStation, for instance, announced R4000 machines with close-to-Intel-PC prices before NT was even released—a DeskStation rPC 401e/50, with a 50 Mhz R4000 chip was priced at $3995.

Some industry analysts are predicting that we're seeing the end of the familiar PC, as these more advanced workstations drop in price and users' expectations rise. But the PC itself will change too. Hardware manufacturers are planning a new use for the Overdrive upgrade socket. While the socket has been used to allow an upgrade to a newer CPU—adding a 486 chip to a 386 machine, for instance, disabling the 386 chip—some new Pentium-based machines will come with an upgrade socket that lets you add another Pentium chip, turning the machine into a multiprocessor computer.

All these features let you use a computer in several different ways: as a stand-alone workstation, as a networked workstation, or as a network server. As a workstation, NT provides excellent performance, along with many useful features such as system security. As a networked workstation, NT provides simple access to networked resources through File Manager and Print Manager. And, as a server, it allows other computers on the network to access the computer's files, directories, and printers.

Windows NT may not be entirely New Technology—many of the ideas we see in NT were borrowed from other operating systems. The NT team was led by Dave Cutler, who had worked at DEC developing operating systems such as VAX/VMS, and Microsoft licensed and studied the Carnegie-Mellon's MACH system to get ideas for NT. But its name is valid in the sense that it is a completely new operating system for the masses, intended for a wide variety of platforms and likely to be found on millions of computers within a relatively short time. Microsoft released over 55,000 copies of the final Windows NT beta release—mostly to paying customers. By April 1993, over 58 development tools were available for NT programmers, with another 200 on their way. When the computer business shows that much interest in a new product, its success is all but guaranteed.

Over 500 32-bit applications were announced at the 1992 COMDEX convention, more than 9 months before NT's final release. In April 1993 Microsoft estimated—based on a survey of beta sites—that within 12 months, over 2,000 32-bit NT applications would be available through retail channels. Another 6,000 or more would be released by large organizations for internal use. Clearly, a lot of businesses believe NT will be important to their future success.

2

Preparing for Windows NT

Before you load NT, you need to spend a little time thinking about how you are going to do so. You are not loading a program, remember, but an operating system, and you have several things to consider—whether you want to keep another operating system on your computer, for instance, and whether you want to use the NTFS file system, or stick with DOS' FAT system or OS/2's HPFS system.

Multiple Operating Systems

The most important decision you must make is whether you want to keep another operating system on your computer. You can have NT coexist with MS-DOS or OS/2 by having NT install a program called *Flexboot*—also known as *boot loader*—which lets you decide which operating system to boot each time you turn on your computer.

In many cases, the choice is simple. If you have a computer which is **used for only one task** such as a CAD workstation, and the program used for that task will run on NT, you don't need any other operating system. You can load NT directly onto the computer's hard disk, without any concern about which partition to load it onto. However, if there's already data on the hard disk, you should back it up, as NT will format the drive when you install. You can load your data back onto the disk afterward.

If **security** is of paramount concern, then you should use only NT. NT has extensive built-in security features that can only operate on disk partitions formatted with NTFS. If you use another operating system, the partition or partitions formatted with that file system will not be protected by NT.

17

If you are already running MS-DOS or OS/2 and have **existing programs you want to continue using**, you may want to keep that operating system on the computer. Why? Well, although NT can run DOS, Windows 3.1 and OS/2 programs, many people are naturally suspicious of a brand new product, and don't want to risk finding themselves in a situation in which they can't use a program or get to data they need. And the last beta before NT's release still had problems running some Windows 3.1 and DOS programs. While most of these problems were fixed for the final release, some may have slipped through. So why not leave the operating system where it is, and load NT in addition? After you've worked with NT for a few months, and are satisfied that it does what you need it to do, you can always remove the other operating system if you want.

Also, the current version of Windows NT does not run all **OS/2 programs**— only text-based OS/2 1.x programs. If you are running more recent programs, you will need to keep OS/2 installed.

Missing Hardware Drivers?

There's another reason to keep your old operating system. NT may not yet be able to use all the **hardware** that your old operating system does. Although thousands of drivers have already been created for NT, there are still some missing.

Check your NT documentation for the latest hardware-compatibility list, and if you can't find your hardware listed, check with the device's manufacturer. You'll find that SCSI devices and most printers will work fine in NT. Microsoft started by creating SCSI (Small Computer Standard Interface) drivers as a quick way to interface with lots of devices. Because SCSI is a recognized standard, and because there are already many devices that use the SCSI interface, all Microsoft had to do was interface with a handful of SCSI adapter cards to automatically interface with hundreds of different devices. (SCSI's going to become even more prevalent, as hardware manufacturers start putting SCSI adapters on computer motherboards. The Macintosh has had built-in SCSI support for a while now, and it won't be long before the PC world gets it, too.) But that means if you have a device that is non-SCSI, you may not be able to use it in NT. In particular, most non-SCSI **CD-ROM** drives won't run in NT at this time—you may be lucky and find that your drive's manufacturer has created proprietary drivers for its non-SCSI CD drives, but there's a good chance they haven't. Sony engineers, for instance, are currently creating NT drivers for their *new* range of non-SCSI CD drives, but those drivers won't work for existing Sony non-SCSI drives, and it may be a while before drivers are available for these devices—if ever.

Note   Even if you have a CD-ROM drive that is not supported by NT, you can still install NT from the CD. If you ever have to reinstall NT, however, you may not be able to do so from the CD. See Chapter 3 for more information.

As for **tape drives**, you may be lucky and find that your non-SCSI drive (most small-capacity drives—under 700 MB—are non-SCSI) can be connected to a SCSI adapter board's floppy-disk port. Colorado Memory's Jumbo range of tape drives (one of the most popular small-capacity drives) can be connected to a SCSI board and use the QIC-40/QIC-80 driver provided with Windows NT. See Chapter 19 for more information.

Missing Software Drivers?

Although NT can run most MS-DOS, OS/2 1.x, and POSIX applications, some may require special **device drivers** that are not available in NT. And some programs may try to **access the hardware directly**, which NT will not allow. Some MS-DOS disk utilities won't run in Windows NT because of this. Some applications that use **unofficial programming methods** on the other operating system may not run in Windows NT. You may want to leave another operating system on your computer if you have to **test applications** based on that system, to ensure total compatibility. And if you **write programs** for another operating system you will also want to retain that system on your computer.

Finally, MS-DOS-based **disk compression systems** won't currently work with Windows NT. For example, if you use Stacker, a product sold by Stac Electronics, you can't install NT on a "stacked" drive, and NT won't be able to access data on any stacked drive. You could unstack the drive and load it elsewhere, but you're probably short of disk space (which is why you stacked the drive!). Your only other option is to move data around, putting data you won't need while working in NT onto the compressed drive, and making sure the data you will need is on an uncompressed drive. Hopefully it won't be too long before there is some sort of disk-compression system available for NT. In fact, by the time you read this book, this may be a moot point, so check with the manufacturer of your compression system.

Shortly before NT was released, Microsoft released DOS 6.0, which also has a disk-compression system. Microsoft intends that NT *will* read drives compressed with this system, but the required software was not available when NT was released.

There is one way in which NT *can* read from a "stacked" or compressed drive, by the way—over a network. If you have NT on one computer, and a compressed drive on another computer to which the first is networked, NT will be able to read the data from the compressed drive. NT has no way to know what sort of drive it is, of course, and the network software makes the data available to any computer that is compatible with that network protocol.

NTFS vs. FAT vs. HPFS

When you install NT you'll have the option of selecting the file system. You can stick with FAT (File Allocation Table), the MS-DOS file system, with HPFS

(High Performance File System, if you are using OS/2), or use NT's own NTFS (NT File System). Even if you choose NTFS, NT will still be able to read and write HPFS and FAT files.

Of the three file systems, FAT is the most popular. Let's rephrase that: It's the most used. Because of the growth of PC use in the past decade, more computers use FAT than any other system, although it is a relatively primitive system. The most obvious shortcoming to the user is the 8.3 filename limitation (8-character name, 3-character extension), but it also has limited error-correction and file-attribute capabilities. HPFS—introduced with OS/2—is much more advanced than FAT, allowing long filenames, the ability to store more attribute information with each file, and some error-correction features.

NTFS is the most advanced of the three. It, too, allows long filenames and stores more attribute information, but has a much more sophisticated error-correction system, and built-in security features. Without NTFS, the security system we talked about in Chapter 1 *won't work*.

Let's look at NTFS's advantages:

Security: The ability to restrict access to files and directories. This only works in disk partitions formatted as NTFS.

Fault Tolerance: NTFS uses *transaction logging* to make sure that data is correctly copied to disk. If a problem occurs during a disk write, NT uses the transaction log to recover.

Disk mirroring: The ability to write the same data onto two disk drives at the same time. (This feature is only available on NT Advanced Server machines.)

Disk striping: The ability to combine partitions on different disk drives into one virtual partition. If one partition fails, the data can be recreated from the other partitions.

Long directory and filenames: Up to 256 characters, uppercase and lowercase, including spaces and many special characters, and multiple extensions. NT also provides each file with a short DOS name for compatibility with DOS and Windows 3.1 programs.

Multiple file systems: NTFS can read and write NTFS, FAT, and HPFS files.

There are, of course, disadvantages:

Long filenames: Applications created for MS-DOS or 16-bit Windows (Windows 3.1 or earlier) will remove the long filename and keep only the short DOS filename, negating the benefits of this feature.

No access to other operating systems: When you are running another operating system, it won't be able to access files on the NTFS partition. Other operating systems' programs can access the data only when running in NT.

Non-NT Floppy Disks: Windows NT only formats floppy disks in the FAT format—they can be used with NT, MS-DOS, and OS/2, but files copied onto these disks will lose their NT security attributes and long filenames.

Which Do You Choose?

So which do you choose? If NT will be the **only system** on your computer, you will probably want to use NTFS, if only for the long filenames and fault tolerance. (As wonderful as the other features are, many users simply won't need disk striping and file security.) NT still formats DOS disks, so you can copy data from NT to transfer to MS-DOS and OS/2 computers (OS/2 reads DOS).

If you decided to leave **another operating system** on your computer, you now have two choices: You can either use that operating system's file system, so that all files will be accessible from all operating systems, or you can put NT in a separate partition, format that partition as NTFS, and make sure that files you want to access from the other operating system will be on a non-NTFS partition.

If you want to make sure your NT data is **totally secure**, you should use NTFS. You'll be able to limit access to files, directories, programs, and so on. Remember, though, the data on non-NTFS drives will not be protected in any way. Not only will using another file system stop you from using NT's security features, but all files and directories will be accessible while running MS-DOS. If you use NTFS, other users won't be able to get to those files unless they have a valid account on the NTFS partition.

If you are on a **network**, and all the other systems are using NTFS, you should probably go with NTFS. If you have a stand-alone system, but one which **several people** will use, you may want NTFS, so you will be able to use the security system features which allow you to limit user access to files, directories, and system maintenance procedures.

Think carefully about your decision, because it's not easy to change later. You can convert a partition that doesn't have the NT system files relatively easily—assuming you have a quick way to back up all the data first—but in order to "convert" the partition containing the system files you'll have to reinstall.

Where Do You Put NT?

If NT is going to be the **only operating system** on your computer, you will put it in the system partition of your primary hard-disk drive, drive C:. If it's going to **coexist with another operating system**, you have several choices. First, if you plan to use the **same file system** as the other operating system—FAT or HPFS—you can put NT anywhere: on the same partition or in a different one. In fact the installation program recommends that you place it in the **Windows 3.1** directory. Both systems will coordinate with each other, so Program Manager has the same groups and icons in both. Of course, you can only do this if you are going to use the FAT system, not NTFS.

If you want to use **NTFS**, though, you must isolate NT—you can't put it in the same partition as the other operating system, so you must create a partition just for NTFS. (A few notes about partitions: A partition can be thought of as a virtual disk drive. For instance, you may have one disk drive [Drive 0], which is partitioned into three sections: disk C:, disk D:, and disk E:. Your computer treats each partition as a separate drive, though the data share the same physical disk. You could also have two drives [Drive 0 and Drive 1], one of which has two partitions [C: and D:], and the other of which is a single partition [E:]. Now the partitions are on two disks, but your programs don't know that. They still regard them as three separate disk drives.)

The original operating system must remain in the *system* partition on the first internal hard-disk drive (the physical drive is known as Drive 0), the one from which your computer boots. On an Intel-based machine that will be drive C:. You will load NT into another partition.

If you don't have an available disk partition, you will have to create one. This is not always simple. If you have a single disk drive with a single partition—the entire drive is disk C:—you will have to back up all the data, use the operating system's disk-formatting commands, and create a new partition. The partition must be at least 75 MB, officially, though you can actually install on 71 MB, which would leave about 19 MB free once NT is installed. On a RISC system you'll need 92 MB. See your MS-DOS or OS/2 documentation for information on partitioning the drive. You can also install onto a partition that is full, as long as it's total size is 71 MB or more, and you don't mind losing all the existing files. During the installation you will be able to reformat the partition to DOS or NTFS. *However,* if you are installing from a non-SCSI CD-ROM drive, the situation is a little different. NT won't be able to read the drive. To get around this problem, Setup begins by copying all the files it needs from the CD, placing them onto a hard disk that the NT portion of Setup *can* read. Setup has to copy 85 MB of files from the CD, so you are going to need that much free hard-disk space. You can load these files into the partition you are planning to use as the NT partition, if you wish (that *doesn't* mean you need 85 MB *plus* 71 MB, just 85 MB will do).

Once you've loaded NT, you'll have to restore your backed-up data, if necessary. You might copy some of the data into the NT partition, and some into the original operating system's partition. (You'll leave the other operating system on the C: drive, and put NT in the D: or higher drive.) Of course you may have too much data, in which case you are going to have to find somewhere else to put it all, or perhaps buy another disk drive.

MS-DOS and OS/2?

If you have your computer set up so that you can boot both MS-DOS and OS/2, NT's installation program will have to pick one with which it will share the computer—NT's Flexboot procedure has not been designed to allow *three* operating systems on one computer. NT will choose the *last* operating system you used. So if you want to use MS-DOS with NT, for instance, boot MS-DOS immediately before loading NT.

It *is* possible to run MS-DOS, OS/2, and NT on the same system, although it's not a procedure devised—or even recommended—by Microsoft. However, it was created by Arthur Knowles, an NT "guru" well known to many NT developers and well respected by Microsoft's own programmers. If you would like to find out more about this system (it's free), download DOSNT.OS2 from the CompuServe WINNT forum. It's currently in Library 1. (WINNT is a forum used to help with NT during it's beta phase, so by the time you read this, there may be some new NT forums available. You'll just have to search around a bit. For more information on CompuServe, see Chapter 22.)

Designating an Administrator

If you own the computer onto which you are about to load NT, you already know who the Administrator is. But in a situation in which one computer will be used by several people, or in which an office has several non-computer-literate people using their own terminals, someone must be designated as an Administrator. In fact *all* NT computers must have an Administrator, because NT provides the Administrator with special privileges. The Administrator can do anything on the computer. Other users have limited rights. They may not be able to change the system time, display security data in the Event Viewer, or create new user accounts, for example.

The first person to log onto NT automatically becomes the Administrator and will be given the Administrator's privileges—full control over the system. That Administrator can create another administrative account during the installation procedure, and then create other administrative accounts later (you'll learn how in Chapter 5), giving other people full privileges if necessary. Or perhaps the Administrator may wish to give certain administrative privileges to one person—the ability to create printers, for instance—and the right to create new user accounts to another.

Important—Don't Lose Your Password!

If a computer has only one Administrator, and that Administrator's password is lost, perhaps because the Administrator leaves the employment of the company owning the computer, Windows NT may eventually become unusable. Certain areas of the hard disk drive, for instance, may be out of reach of other users, printers cannot be configured, certain services cannot be modified or started, new accounts cannot be created. It is essential that it be possible for *someone* to log on as the Administrator. There are three options:

> Don't use the security system—don't use a password for the administrative account, so anyone can log on as Administrator.

> Have one administrative account, but make sure more than one person knows the password.

> Have two or more administrative accounts.

Chapter 5 explains how to create an account without using a password, and Chapter 22 describes Desktop+, a freeware utility that lets you bypass the login procedure entirely.

A Word About Passwords

Passwords can be a problem. The most effective password is, unfortunately, one that is easy to forget. It should have these characteristics:

It's not written down.

You don't put it in any electronic mail (intruders have sometimes scanned email for passwords).

It's known to only one person.

It's not a real word or name.

It's changed regularly, either weekly or monthly.

It contains as many characters as possible (NT allows 14 characters).

It's used for only one system—don't use the same password for all systems to which you have access.

You will have to figure out some kind of compromise between security and your ability to remember your password. For instance, if you use your computer at home, you may feel a password is not necessary at all and won't want to use one. If you share your computer at work, and you work with data of a noncritical nature—it doesn't matter if someone reads your memos, and nobody's likely to try—you may want to use an easily remembered password, and perhaps even write it down at home. If your work is in a confidential area of national security, you will have to take the password thing a little more seriously. You should pick a difficult-to-guess password, change it frequently, and not write it down. Remember also that an NT password is **case sensitive**. In other words, if you create the password *AbcDefG*, you won't be able to log on by typing *ABCDEFG* or *abcdefg*.

Here's a tip for picking a difficult-to-guess yet easy-to-remember password. The ideal password is a totally random collection of characters, such as **1-=jnm(<3d**. That's hard to remember, but you can create what appears to be almost a random sequence by creating an acronym, **ttj&si**, for instance (Take This Job & Shove It). Of course, you wouldn't pick this acronym if your coworkers knew this was your favorite phrase! Or select three or four short words at random from a dictionary, and merge them with special characters: **job/this&it@@**.

The rule that "it's not a real name or word" precludes the worst password-selection habit—using a child's name, your favorite fictional character, your maiden name. You should also avoid using common numbers—your telephone number, car license-plate number, date of birth, and so on. And don't combine these in the manner we just suggested. Don't, for instance, use your kids' names, as in **Sue/Joe*Jim.**

Here are a few more rules for passwords:

- If your Administrator gave you a password, don't keep it; change it the first time you log on. (In Chapter 5 you'll learn how the Administrator can ensure that you can't even log on the first time without entering your password and then changing it.) When Administrators create new accounts, they typically select simple passwords, like PKENT. This is merely intended to let the user get started easily, not to be used as a permanent password.

- Don't give your password to someone else unless you really have to. If someone has to use your account for a short time, change your password as soon as he or she has finished. Better still, ask the Administrator to create a new account for that person.

- Don't let someone watch you enter your password. If you think someone may have seen you, change it immediately.

- If you are the Administrator, keep a close track on password use. User Manager lets you define how long passwords can last, and even how soon passwords may be reused. When someone quits or is fired, immediately close that account. You can even temporarily disable accounts while people are on vacation.

It's easy to get paranoid about passwords, though in general people have the opposite inclination, to treat them lightly. Many people are at no great risk—nobody's going to try to break into their account as soon as they walk away, and the data on the computer would be of little use to anyone else, anyway. On the other hand, many people are in positions in which the data on their computer could be valuable to someone else, and there *are* people who would love to break in and get to it.

There's another threat that is perhaps more important to some people: An intruder may be more interested in malicious damage than in stealing something. NT's security system is a great way to keep users from destroying data, if you've created an NTFS partition. Only an Administrator can format a partition, for example, and any user can make sure other users (excepting the Administrator) can't touch their data files. If you use a sloppy password, though, anyone can get into your account and destroy whatever they want.

Who Does What?

As you've seen, if you are the owner of this computer, or perhaps the sole user of a business machine in a company in which you will be expected to look after the machine, you will have the Administrator's account, allowing you to do anything you wish on this computer.

If you are administering computers used by other people, you will need to decide what rights to give those people. (How to actually define those rights is discussed in Chapter 5—right now we're interested in the planning.) Even if only one person will be using the computer, you don't necessarily want to provide that person with the ability to act as an Administrator—he or she may not have enough knowledge about computers to do so, and you may want to limit access to certain areas of the hard disk. You may want to provide the user with enough rights to get his or her work done, but no more. You probably wouldn't want the average user to have access to the Configuration Registry, a database that contains information critical to NT operations (see Chapter 11).

If several people will be using the computer, they can each have different rights. You may want to let a user who is quite knowledgeable about computers create printer configurations and do tape backups, for instance, while limiting others to the applications they require to get their work done. You can remove Program Manager icons, stop users from modifying Program Manager or running programs with the File|Run command, and deny access to File Manager, effectively controlling what programs the user may run. Before creating accounts you should find out what each user needs to do, and what each is capable of doing, and then base you decisions on that information.

By the way, NT lets you create *user groups*, and it's often easier to create a group and then assign users to it, rather than trying to assign the same or similar privileges to each user in turn. You can learn more about user groups in Chapter 5.

What Next?

Before you install Windows NT, you may have a little work to do. If you plan to install NT as the **sole operating system**, you can install now, without further ado.

If you plan to install NT and **keep the previous operating system**, and you want to **use the NTFS** file system, you must make sure you have an empty partition you can use for NT. Microsoft says that you must have at least 75 MB free (you can actually squeeze into 71 MB, but no less). This is a bare minimum— once you've installed NT you won't have much room to move—with only 19 MB free. (On a RISC system you'll need more, 92 MB.) Remember that you'll need space to store NTFS files. You'll be able to store files in the other, non-NTFS, partitions, of course, but those files will lose the benefits of NTFS. For more information about preparing your disk drive, see your operating system's documentation.

If you are going to **keep the previous operating system**, and **use the FAT or OS/2** file system, you can put NT wherever you want. You don't need to create a new partition if you don't want to—and you can even load NT into the Windows 3.1 directory, where they will "coexist."

The situation for **RISC-based** computers is a little different. These can have several *system* partitions—partitions containing an operating system's boot files. Your hard disk must have been initialized and at least partly partitioned (see your computer's documentation), and all the system partitions must be formatted for FAT. You must have at least one 2 MB system partition. The installation program will install a couple of boot files in the system partition, and you can then install NT in another partition (or in the system partition if it is large enough—71 MB or more).

Hardware Requirements

Windows NT won't run on just any machine, of course. You'll need one of the following (or better):

Computer	An Intel 80x86-based computer (386 PC or better) or a RISC MIPS ARC/R4000 computer (more machine types will be supported soon).
Video	VGA or higher.
Hard disk	One or more hard disks, with at least 85 MB free on the partition containing the NT system files.
Floppy drive or CD-ROM	An Intel x86-based machine must have a high-density floppy-disk drive (either size). You don't have to have a CD-ROM drive, though you can install from either a SCSI CD-ROM drive or a non-SCSI CD-ROM drive.
Memory	8 MB.
Mouse	As with Windows 3.1, it's optional for NT itself, though you may find some NT programs require it.
Other components	Many network cards, printers, display adapters, and SCSI devices are supported. See the hardware compatibility list that comes with your software.

As usual, the recommended configuration is not the same as the bare minimum. You probably wouldn't want to run NT on a 386, for instance. This is what Microsoft *recommends* as the minimum core components for a PC running NT:

Computer	A 486-25 or RISC MIPS ARC/4000
RAM	8 MB
	16 MB for RISC systems
Hard disk	100 MB

A good rule of thumb is, the more the better! Your computer can never be too fast, have too much RAM, or have too large a hard disk, especially when you're running sophisticated software like NT. And if you are using the computer as a server, you'll want as much of everything as possible, of course. The Server service will not start automatically on boot-up unless the computer has at least 12 MB of RAM.

3

Installing and Starting Windows NT

We're going to assume you've read Chapter 2, so you know what you have to do to get ready for Windows NT. If necessary, you've prepared an empty disk partition into which you can place NT, and you've designated the system Administrator. (Presumably, if you're reading this chapter, you're the Administrator.) You've also decided whether you intend to keep the computer's original operating system on the computer, and if you are going to use the NT File System.

Here's what you need to know before you install NT:

- Disk partition into which you will install NT
- File system you will use (NTFS, FAT, or OS/2)
- Name of the System Administrator (optional)
- System Administrator's password (optional)
- Type of video card your computer has
- Keyboard layout ("nationality")
- Type of mouse
- Type of SCSI adapter
- Type of printer and port to which it is connected
- Network card's configuration (IRQ interrupt number, base I/O, etc.)
- Name of the network domain or workgroup you will be joining
- Time zone in which you are operating, and the current time and date
- Username and computername assigned to your system

You'll also need a blank high-density floppy disk for drive A:—this will be used to load the Emergency Repair data.

Note   Before installing NT it's a good idea to back up your disk drives entirely. The NT installation program lets you create partitions and format drives, so if you make a mistake you can destroy a lot of information.

Beginning Installation

If you are installing onto a RISC-based computer, you will be installing from the CD-ROM. If you are installing on an IBM-compatible PC, you may use either floppy disks or a CD-ROM drive (even if that CD-ROM drive is not supported by NT). When you first start the installation program it will be running in your current operating system—DOS or OS/2. At some point in the procedure, however, NT takes over. At that point an incompatible CD cannot be used. To get around this problem the installation program loads all the data onto the hard drive during the DOS or OS/2 phase; then, when it enters the NT phase, it will no longer need the CD-ROM drive. However, there's one problem with this method. If you have installed NT onto an NTFS partition, and you need to *reinstall* NT onto that partition, you have to remove all the data from another partition in order to use the CD. Then the installation program can load the data into that partition during the DOS and OS/2 phase, and reload it into the NTFS partition during the NT phase.

To begin installation on a **RISC-based** computer, your hard disk must have been initialized and at least partly partitioned (see your computer's documentation). The *system* partition—the one used by the computer to boot from—must be a FAT partition, 2 MB or larger. RISC computers, unlike Intel-based computers (386, 486, and Pentium) can have more than one system partition—each must be formatted for FAT. You can then install NT in another partition (or in the system partition if it is large enough—71 MB or more). You will run the NT setup program as you would any other program. That may vary slightly between computers, but it's probably a procedure similar to this: place the CD in the CD-ROM drive, choose Run A Program from the computer's menu, type `cd:\mips\setupldr` and press Enter. Then follow the instructions. (On some machines you may require a device name instead of CD: See your computer's documentation.)

To begin installation on an **80x86-based** computer—a 386, 486, or Pentium—you have four options. You can install from **floppy disks**, from a **SCSI CD-ROM drive**, from a **non-SCSI CD-ROM drive**, or from a **network drive**.

Starting from Floppies

Windows NT comes with a set of 3.5-inch disks and a CD-ROM. In order to begin the floppy installation you have to boot the computer with Disk 1 in the A: drive. That's no problem, because the installation kit also has a 5.25-inch Disk 1. If your Drive A: is a 3.5-inch disk drive you'll use only the 3.5-inch set. If your computer's Drive A: is a 5.25-inch drive, though, you'll place the 5.25-inch Disk 1 in Drive A:, then use the rest of the 3.5-inch disks in Drive B:. In the unlikely event that your computer doesn't have a 3.5-inch drive, you can order a full set of 5.25-inch disks from Microsoft—there's a form in the back of the System Guide. The set is free in the United States.

To begin installing from floppies, turn the computer off, place Setup Disk 1 in drive A:, and turn the computer back on. The setup program will begin.

Starting from a SCSI CD-ROM

To begin installing from a SCSI CD-ROM drive, turn the computer off, place the Setup disk in drive A:, then turn the computer back on. (Your NT installation kit contains both 3.5- and 5.25-inch Setup disks for CD-ROM installation.) When prompted, place the CD in the drive and follow the instructions.

Note If you can't get the installation procedure started, it may be because you have the CD set at SCSI ID 0 or 1. You must change to another ID number.

Starting from a Network or Non-SCSI CD-ROM Drive

If you are installing NT from a network drive or from a non-SCSI CD-ROM drive, start DOS, and then change to the network directory containing the NT files, or to the \I386 directory on the CD. Then place a blank, formatted high-density floppy disk into drive A:.

At the DOS prompt, type **WINNT** and press **Enter**. You will be asked to enter the source directory, the directory containing the WINNT file. This should already be displayed in the text box, so you can just press **Enter**. If you are installing from a non-SCSI CD-ROM drive, Setup will then look for a hard disk on which it can install up to 85 MB of installation files—because NT won't be able to read from the CD once it starts, Setup has to load the files onto a hard disk that NT *can* read from. That disk can be the disk you plan to actually install NT on, or simply a disk you will use to store the files temporarily. If Setup finds enough space, it will ask where you want to place the files. Enter the disk and directory, press Enter, and then follow the instructions.

Note   For more instructions on network installation and how to get the NT files onto the network in the first place, see Installing NT from a Network, later in this chapter.

Installing NT—First Phase

The installation program is very similar to that used by Windows 3.1. It begins with a series of text-based screens, copies files to your hard disk, and then switches to a graphical user interface—it has to reboot your computer to make the switch.

Whichever way you start the setup program, you'll arrive at the **Welcome to Setup** screen. Press Enter to continue, and you'll be given two options: **Express Setup** or **Custom Setup**. The latter gives you more control over what will be installed, of course, so you may prefer to select that option. Express Setup installs all the components—you can't omit any—and it won't give you a chance to modify the video, mouse, keyboard, or virtual memory settings.

For instance, if you don't want to waste disk space by loading the games and "wallpaper," use the Custom Setup, and tell the setup program not to load them. Even if you are not an experienced user, Custom Setup is a good idea—you can just accept all the defaults, but at least you'll see what the setup program is loading.

Next, the installation program searches your hardware to see if it can find any **SCSI adapters**. It will show a list of the ones it finds. You can then continue, or press **S** to select another adapter, perhaps bypassing one which you will be installing later. You can always load the drivers later, using the Windows NT Setup application.

The installation program then looks at the rest of your hardware, and displays a list showing the **computer**, **video display mode**, **mouse**, **keyboard**, and **keyboard layout**. The list will probably be okay. The video mode may not be the one you want to use, though, so you can select another by using the arrow keys to highlight an entry in the list and pressing Enter. However, Microsoft recommends that you load the listed mode's drivers now, and then change to another mode using the Windows NT Setup application later. If you select the wrong adapter now, NT will, in effect, install a system that won't run. You can install another adapter driver later, and, if you get the wrong one, recover from any problems using the "Last Known Good Configuration" procedure, which we explain later in this chapter.

When you continue the program starts loading the files. It also scans for **disk drives** that have been **compressed** with products such as Stacker or DOS 6.0. If you have such a drive you'll see a warning telling you that NT won't read it. (We discussed this in more detail in Chapter 2.) It also warns you that the setup program could damage the compressed volume if you are not careful. This is true of *any* disk volume, compressed or not, as we'll see in a moment.

Next, the program looks for **Windows 3.1**. If it finds that you have Windows on your system, it suggests that you load NT into the same directory. You'll still need just as much disk space, though—at least 71 MB. You should only load into the Windows 3.1 directory if you *don't* want to use NTFS. If you are going to use NTFS you should press **N**, to tell the installation program that you want to select another path.

If you decide to select another location, you will now be able to select the **partition** you want to load NT into. Whichever partition you choose, it must have 71 MB free space, or a total size of 71 MB if you don't mind losing all the data (you'll be able to reformat the partition in a moment, destroying all the existing files). If you plan to use the NTFS file system you have two options: If you want NT to coexist with another operating system, you will have to put NT on a partition other than the system partition (the C: drive on an Intel-based machine); if you don't want to use the original operating system, you can load NT into the system partition and reformat to NTFS.

Note If you load NT into the original operating systems partition and reformat to NTFS, you will be disabling the original operating system. If you load NT into the original operating systems partition and retain the original operating systems file system—FAT or HPFS—NT will assume you want *both* operating systems, and will set it up so that you can boot either operating system.

You'll see a table showing all the available partitions, the size of each partition, and the amount of free space on each one. Be *very* careful at this point. Make the wrong selection and you can destroy the data on the partition you choose. (As we mentioned earlier, you should back up your drives before installing NT.) You may have some free space on your drive. If so, this is shown in the list, and you can select it and press **P** to create a new partition (assuming there's enough free space). You can also delete partitions (select and press **P**). Or simply select the partition you want and press **Enter**. If you have a partition containing an existing NT installation and you want to install on top of it, select that partition and press Enter and Setup will ask if you want to remove the NT files—the data files will remain. After removing the files you will return to the same screen, where you can select the partition again.

You may see **Windows NT Fault Tolerance** in the partition list. These may be stripe sets, mirror sets, or volume sets. Do not delete any of these. (You can learn more about these types of disk systems in Chapter 14.)

Note You can only load NT onto a hard disk, not a removable such as a Bernoulli drive.

If you selected a partition that doesn't have enough free space for NT, or that has a format that NT can't recognize, you can now **reformat** the partition, either as **NTFS** or **FAT**. Of course, you are going to destroy any existing files in that partition when you format it. If you continue, Setup will format the drive and then check it for errors, which may take some time.

Now you are ready to actually install the NT files. Setup suggests the directory **\WINNT**, though you can enter another name if you wish. If you are using floppy disks, Setup will prompt you each time you need to insert a new one. You will soon come to the end of the first part of the installation procedure. You will have to remove the disk from A:, if any, and reboot your computer. Try **Ctrl-Alt-Del**, which should work—if not, use the reset button or power switch.

Note Some beta versions of the Setup program would not work correctly on some computers—Setup would not continue after rebooting. While this problem has probably been eliminated, if you do experience it you can try temporarily disabling BIOS shadowing on your computer. You can do this in the computer's setup screen—see your hardware documentation for more information.

Installing NT— NT Setup Phase

When your computer reboots you enter the next phase of the installation. You will now be running in Windows NT, and will see various dialog boxes prompting you for information. First you must enter your **name** and, if you wish, **company name**. This name is *not* an account name; in fact after Setup is finished you won't see this information again. When you click on OK you'll then see a dialog box showing what you entered and asking you to confirm the entries.

Next you'll be asked for your **computer's name**. This name will be used to let other computers find yours on a network—even if you aren't on a network you must enter a name. The name can be up to 15 characters, without spaces. It must be unique to your network, of course. You should ask the network Administrator what name to use—one may already have been assigned, or there may be a preference for a particular format. This name can be changed later using the Control Panel's Networks dialog box (see Chapter 15).

You will then be asked for the **language** and **location**. Select from the drop-down list box, if necessary, though the default will usually be the correct setting. The selection determines various date, currency, time, and other formats that are used by NT and NT applications. For instance, it determines the manner in which a date is displayed, whether the month or the day of the month should appear first. If you ever need to change your selection you will do so using the Control Panel's International dialog box.

Next you'll see a dialog box that lets you deselect several options (all are selected initially). The options are **Set Up Only Windows Components You Select**. That means you'll be able to select which items you want to install and which you don't—components such as the applets (Cardfile, Notepad, etc.), wallpaper, readme files, and so on. You should do this, because you can save disk space by omitting things you will never use. You can **Set Up Network**—deselect this if you're not on a network, of course. You can select **Set Up Printers**—deselect this if your computer doesn't have a printer connected to it, if for instance, you are on a network and only use a network printer. Finally there's **Set Up Applications on the Hard Disks**. This means that NT will search your hard disks (you'll be able to specify which ones) looking for program files—.EXE files. When it is done, you can select which ones you want to add to Program Manager. If you are installing in an existing Windows 3.1 directory you don't have to do this, because NT will use the existing Program Manager settings anyway.

We are going to assume that you left all the options selected. So when you continue, you will see the Optional Windows Components dialog box, as shown in Figure 3.1. (This dialog box is also available from the Windows NT Setup application, as we'll see later in this chapter.) This box lets you decide which of the **optional files** you are going to install. The files have been grouped into various categories—Readme files, Games, Accessories (such as Paintbrush, Notepad, Write, and so on), Screen Savers, and Wallpaper & Misc. (sample sounds and desktop wallpaper).

The dialog box also shows you how much hard-disk space each category takes up, the total of all the selected files, and how much space you have available. If you want to install all the files in a category, make sure there's an **X** in its check box. If you don't want *any* of the categories files loaded, click on the check box to remove the **X**. If you want to select specific files, click on the appropriate **Files** button to see another dialog box with a list of file types. To select files that you *don't* want to load, click on them in the right-side list box, then use the Remove button to move the files to the left list box, and click on OK to continue.

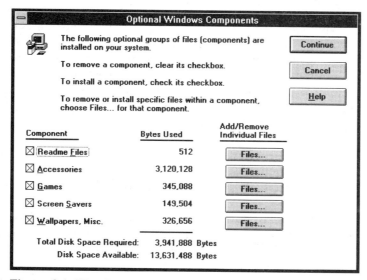

Figure 3.1 The Optional Windows Components dialog box

Click on each Files button and spend a few minutes looking through these options. You can save a lot of disk space by removing the options you will simply never need. Will you ever use Cardfile or Media Player, for example? If you are not on a network, you can also remove Chat. Just removing these few items and their help files will save 1.3 MB. (Not all accessories can be removed, though.) You can save up to almost 4 MB by removing options you don't want. And if you ever change your mind, you can add them later using the Windows NT Setup application.

Next, you'll **set up your printer**. This is a *local* printer, one you have connected directly to your computer. If you are using a *networked* printer only, you can skip the printer setup. Otherwise, give the printer a **name**. Windows NT treats printers differently from Windows 3.1. In Windows 3.1 you select a print driver—the driver name is, in effect, the printer name. But in NT you create printer profiles, and the driver name is only one part of the profile. So, for instance, you might call the printer the Accounting Printer, or Dot Matrix, or Documentation Printer, or whatever best describes the printer's usage. Then you'll select a **printer model**—the actual driver—from the drop-down list box, and select the **port** to which you have connected the printer. You can change all this later, using Print Manager.

The next step is **network-adapter** configuration. Of course you will skip this if you are not connected to a network. You have two options—you can tell Setup to **Continue**, and search for the network adapter you have installed, or you can select **Do Not Detect**, in which case you will be able to select the adapter manually. If you select Continue, Setup looks at your hardware and then reports the first adapter it finds. You can then select **Continue** (to load the driver for that board), **Find Next** (to ignore the one it found and search for another adapter), or **Do Not Detect** (so you can enter the information manually).

Once you've selected the adapter you want to use, you will have to enter **Adapter Setup** information—values such as the IRQ and I/O Port Address. The information Setup requests may vary depending on the adapter board installed.

Next, Setup will load the system files and then display the **Network Settings** dialog box. You can now add other network options. You should probably leave this for now, unless you have specific instructions from an adapter-board manufacturer about adding a particular driver. Setup has probably loaded everything correctly, and if you do need to make any changes later you can return to this dialog box by clicking on the Control Panel's Networks icon. (See Chapter 15.) When you continue, Setup will configure and start the network connections.

Now you will be asked about the domain or workgroup settings. If you are on a network that uses workgroups, just type the workgroup name into the **Workgroup** text box. For instance, if you are connecting to a Windows for Workgroups network, ask the network Administrator for the workgroup name you should use. The workgroup name does not have to currently exist on the network—computers with the same workgroup name can connect to each other, so there's not real central control over workgroup names. If you are connecting to an NT Advanced Server network you will need to enter a **Domain** name instead. A domain name *must* exist. Domains are maintained in a very different way from workgroups, with a server keeping data about each domain. You must either have an account on that domain already, or have administrative rights on the domain. If you are a domain Administrator you can create an account on the domain by entering your **User Name** and your **Password**.

When you click on OK, Setup continues, setting up your network account and then building Program Manager. Now you are going to come to the **Administrative Account Setup**. By default—because you are installing NT—you are now the Administrator. First, NT will create an account with the **username** of Administrator. You are prompted to enter a password for this account, which you enter twice. When you type the password, only asterisks are displayed in the text box for security's sake, so typing it twice makes sure that you really typed what you thought you typed. If you **don't want a password**, simply click on OK without entering one. You'll see a warning, but you'll be able to continue. The password must be 14 characters or less, with no spaces. It's case sensitive, also, so ABC is not the same as abc. We discussed passwords in detail in Chapter 2.

Note By default, passwords expire in 42 days, forcing you to enter a new one. You can turn off password expiration, though. See Chapter 5 for more information.

Now you can create another account, if you wish—just cancel to bypass this step if you *don't* want to create another account. (This step is not available if you added the computer to a domain, because the new user is expected to log on through the domain.) This time you'll be prompted for a **username**. Usernames must be 20 characters or less, and may not include spaces. Typically a username is built from a user's real name—PeterK, PKent, PeterKe, or something similar. This username must be unique on the network, of course. You can also enter a password, though again, you don't have to enter a password if you don't want one. This account will be added to the Administrators group, so anyone logging on to this account will have full access to all features. You can add more accounts, or modify the accounts you have just created, in User Manager. See Chapter 5 for more information.

The next step is to set up **Virtual Memory**, the system's **paging file**. (This is the equivalent of Window 3.1's **swapfile**.) NT will suggest a pagefile size, so you may want to simply continue, accepting the recommendation. You definitely need a pagefile—running without a pagefile can make NT so slow it's virtually unusable. You can change the pagefile later, if necessary, from the Control Panel's System dialog box. See Chapter 6 for more information.

Now you can **Set Up Applications**. If you are installing NT into a Windows 3.1 directory, Setup will simply copy the program icons from your Windows 3.1 Program Manger. Otherwise you can use this dialog box to search for applications in your DOS path, or on any or all of your hard-disk drives. Setup will look for .EXE files. If it finds one it recognizes it will ask you if it is correct. Finally it lists all the files it has found in a dialog box. You can then select the ones you want to add to your Program Manager Applications program group (or groups, if there are a lot of them). If you decide not to use this procedure right now, you can always do it later, using the Windows NT Setup application.

The next step is to place a high-density disk in drive A:. This doesn't have to be formatted or blank—NT will format the disk for you—but you will lose any data on the disk. NT uses the disk as the Emergency Repair Disk, copying configuration information to the disk. You'll find out more about this disk later in this chapter.

Note   Label the disk Emergency Repair Disk, and also include information identifying the computer from which the disk comes. An Emergency Repair Disk should be used only for the computer on which it was created.

After creating the Emergency Repair Disk, Setup asks for information about the **date and time**. Enter the correct date and time, and the correct time zone. You can also tell NT whether you want to **Automatically Adjust for Daylight Savings Time**. Of course the time zone is not really important if you are not on a Wide Area Network, or if you didn't select the Daylight Savings Time option (which needs to know the time zone in order to adjust on the correct date). For detailed information about this dialog box, see Chapter 6. You can change this information later using the Control Panel's Date/Time dialog box.

You've now finished. NT will reboot. If you told Setup to install NT on an NTFS partition, the partition will now be converted, and then NT will reboot again.

Tip   What if you want to convert other partitions to NTFS? You'll have to back up all the data, use the Command Prompt FORMAT command (see Chapter 9 for information about Command Prompt), and then restore the data to the newly formatted partition.

Installing NT from a Network

If you are installing NT on several computers on a network you can install directly from the network. Begin by installing NT on the server. You can do this from the server itself or from a workstation. You begin by installing NT on a single machine, and then use that machine to install a network drive to which other MS-DOS users have access.

First, use the instructions earlier in this chapter to install NT on a workstation or the server. Then log on to NT, go to File Manager and create a directory on the server into which you will save the NT "master" files. (See Chapter 7 for more information on File Manager.)

Double-click on the Command Prompt icon in Program Manager. At the command prompt, type:

```
setup -n -i initial.inf -s source -d destination
```

and then press Enter.

These are the command parameters:

-n	tells Setup to copy files to a network "sharepoint."
-i initial.inf	tells Setup to use the INITIAL.INF file.
-s *source*	tells Setup which drive and directory contains the Windows NT Setup CD or floppy disks.
-d *destination*	tells Setup to which network drive and directory to copy the master files.

For instance, the following command would tell Setup that the Setup disks are in drive B:, and that you want to copy the files to network drive G: and the directory NTADMIN:

```
setup -n -i initial.inf -s b: -d g:\ntadmin
```

In the following example a CD contains the source files:

```
setup -n -i initial.inf -s f:\i386 -d g:\ntadmin
```

Notice that you define the destination using the network drive letter, not the name of the computer containing that directory. Of course if you are working at the server, you will be copying the files to the computer's own hard disks.

When you press Enter the installation begins. Follow the instructions. When the installation is complete you can then install NT on other computers from the network drive, using the instructions earlier in this chapter under Starting from a Network or Non-SCSI CD-ROM Drive.

Logging On

When NT boots, you'll see the **Windows NT panel**, a box centered in the desktop with a picture of the Windows NT logo. This is the image in the file WINNT.BMP. However, you will be able to replace the image in the WINNT.BMP (it's in the WINNT directory) with anything you want—your company logo, a cartoon, photograph, message, or anything else you'd rather see. Simply rename WINNT.BMP, then create a new file—in Paintbrush, for instance—and name it WINNT.BMP.

Note If you installed NT in the Windows 3.1 directory, you'll see the Windows 3.x Migration dialog box. You can choose to **Migrate Windows 3.x WIN.INI and SYSTEM.INI** files, so that the NT's configuration data is updated with your Windows 3.1 INI-file information, which controls the way in which Windows

3.1 applications run. You can also choose to **Migrate Windows 3.x Program Manager group files**, so that NT's Program Manager will have the same groups as 3.1's.

A second or two later you will see a dialog box telling you to press **Ctrl-Alt-Del** to log on. Of course in DOS this would reboot your system, and in Windows 3.1 it would provide the option of closing a stalled application. But in NT this is the security method used to ensure that a "Trojan horse" program is not running, just waiting for someone to come along and enter a password. (A Trojan horse is a program that appears to be providing a necessary or useful function, while in fact it really has an ulterior motive, such as stealing information or causing damage.) When you use Ctrl-Alt-Del, Windows NT clears the system for a moment and runs the logon program. Any unauthorized program running at that time would stop. Incidentally, many computers these days have programmable keyboards—you could, if you wished, program one key as the logon key, to "press" Ctrl-Alt-Del for you. (The Ctrl-Alt-Del sequence is also used within NT, to reboot, shut down, lock the workstation, and change passwords.)

Within a second or two you will see the **Welcome** dialog box (Figure 3.2). The first text box will show the **Username** of the last person who used the computer—in this case the username you created during Setup. (In subsequent logons a user can press Shift-Tab twice [or Tab thrice] to move to the Username text box, and type an account name. Subsequent users cannot log on until provided a username and password by an Administrator.) If you created a password during Setup, type the **Password** and then click on OK. Remember that passwords are case sensitive—you must type the exact same password that you created, including using lowercase and uppercase as you did in the original setup. (If you didn't create a password during Setup, just leave the password box empty, and click on OK.) Incidentally, if you don't enter any logon information, or don't press Enter or click on OK, NT will wait several minutes and then remove the Welcome dialog box, displaying the Ctrl-Alt-Del box again.

Note You can change your password any time while working in NT by pressing Ctrl-Alt-Del and clicking on the Change Password Button in the Windows NT Security dialog box.

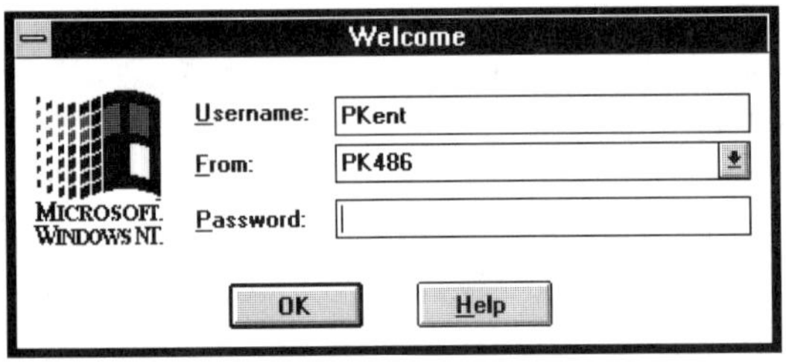

Figure 3.2 The Welcome dialog box

When you click on the OK button the Welcome dialog box disappears, and the NT logo panel is replaced with the system wallpaper, the picture (or colored background) that appears on your computer screen underneath all the windows and dialog boxes. By default the wallpaper is WINNT.BMP, so you won't see anything different. However, you can use the Control Panel's Desktop dialog box to modify the desktop (it works in the same way as in Windows 3.1). You can select another wallpaper file (a .BMP file you created yourself, if you wish); you can select a wallpaper of None (so the desktop is set to the default desktop color defined in the Control Panel's Color dialog box); or select a *pattern* instead of a wallpaper.

Then Program Manager loads, and any applications in the Program Manager's Startup program group are loaded, just as in Windows 3.1.

Tip To stop applications in the Startup group loading automatically, press **Shift** *before* clicking on OK, and continue holding Shift until Program Manager has been completely loaded—keep holding Shift as long as you hear your hard drive churning or see the drive light flashing.

We're going to take a close look at Program Manager in Chapter 4. For now, let's look at how to get out of NT and how to get back in.

Leaving NT

There are a couple of ways to "leave" NT. In Windows 3.1, exiting Windows is a simple matter: Selecting File|Exit Windows closed Windows and returned you to the DOS prompt (Windows 3.1, remember, is not a true operating system, but an application program running in DOS). In Windows NT, though, you have two choices. You can log off the system, closing all your applications and Program Manager but leaving the Windows NT operating system running. Or you can close NT entirely, closing applications, Program Manager, and the operating system.

To log off, select **File|Logoff**, press **Alt-F4**, or double-click on Program Manager's **Control** menu. Your applications close—you'll be able to save data if necessary—and Program Manager closes. You'll be left with the Windows NT banner on your screen, and the "Ctrl-Alt-Del" dialog box. Now, if you want to run applications, you'll have to press Ctrl-Alt-Del and log back on.

If you want to turn off your computer or switch to another operating system, you should select **File|Shutdown**. You'll see the dialog box shown in Figure 3.3. If you want to reboot your computer—so you can use *Flexboot* (also known as *boot loader*) to select another operating system—make sure the **Restart when shutdown is complete** check box is selected. If you are going to turn the computer off, leave the check box unselected. Now, when you click on Yes, the system logs off, closing your applications, and then closes the Windows NT operating system itself. You will either see a dialog box with a large **Restart** button—you can click on

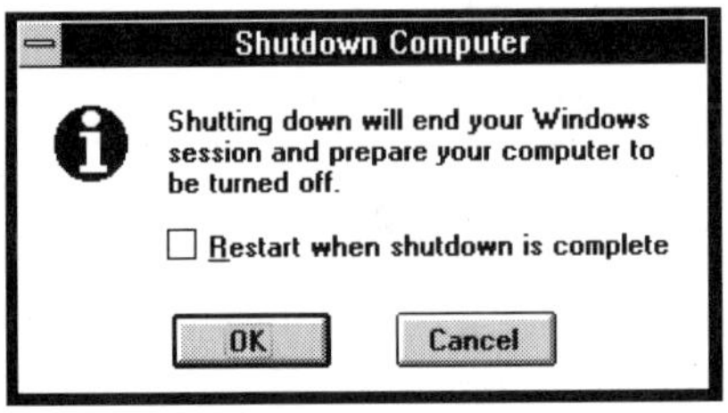

**Figure 3.3 The Shutdown Computer dialog box,
shown when you select File|Shutdown**

the button to reboot your computer, or turn the computer off—or, if you selected the Restart check box, the computer automatically reboots, and if you have a dual-operating system setup, Flexboot appears, letting you choose operating systems.

Note   The Shutdown is sometimes aborted if an application has a dialog box open. You may have to close the dialog box and then select Shutdown again.

Don't be tempted to use File|Logoff and then turn off or reboot your computer; NT needs to shut down its files and services properly. Use Shutdown and wait for the dialog box telling you that you can switch off your computer.

Tip   There's a quick way to shut down or log off without returning to Program Manager first. Press **Ctrl-Alt-Del**. When you see the Windows NT Security dialog box, click on the Shutdown or Logoff button. There are also a couple of shareware applications that can speed up the process—clySmic Software's Drag 'n' Drop Utilities and Silverware Consulting's WinEXIT. See Chapter 22 for more information.

Starting NT

There are, of course, two ways to start Windows NT. If it's the only operating system on your computer, when you turn on your computer it will automatically boot, in the same way that MS-DOS and OS/2 systems do. If it's a dual operating-system computer, though, you'll see Flexboot appear on your screen as soon as your computer finishes its initial startup tests. You'll see a few lines of text, like this:

```
OS Loader V2.10

Please select the operating system to start:

Windows NT

MS-DOS
```

```
Use ↑ and ↓ to move the highlight to your choice.
Press Enter to choose.
Seconds until highlighted choice will be started automat-
ically: 30
```

You'll notice that a counter is counting down the seconds—you can wait for Flexboot to start the highlighted operating system (as soon as the counter reaches 0). By default, NT is highlighted (though you can change the default using Control Panel's System dialog box). You can also press Enter to select the highlighted system immediately, or use the arrow keys to select the other operating system and then press Enter.

Warning and Error Messages

NT has a "service" called EventLog which monitors various system, security, and application events, and keeps a record of problems and possible problems. By default EventLog is set to start automatically when you boot NT, so if it finds a problem during the boot procedure you will see a message box appear over Program Manager when the boot is almost complete. You might see a message telling you "At least one service specified to start at boot time has failed to start." You might also see a message saying that the "Security log is full." In either case you should open Event Viewer—the application that lets you view the event log—and read the messages. For more information, see Chapter 13.

The Guest Account—A Trojan Horse

Setup automatically creates an account called Guest. This account has very limited rights. The user can't damage existing files on NTFS disks, for instance—he can open them, but can't save them—and he can't connect to other computers on the network. Of course he *can* damage files on FAT or HPFS disks, because NTFS's security system can't protect these files systems.

The Guest account has no password, and can't be removed from the system (though it can be renamed). If you are running NT on a machine with one or more non-NTFS disks, you should use User Manager (Chapter 5) to provide the Guest account with a password, so no one can use this account without your approval.

Stop Access to Registry Editor

Another potential problem you should consider is that all users are able to access the Registry Editor. This application lets you play with the system's configuration registry, the basic operating instructions for NT. While users may not be able to get to all the information in the registry, they are still able to get to enough to create serious havoc if, through accident or intention, they change the wrong thing.

You can stop users from using Registry Editor quite simply, by using File Manager to restrict the use of the REGEDT32.EXE file (it's in the \WINNT\SYSTEM32 directory). Use the Security|Permissions command to see the File Permissions dialog box, and remove **Everyone** from the list of users allowed to use the application. Then only Administrators will be able to do so. See Chapter 7 for more information.

Modifying Flexboot

You have a certain amount of control over Flexboot. You can change the countdown time, the default operating system, and even the names of the operating systems displayed on your screen. Change the default operating system and the countdown time in Control Panel's System dialog box (see Chapter 6). For other changes, follow this procedure.

The information is saved in the root directory of your primary hard-disk partition (usually in the root of drive C:\), in a system file named **BOOT.INI**. You can open and edit this file in a text editor such as Notepad. (Remember that in File Manager you'll have to use the View|By File Type command to Show Hidden/System files in order to see BOOT.INI—system files are hidden). You can then load it into Notepad from there, or change its attributes with the File|Properties command. BOOT.INI looks like this:

```
[boot loader]
timeout=30
default=multi(0)disk(0)rdisk(0)partition(3)\winnt
[operating systems]
multi(0)disk(0)rdisk(0)partition(3)\winnt="Windows NT"
c:\="MS-DOS"
```

To change the name of the operating systems, modify the lines under [operating systems]. For instance, you could change **C:\ = "MS-DOS"** to **C:\ = "Windows for Workgroups"**. Don't change the information on the left side of the = sign, though, just the information in quotation marks. You can also change the **timeout** (countdown time) and the default system in this file. To make the previous operating system the default, simply change the third line to show the boot information for that operating system. This is the information to the *left* of the = sign in the [operating systems] section. For instance, enter **default = C:** if you want to set DOS as the default. If you don't need to go into BOOT.INI to change the operating system names, you'll probably find it easier to change the timeout and default system from the Control Panel, of course.

BOOT.INI is also a read-only file, by the way, so before you can save your changes you'll have to use File Manager to change the attributes. (Hold Alt, double-click on BOOT.INI, and click on the Read Only check box. Remember to change it back to read-only after saving the changes.)

Tip If you want to temporarily "disable" flexboot, and boot directly to the default operating system, simply set the countdown time to 0 in the Control Panel's System dialog box.

Bypassing the Logon Procedure

If you don't want to use NT's security features, there's a way that you can bypass the logon procedure entirely, so that your computer boots straight into Program Manager without asking for an account name or password. First, get Desktop+— it's a "freeware" program from Babarsoft (you can get it from an electronic bulletin board such as CompuServe—see Chapter 22). Install the program, open Control Panel, then double-click on the Desktop+ icon. In the Desktop Settings dialog box click on the LogOn button. In the Log On Settings dialog box select Automatic Administrator Log On.

Autoadmn

Place AUTOADMN.EXE in your WINNT\SYSTEM32 directory, then add the program to your Startup group. Now go to User Manager (see Chapter 5) and select the Administrator account. Remove any password from the account. Now, when you boot your computer, you will see a small message box telling you that the automatic logon is being used, and NT will open Program Manager for you. Of course this effectively disables the Logoff commands—if you log off NT with this system in place, NT simply logs right back on, because there is no longer any "logged off but still running NT" state.

The Boot Files

When you install NT on a 386, 486, or Pentium, Setup creates several files in the root directory of the C: drive. These are BOOT.INI, BOOTSECT.DOS (if another operating system remains on your computer), NTDLR, NTDETECT.COM, and, if you are using a SCSI hard disk, NTBOOTDD.SYS. These are Read Only, System, and Hidden files. You won't see them unless you use File Manager's View|By File Type command to select Show Hidden/System Files. Setup also creates PAGEFILE.SYS, the NT pagefile (similar to Windows 3.1's swapfile). On RISC-based computers NT places HAL.DLL and OSLOADER.EXE in the \OS\NT directory on the system partition. All these files are essential, so they must not be removed.

Setup changes your system's boot record so that each time your computer boots it looks for NTLDR. NTLDR runs NTDETECT.COM, which puts together a list of your computer's hardware. NTLDR also reads the information in BOOT.INI, and uses it to create the "menu" of operating systems that you see when you boot. BOOTSECT.DOS contains the boot record for the other operating system.

Future Changes—Using Windows NT Setup

Windows NT
Setup

If you need to modify your setup information in some way at a later date, you'll generally use Windows NT Setup. Double-click on the icon in Program Manager's Main program group. You'll see the dialog box shown in Figure 3.4. This is very similar to the Setup dialog box in Windows 3.1. It doesn't have a network setting, because NT controls that through another dialog box.

Change System Settings	Lets you select another video-display driver, mouse, or keyboard.
Set Up Applications	Lets you search for applications that you can add to Program Manager, using the same dialog box that appears during the NT installation procedure.
Add/Remove Windows Components	Displays the dialog box shown in Figure 3.1, so that you can add or remove applications, readme files, wallpaper, and so on.
Add/Remove SCSI Adapters	Lets you add SCSI adapter-board drivers.
Add/Remove Tape Devices	Lets you add tape-drive drivers.
Delete User Profiles	Lets you remove user profiles.

Tip The shareware application named Add Applications To Program Manager is easier to use and a little more sophisticated than Windows NT Setup's Set Up Applications command. It lets you define to which program group programs should be added.

Where do you go to make other configuration changes? Use the **Control Panel** to install **network adapters** and **protocols**; to install any **drivers**, such as **MIDI**, **sound boards**, and **video**, other than the ones Setup controls (video, mouse, keyboards, SCSI adapters, and tape drives); and to configure an **uninterruptible power source**. Use **Print Manage**r to install printers.

```
 ═                    Windows NT Setup                     ▼
 Options   Help

   Display:     ATI 640x480, 256 colors

   Mouse:       Microsoft Serial Mouse

   Keyboard:    XT, AT or Enhanced Keyboard (83-102 key)
```

Figure 3.4 The Windows NT Setup dialog box

Removing User Profiles

A network user can log onto another computer from your computer. When the Welcome dialog box appears the user enters his username and computer name, and the network logs him onto the other computer.

When this happens, that person's user profile is copied to your computer, so your computer knows how to run the session for that person. This copied profile will stay on your computer until you remove it—it is not removed automatically when the person logs off. You can remove such profiles from the Windows NT Setup using the **Options|Delete User Profiles**. You'll see a list showing all user profiles on your machine, including the ones you want to keep. You can select one you want to remove and click on the Delete button. You can't delete the Administrator account, or the account under which you are currently logged on.

Converting File Formats

After installing NT you may later decide that you want to convert the system's file format, or just the format used on a particular partition, perhaps converting from FAT to NTFS, or even back from NTFS to FAT. There are several ways to do this.

Removing the Other Operating System

If, as many users will, you decide to retain your original operating system on your computer in combination with NT, you can always convert to an all-NT system later. In fact, you have two options. You can simply **remove flexboot**, the system that lets you select which system you want to boot when you turn on your computer. Or you can **remove the other operating system** entirely.

Removing the other operating system is a drastic move, one you shouldn't make until you are absolutely sure you are ready. Reinstalling it will be a lot of work, as you'll also have to reinstall NT as a multiboot system. As a temporary measure you could simply disable Flexboot—open NT's **Control Panel**, double-click on the **System** icon, and change the **Show list for** setting to 0. Make sure the **Startup** options shows Windows NT. This will ensure that NT boots immediately when you turn on your computer.

To remove the other operating system entirely, follow the preceding instructions to disable Flexboot and delete BOOTSECT.DOS and all the other operating system's files. Once you've removed the operating system you will probably want to convert the disk partition to NTFS.

Converting to NTFS

You can convert FAT and HPFS disk partitions to NTFS using a command called CONVERT.EXE. It's a good idea to back up all your data first, of course, but the command shouldn't cause any data loss. At the Command Prompt, type CON-VERT E: /FS:NTFS and press Enter. You may see a message saying that NT can't convert immediately, but you can tell NT to do it the next time you boot the computer (just type Y and press Enter). The next time you boot the partition will be converted, and the system will then reboot again. When Program Manager starts, you'll find that the partition is now NTFS.

You can't use this method to convert the partition that contains the NT system files themselves, though. You will have to reinstall NT to do this, because the system is running from those files, and has them read locked.

Converting from NTFS to Another Operating System

There is no direct way to convert from NTFS back to FAT or HPFS. On a nonsystem partition your will have to back up all your data, go to Disk Administrator (see Chapter 14), delete the disk partition, create a new partition, and then close the Disk Administrator. The system will reboot automatically.

When you get back to Program Manager you have two options. If you are converting a removable disk, such as a Bernoulli drive, open File Manager and click on that drive's icon. You'll see a message telling you that the drive is not formatted and asking if you want to format it now. Click on OK, and when the Format Disk dialog box appears, select the appropriate disk drive from the Disk In drop-down list box and click on OK. The drive will now be formatted in FAT.

If you want to format the disk in HPFS, or if the disk is a hard disk, you'll have to use the Command Prompt's FORMAT command. Open the Command Prompt from the Program Manager's Main program group, type FORMAT X: and press Enter if you want to format in FAT (where *X* is the disk drive you are formatting), or FORMAT X: /FS:HPFS and press Enter if you want to use HPFS. Once you've formatted the partition you can reload the backed up data.

You can't use this method to convert the partition containing the NT system files to FAT. In fact there's no direct way to do this; you would have to reinstall NT.

Removing NT

As we mentioned earlier, you can temporarily **disable Flexboot**, so that you automatically boot the chosen operating system. Open NT's **Control Panel**, double-click on the **System** icon, and change the **Show list for** setting to 0. Make sure the **Startup** option shows the other operating system. This will ensure that NT does not boot, and the other operating system boots immediately when you turn on your computer.

To **completely remove NT** from your machine, first boot DOS, type sys c:, and press Enter. This will change the computer's boot record so it no longer looks for NTLDR. Then delete these files in the root directory of drive C:

BOOT.INI

BOOTSECT.DOS

NTBOOTDD.SYS (only there if it's a SCSI disk)

NTDETECT.COM

NTLDR

PAGEFILE.SYS

All of these files but PAGEFILE.SYS are Hidden and Read Only. In File Manager select View|By File Type and make sure Show Hidden/System Files is selected.

Now you can delete the NT files and directories. Of course if it's in an NTFS directory, you have another problem, because your other operating system won't be able to see it. You'll have to run the NT installation program, converting the partition to a FAT partition. *Then* delete the files we listed above and the NT files.

Recovering from Problems

NT provides several ways to recover from serious configuration problems. First, you have an option called **Last Known Good Configuration**, which lets you return to a previous configuration setting if you have changed something that caused problems. There's also the **emergency repair disk** that Setup created during the installation. And if you use **Backup** (NT's tape-backup utility) you can save configuration data and restore it to your NT partition (of course, this assumes that you can run NT and get to the Backup program). See Chapter 19 for more information about Backup.

Last Known Good Configuration

If you change your configuration—select a different video driver, for instance—and make a mistake, you may find that when NT reboots (as it has to, to make configuration changes take effect) your system won't run properly. In the case of the video driver, you won't be able to see your screen correctly. In Windows 3.1, you use an ASCII editor to open WIN.INI and SYSTEM.INI files and change back to the previous settings, or to copy backups of the previous WIN.INI and SYSTEM.INI files over the existing ones. Then, when you rebooted you would get the last good configuration.

Well, NT has automated this whole process for you, in a procedure called Last Known Good Configuration. If you find, when you reboot your system, that you have serious problems, reset your system, begin booting NT, and just after NT begins booting press **Spacebar** for a moment—don't hold it down. (If you are using Flexboot, press Spacebar immediately after selecting the NT line and pressing Enter. If NT is the only system, press Spacebar as soon as you see "OS Loader" appear on your screen.) You'll see the **Configuration Recovery Menu**, with these options:

- Use Current Startup Configuration
- Use Last Known Good Configuration
- Restart Computer

The first option simply continues the boot process as normal. The last, Restart Computer, returns to the Flexboot menu, or, if you are not using Flexboot, reboots again (the same as the first option, really). If you are having configuration problems you will select the second option, **Use Last Known Good Configuration**, and then press Enter. This will automatically boot NT using the previous configuration, the last one used to successfully log onto NT. (How does NT know it was good? Each time someone completes the logon procedure by entering a correct username, computername, and password, NT saves the configuration data, assuming that if a user got that far, the configuration must be okay.) The current configuration is replaced by the Last Known Good Configuration, so you'll lose all changes, both good and bad. The next time you boot NT, this previous configuration will be used as the current configuration.

Note It's possible for NT to automatically jump to the Configuration Recovery menu in some situations, if it encounters a Severe or Critical device-driver loading problem.

Configuration data is saved in the configuration registry (see Chapter 11). The current configuration—the one that is used if you *don't* press Spacebar when you boot—is saved in the HKEY_LOCAL_MACHINE\SYSTEM\CurrentControlSet key. The Last Known Good Configuration setting is defined in the HKEY_LOCAL_MACHINE\SYSTEM\Select key. This key saves a number. For instance, if the number is 3, it means that the HKEY_LOCAL_MACHINE\SYSTEM\ControlSet003 key should be used as the Last Known Good Configuration.

There's a situation that Last Known Good Configuration can't deal with. If you have a portable machine that you use hooked up to both a desktop monitor and a portable monitor, and if those monitors have different video modes, when you swap monitors you may have a situation in which you can't see anything on the screen, because the computer is running a mode that the monitor can't use. Last Known Good Configuration won't help, because the last configuration *was* good, and you've changed the hardware, not the software. The solution is to change to a video mode compatible with *both* screens, then shut down NT and change screens, checking to see that it all works before leaving.

Using the Emergency Recovery Disk

If you ever have serious problems caused by damaged or missing system files, problems from which you can't recover by merely using Last Known Good Configuration, you may be able to use the Emergency Recovery Disk to get back to normal.

Start the Setup program as if you were installing NT all over again—see earlier in this chapter for instructions on starting Setup. When you see the first Setup screen you'll notice that one of the options is **To attempt repairs on a damaged Windows system, press R.** When you press R you may be prompted to insert one of the Setup disks, depending on the manner in which you are running Setup. Setup begins scanning for SCSI adapters, and then tells you to insert the Emergency Repair Disk. Setup loads some files, and then displays a list of optional tasks:

```
[x] Verify Windows NT system files
[X] Verify boot files on your C: drive
[X] Inspect configuration registry files
[ ] Unsecure Windows NT system files
Continue (perform selected tasks)
```

The last line is selected, so when you press Enter the procedure will begin. If you want to modify one of the options, use the Up Arrow to move to it and press Enter. The last option, **Unsecure Windows NT system files**, is *not* selected and should not normally be used. If you select this option when the system repair is finished the system files will no longer have restrictions on them—anyone will be able to work with them.

When you continue, Setup runs CHKDSK on the NT partition, to check for disk errors, and then begins examining the files in the NT partition for any evidence of corruption. If you are using a floppy-disk set you'll be prompted to insert disks now and again, and Setup will fix any corrupt files. That means that if you've modified any of them—if you changed the WINNT.BMP file that displays the startup panel, for instance—you'll lose your changes. When Setup has finished looking at all the files, it displays its recommendations for fixing the configuration registry, which is the data that determines the manner in which NT operates (the equivalent of Windows 3.1's .INI files):

```
[ ] SYSTEM (System Configuration)
[ ] SECURITY (Security Policy)
[ ] SAM (User Accounts Database)
[ ] DEFAULT (Default User Profile)
[ ] SOFTWARE (Software Information)
Continue (restore selected files)
```

If there are no Xs in the brackets, then Setup found no problems. An X in a bracket means that Setup is recommending that you replace that configuration data. (For a list of the characteristics controlled by any of these file systems, press F3 to see the Help system. Each entry in this list is explained on a separate screen.)

When you press Enter (while Continue is selected), Setup begins restoring the selected data from the Setup CD or floppies—you'll be prompted to change disks if necessary. Of course if there are no problems, and none of these options have Xs in their brackets, you've come to the end of the Emergency Recovery procedure and your computer will reboot. If the Emergency Recovery Disk does not fix your problems—if you still can't run NT—you have no option but to reinstall Windows NT. Run the Setup program over again, and completely restore the NT installation. Before doing this, you should make sure that a hardware problem is not the cause.

Reinstalling NT

If you ever need to reinstall NT, you'll have to run the installation program again. That's not necessarily a problem, but it may be in one situation—if you are reinstalling from non-SCSI CD-ROM drive. As we explained earlier, because NT can't read the files from the CD, Setup has to load them onto a hard disk with 85 MB of free space first, then run the installation program.

Let's say, for instance, that you have disk C:, containing MS-DOS, and disk D:, containing NT. If disk D: is formatted as a FAT drive, you can use MS-DOS to delete the files you don't want, and save the data files, then use the free space for the installation. But if you formatted drive D: as an NTFS drive, and if you can't get NT to run, you've got problems. First, you can't get to your data, because MS-DOS won't be able to recognize drive D:, let alone get in and save data. Second, you can't reinstall NT easily because you probably don't have room to store all the installation files. What you may have to do is remove as many of the files on drive C: as possible, leaving just enough to run DOS, then use Setup and copy the installation files onto drive C:. During Setup you'll reach a stage when drive D: *is* recognized, and you can install in that drive. (However, you may have to reformat it to free enough room for the installation, and lose your data.) Once you've finished the installation, Setup will remove the temporary files from drive C:, and you can restore your MS-DOS data to that drive.

Of course, the easiest way around this problem is to install from the floppy disks instead of the non-SCSI CD-ROM drive—or to get a SCSI drive!

4

Program Manager

Program Manager in Windows NT looks almost exactly the same as it does in Windows 3.1, and to a great degree it functions in the same way (see Figure 4.1). You create program groups and program icons in the same way, arrange groups and icons in the same way, and run programs in the same way. There are a few differences, however. There are three new menu options, a new program group, and a few new program icons. These are the new menu options:

File|Logoff (Alt-F4)

Logs off, closing Program Manager, but the operating system remains running. If other computers on the network are working with your system's resources they can continue. Use Logoff if you want to let someone else log on, or if you want to leave your computer unattended but don't want to turn it off (there's also a Lock Workstation command, which we'll look at later in this chapter).

File|Shutdown

Shuts down the operating system. Use when you want to turn off your computer or select another operating system.

Options|Save Settings Now

Saves the Program Manager settings—program icon and group positions, and the first three Options menu settings—immediately. In Windows 3.1, this is performed by holding Shift and double-clicking on the Control menu, or by holding Shift and selecting File|Exit Windows, but there is no actual menu option. You can use these alternatives in NT, too, though you'll use File|Logoff instead of Exit Windows.

53

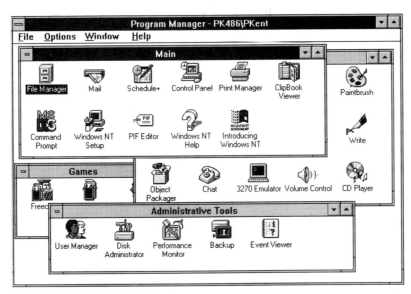

Figure 4.1 Windows NT's Program Manager

Tip The Save Settings Now command doesn't save program-group icon positions, only the size and position of *open* program groups and the positions of the icons within them. To save the positions of the program-group icons, press **Shift-Alt-F4**.

The new program group is the **Administrative Tools** group, which contains the following program icons:

User Manager	Set-up and administer user accounts. User account profiles define what a user may do to the system—which files and directories the user can use, what system settings may be changed, and so on. See Chapter 5.
Disk Administrator	Create and modify disk partitions, set up disk volume sets and striping. See Chapter 14.
Performance Monitor	View a variety of system parameters. See Chapter 12.
Backup	Back up data to tape-backup systems. See Chapter 19.
Event Viewer	View logs of important system, security, and application events, including error messages. See Chapter 13.

There are also several new program icons in other program groups:

Windows NT Help	(Main group) An entry to the Help system that lets you quickly find information about NT's command-prompt commands, view a glossary, view information

about support services and disability services, and search all NT's help files for information.

Command Prompt   (Main group) Similar to Windows 3.1's MS-DOS prompt window, except that additional, non-MS-DOS commands may be run.

Mail   (Main group) A network email system (originally released in Windows For Workgroups).

Schedule+   (Main group) A network scheduling program, to help you coordinate deadlines and meetings (originally released in Windows For Workgroups).

ClipBook Viewer   (Main group) An "extended" clipboard application, which lets you share clipboard data across the network and save Clipboard data for future use (originally released in Windows For Workgroups). This replaces the original Clipboard Viewer application.

Introducing Windows NT   (Main group) A Windows NT demo. It's a good idea to run this to get a simple overview of some basic NT features, such as file and directory security and user groups.

CD Player   (Accessories group) An application which plays music through your computer's CD-ROM player.

Volume Control   (Accessories group) An application which controls your sound board's volume.

Chat   (Accessories group) A "real-time" network message system, which allows you to communicate with another person by typing messages which appear on their computer immediately (originally released in Windows for Workgroups).

Freecell   (Games group) A solitaire-like card game.

A couple of icons (and their related applications) have been *removed*. You won't find **Calendar**—you simply don't need it anymore, because NT comes with a much more powerful application, Schedule+, which does everything Calendar could do plus a lot more.

Tip   If you still want to use Calendar, run your Windows 3.1 version. Or you can import your existing data into Schedule+. See Chapter 17.

And **Recorder**, the application that lets you create Windows macros, is no more. If you want to create your own Windows NT macros, you'll have to buy an add-on application, because the Windows 3.1 version won't work in NT.

Creating Program Groups

 Windows NT has two types of program groups, *personal* and *common* program groups. A **personal program group** is one which will appear for only one person; log off Windows NT and log on under a different name and that group will no longer be available. The program groups that Windows NT installs for you are all regarded as personal groups. If you log on under a different name you will find groups of the same names, but if you modify these groups, or add other personal groups, those changes will not appear in Program Manager when someone else logs on.

 Common program groups are available to all users, regardless of who they are. If five people have logon accounts on a machine, all five will see the same common program groups. Only an Administrator may create or modify common groups.

Creating groups is the same as in Windows 3.1; select **File|New**, click on Personal Program Group or Common Program Group (which is disabled if you are not an Administrator), type a program-group name, and click on OK. By the way, users without Administrative rights can still copy icons from a common group to a personal group—by holding Ctrl and dragging the icon—but they can't actually remove them from the common group, nor can they copy icons *to* the common group.

Tip   There's a way to further restrict the way in which users can work with Program Manager, stopping them from creating new groups and icons, copying or moving icons, and so on. See later in this chapter.

Hidden Applications

 There are a few icons you may want to add to Program Manager, applications that Microsoft keeps hidden—perhaps because some of the applications allow users *too much* power over the system. If you don't know what you are doing, you can get yourself into trouble. **SYSEDIT** is the same as in Windows 3.1—it is a Notebook-type application that opens four document windows, containing SYSTEM.INI, WIN.INI, CONFIG.SYS, and AUTOEXEC.BAT. Of course these are only useful if you are running DOS and Windows 3.1 applications.

 REGEDIT opens the Registration Info Editor, which lets you edit information about application-integration—applications that support OLE and File Manager's drop-and-drag functions. It also contains the information entered when you use File Manager's File|Associate command. There's also an advanced version of REGEDIT—use the command line **REGEDIT /V**—so you may want to create two icons. The advanced version lets you get into some pretty complicated system configuration information. You will rarely need to use this application, if ever, though you may have to change settings if advised to do so by an application vendor.

Note You can't have both types of Registration Info Editor open at the same time. So if you open the standard type, then try to open the advanced type, you'll still see only the standard Editor.

Regedt32

You may also want to create an icon for **REGEDT32.EXE**. This will open the Registry Editor, which contains all sorts of information about your system. Again, Microsoft doesn't want you to get into here unless you know what you are doing, but there may be occasions in which you will want to modify something. As you'll see later in this chapter, for instance, the Registry Editor lets you control the use of Program Manager, disabling menu commands. You can learn more about Registry Editor in Chapter 11.

Winmsd

You'll probably want to add Windows NT Diagnostics (WINMSD.EXE). This is a Windows NT version of Microsoft Diagnostics, which shipped with Windows 3.1. You can find lots of different types of information using this program, from the NT version number to memory configuration.

Qbasic

If you program in BASIC, you may want to create an icon for **QBASIC.EXE**, a program that lets you write code and compile it into executable computer code. The program also has online help and converts BASICA programs into QBASIC, and comes with a small program called REMLINE.BAS which removes line numbers from Microsoft Basic programs.

Even if you don't need to use QBASIC, you may want to use some of the sample applications. There's **Gorilla**, a game in which two giant apes, standing on skyscrapers, lob exploding bananas at each other, and **Nibbles**, in which you direct snakes across the screen as they gobble up numbers. (See Chapter 20 for more information about these games.) There's also Money Manager, a simple financial management tool—probably too simple. (Run QBASIC and open MONEY.BAS.)

Msrmnd32

If you use Schedule+, but don't want to open it every day, you may want to place the **MSRMND32.EXE** icon in your Startup program group. This runs a program in the background that checks your Schedule+ data for appointments, and displays a reminder dialog box at the appropriate time. See Chapter 17 for more information.

Drwatson

As in Windows 3.1, Dr. Watson, the software diagnostics program, is also hidden yet available in Windows NT. In fact, NT contains both versions of Dr. Watson, DRWATSON.EXE, the Windows 3.1 version, and DRWTSN32.EXE. You'll probably want to use the latter version. If an application error occurs, it automatically starts and creates a log called DRWTSN32.LOG—a log file that can be given to technical support personnel to help them track the problem. DRWTSN32.EXE has lots of options which control the method in which you are notified of a problem (you can assign a sound file if you wish), the type of data that will be saved, and the location of the log file. For more information run the program and view the Help file.

Finally, there's another application you may be interested in if you work with graphics much. NT's Print Manager has a halftone-management system that is used to adjust the manner in which your printer prints color and grayscale images. This lets you load a graphic, then adjust it for contrast, brightness, color, and tint. You can even adjust for various different types of lighting (noon sunlight, bond paper, cool white light, and so on). Then you can save the sample file with a different name. See Chapter 8 for more information.

Ctrl-Alt-Del — Windows NT Security

Before we move on, let's take a quick look at the Windows NT Security dialog box (Figure 4.2). Press **Ctrl-Alt-Del** at any time to view this box. (Press **Esc** to return to your applications.) This is a quick method for carrying out several operations. First, you'll notice that it shows you who is logged onto the machine. (This may be useful for an Administrator wanting to know who walked off and left the system up and running!) It also shows you the date and time of the logon.

In Windows 3.1, if an application ever locks up your system, you can use Ctrl-Alt-Del to close the application. In NT, however, there's no need to use Ctrl-Alt-Del. Simply press Ctrl-Esc to see the Task List dialog box and then use the End Task button to close the application.

Occasionally, your system may lock up so you can't use Ctrl-Esc. In this case you can press Ctrl-Alt-Del, then click on the Task List button in the Windows NT Security dialog box. Only rarely does a system ever lock up so totally that you can't even get to the Windows NT Security dialog box. (If it ever does, your only option is to reboot.)

The Windows NT Security dialog box has six options:

Lock Workstation	A sort of temporary logoff.
Logoff	The same as Program Manager's File|Logoff.
Shutdown	The same as Program Manager's File|Shutdown.

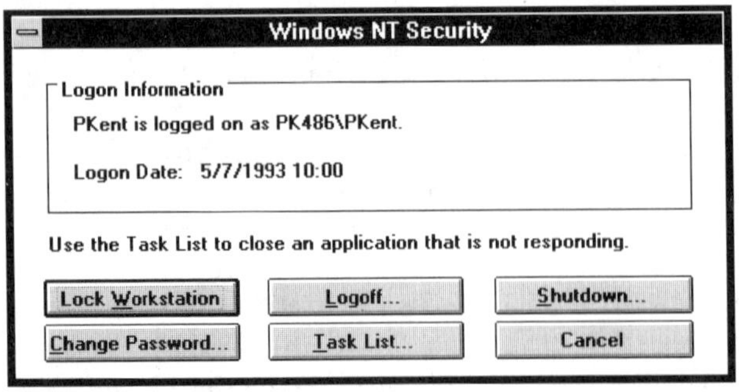

Figure 4.2 The Windows NT Security dialog box

Change Password	Lets you change your password.
Task List	Displays the Task List, the same as pressing Ctrl-Esc.
Cancel	Closes the dialog box and returns you to your work. (Or simply press Esc.)

The **Lock Workstation** option is a quick way to secure your workstation without going through the hassle of logging off. As soon as you select the option a dialog box appears, telling you that the workstation has been locked—it tells you who locked it, and at what time and on what date they did so. In order to use the computer again you must press Ctrl-Alt-Del and type your password into a dialog box, similar to the Welcome dialog box that appears when you logon. When the system is unlocked, the workstation will appear as it was before you locked it, with all the same applications open. An Administrator can also unlock the workstation, by entering his name and password, but he can't actually log back in at the same time—the system will unlock and log the current user off, possibly losing data in the process! Then the familiar "Press Ctrl-Alt-Del" message will appear on the screen, letting the Administrator log on using his own password.

The **Change Password** button lets a user change his password, or an Administrator change his or another person's password. (Actually, anyone can change anyone else's password, as long as they have that person's current password.) You'll see the dialog box shown in Figure 4.3. If you are an Administrator and want to change another person's password, enter the **Username** and, if necessary, the **From** computer (if that user's account is on another computer). Then type in the **Old Password**—to confirm that you have the right to change the password, and you're not just someone who walked up when the real user went to the bathroom. Then type the **New Password**, and type it again in **Confirm New Password**, confirming that you typed what you thought you did (remember, NT displays asterisks when you type). Passwords may be up to 14 characters long, must not include spaces, and are case sensitive. See Chapter 2 for more information about passwords. (Actually, a bug in this dialog box lets you use much longer passwords if you wish—40 characters or more. Because this is a bug, this is the only place where you can create such long passwords. You can't do so in User Manager.)

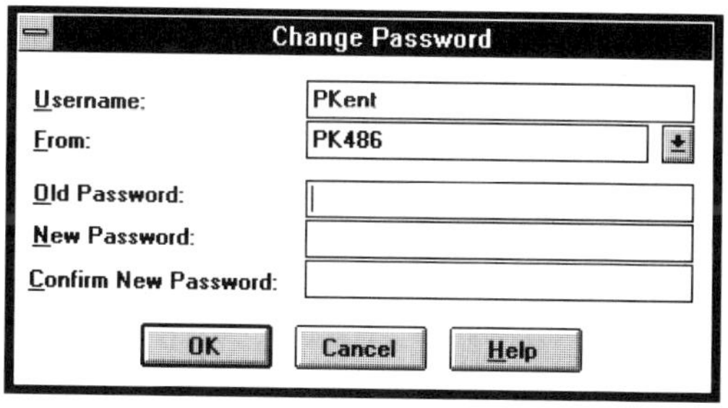

Figure 4.3 The Change Password dialog box

Note   Even an Administrator who is changing someone else's password must know that person's current password. But Administrators may also change passwords in User Manager, where they *don't* need to know the old password in order to create a new one. See Chapter 5.

Starting Applications and Multitasking

You will start applications from Program Manager in the same way you are used to from Windows 3.1—double-click on a program icon. There's something important that may take a little while to get used to, though. As soon as you tell NT to do something for you, it runs off and does it in the background, so you can continue working on something else.

In Windows 3.1, for instance, if you wanted to open several applications, you would double-click on an icon, wait until it opened, then return to Program Manager and click on the next. In NT you can open them all at the same time. You will double-click on the first icon, and NT starts opening the application. But before anything appears on your screen, you can double-click on the next icon, and the next, and NT will open all three for you.

This can be confusing for Windows 3.1 users, and in fact Microsoft had to create a new mouse pointer because of this confusion. In the early beta versions of NT, users would double-click on an icon, and the mouse pointer would turn to an "hour glass" for a moment or two and then turn back to an ordinary pointer. Users, thinking they hadn't double-clicked correctly, would then double-click again, not realizing that NT was working in the background, preparing to display the window belonging to the application they were opening.

So Microsoft created a new pointer—when you see an ordinary arrow pointer, with an hourglass next to it, it means that something's happening in the background. In the case of double-clicking on a program icon, it means NT is telling you that "yes, you double-clicked correctly and I'm opening the application, but you can do something else for a few seconds before I display the window."

When NT is ready it will display the windows of the applications you opened, but not necessarily in the order in which you opened them. Rather, as soon as one is ready, the window appears. Some applications take longer to open, so they won't appear for a while even if you double-clicked on their icons first.

There's another characteristic of multitasking that you will notice: When you click on a window you will find the cursor jumps to the position on which you clicked. In Windows 3.1 the first click would select the window, but have no effect on the cursor position.

Overall these characteristics of multitasking are a boon, because they let you get on with things instead of twiddling your thumbs. Generally task switching is much "snappier." You'll find some of the characteristics of multitasking irritating, though, such as when another application grabs control when you're in the middle of something (when you open the Task List dialog box, for instance, just as another operation finishes, the Task List box closes before you have a chance to get to it). There are many minor irritations related to multitasking in NT. Perhaps Microsoft will find a way to make future versions of NT operate a little more smoothly.

Starting Applications from Task List

There's a new way to start an application in Windows NT—from the Task List dialog box. Press **Ctrl-Esc** to open the Task List box, click the cursor in the **New Task** text box, type the name of the application—and path, if necessary—and press **Enter**. The application will open. This is a quick way to run an application, without having to return to Program Manager or File Manager.

Limiting Access to Features

If you are an Administrator, you may want to know how to limit a user's ability to work in Program Manager. For instance, you may wish to set up Program Manager with the program icons and groups that the user needs, but ensure that the user cannot create new ones, or run programs with the File|Run command.

In Windows 3.1 you can use PROGMAN.INI to do this, but Windows NT doesn't use this file anymore. These commands have been moved to the Configuration Registry. It's actually easier to modify the settings in NT, once you know where to go.

We're going to talk more about Registry Editor in Chapter 11, so these instructions are only a quick outline of what you need to do. Begin by opening Registry Editor, using the icon if you created one (NT doesn't do so automatically) or by running REGEDT32 with the File|Run Command. When Registry Editor opens, select the **HKEY_USERS on Local Machine** document window. Maximize it to make it easier to use.

Now, if you are going to have several people working on the machine, most of whom will have restricted Program Manager rights, you will want to change the defaults. So double-click on the Defaults directory. Then "travel" down the directory "tree," by double-clicking on the file-folder icons, along this path: **Default\Software\Microsoft\WindowsNT\CurrentVersion\ProgramManager \Restrictions**.When you get to Restrictions you'll notice several items in the panel to the right of the directory tree (see Figure 4.4). Here's what they are:

NoRun   =1 will disable the File|Run command.

NoClose   =1 will stop the user from closing NT by using Con-
                    trol|Close, Alt-F4, File|Logoff, or by double-clicking on the
                    Control menu. The user can still Shutdown the system,
                    though, and can also press Ctrl-Alt-Del and then click on
                    the Logoff button in the Windows NT Security dialog box
                    (though this is a bug).

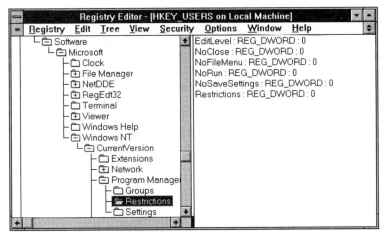

Figure 4.4 The Program Manager entries in Registry Editor

EditLevel	=1 The user cannot create, delete, or rename groups.
	=2 Same as Level 1, plus restricts actions carried out on program items. Disables File|New, File|Move, File|Copy, and File|Delete.
EditLevel	=3 Same as Level 2, plus disables the Command Line in the Program Item Properties dialog box, so the user can view icon information, but not create new ones.
	=4 Same as Level 3, plus disables all areas in the Program Item Properties dialog box, so the user can still view the information but not change it.
NoFileMenu	=1 Removes the File menu entirely.
NoSaveSettings	=1 Disables the Options|Save Settings on Exit and Options| Save Settings Now commands.
Restrictions	This entry is a bug and can be ignored.

You've just restricted access for *all* users. Now you can log on as the user you want to provide with more Program Manager rights, and open Registry Editor again. You'll open the **HKEY_USERS on Local Machine** document window again, but this time you will look below the DEFAULT *key* or "directory" and open the key that has a number. For instance, you might see S-1-5-21-21-2143564435-27001123-501965909-1000. Go down the tree in the same direction as before: **\Software\Microsoft\Windows NT\CurrentVersion\Program Manager\Restrictions**. Now you can remove the restrictions you added to the default setting. When you do so you are removing those restrictions from the user who is currently logged onto the computer.

Of course, you can do all this the other way around—leave the default settings with full access, and just limit the individual user's settings.

Remember, that if you leave a **File Manager** icon in a program group, a user can bypass some of these restrictions by opening File Manager and running programs from there. Of course you can also use File Manager's security features to restrict the user's access to certain files and directories—although you won't be able to stop the user getting to directories which are not on NTFS drive partitions. (See Chapter 7 for more information.) Another way to restrict Program Manager is to remove all **personal program groups** from users accounts, and only provide **common program groups**, so only an Administrator can make changes.

Jumping to Program Manager

Here's a tip that will help you swap back to Program Manager from other applications. Create an icon in the Startup program group for Program Manager (type PROGMAN in the Program Item Properties dialog box's Command Line text box). At the same time enter a Shortcut Key, in the same way you would create a shortcut for any application.

Now, when you log onto NT, Program Manager will start as an application. The only difference you will see is that the Program Manager title bar will no longer show the username and computer name (it'll show Progman, or whatever you enter into the icon's Description text box). Whenever you need to jump straight to Program Manager, press the shortcut you entered when you created its icon.

Program Manager's Menu Options

Finally, here's a quick summary of Program Manager's menu options:

File|New	Lets you create a new group window or icon.
File|Open (Enter)	Starts the application represented by the selected icon.
File|Move (F7)	Lets you move an icon from one group to another.
File|Copy (F8)	Lets you copy an icon from one group to another.
File|Delete (Del)	Deletes an icon or program group.
File|Properties (Alt-Enter)	Displays the selected icon's properties.
File|Run	Lets you enter the name of an application you want to run.
File|Logoff (Alt-F4)	Logs off Windows NT.
File|Shutdown	Logs off Windows NT and shuts down the operating system. Used when you want to switch off your computer or switch to another operating system.

Options|Auto Arrange	Makes Program Manager keep the program icons lined up tidily.
Options|Minimize on Use	Makes Program Manager minimize itself whenever you run an application.
Options|Save Settings on Exit	Makes Program Manager automatically save its settings—its program icon and program group positions, each time you close Windows.
Options|Save Settings Now	Makes Program Manager save its settings immediately. This is the same as holding Shift while you select File|Logoff, or holding Shift while you double-click on the Control menu.
Window|Cascade (Shift-F5)	Places the open group windows on top of each other, with each title bar visible.
Window|Tile (Shift-F4)	Places the open group windows so that all are visible, and all have the same amount of space.
Window|Arrange Icons	Tidies up the icons, placing them in lines, and equally spaced.
Window|*group names*	Opens the selected group window.
Window|More Windows	Lets you select and open a group window. This option only appears if you have more than nine group windows.

5

User Manager

Windows NT uses an application called User Manager to manage user accounts and groups. It's here that you will create and modify accounts, assign rights and passwords, and set up security logging.

If a computer has several users, you can let each user have different *rights* or *privileges*. One user may be able to do anything on the machine—from creating new printer profiles, to determining who can use what directories on the hard disk. Another user may have very restricted access, being allowed to run only one program and access only one file. Yet another might be able to access several directories and programs, but not others.

An **account** is created for each user on a computer, and a *username* is assigned to each account. As you've seen, the user must type his username—and an optional password—in order to log onto NT. Each user account may be a member of one or more *user groups*—or none. **User groups** let you define user rights for several users at once. For instance, if several users of one computer all do exactly the same thing—perhaps they are all accountants, or telephone-sales clerks—you can create a group, define the user rights for that group, and then assign each user to the group. That's much quicker than defining rights for each user, one by one. You can then assign **permissions** to the group as a whole. A *permission* is the ability to use a particular resource—a file, or directory, or printer. For instance, you can assign a permission to use a particular printer to a group, so that all members of that group can use it.

 There are two types of groups: **local groups** and **global groups**. A local group is the sort that you can create on your NT workstation. It can only have rights and permissions on its own computer, not on other computers on the network. Its members can be the workstation's user accounts, the domain's user accounts, the domain's global groups, and even users and global groups from "trusted" domains.

A **global group** is one which can operate on various workstations and servers in its domain and in other, "trusting" domains. The global group's members are user accounts from various workstations on the domain, and it may be a member itself, of local groups on various computers.

Administrators—users whose accounts are members of the Administrators group—have special rights that other users do not have. Most importantly, they have the right to determine what rights should be extended to those other users! When you first installed NT, Setup created one **Administrator account** automatically—named, aptly, *Administrator*. You may also have had the opportunity to create another account (the **initial account**), and enter whatever username you chose—this account is also a member of the Administrators group, so it has just the same rights as the Administrator account. (If you added the computer to a network domain the initial account was *not* created.) Setup also automatically created another user account, the **Guest** account. As you'll see later, this account has very limited rights on the system, and can be used for a short-term or one-time user. This account has no password, and can't be deleted.

Once you have logged on with one of the Administrator accounts, you can use User Manager's File|Rename command to change the Administrator username to whatever you wish—your own name, for instance. You can also create other Administrators. Simply create another account, then assign the account to the Administrators group (you'll see how a little later in this chapter).

The primary place in which you administer user accounts is User Manager, and most of this chapter is taken up with that application. However, there are other important places you must know about if you want to retain an iron grip on your users:

User Manager	This is where you add or modify information about users and their passwords, and create groups of users with similar rights. Although non-Administrators may *open* this application, much of it is off-limits to them.
Program Manager Restrictions	Stop users from accessing File Manager, running programs with the File|Run command, creating or modifying icons, and so on by modifying the Restrictions settings in the Registry Editor. See Chapter 4.
File Manager	Stop a user from getting to specific NTFS files and directories, and determine the *type* of access to others—read only, read and write, run programs, change access permissions, and so on. See Chapter 7.
Windows NT Security	Passwords can be changed from the Windows NT Security dialog box (press Ctrl-Alt-Del to get there), though you must know the

Windows NT Setup

person's current password to do so. Administrators can use User Manager to create a new password without knowing the current one.

User accounts can be removed using the Windows NT Setup application (see Chapter 3). This is where you will remove accounts created when users logged onto another computer from your computer.

Using User Manager

User Manager controls users and groups. It is used for assigning and modifying group names, usernames, and passwords. It is in this application that you also assign rights to users. User Manager is not fully available to all users, of course. It is only fully available to users who have **Administrator** rights, though **Power Users** can create new accounts and groups. Members of the **Users** group will be able to create groups, and assign existing accounts to those groups, but they won't be able to create or modify accounts, nor can they modify existing groups.

User Manager

Start User Manager using the icon in the Administrative Tools program group. Figure 5.1 shows User Manager. As you can see, it's split into two panels: The upper panel shows all the users, while the lower panel shows the groups. The users may be assigned to one or more groups, or to none at all. It's not obvious from this window which users belong to which groups. The easiest way to see the members in a particular group is by **double-clicking** on the group (or by selecting **User|Properties**). This displays the Local Group Properties dialog box. Unfortunately there's no way to see an overall picture of the different groups and members.

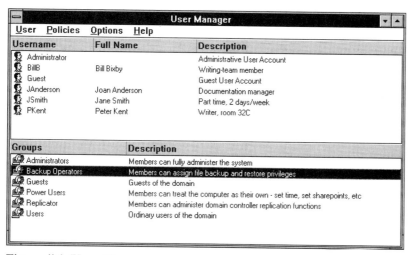

Figure 5.1 User Manager

Creating Groups

Let's begin by creating a new group. Simply select **User|New Local Group**. When the New Local Group dialog box appears (Figure 5.2), type a **Group Name** into the first text box—Documentation or Accounting, for instance. You can then type a **Description** if you wish, perhaps a short explanation of that group's function or what rights the group will have. Try to limit this description to about 45 characters, because a description longer than that can't be read in some of the dialog boxes in which it will appear. Now you may click on OK to finish creating the group, or click on the **Add** button to see the Add Users and Groups dialog box (Figure 5.3) and begin adding members to the group.

First, select the computer that contains the accounts you want to add to this group from the **List Names From** drop-down list box. Now select the users you want to add—you can quickly find the first name you want to select by typing the first character in that name. To select from the list, press **Ctrl** while you click on the names you want. Or press **Shift** and **drag** the mouse down a group of names. (You can also press **Shift** and the **up** or **down arrow key**.) Click on the **Add** button and the selected names are placed in the **Add Names** list.

INTERACTIVE   If your computer is an NT Advanced Server, you can add *global groups* to the group you are creating. So this list might include global groups as members. If it does, you can select a group and click on the **Members** button to display a list of all the members of that group.

You can also click on the **Search** button to see the Find Account dialog box (Figure 5.4). Type the name of the account or group you want to add, then select one of the option buttons—select **Search All** if you would like to look in all the computers on the network, or **Search Only In** if you want to select one of the computers from the list (only NT Advanced Server domains and NT workstations, of course). Then click on the **Search** button, and the matching entry, if any, will be placed in the **Search Results** list. Click on the **Add** button to return to the Add Users and Groups dialog box and add the account or group you found.

When you've finished in the Add Users and Groups dialog box, click on the **OK** button. The names in the **Add Names** list will be added to the New Local

Figure 5.2 The New Local Group dialog box

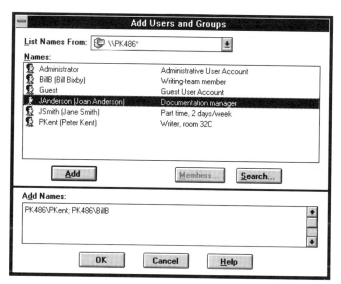

Figure 5.3 The Add Users and Groups dialog box

Group dialog box's **Members** list. The **Show Full Names** button in this dialog box, by the way, makes the list show not only the usernames but also the full name entered into the users' properties. We will learn about that in a moment.

You don't have to add members when you create a group. It doesn't matter which way around you do it. You can create a group first, then create user accounts and assign each user to a group at the same time you enter their username

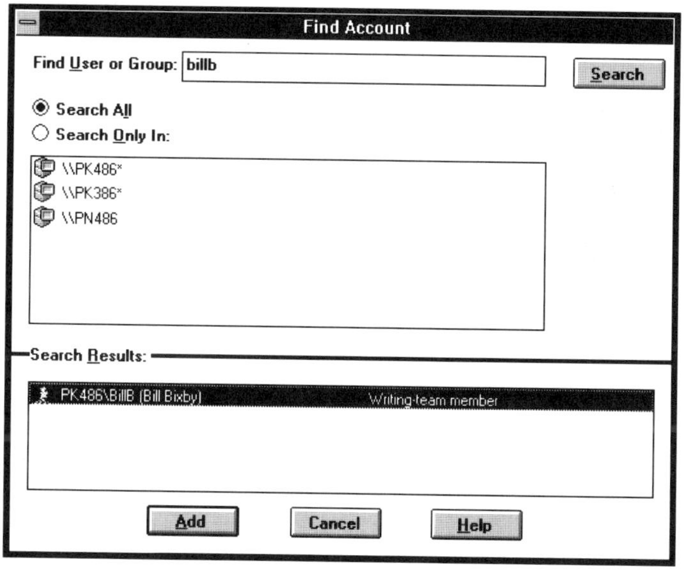

Figure 5.4 The Find Account dialog box

and password (as we'll explain in a moment). Or create all the user accounts first, then create groups and assign users.

More About Groups

NT automatically creates the following groups for you, and creates profiles for each one that allow their members special privileges or rights:

Administrators	Members of this group can carry out any operation on the system.
Backup Operators	Members of this group can use the Tape Backup program to both back up and restore data.
Guests	Members of this group have very restricted rights. They can log on and off, and create new files, but they can't change existing files or connect to another network computer.
Power Users	Members of this group have a few administration rights. They can create new accounts and groups (but not change existing ones), share directories and printers, change the system time, access the computer from another one, and create common program groups in Program Manager.
Replicator	This is a special-purpose group used by NT Advanced Server for directory replication (the automatic copying of data from one machine to another across the network). Its sole purpose is replication, so you wouldn't assign a real user to this group. Its only member will be a domain user, and this account should be given the "Log on as a service" privilege in the User Rights Policy dialog box (explained later in this chapter).
Users	New accounts are automatically added to this group. If the computer is part of a network domain, the Domain Users group is also a member of the local Users group, providing all domain members with access to this computer. (Remove the Domain Users group from the Users group to stop users on other computers from getting to this computer.) Members have fairly limited rights; they can create and modify their own files, however.

Note You cannot delete any of the above groups.

There are several other "groups" that you won't see listed. These are the *special* groups, groups that don't need to be administered, so they don't appear in User Manager. They *do* appear elsewhere in NT, however. You'll see them in the Add Users and Groups dialog box in File Manager, for example, when assigning file access, so you can modify or limit the type of access that these groups can have.

Everyone	Everyone	Everyone means just that, everyone, regardless of group membership, who is using the computer, unless they have one of the groups special rights specifically denied to them. For instance, members of the Guests group cannot access the network, though members of the Everyone group can.
INTERACTIVE	Interactive	Anyone using the computer locally.
NETWORK	Network	Anyone using the computer over the network.
SYSTEM	System	The operating system itself.
CREATOR OWNER	Creator Owner	The user who created or owns a directory, file, printer, or a document sent to a printer. You'll learn in Chapters 7 and 8 how users can "own" directories, documents, and printers.

Rights vs. Built-in Abilities

There are two classes of features that can be assigned to users: *rights* and *built-in abilities*. A **right** is a feature or capability that can be assigned to a user. The default groups already have certain rights assigned to them, but you can assign more rights to these groups, or to individual users or other groups, using the User Rights Policy dialog box, explained later in this chapter. These rights are listed later, and include such things as the ability to take ownership of files and printers, and the ability to back up and restore files and directories.

The **built-in ability** is something that cannot be assigned to an individual user or to other groups—if you want a user to be able to carry out one of these operations, you must add the user to the applicable group. For instance, Administrators and Power Users can create common program groups in Program Manager—program groups that are available to all users. You can't assign that right to other users or other groups—you must assign a user to the Administrators or Power Users group, instead.

These are the built-in abilities:

Create user accounts and groups	Administrators and Power Users
Modify the Administrators or Backup Operators groups	Administrators
Modify the Power Users, Users, and Guests groups	Administrators and Power Users

Assign user rights	Administrators
Lock the workstation	Administrators, Power Users, Users
Override the lock of the workstation	Administrators
Open Disk Administrator	Administrators
Format a hard disk	Administrators
View a security log in Event Viewer	Administrators
Create common program groups (Program Manager)	Administrators, Power Users
Keep Local Profile	Administrators, Power Users, Users, Back-up Operators
Share directories and printers	Administrators and Power Users

To "Keep a Local Profile" means to store information about the setup in the configuration registry. Because members of the Guest account cannot keep a local profile, when they log off no configuration information is stored for their accounts—changes made to the Control Panel, for instance. The next time they log on they are starting with a "clean slate."

Creating User Accounts

To add a new user to the system, select **User|New User**. When the New User dialog box appears (see Figure 5.5), begin by entering a **Username**. The username is simply the account name, the way the user will identify himself to the computer, telling the computer where to look for more detailed information when he logs on. It doesn't have to be the person's real name. In fact you can even assign one user account to several people if you wish (in the way that the Guests account may be used for different people). Generally, though, you'll assign a name that is close to the person's real name. For instance, you might assign the name **Pkent** or **PeterK.** Or you might prefer **Kentp** or **Kpeter**, because the names are going to be sorted alphabetically in the User Manager list. You can use up to 20 characters, including spaces, but you can't use the following characters:

" / \ [ ] : ; | = , + * ? < >

Of course, this name must be unique, a different name from the others already assigned to this machine or the domain of which the computer is a member.

On the next line you can enter the person's **Full Name**, though you don't have to. You can enter dozens of characters, including spaces or any other character you wish, but should restrict the name to 31 characters or less. This will allow it to fit in the dialog boxes in which it will have to be displayed. On the line after that you can enter a **Description**—a short explanation of the person's duties on the computer, for instance, or of the user's rights. Again, this line is optional, and can include up to 48 characters, though you should limit it to about 45.

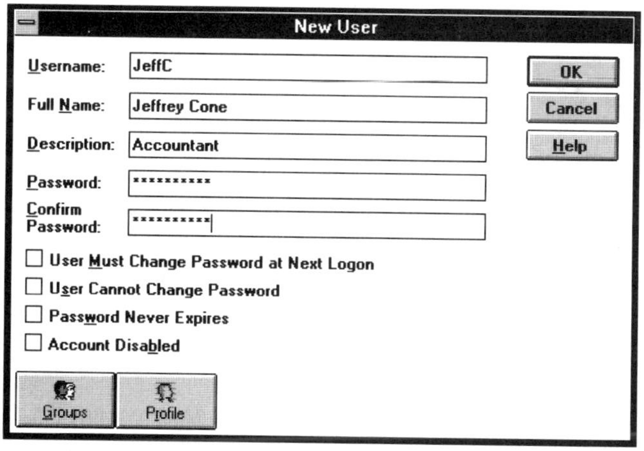

Figure 5.5 The New User dialog box

The next line—**Password**—is also optional. By default you don't need a password (though it's possible to "ban" blank passwords—we'll see how in a moment). If you do enter a password, you won't see the characters as you type, you'll see asterisks instead. This is a common security measure that stops someone from peering over your shoulder to look at your password as you type it. But because you can't see what you are typing, you may make a mistake and not know it, so NT has another line, **Confirm Password**. You must type the same password again. If you type a different one, it means you made a mistake somewhere, and you won't be able to continue—go back to the Password line and try again.

The password can be up to 14 characters, can include any character on the keyboard (including spaces), and is case sensitive—that is, the user will have to type the password exactly as you defined it, using the same case. If you type #RttBYE, the user won't be able to type #rttbye. (The username, by the way, is *not* case sensitive.) There's more to know about passwords. We'll look at them again later in this chapter when we cover the Account Policy. (Incidentally, there's a bug in NT that allows you to create much larger passwords, 40 characters or more. Press Ctrl-Alt-Del to see the Windows NT Security dialog box, then click on the Change Password button. The dialog box you see accepts long passwords. See Chapter 4 for more information.)

Note For a detailed discussion about picking secure passwords, see Chapter 2.

Now look at the check boxes at the bottom of the dialog box. The first one, **User Must Change Password at Next Logon** means exactly what it says. NT will force the user to select a new password the first time he logs on. If you, the Administrator, assign a password to a new user you will probably either write it down, or make it a simple, easy-to-remember password. It's much safer to require that the new user choose a unique password of his own.

You may select **User Cannot Change Password** instead, if you wish. This cannot be used at the same time as the first check box, of course. Although selecting one doesn't automatically deselect the other, when you close the dialog box you'll see a message telling you that you can't use both. Again, this means exactly what it says—the user will be unable to change the assigned password. Note that this provides a way to create an account that is automatically disabled after the password expiration period. When the password expires, NT will ask the user to create a new one—but won't accept the new one!

Note   Select the User Cannot Change Password option when creating accounts that will be used by more than one person, so no one can lock the others out of the account.

The **Password Never Expires** check box will override any expiration setting in the Account Policy dialog box. This dialog box (which we'll look at later) lets you make all passwords expire after a certain number of days. If Password Never Expires is checked in the New User dialog box, though, that user is an exception, and does not need to change the password after the normal expiration period. You should use this option for special system accounts such as Replicator, so that the system won't force Replicator to choose a new password, effectively locking Replicator out.

The Password Never Expires check box also overrides the User Must Change Password at Next Logon check box. In other words, if *both* are checked, the user will *not* have to enter a new password at logon (and the check mark will be removed from the first box when you close the dialog box).

The last check box, **Account Disabled**, is used to stop the user from logging on. You are more likely to use this box when editing account information than when creating a new user, of course. However, you may want to create an account and leave it disabled until you are ready to use it. Or you may want to create a template account, disable it, and then use it to create new accounts (with the User|Copy command).

Having created a new user account, you can now assign it to a group. Click on the **Groups** button to see the Group Memberships dialog box (Figure 5.6). You'll notice that the new account is already a member of the Users group. This gives this new user fairly limited rights, enough to work in applications but not to modify NT's operating characteristics or back up data to tape, for instance. On the right side of the box is a list of groups of which the new user is not a member. You can select any of these groups and click on the **Add** button to move that group name to the Member Of list box. If you want the user to be able to make tape backups, for instance, click on Backup Operators and then click on Add. To remove a name from the Member Of list you do the opposite, select the name and click on **Remove**.

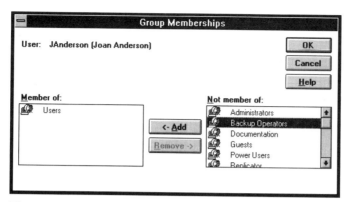

Figure 5.6 The Group Memberships dialog box

Tip You can also drag entries between the two lists. You must drag the *icon*, not the name of the group.

The **Profile** button at the bottom of the New User dialog box displays the User Environment Profile dialog box (see Figure 5.7). This lets you assign a script that will be run when the user logs on, and lets you assign a "home" directory, one that applications will use as the default when the user tries to open or save files.

To run a script, simply enter a .CMD, .BAT, or .EXE name in the **Logon Script Name** text box. The script is similar to AUTOEXEC.BAT in DOS—it runs various programs and commands that you use to set up the system configuration before beginning work. Don't enter the script's path here, just the name of the file. The file must be in the \WINNT\SYSTEM32\REPL\IMPORT\SCRIPTS directory, or you may create a subdirectory in the SCRIPTS directory, then enter *subdirectory-name\filename* in the Logon Script Name box.

This feature runs a program in the same way the Startup program group in Program Manager does, so you can run your Logon Script by creating an icon and placing it in the Startup group. You will have more control over the directory

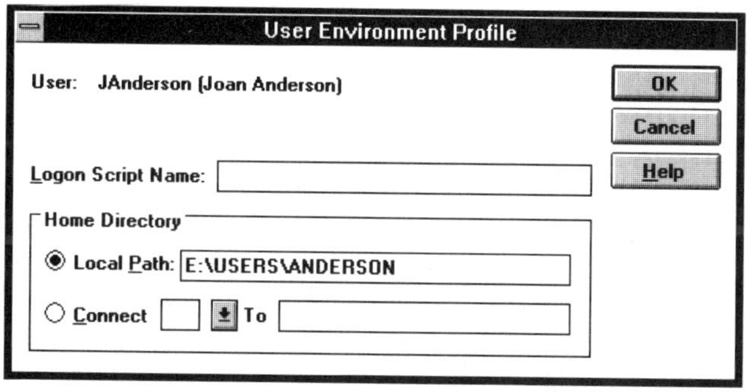

Figure 5.7 The User Environment Profile dialog box

in which the file is stored, too. The difference is that the Logon Script is not under the control of the ordinary user, though the Startup group *is* (although it can be placed out of the user's control in various ways).

A **Home Directory** is similar to the *working directory* that you can define in an application's program icon. But the home directory affects *all* applications. For instance, when you type a filename—without a drive letter and path—into the Program Item Properties dialog box, NT will assume that file is in your home directory. This home directory will also be used by the Command Prompt. Windows NT Setup creates a directory called \USERS—you might want to create individual user's directories as subdirectories of \USERS.

To set the default home directory, type its path name into the **Local Path** text box. Now all applications will use this as the default, *unless* you enter a different path in the Program Item Properties dialog box when creating a new program icon, or you enter one into a DOS application's PIF (Program Information File).

Note   If you are assigning an existing directory as the home directory, go to File Manager and make sure that the user has the right to use that directory. See Chapter 7.

You can name a **nonexisting home directory**, and User Manager will create it for you, and assign the user full control over that directory. You can also make NT use a **network drive** as the home directory. Click on the **Connect** option button, select a drive letter from the drop-down list box, then type the directory to which you want to connect. For instance, if you type **\\PK386\C\1-winnt\book,** when you next log on NT looks across the network for a computer called PK386, then looks for the BOOK subdirectory, in the 1-WINNT directory, on the C: drive (don't include a colon after the drive letter). NT then connects you to that directory (assuming the directory exists and your network features are set up correctly to allow access to it), and it will even add a drive icon to File Manager for you. That drive will be your default working directory.

Note   You can change between a local and a network drive without retyping the path each time. If you type a path into the network text box, then click on the Local Path option button, the text in the network box will disappear. It will reappear when you click on the Connect option button.

As you'll see later, you can use this dialog box to configure **several accounts** at once—you can do so when modifying accounts by selecting several accounts and then selecting User|Properties. You can still specify individual Home Directories, by using **%USERNAME%** as the name of the directory (for instance, you might enter E:\USERS\%USERNAME%). User Manager will then substitute the username for each account, and create all the necessary directories for you.

Copying User Accounts

There's a quick way to create a new user account—you can **copy** another account. Select the account with the profile you want to use, and then select **User|Copy** (or press **F8**). You'll see a New User dialog box (although its name will be Copy of . . .). The Description will be the same as the copied account, as will the check boxes at the bottom of the dialog box. Now all you need to do is enter a new username, full name, and password. The account's **group memberships** will be the same, also, though you can make any changes you want.

The **Home Directory** in the User Environment Profile is a special case. When you copy the account, User Manager looks at the last directory in the path. If the name of the last directory is exactly the same as the username, then User Manager will create a new directory using the new username. For example, you copy the account named PKent, whose home directory is E:\USERS\PKENT. When you create a new account—with the username RPetrush—User Manager creates a new directory: E:\USERS\RPETRUSH.

User Manager *will not* copy **rights and permissions**, only group memberships. (A right is the ability to carry out an operation, set in the User Rights Policy dialog box, as explained below. A permission is the ability to work with a particular resource—a printer or file, for instance—and is set in another application—in Print Manager and File Manager.)

You may want to create several template accounts, accounts set up with particular user settings, and then use these templates to create new accounts when needed. You can use the Account Disabled check box in the User Properties dialog box to make the templates nonfunctioning accounts. (When you create a new account by copying, User Manager will automatically turn off the Account Disabled check box in the copy.)

Modifying Information and Deleting

Administrators can modify information related to any user on the computer, including themselves. To change a username, simply select the name, select **User|Rename**, and type a new name into the box. (You can only change usernames, by the way, not group names.) To change descriptions, full names, group memberships, environment profiles, and password options, double-click on the user in the User Manager (or highlight the user and then press **Enter**, or select **User|Properties**) to see the User Description dialog box, which is almost exactly the same as the New User box (the only difference is you can't change the username). You can also select several accounts at once (drag the mouse across them or hold Ctrl while you click on them). Then press **Enter** or select **User|Properties**. (You can also double-click on the last one while still holding Ctrl to open this dialog box.) This time you'll see a User Properties dialog box with a list of the selected users at the top (see Figure 5.8). You can't change usernames or full names, but you can change the Description for all the accounts at once. Also, the

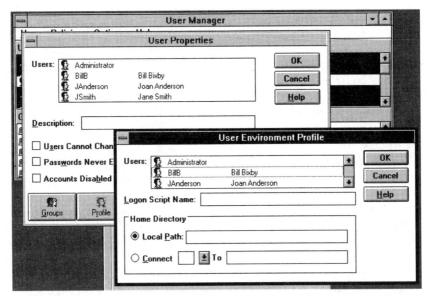

Figure 5.8 The User Properties dialog box, after selecting several users

Groups and User Environment Profile information will not be correct, of course, because it's probably different for each account. You can, however, use these dialog boxes to change all the selected accounts to the same settings.

This can be a little confusing. The Group Memberships dialog box, for example, will show two lists: All Are Members Of and Not All Are Members Of. The first list shows groups of which all selected users are members—that's clear enough. If you want to make sure all the accounts are members of a particular group, select from the Not All Are Members Of list and click on the Add button. The Not All Are Members Of list, however, includes all groups that have only some or none of the selected users as members. To make sure all the selected users are *not* members, select the group, click on Add, close the dialog box, reopen the dialog box, select the group in the All Are Members Of list, click on Remove, and close the dialog box.

To **delete** a user account or group from the User Manager window, select it and press **Del** (or select **User|Delete**). You'll see a warning box telling you that you'll never be able to restore the exact same user account, even if you create a new account with the same name—click on OK, then click on Yes in the confirmation box. (You cannot delete the default accounts—the Administrator and Guest, for instance—though they can be renamed.)

Each user account is assigned a SID, a *security identifier.* It is the SID that is actually used when you assign permissions to an account—when, for instance, you assign the right to use a particular file or directory in File Manager—not the name of the account. So if you delete an account, then later decide you want to restore the account, you can recreate it with exactly the same name, but the permissions you assigned are lost because the new account will have a new SID. If you are not sure yet if you really want to delete an account, just disable it instead using the Account Disabled check box in the User Properties dialog box.

Forgotten Passwords

What happens if a user forgets his **password**? There's no way he can get into the system without the help of the Administrator. The Administrator can assign a new password to any user, without knowing the old one. He simply enters a new password in the User Description dialog box, types it into the Confirm Password text box, clicks on OK, and is finished. Note, however, that whenever you assign a new password, the User Must Change Password at Next Logon check box is automatically selected, so you'll have to uncheck it if you don't want to use this feature.

The Administrator can also change his own password in the same way. Of course to change his password he has to log on first—which requires a password. So there is no way that an Administrator can change his password without using the existing one. In other words, if he forgets his password, he can't assign a new one. Losing the password is a very serious problem for a system that has only one Administrator and the only way to solve the problem is to reload NT. However, you can assign Administrator rights to another person, by simply assigning him to the Administrators group. Then if one Administrator forgets his password the other can assign a new one. Remember that we're all mortal, and no system should be dependent on the presence of one person. There should be someone else who either has user-profile privileges, or who knows the Administrator's password.

Assigning Rights to Users

There are two ways to assign rights to a user. You can assign the user to a group—and the user automatically gets the rights assigned to that group—or you can assign specific rights to the user. When you assign a user to a group, he automatically assumes the rights that all members of the group share. (When you create a new user's account, the user automatically becomes a member of the User group, and has the rather limited rights assigned to that group.)

You can modify the rights that any group has, or even assign special rights to individual users independent of their group memberships. You've already seen how to assign users to groups. When you want to modify a group's rights, or to assign rights to an individual rather than a group, select **Policies|User Rights**. You'll see the dialog box shown in Figure 5.9. The **Right** drop-down list box lists the various types of rights that are available, while the **Grant To** list box shows who has the currently displayed right. Initially the Right drop-down list box holds only a limited number of basic rights. Click on the **Show Advanced User Rights** to add all the advanced rights to the list.

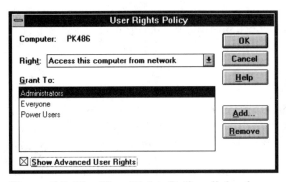

Figure 5.9 The User Rights Policy dialog box

These are the basic rights listed in the Right box:

Right	Description	Groups
Access this computer from network	Access the computer from another network workstation.	A E P
Backup files and directories	Use Backup to back up data to tape. This overrides any security settings in File Manager.	A B
Change the system time	Use the Control Panel to change the computer's time and date.	A P
Force shutdown from a remote system	Shut the computer down from another computer on the network. (This feature will be added to future revisions of NT.)	A P
Log on locally	Log onto and off the computer from the computer's own keyboard.	A B E G P U
Manage auditing and security log	Specify what events should be logged in the security log (in File Manager, ClipBook Viewer, Print Manager, and User Manager), and view and clear the security log. See Chapter 13.	A
Restore files and directories	Use Backup to restore files from tape backup. Caution: This overrides any security settings protecting files in File Manager— someone with the right to restore files can overwrite files that he has no right to modify.	A B

Right	**Description**	**Groups**
Shut down the system	Shut down the computer.	A B E P U G
Take ownership of files or other objects	Use File Manager to take over files and directories.	A

The groups in the preceding table are as follows:

A   Administrators

B   Backup Operators

E   Everyone

G   Guest

P   Power Users

U   Users

Most of the advanced rights are of interest only to programmers and testers. The following are the rights that are added to the dialog box if you select the **Show Advanced User Rights** check box:

Act as part of the operating system

Bypass traverse checking

Create a pagefile

Create a token object

Create permanent shared objects

Debug programs

Generate security audits

Increase quotas

Increase scheduling priority

Load and unload device drivers

Lock pages in memory

Log on as a batch job

Log on as a service

Modify firmware environment values

Profile single process

Profile system performance

Receive unsolicited device input

Remote Access

Replace a process level token

The only ones you are likely to ever need are **bypass traverse checking** (a user can view a directory tree, moving through directories in which he has no rights), and **Log on as a service** (used by special system accounts such as Replicator, accounts that are used for services rather than actual users).

Notice that some of these rights are assigned to Everyone, *and* to other groups as well. Isn't that redundant? Well, not exactly. You might decide that you don't want Everyone to have access to a certain procedure and remove the right from that group, but it's important to remember that the right is still assigned to the other groups. The overlapping of groups lets you deny rights very selectively. Notice also that the Guest group has no rights except that of logging on and off, though of course users in the Guests group are also members of the Everyone group, and have the rights assigned to that group.

To assign a right, begin by selecting the right from the drop-down list box. Then click on the **Add** button to see the Add Users and Groups dialog box. This is almost the same as the one shown in Figure 5.3, except that it has a **Show Users** dialog box. When you first open the dialog box it lists only groups—if you want to assign the rights to individual user accounts, click on the **Show Users** button and the dialog box adds all the users. You can now select the user—or select a combination of users and groups—and click on **Add** to add them. There's a shortcut to get to the name of a group or user—type the first character of the name, and the highlight will move to the first name that begins with that letter.

You can also select a group and click on **Members** to see a list of all the members in that group, or use the **Search** button to search for a particular group or user, as we described earlier in this chapter (see Figure 5.4).

There's also a **Remove** button in the User Rights Policy dialog box, which lets you remove a right from a group or person (or remove that group or person from the right, functionally speaking). Select the right, select the group or person, and click on Remove.

As we discussed earlier (**Rights vs. Built-in Abilities**), there are certain procedures that cannot be assigned to a user—to use one of these built-in abilities, a user must be assigned to a group which has them. For instance, if you want a user to be able to create and manage accounts, you cannot simply assign this as a "right." The user must be assigned to either the Administrators or Power Users group. (Power Users can create and manage their own accounts, but cannot change existing accounts.)

Changing Account (Password) Policies

Select **Policies|Account** to see the dialog box shown in Figure 5.10. This dialog box only handles password policies, determining how users will work with passwords. In the top left you can decide whether or not you want the password to expire, and, if it will, the **Maximum Password Age**. You can determine any duration from 1 to 999 days, and at the end of that period users will have to renew their password when they log on. Remember, however, that the Password Never

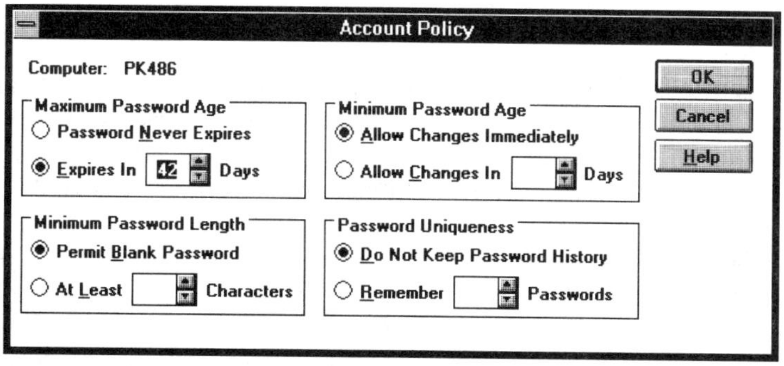

Figure 5.10 The Account Policy dialog box

Expires check box in a user's User Properties dialog box will override this expiration period. You may also select the **Password Never Expires** option button, instead, so nobody's password will ever expire.

You also have the option of assigning a **Minimum Password Age**, so that users *cannot* modify their passwords until the period has passed. Again, you can set a period of up to 999 days. If you don't want users to modify passwords, though, you should probably check the **User Cannot Change Password** check box in the User Properties dialog boxes. There are no great advantages to denying users the ability to change passwords. It may save the Administrator the minor irritation of having to assign new passwords to users who have forgotten their most recent ones, but at the expense of reduced security. Passwords are more secure when they are constantly changing.

The **Minimum Password Length** is, by default, set to 0 characters, because the **Permit Blank Password** option button is selected. This allows any user to simply enter his or her username at the logon prompt and then press Enter, without bothering to type a password. This is not very secure, though it does have advantages, especially on a computer that is used by only one person, and in a secure location. (There's also a way to bypass the logon prompt entirely, using a program called Desktop+. See Chapter 22 for more information.) If you don't want to allow users to have blank passwords, enter a number into the **At Least** incrementer box. You can enter any number up to 14, the maximum length of a password. By the way, if you allowed blank passwords but then assign a minimum length, existing passwords—whether blank or simply shorter than the new limit—remain in effect unless you assign new ones.

Finally, you can stop users from reusing recent passwords. The **Do Not Keep Password History** option button is selected by default, which means when a user is forced to change a password he can reuse one he's used in the past (except the one he's currently using, of course). But you can tell NT to **Remember** passwords, any number up to eight. That means the user will be unable to re-use any of the last eight passwords—he'll be forced to come up with a new one.

Auditing Security Events

NT lets you create a security log, a file called SecEvent.EVT in the WINNT \SYSTEM32\CONFIG directory. This file stores information about particular events related to the security of the system, and can be viewed using the Event Viewer (see Chapter 13). Several applications, including User Manager, let you set up security logging.

When you select **Policies\Audit** you will see the Audit Policies dialog box, as shown in Figure 5.11. If the **Do Not Audit** option button is selected the auditing system is turned off, and you won't be able to select audit events.

You can log these events by clicking on the **Audit These Events** and clicking on the check boxes:

Logon and Logoff	A user logs onto or logs off the computer or a network.
File and Object Access	A user accessed a directory, a file, or a printer set for auditing in File Manager or Print Manager.
Use of User Rights	A user used an assigned right (other than logging on or off).
User and Group Management	A user account or group was created, modified, or removed, or a password was set or modified.
Security Policy Changes	A change was made to this dialog box or in the User Rights Policy dialog box.
Restart, Shutdown, and System	The system was restarted or shut down, or a system security or security log event occurred.
Process Tracking	Events such as program activation, indirect object access, and process exits.

In each case, you can log both **Success** (events in which a user succeeds in carrying out the procedure) and **Failure** (events in which the user tries but is unable to complete a task).

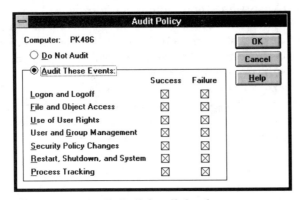

Figure 5.11 Audit Policies dialog box

Assigning Permissions to Files and Directories

You can restrict user's *permissions* to files and directories using File Manager's Security menu. You've looked at **rights** in this chapter—a right is the ability of a user to carry out some kind of procedure. A **permission**, though, is the right to work with a particular "object," a file, directory, or printer.

This is a very useful feature, because it can severely limit a user's options. If you want a particular user—or the Guest group, for instance—to be able to use only a word processor and a directory for storing documents, you can make sure that the user cannot get to anything else—she will be unable to run programs, view, copy, delete, or move files, and so on. Using this method, you can place anything off limits, preventing a user from getting to File Manager, for instance, or from using the Command Prompt.

Only NTFS (NT File System) drives are supported by this feature, so if you have a drive that is non-NTFS (even if it is running NT), you won't be able to protect that drive. Also, restricting access to directories can lead to problems if you're not careful. It's one of the few areas of the system where it's possible for someone to completely lock out everyone. If, for example, the Administrator takes control of a directory and then forgets his password—or quits the company—no one but another Administrator will be able to get into the directory. For more information, see Chapter 7.

"Disabling" User Management

Some users won't want to set up different accounts, and allow users different rights. In some cases, of course, the computer will have only one user and he will want full access. Perhaps the easiest way to do this is to use the method described in Chapter 3 to bypass the logon screen, and automatically log on as an Administrator—anyone using the computer will then have full access to all procedures.

You can also simply create all user accounts as members of the Administrators group, again providing full access to all features.

User Manager's Menu

Here's a quick summary of User Manager's menu:

User|New User	Creates a new user account.
User|New Local Group	Creates a new user group.
User|Copy (F8)	Creates a new account or group, copying the settings from an exisitng one.
User|Delete (Del)	Deletes the selected user account or group.

User|Rename	Renames the selected user account. (You can't rename a group.)
User|Properties (Enter)	Displays user properties or group properties, and lets you modify them.
User|Exit (Alt-F4)	Closes User Manager.
Policies|Account	Lets you define password policies for all accounts.
Policies|User Rights	Lets you define who should have what user rights.
Policies|Audit	Lets you define what events should be audited (if any). Audited events can be viewed in the Event Viewer's Security log.
Options|Confirmation	Toggles confirmation boxes on and off. Confirmation boxes appear when you carry out certain operations, such as deleting accounts.
Options|Save Settings on Exit	If this option is selected, User Manager saves the window's nonmaximized size and position and the Confirmation setting when you close User Manager. (You can't hold Shift and select File|Exit, as you can in File Manager.)

6

Control Panel

Windows NT retains the Control Panel that you are familiar with from Windows 3.1 (see Figure 6.1). Of course it's changed somewhat—icons have been added, and dialog boxes modified. These are the icons that match the ones in Windows 3.1:

Color	The same as Windows 3.1.
Fonts	A minor change in function: No Enable TrueType Fonts check box.
Ports	A minor change in format.
Mouse	A minor change in function: no Mouse Trails check box.
Desktop	The same as Windows 3.1.
Keyboard	The same as Windows 3.1.
Printers	Now opens Print Manager (see Chapter 8).
International	The same as Windows 3.1.
Date/Time	The dialog box now contains time zone information.
MIDI Mapper	The same as Windows 3.1.

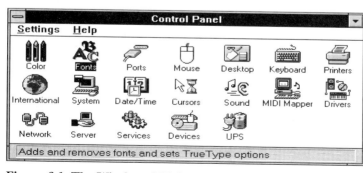

Figure 6.1 The Windows NT Control Panel

Drivers   The same as Windows 3.1.

Networks   Very different—see Chapter 16 for more information.

Sound   Similar to Windows 3.1, but with some extra sounds.

These icons are new to Windows NT:

System   NT's equivalent to the 386 Enhanced icon. The dialog box lets you control Flexboot, determining which operating system should boot automatically; set system- and user-environment variables; and control virtual memory.

Cursors   Lets you select the type of mouse pointer you want to use for various functions.

Server   Lets you monitor and administer network connections using your computer's resources. See Chapter 15.

Services   Lets you control special services such as a UPS, the event log, and various network services, stopping, starting, and pausing those services.

Devices   Provides control over system software devices, starting and stopping them, and setting them to start automatically.

UPS   Lets you set up the interface between your computer and an "intelligent," uninterruptible power supply.

Notice also that Windows NT still has a **Printers** icon in the Control Panel, but it is there merely for convenience. It now opens Print Manager—unlike Windows 3.1, there is no separate Control Panel function that administers printing, because everything is done from the Print Manager (where, many people would say, it should have been all along!). You can, of course, also open Print Manager with the icon in Program Manager.

There's no **386 Enhanced** icon. Some of the functions of that dialog box are no longer relevant, and the ones that are—the virtual memory configuration—are controlled by the System dialog box.

The rest of this chapter describes each of the Control Panel dialog boxes in the order in which they appear in the panel, except in those cases in which the dialog box is exactly the same as in Windows 3.1 (Color, Desktop, Keyboard, International, MIDI Mapper, and Drivers), and in the case of Printers (see Chapter 8), and the Network and Server dialog boxes (see Chapter 15).

Fonts

 This dialog box is almost exactly the same as in Windows 3.1. The only exception is that when you click on the TrueType button you'll see a dialog box with one option—Show Only TrueType Fonts in Applications. In Windows 3.1 you also have the option to Enable TrueType Fonts. In Windows NT the TrueType fonts are permanently enabled.

Ports

Ports

The format of the Ports dialog box is different in Windows NT. Instead of seeing four icons, one each for COM1 through COM4, you see a list of the ports (see Figure 6.2). Click on the port you want to work with and then click on the Settings button to see the same dialog box you would see in Windows 3.1. It allows you to set Baud Rate, Data Bits, Parity, Stop Bits, and Flow Control. In some cases you may also be able to modify "advanced" settings for the ports.

Mouse

Mouse

Windows NT's Mouse dialog box is almost exactly the same as the Windows 3.1 box, its only difference being that it doesn't have the Mouse Trails check box. You can still swap buttons and adjust the tracking and click speeds.

System

System

The System dialog box (see Figure 6.3) lets you control Flexboot (also known as *boot loader*), assign environment variables, define virtual memory, and control multitasking. The Operating System area at the top is where you define how Flexboot will work. Flexboot is the utility that lets you decide which operating system to use when you turn on or reset your computer (your computer won't use Flexboot if NT is the only operating system you have). Flexboot displays a list of operating systems, and waits for you to choose the one you want. If you don't select one within a certain time (the number of seconds shown in the **Show list for** incrementer box), Flexboot runs the default operating system—the one selected in the **Startup** drop-down list box. This information is stored in a file called BOOT.INI, in the root directory of your primary partition. As explained in Chapter 3, you can also edit BOOT.INI directly.

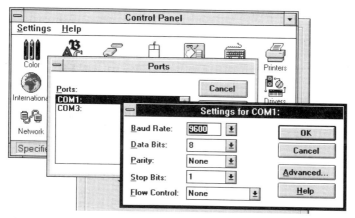

Figure 6.2 The Ports and Settings dialog boxes

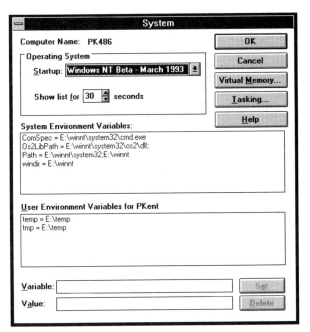

Figure 6.3 The System dialog box

Tip To disable Flexboot entirely, enter 0 into the **Show list for** incrementer box.

Environment variables are used to setup the NT environment (just as the SET and PATH commands are used to setup the environment in DOS), providing information to programs about such things as drives, paths, memory allocation, and filenames. The System dialog box shows both **system** and **user** environment variables—you can't change the system variables, but you can modify the user variables (and override the system variables, as you'll see in a moment).

To add a new **User Environment Variable**, just type the name in the **Variable** text box, type the **Value** into the box below, then click on **Set**. To edit a variable, select it in the list and modify the information in the Value text box. You can remove a variable entirely by selecting it and clicking on the **Delete** button. User environment variables include those you set yourself, and those set by programs you install.

When you close the dialog box NT saves any changes you have made, so be careful with how you modify this information. Environment variables are set in this sequence: the system environment variables, then the AUTOEXEC.BAT (if available and where appropriate) file variables, and finally the user environment variables. If any variables have the same name, the last one set overrides the previous one, so even system variables can be overridden if you duplicate a name in the AUTOEXEC.BAT or user variables.

Virtual Memory

Like Windows 3.1, NT uses a swapfile (though it calls it a *paging file* or *pagefile*). Click on the Virtual Memory button to see the dialog box shown in Figure 6.4. Unlike Windows 3.1, with NT you can put one paging file on each hard drive if you wish.

Note You can modify virtual memory only if you have Administrator privileges.

Virtual memory management is the process by which data is taken from memory when the memory becomes full and is placed on the hard disk. When the data is needed again it is taken from the hard disk and placed back into memory. Unlike the early days of computing, when the size of a computer's memory effectively limited the size of the program that could be run, virtual memory allows more and larger programs to operate, even when they exceed the available memory.

NT uses a system called *paging*, by which a block (or *page*) of data on disk is swapped to a *page frame* in memory, and vice versa. On the PC each page is 4 KB, while on the MIPS R4000 the page size may be adjusted by software. NT's virtual-memory manager can work with page sizes up to 64 KB. These pages are stored in a paging file, the size of which is determined by you in the Virtual Memory dialog box.

You'll notice that paging files have a size range, unlike Windows 3.1 swapfiles which have a set size. For instance, a paging file may show an **Initial Size** of 27 MB, but a **Maximum Size** of 77 MB. 27 MB will be the size with which the file is initially created, and the amount of disk space it will take up when you are running an operating system other than NT. But if NT needs more room, it can expand

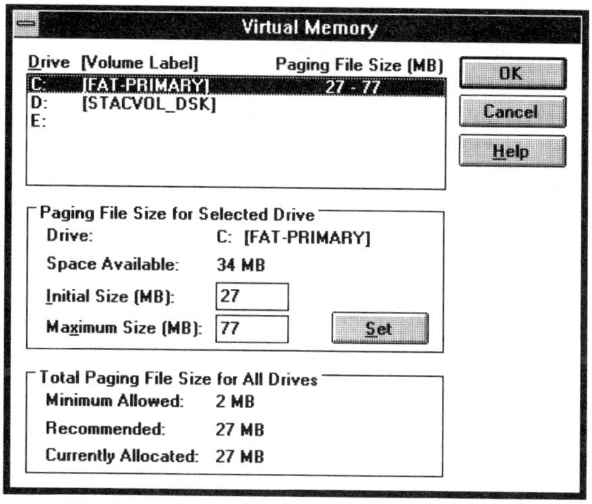

Figure 6.4 The Virtual Memory dialog box

the file up to the maximum size, assuming there's still room on the disk. Of course, you can make the Maximum size the same as the Initial size if you wish.

NT will **Recommend** a paging file size (on the second to last line of the dialog box). According to Microsoft it calculates this size by adding 12 MB to the amount of RAM your system has, also taking into consideration the amount of free disk space you have. Whatever number it comes up with, it's unlikely to be a good recommendation because NT doesn't really know how you plan to use it. And recommending a large file if you have lots of RAM is not always best anyway—after all, the less RAM you have the larger the pagefile you need because the more likely you are to run out of RAM.

Tip   Accept the recommended size now, then use Performance Monitor to track the actual use of the pagefile. You can then adjust the pagefile later to a more logical size. See Chapter 12 for information about Performance Monitor.

To set or modify a paging file, select the hard-disk **Drive** from the list at the top of the box, type the values into the **Initial Size** and **Maximum Size** text boxes, and click on **Set**. Paging files are called PAGEFILE.SYS—you can only have one per disk. You can't delete a paging file while running NT (except by using the Virtual Memory dialog box, of course), and if deleted while running another operating system it is restored when you run NT.

NT needs **contiguous space** on your hard drives for paging files. You may notice that the Virtual Memory dialog box shows a disk drive as having less space available than File Manager indicates; that's because not all the space on the drive is contiguous. If you don't have enough contiguous space you should remove unnecessary files and then defragment the drive using a disk "optimization" or defragmentation utility. The pagefile may be on an MS-DOS FAT disk, in which case you can use an MS-DOS utility. NT itself has no defragmentation utility, though third party utilities may be available.

It's a good idea to create **several pagefiles**, one on each hard disk. That way NT can write to multiple files simultaneously (if your disk-drive controller allows this), speeding up operations. It can also expand pagefile size more easily, as it can expand them all just a little bit instead of expanding one file a lot.

After you close the Virtual Memory box you must shutdown the system and reboot NT for the changes to take effect—simply logging off and back on is not enough. These virtual memory settings, by the way, are for the computer, not a single user, so all users have the same size paging files.

Multitasking

Click on the System dialog box's **Tasking** button to see the Tasking dialog box (Figure 6.5). This dialog box lets you adjust how NT will multitask applications—which applications get how much of the processor's time.

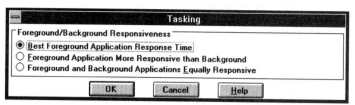

Figure 6.5 The Tasking dialog box

You have three options. Selecting **Best Foreground Application Response Time** tells NT that you want the application you are working in to always run quickly. **Foreground Application More Responsive than Background** tells NT that although you want the applications in which you are working to run more quickly than the ones in the background, you're prepared to accept a little slow-down to get the background work done. And **Foreground and Background Applications Equally Responsive** means, of course, that all applications should be treated equally, regardless of which is active.

Tip The problem with setting multitasking priorities here is that you will often want to change them—one moment you will want your active applications running quickly, a little later you may want all running equally. See the instructions later in this chapter on how to open the System dialog box without opening Control Panel first. (See Fast Access To Control Panel Dialog Boxes.)

Date/Time

Date/Time
The Date/Time dialog box (see Figure 6.6) is different from the Windows 3.1 box. You can still change the time and date, of course, in much the same way you would in Windows 3.1. But now you can also enter time-zone information. This may be important if you are on a large network that spans more than one time zone. In such a case the time-zone information may be used to synchronize the network.

Select a time zone from the list box. Notice that all times are referenced to Greenwich Mean Time (GMT). Greenwich is a small town near London with a very old Observatory, and has been used for centuries as the 0 meridian. (Look at an atlas and you'll see the 0 degrees line of longitude running through Greenwich.) Greenwich is also universally used as a reference point for time zones— that is, all times zones are described as being so many hours after GMT, or so many hours before GMT. For instance, U.S. Mountain Time is "GMT -7 hours," meaning it's 7 hours behind GMT. So when it's 7 PM in London, it's only noon in the U.S. Mountain Time area.

There are a lot of entries in this list, to help you select the zone you are in. For instance, there are separate entries for both Hong Kong and Chongqing, though both are in the same time zone. Different areas in the same time zone may treat

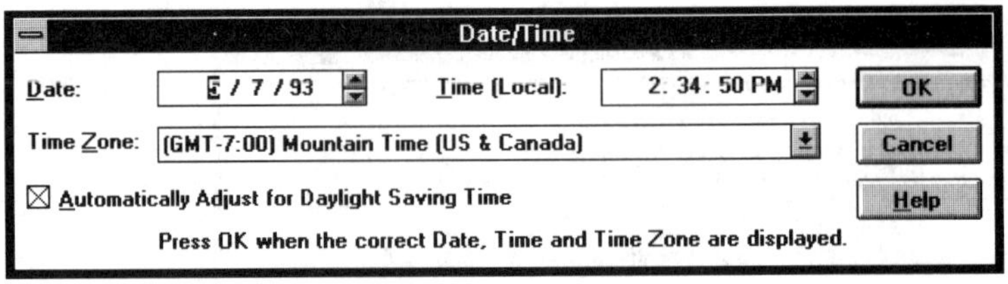

Figure 6.6 The Date/Time dialog box

daylight-savings time differently—some may use it, some may not, and the areas that do use it may set their clocks forward on different dates. So make sure you select the correct area: If you live in Saskatchewan, don't select "Central Time" (US and Canada), even though Saskatchewan is in the same time zone.

Select the **Automatically Adjust for Daylight Savings Time** if you want the computer to automatically adjust the time for you on the days when the clocks "spring forward and fall back." For this feature to work correctly you must have selected the correct time zone—or you may find your computer adjusting its time on the wrong date, or not at all.

Note The date and time formats are defined in the International dialog box.

Cursors

The Cursor dialog box lets you view the default pointer selections, and choose different ones for each situation. As you can see in Figure 6.7, there are different pointers for different situations—the default cursor, the Wait and Application Starting Cursors, and so on. Scroll down the list and you'll see more—various window-sizing cursors, for example.

You can change a cursor by clicking on it in the list and then clicking on **Browse**. Then you select the cursor file you want to use—either a .ANI (animated) or .CUR (static) pointer. There's a sample box in the Browse dialog box, so you can see what you are getting. NT only comes with animated cursors, though they can be fun (try changing a colleague's pointer to a peeling banana or a hand with fingers "drumming" on a desk, for example—there again, if you are all using NT's security features properly, you won't be able to get near your colleague's computer).

When you change a pointer, the title, creator, and file name appear at the bottom of the Cursors dialog box. If you ever want to change back to the default, though, simply select that entry in the list and click on **Set Default**.

The .CUR format is the standard cursor format, by the way. The .ANI format is created by merging several .CUR files. The Microsoft Windows Software Development Kit contains a utility for creating .CUR files, and the Windows NT Resource Guide contains a utility for creating .ANI files (see Chapter 21). See Chapter 22 for a description of a shareware cursor editor.

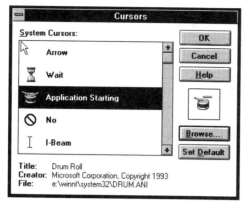

Figure 6.7 The Cursors dialog box

Sound

Sound

The Sound dialog box looks almost exactly the same as the one you are familiar with from Windows 3.1. The only difference is the list of possible Events. You can now add sounds to the following additional events:

New Mail Notification	The sound played when you receive a Mail message.
Schedule+ Reminder	The sound played when Schedule+ (or its ancillary program, MSREMIND) pops up a reminder box.
Chat Incoming Ring	The sound played when a Chat message arrives.
Chat Outgoing Ring	The sound played when you send a Chat message.

Other applications may also add events to this dialog box. For instance, the shareware application While You Were Out, described in Chapter 22, adds a "WYWO Notification" event.

Services

Services

The services dialog box (Figure 6.8) lets you determine how a system service will operate. You can start, stop, and pause services, or configure them to start automatically. Windows NT has a variety of special services, such as UPS monitoring and the Event Log, though the ones that appear in the list box will vary depending on your system configuration. When you install certain options, such as network protocols, other services may be loaded. Here are the ones included automatically with NT:

Alerter	Sends alerts to other users and computers. This requires Messenger to run, and is used by Server.
ClipBook Server	Allows the sharing of Clipboard data between networked computers. See Chapter 18 for more information.

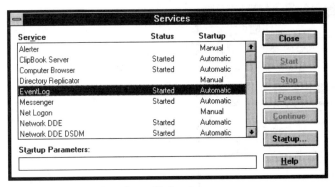

Figure 6.8 The Services dialog box

Computer Browser	Keeps a list of computers and can provide that list to applications when requested. For instance, it provides the list to the Select Domain and Select Computer dialog boxes used in various places.
Directory Replicator	Allows the replication of network directories, copying directories from one computer to another. This feature requires the NT Advanced Server.
EventLog	Logs system, security, and application events. The logs can be viewed in the Event Viewer.
Messenger	Sends and receives messages sent by Alerter or Administrators.
Net Logon	Authenticates a domain's logon attempts.
Network DDE	Provides a way for Dynamic Data Exchange to work over a network.
Network DDE DSDM	The DDE Shared Database Manager, used by Network DDE to manage DDE connections over the network.
Remote Procedure Call (RPC) Locator	Used by "distributed applications." The applications "server side" can "register" with the Locator, which can then provide the information to the "client side."
Remote Procedure Call (RPC) Service	Provides various RPC services for use by distributed applications.
Schedule	Required to allow the AT command to operate. AT schedules operations, carrying them out automatically at the scheduled time and date. For an example, see Unattended Backups in Chapter 19.
Server	Lets the computer operate as a server, allowing other networked computers to use the computer's resources (such as printers and files).

| UPS | Lets NT interface with an "intelligent" UPS (uninteruptible power source). See the UPS dialog box, later in this chapter. |
| Workstation | Lets the computer operate as a workstation, using resources on other networked computers. |

In many cases you won't need these services. Most users probably won't need to use the RPC Locator and RPC Server, for instance. It all depends on the configuration you are running.

Notice the **Startup Parameters** text box at the bottom of the dialog box. The services listed above don't require start up parameters, but some optional services may.

The **Start**, **Stop**, **Pause**, and **Continue** buttons do just that—select the service and click on Start to start it running, Stop to stop it, Pause to stop it temporarily, and Continue to start it after it's been paused. You can only use these buttons if you are an Administrator, and you can't use them at all if the service has been disabled—you'll have to change the startup options first.

It's important to know that these services depend on each other. For instance, if you try to stop the Network DDE DSDM service, you'll see a message saying that the ClipBook Server and Network DDE services depend on Network DDE DSDM. If you continue, you will close those services down, too.

When do you ever need to use these services? Not often. If you decide you want to set up automatic backups using the AT command, you'll have to turn on the Schedule service (it's off by default). However, it makes more sense to change the startup options to do that, so that Schedule starts automatically when you boot. You might also want to use the Services dialog box to turn EventLog off, if you never use the Event Viewer to see the data—again, though, you'll want to change the startup options so it never starts. In general, you won't need to work in the Services dialog box very often.

Startup Options

If you have Administrator privileges, you can set the services' Startup options: Select one and click on the **Startup** button. You'll see the *servicename* Service on *computername* dialog box (see Figure 6.9 for an example). Select one of the **Startup Type** option buttons; select **Automatic** to make the service start when you boot NT, **Manual** to make it start only when selected from the Services dialog box, or to totally disable it select **Disabled**. Once disabled, no nonadministrative user will be able to start the service (remember, they can't use the Startup button, either), nor will any other service be able to run it.

Some services may let you define with which user account the service should run. Normally the **System Account** runs the service—that is, the system itself runs the service when NT boots. However, you can link a service to a particular account—no longer is the service dependent solely on NT booting, it also can't run until a particular account is logged on.

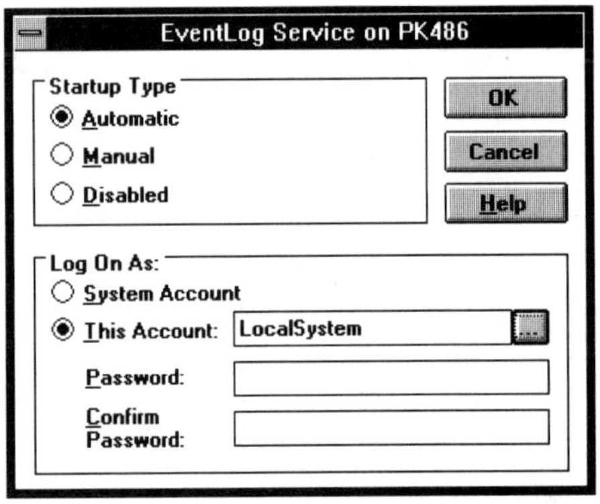

Figure 6.9 The EventLog Service dialog box

Only a few services can use—or need—this feature. Most must be assigned to the System Account. Advanced services such as Directory Replicator use an alternative account, usually created for the express purpose of running the service. Schedule can also be assigned to another account, though it doesn't need it. You will only need to assign a service to another account for networking purposes—when configuring services to run with NT Advanced Server, for instance (Directory Replicator requires NT Advanced Server to run).

If you do need to assign a service to an account, click on the button at the end of the **This Account** text box. You'll see an Add User dialog box. Select the computer that has the account you want from the **List Names From** drop-down list box, and then pick the name from the **Names** list and click on the Add button. You can also Search for a particular account. When you click on the OK button the account is added to the **This Account** text box.

Now, of course; you must enter the **Password**, and then **Confirm** the password.

A Word About Accounts

When you create an account to which you plan to assign a service, you must make sure that certain account features are initialized. The account must have a password that will not expire, it must not be set to "Change Password at Next Logon," and the account must have the right to "Log on as a service." That right is one of the Advanced User Rights, selected by opening the User Manager's User Rights dialog box, clicking on the Show Advanced User Rights check box, and choosing it from the Right drop-down list box. See Chapter 5 for more information.

An account that is to be assigned to Directory Replicator must be part of the domain's Replicator, Domain Users, and Backup Operators groups, and of the Replicator group in each computer that will be using import replication. Furthermore, the Replicator group must be assigned the "Log on as a service" right. Replicator is a Windows NT Advanced Server feature; see that system's documentation for more information if necessary.

Devices

Devices

The devices (Figure 6.10) dialog box displays the status of dozens of different software and hardware devices that are essential to the running of your system. What devices? Well, that depends on your system configuration, and it may not be immediately apparent what each item is when you view this list. Some will be obvious—things like Busmouse, Cdaudio, and Intel EtherExpress16 LAN Adapter Driver are fairly clear descriptions of the devices. But others are most certainly not—Jazzg300, Mup, Spock, T13B, and Sparrow will not mean anything to most users.

Here are the meanings of just a few of the devices:

Pinball	HPFS driver
Rdr	Network Redirector
Sparrow	Adaptec 1502 and 1510 SCSI drivers
Spock	SCSI miniport driver
Aha154x	Adaptec SCSI driver
Serial	Serial driver for all serial communication devices

Luckily, you will rarely need to know what these devices are, unless you are doing some fairly sophisticated tweaking of your system. And Microsoft representatives have said that *if* you do need to know what they are, you'll have to check with technical support.

You can move around the list by pressing letters—press P to move to the devices starting with P, for instance. Once you've selected a device the dialog box lets you **Start** and **Stop** devices, and configure the startup option for each device. Click on the **Startup** button and you'll see a dialog box similar to the one on top of the Devices dialog box in Figure 6.10. You have five startup options:

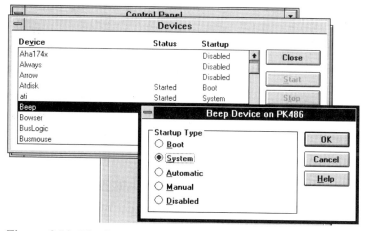

Figure 6.10 The Devices and Beep Device On dialog boxes

Boot	One of the first devices to start when NT boots. This is reserved for the devices that are essential for system operation.
System	The next group of devices to start when NT boots. They are not essential for booting, but are essential for system operation.
Automatic	The next group of devices to start when NT boots. They are not essential to system operation.
Manual	The device will not start automatically—it must be started manually, with the Start button in the Devices dialog box.
Disabled	Only an Administrator can start the device.

Be *very* careful when playing in the Devices dialog box. A good rule of thumb is that if you're not sure, *don't do it*. If you *do* decide to change something, you may see a message that says "Changing the Startup Type for the *devicename* device may leave the system in an unusable state." In many cases it *won't* leave the system unusable, but it might. Making the wrong move here can make NT literally unusable. So unless you've got a good reason to change something, and you know what and how it must be changed, *don't!*

Note If you make a change here and the system *does* become unusable, you will probably be able to use the Last Known Good Configuration procedure, as explained in Chapter 3.

UPS

If you are using an Uninterruptible Power Supply (UPS) that communicates with your computer via a serial port, you may be able to use the UPS dialog box to interface it with NT (see Figure 6.11). Some UPSs are not able to communicate with the computer—they simply continue sending power to the computer for a certain time, and may have their own alarms or warnings, but are unable to interact with the computer. And some may not be compatible with NT. Others, however, can communicate by sending simple signals to your computer's serial port. Depending on the UPS, it may be able to inform you of a power cut, warn you that the UPS's battery is running down, and even be shut down automatically. NT can also use the information from the UPS to carry out an unattended shutdown of your computer. Most UPSs provide enough time for you to shut down your system in the event of a power cut—5 to 15 minutes—but not enough to continue working for long.

Note Only an Administrator can open the UPS dialog box.

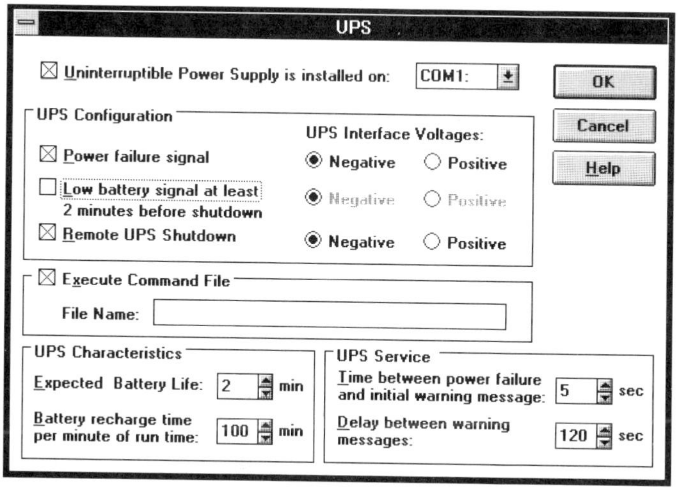

Figure 6.11 The UPS dialog box

If you are using one of these "intelligent" UPSs, open the UPS dialog box and begin by selecting the **Uninterruptible Power Supply Installed On** check box—until you do so the rest of the dialog box is disabled. Then, in the drop-down list box, select the serial port to which you have attached the signal line from the UPS. Now select the UPS' features. The UPS may send a **Power failure signal**, a **Low battery signal**, and may be able to carry out a **Remote UPS Shutdown**.

The **Power failure signal** simply tells NT that power has failed and that the UPS is taking over. NT can then send a warning message to the computer's user. The **Low battery signal** tells NT that the UPS cannot continue running the computer for much longer, giving NT a chance to shut all the applications and close itself down.

Some UPSs may be able to receive a signal from NT, telling them to shut themselves down. When NT has closed all the applications and shut down virtually all of its own operations, the last thing it will do is to send a signal to the UPS. The UPS can then turn itself off, removing power from your computer. This is simply a way to save UPS power. If your UPS can receive this signal, select **Remote UPS Shutdown**.

Check the UPS's documentation to see which features it is capable of, and which **UPS Interface Voltage** it uses for each, **Negative** or **Positive**.

The UPS will send a signal, negative or positive, along a particular line on the serial connection, or in the case of the Remote UPS Shutdown, will receive a signal from the computer along a particular line. These are the lines which Windows NT uses for those signals:

Power failure signal   CTS (clear-to-send line)

Low battery signal   DCD (data-carrier-detect line)

Remote UPS Shutdown   DTR (data-terminal-ready line)

Check the UPS's documentation to make sure that it uses those lines also. You could, of course, create a cable to switch lines if necessary.

If you select the **Power Failure Signal** check box, the **UPS Characteristics** and **UPS Service** areas at the bottom of the dialog box are enabled. If you also select the **Low battery signal at least 2 minutes before shutdown**, the **UPS Characteristics** area will be disabled, because NT will wait for a shutdown signal rather than estimate the shutdown time.

If you *don't* select the Low battery signal option, refer to your UPS documentation and enter the **Expected Battery Life** and the **Battery recharge time per minute of run time** (make sure you don't enter the time for a full recharge—if that's the only number provided by your documentation, divide it by the battery life). Windows NT can then use this information to track how long you have before the UPS will turn off, and warn you to shut down the computer, and also estimate how much life is left in the battery the *next* time power goes down. By default, the Expected Battery Life is set to 2 minutes, which means that as soon as NT receives a Power Failure signal it will start shutting down the system.

Now enter the **UPS Service** information. You can enter the **Time between power failure and initial warning message**—the time that NT should wait before informing you of the power failure, any interval up to 120 seconds. Why not inform you immediately? Because the power may drop for a second or two and then come back. You can also tell NT how often you want it to warn you of the power failure, the **Delay between warning messages**. NT will continue sending warning messages until you shut down or the UPS drops its power-failure signal; you can set any interval up to 300 seconds.

Finally, notice the **Execute Command File** option. This tells NT to execute a command file immediately before carrying out an automatic shutdown. You might want to carry out a network command, informing workstations that the server is shutting down, for instance, or closing remote connections. This command must be completed within 30 seconds of being issued. If you want to use this feature, select the check box and type the .BAT, .CMD, .EXE, or .COM filename in the **File Name** text box. NT assumes this file is in the \WINNT\SYSTEM32 directory—you can't use a pathname in this text box.

When you click on **OK** you'll see a message asking if you want to start the UPS service immediately. The service will then start, assuming the UPS is connected correctly. If it isn't, you'll see a message telling you to check the connections and interface signals. Read your UPS documentation and make sure it's connected correctly. NT also configures the service so that it starts automatically when you boot. You can confirm this by looking at the UPS entry in the Control Panel Services dialog box.

You also need to start the **Alerter** and **Messenger** services, if you need your computer to generate a network message when you get UPS problems. First, go to the Control Panel's **Services** dialog box and set these two to run automatically. You can also make sure that **EventLog** starts automatically, so UPS signals can be logged and viewed with the Event Viewer. Then use the Control Panel's **Server** dialog box (described in the networking chapter, Chapter 15) to determine who will receive Alerts. And on each computer that you designate to receive alerts, make sure the Messenger service is also set to start automatically.

Testing the UPS

You'll probably want to test the UPS once you have everything set up. Some UPSs have test buttons which simulate power loss. Otherwise simply disconnect UPS power. Make sure your computer remains running, and that the warning message appears. When the battery level reaches a low level and the UPS sends a battery-low signal, or when the Expected Battery Life has been exceeded, your computer should shut down automatically.

If you entered a command file into the UPS dialog box, make sure it completes its execution within the 30-second limit, carrying out everything it needs to do before the system shuts down—experiment with different situations, making sure the command always finishes, however much work it needs to do.

If NT is supposed to send a Remote UPS Shutdown signal, make sure the UPS does indeed shut down. Finally, when you turn power back on, look in the Event Viewer to read the UPS signals. (See Chapter 13.)

Fast Access To Control Panel Dialog Boxes

Here's a way to quickly open a Control Panel dialog box, without opening the Control Panel directly. For each dialog box that you use frequently, duplicate the Control Panel icon. Hold Alt while you double-click on the first icon, then—in the Command Line of the Program Item Properties dialog box—add the name of the dialog box to the end of the Command Line.

For instance, the Command Line might say CONTROL.EXE NETWORKS. Close the dialog box, then double-click on the icon, and you'll find that the Control Panel opens, followed by the Networks dialog box. Closing the Networks dialog box automatically closes the Control Panel.

In most cases, use the name that appears below the icon in the Control Panel—system, data/time, international, and so on. One or two cases are different, though. For the Time Zone dialog box, enter GMT.CPL. And for MIDI Mapper, enter MIDIMAP.CPL. In both these cases the dialog box will open without even opening the Control Panel first.

You can even use the correct icons, the ones that appear in the Control Panel. Use the Change Icon button in the Program Item Properties dialog box, click on the Browse button in the Change Icon dialog box, then enter *.CPL into the File Name text box. Look for the .CPL files in the WINNT\SYSTEM32 directory. You'll find most of the icons in MAIN.CPL. You'll find the Server, Services, and Devices (and some clock icons) in SVRMGR.CPL. The Networks icon (along with the Windows NT Setup icon) is in NCPA.CPL. And several icons are in .CPL files of the same name—MIDIMAP.CPL, UPS.CPL, and CURSORS.CPL, for instance.

You might want to create a Control Panel program group, icons and all, that exactly duplicates the Control Panel. Or simply create an icon for each one you use frequently, and put the icon in an easily accessible program group.

7

File Manager

Windows NT's File Manager varies significantly from that found in Windows 3.1. It incorporates many of the features found in Windows for Workgroups, but of course it also has a number of other significant changes, such as security features that let you assign file and directory permissions to groups and users, and a customizable toolbar.

The Menus and Toolbar

There are a number of new menu options in File Manager. They let you connect and disconnect network drives, set up file and directory sharing, change the toolbar, and so on. We'll cover each one in detail later in this chapter, and we've marked the new menu options with asterisks in the table at the end of this chapter.

Windows NT's File Manager has a special toolbar that automates various functions (see Figure 7.1). If you have used Windows for Workgroups 3.1 you've probably already seen this toolbar, though Windows 3.1 doesn't have it. These are the icons and the commands that they duplicate:

    Disk|Connect Network Drive

    Disk|Disconnect Network Drive

    Disk|Share As

    Disk|Stop Sharing

▣	View|Name
▣	View|All File Details
▣	View|Sort by Name
▣	View|Sort by Type
▣	View|Sort by Size
▣	View|Sort by Date
▣	Window|New Window
▣	File|Copy
▣	File|Move
☒	File|Delete
▣	Security|Permissions

These buttons speed up File Manager operations. If you want to delete a file or directory, select it and click on the button with a big **X** on it (instead of selecting File|Delete). To set permissions for a directory, select it and click on the button with a picture of a key (instead of selecting Security|Permissions).

There's also a disk-drive drop-down list box on the left side of the toolbar, which you can use instead of the Disk|Select Drive to select the disk drive you want to see displayed in the directory window. Unfortunately this can't be removed from the toolbar, though it's rather redundant.

Customizing the Toolbar

File Manager lets you customize the toolbar, selecting the commands you want and placing them where you want. For instance, if your computer is not on a network, you don't need the first four toolbar buttons—the ones that let you connect and disconnect a network drive, and share your files and directories. You may not want the last button, the one which lets you set permissions on files and directories, especially if you don't have an NTFS drive (in which case the button

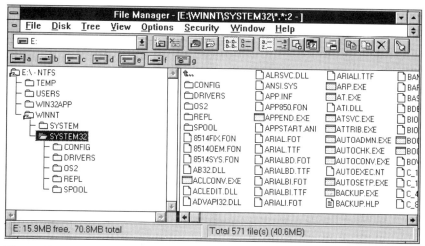

Figure 7.1 The File Manager window

is inactive). So you can remove the useless buttons and replace them with commands you use more often.

Select **Options|Customize Toolbar** or simply double-click somewhere on the toolbar to see the dialog box in Figure 7.2. The **Toolbar Buttons** list shows the existing toolbar. To remove a button, click on it and click the **Remove** button. You can remove the **separators** in the same way (except the first and last separators, which are fixed). The separators are simply the spaces between the buttons on the bar.

Tip   You can also remove toolbar buttons directly from the bar. Press and hold Shift, drag the button off the bar, and release the mouse button.

To add a button, start by selecting a position in the Toolbar Buttons list— select the button *before which* you wish to place the new button. Then click on the

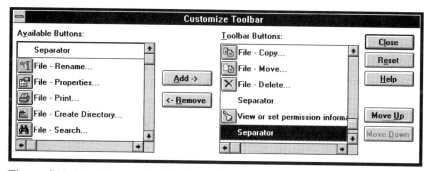

Figure 7.2 The Customize Toolbar dialog box

button you want in the **Available Buttons** list, and click on **Add**. You can add as many buttons as you wish, though of course they may not all be displayed on the toolbar, depending on the size of your monitor and the video resolution you are using. The larger the screen and the higher the resolution, the more buttons that can be displayed. To change the toolbar back to its default settings, simply click on the **Reset** button.

You can also shuffle buttons around on the toolbar. Select the button you want to move and then use the **Move Up** and **Move Down** buttons to move it around. There's an easier way, though; you can move the button on the toolbar itself. Close the dialog box, hold **Shift**, and **drag** the button along the toolbar to the new position.

Finally, Long File and Directory Names!

One of the most common complaints about DOS—and, by extension, Windows 3.1—has always been the way it restricts users to 11-character filenames. As three of those characters are an *extension*, usually used to identify the file type, only eight are left for a real name, far too few to allow one to use sensible, easily identifiable names. Well, finally PC users will be able to use long file and directory names, up to **256 characters**, including the extensions (yes, that's right, you can have multiple extensions).

Here are the rules:

- You can use a maximum of 256 characters.
- Don't use these characters: ? " / \ < > * | :
- You *can* use *spaces*.
- You can use *multiple extensions*.
- You can use uppercase and lowercase letters, and NT will preserve them (for display only—it won't consider *this.file* and *THIS.FILE* as different names).
- You can't use the excluded DOS names: AUX, COM1, COM2, COM3, COM4, CON, LPT1, LPT2, LPT3, NUL, and PRN.

When you create a file or directory with a long name, Windows NT automatically assigns a **DOS name,** also. It does this by taking the first six characters of the NTFS name (less if there's a period in the name before the sixth character) and adding a ~ and a number, usually 1. It then takes the first three letters of the NTFS name's first extension, and adds those characters to the DOS name. If there are any spaces, Windows NT ignores them. If there are any special characters, DOS can't work with they are replaced by an underscore. And if there's already a file with the same DOS name, NT uses a different number after the first six characters. For instance, you rename a file using the following NTFS filename:

```
+this is a sample.firstextension.secondextension
```

Windows NT will create the DOS name, `_thisi~1.fir`.

Why do you need DOS filenames? Some people may prefer them, perhaps, but they are also there for **compatibility** purposes. Some programs can't use long names, so if you are running a Windows 3.1 program and want to use a file on a NTFS drive you'll need a DOS name. And if you want to copy an NTFS file onto a DOS floppy disk, you'll need the DOS name. Also, it allows non-NT workstations to access documents on an NTFS drive. For example, a workstation running Windows for Workgroups will use short names to see the directories and files on a Windows NT server.

By default File Manager will display these DOS names. If you don't want to see them, select **View|Partial Details** and clear the **MS-DOS File Names for NTFS** check box in the Partial Details dialog box. File Manager will display DOS names in the directory side of the directory window, immediately after the NTFS name (so if you want to see the DOS name for a *directory*, you won't find it in the tree itself— select the directory's parent directory and then look in the directory panel). You'll also notice that all the NT files and directories installed by Setup use DOS names.

Using NTFS may take a little getting used to. We've waited for long filenames, but now that they're here we're going to find that all those characters make a clear, organized File Manager difficult to arrange. For instance, when viewing files with View|All File Details selected, the files are displayed in one column. But when you select View|Name, the vertical scroll bar disappears, because NT places the filenames in several columns, and expects you to use the horizontal bar to scroll to the right to view the ones off screen. That's okay in Windows 3.1, because with those short DOS filenames you can usually see three or more columns. But with NT the names can be so long that only one column may appear in the window, with the others hidden off to the right. At first it appears not that the files have been placed in columns, but that the list has been truncated.

Viewing file details is difficult with these long names—often the details are off screen. There are a few things you can do, of course:

- Move the split bar to the left, squeezing the tree side but giving the directory side more room.

- Use View|Directory Only to remove the tree side.

- Use Options|Font to reduce the font size, so more text will fit in the window.

- Use a higher resolution video mode, so more fits on your screen.

- Forget about seeing file details, and rely instead on File Properties (Alt-double-click on file).

- Forget about seeing file details, and use FExtend, the file-management utility described in Chapter 22.

- Get used to navigating through the tree and Shift-double-clicking on the directory you want to view. This opens a directory window that can be quickly maximized to show all the details.

- Select View|Partial Details, then deselect the **MS-DOS File Names for NTFS** check box, removing the DOS name and freeing some space.

Simply using View|Directory Only (removing the tree) provides a lot of room. You can still see directories as long as they are selected in the By File Type dialog box by using View|By File Type. Unfortunately, the directories only use the little + and – signs in the tree, not in the directory-only view.

Of course, all this depends on the names being long, but not too long. If you use 40-character names you'll probably be okay. But use 50, 100, 200, or even 256, and the name is going to shoot off the right side of the screen. Unfortunately, File Manager cannot wrap these long names onto two or more lines, so if just one name is very long, it's going to make the directory contents difficult to read, shifting all columns—file size, date, time, and attributes—over to the right so you have to scroll to find them.

If you are really eager to use very long names, try reducing the font size down as far as it will go while still being readable (hey, the Macintosh uses small text for file names!), and forget about displaying file attributes all the time. However, there's still a problem. If you select View|Name, you won't be able to scroll to the right to see the rest of a long name, because clicking on the scroll bar moves the view to the next column of files, not along the name. (The only way to be able to scroll and view the entire name is to use View|All File Details or View|Partial Details.) You won't be able to see the name in the Properties dialog box at first, either (though you can scroll through the name). So although NT has brought us long names, it hasn't made them very easy to work with. We recommend that you limit yourself to about 40 characters (more if you have a high-resolution monitor or don't mind small text), at least until you find a file-management program that handles them well.

Viewing File Properties

The File Properties dialog box has been modified to account for the new features in Windows NT. Click on a file and select **File|Properties**, or hold **Alt** while you **double-click** on the file, or hold **Alt** while you press **Enter** to see the dialog box shown in Figure 7.3. In this figure you'll notice that we've used a file with a long filename. Of course, it won't all fit in the title bar, nor in the **File Name** text box. However, you can place the cursor in the File Name text box and drag along the name to scroll to the right, or use the arrow, Ctrl-arrow, Home, and End keys to move through the name.

This dialog box has the same information as in Windows 3.1—**Size**, **Last Change**, **Path**, and **Attributes**. It also has the **Version** and **Copyright** information area, displaying information that may be embedded into some executable files by the software publishers. You may see the version number, company name, software name, and other comments here—anything they cared to add. Select an item from the left list box, and the right list box will show more information related to that item.

If you are on a network you can also click on the **Open By** button to see who, if anyone, is using this file (see Figure 7.4). This box shows you the **Total Opens** (the number of users working with the file), **Total Locks** (the total number of

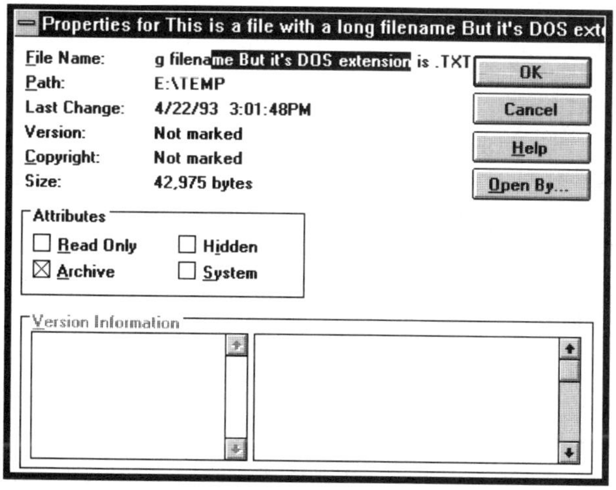

Figure 7.3 The Properties For dialog box

locks on the file, locks placed by applications that restrict other applications from using the file), and an **Open By** list, which shows the usernames of the people working with the file.

For each user, you'll see **For** (the type of access, such as Read or Write), **Locks** (the number of locks the user placed on the file), **File ID** (an identification number assigned to the file). If you are an Administrator or Power User, you can close connections. (See Chapter 5 for more information about the various types of user groups.) Select the users you want to disconnect and click on **Close Selected**. Or click on **Close All** to disconnect all the connections. When you do this, the other person may lose data.

File Manager's Security Options

When you first install Windows NT and create user accounts, everyone has full access to all files and directories, except for users in the Guests group (they can

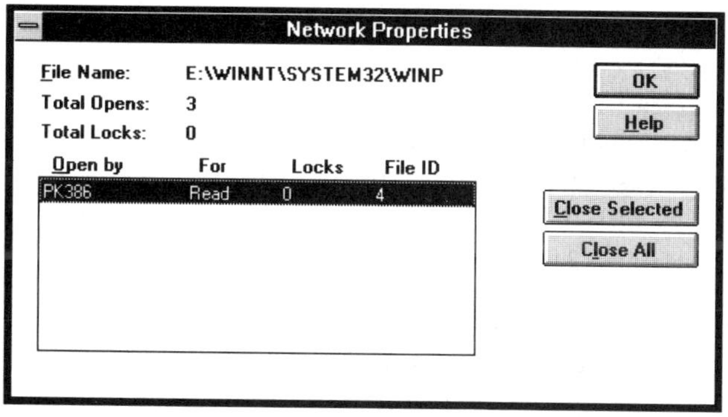

Figure 7.4 The Network Properties dialog box

open existing files, but not modify or delete them). That may not be the way you want it, though. Perhaps you want to limit some users to just one or two directories—a word processor and data directory, for instance. File Manager lets anyone in the Administrators group restrict access to any file or directory. (For more information about the Administrator and Administrators group, see Chapter 5.) It also lets file and directory owners—people who created those objects or assumed ownership using the Security|Owner command—restrict access to their objects.

These restrictions are not only active while working in File Manager—they're active throughout the system, whether you are trying to save or open a file from an application, run an application by double-clicking on an icon, or using the Command Line.

The security features are available only to NTFS files (NT File System). If you configured NT to use FAT (File Allocation Table, the system used by DOS) or HPFS (High Performance File System, OS/2's system), you won't be able to use any of these features. And if your computer has both NTFS and non-NTFS disk drives, you will only be able to use the security on the NTFS disk drives.

Tip   If you didn't install NT, perhaps you don't know if it's using NTFS or FAT. Here's a quick way to check which format a drive is using. Select the drive, then open the Security menu. If the options are disabled, the selected drive is *not* NTFS.

Owning Files and Directories

Each NTFS file and directory on your hard drive is "owned" by someone. When you first install Windows NT it provides the Administrators and SYSTEM groups with Full Control of all NTFS directories and files—that means anyone in the Administrators group, and any internal system process that needs access to a file, can do whatever they want with files, including take ownership. When a user creates a new file or directory, that new object is "owned" by the creator (the creator is, in effect, a member of a special group called CREATOR OWNERS).

Owners can only be overruled by Administrators. That is, an owner can lock out everyone from an object, but cannot be locked out himself—unless, that is, he loses ownership. He can lose ownership by having it taken by an Administrator, or if he grants the permission to take ownership to another user and that user exercises the permission. Any user who has the Full Control or Take Ownership permission can take over ownership.

Once a user takes ownership of an object, that person becomes the CREATOR OWNER—the original CREATOR OWNER will still have Full Control, and can even take back ownership, but that Full Control can be taken away from the original owner, effectively locking the original owner out.

To check current ownership of a file or directory, highlight it and then select **Security|Owner**. The dialog box shown in Figure 7.5 appears, showing the file or

Figure 7.5 The Owner dialog box

directory name, followed by the name of the owner. (If you select several items at once, you will just see a note telling you how many "files/directories" you selected, but it won't show who currently owns them.)

If you simply want to see who owns the file or directory, you can now click on OK to close the dialog box. But if you actually want to own it yourself, click on **Take Ownership**. If you selected a directory, you will see a message asking if you want to take ownership of all the files and subdirectories in the selected directory. Click Yes to do so, or No to take ownership only of the directory itself. This means, by the way, that someone can deny access to a directory to someone else who owns files and directories inside. Still, there can be a purpose—by taking control of just the directory, and not the files or subdirectories, you can temporarily take control of all those files and subdirectories, yet not take ownership, so when you want to allow access again, you don't have to reassign ownership to each original owner. Also, you can let current owners retain their ownership, yet make sure that new files in that directory will be owned by you.

If you don't have the right to take ownership, you will see a message telling you that access has been denied.

Defining Access Permissions

Once you own a directory or file, or if you are an Administrator, you have the right to define permissions. There's also a Change Permissions permission—an Administrator or an owner can give this permission to someone else, so that person, too, can modify permissions for other people.

You can assign a variety of rights, in just about any configuration you want, all the way from no rights at all (the user cannot even view the contents of a directory, or do anything with a file) to full access (the user can do anything, including deleting, taking ownership, reading, and writing).

Select the file or directory for which you want to set permissions—or even several objects at once—and then select **Security|Permissions** (or click on the Permissions icon in the toolbar) to see the Directory Permissions dialog box (see Figure 7.6). In some cases—if your permissions are limited—you will see a message telling you that you can only view this information, and you won't be able to change it.

If you selected a directory, the dialog box will contain the **Replace Permissions on Subdirectories** and **Replace Permissions on Existing Files** check boxes at the top (if you selected a file, these check boxes are not present, of course)

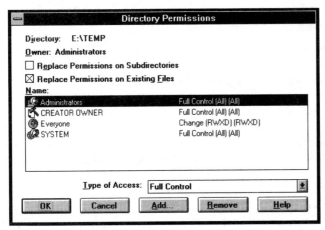

**Figure 7.6 The Directory Permissions dialog box,
after selecting a directory**

Select these check boxes if you want to modify permissions for all files and subdirectories. Leave them blank if you only want to modify the directory itself, and any files or subdirectories created subsequently.

The **Name** list shows who has access to the directory you selected. It also shows who *does not* have access, and this is important. An individual user has the permissions that have been assigned to all of the groups of which he or she is a member, so if you want to make sure one person does not have access, yet still allow access to other members of his group, you have to assign No Access to that particular user (you'll see how in a moment).

In the right side of the box you can see what *type* of access the user has. There are two types of permissions: **standard permissions** and **individual permissions**. Standard permissions are groups of individual permissions. For instance, the Change permission is a standard permission that contains four different individual permissions: Read, Write, Execute, and Delete.

The standard permissions for directories affect both the directory to which they are assigned and the files within that directory. Standard permissions for files only affect the files themselves, of course. These are the standard permissions for **directories**:

Standard permission	Contains these individual permissions for the directory. . .	Contains these individual permissions for the files within that directory. . .
No Access	None	None
List	Read, Execute	Not specified
Read	Read, Execute	Read, Execute
Add	Write, Execute	Not specified
Add & Read	Read, Write, Execute	Read, Execute

Standard permission *(continued)*	Contains these individual permissions for the directory...	Contains these individual permissions for the files within that directory...
Change	Read, Write, Execute, Delete	Read, Write, Execute, Delete
Full Control	All (Read, Write, Execute, Delete, Change Ownership, Take Control)	All (Read, Write, Execute, Delete, Change Ownership, Take Control)

These are the standard permissions for files:

Standard permission	Contains these individual permissions...
No Access	No permissions
Read	Read, Execute
Change	Read, Write, Execute, Delete
Full Control	All (Read, Write, Execute, Delete, Change Ownership, Take Control)

What, then, do these individual permissions mean? Here's what they mean for a directory:

	All	Read (R)	Write (W)	Execute (X)	Delete (D)	Change Permissions (P)	Take Ownership (O)
Display the file-names	✓	✓					
Display the directory's attributes	✓	✓		✓			
Add files and sub-directories	✓		✓				
Change the directory's attributes	✓		✓				
Go to the directory's subdirectories	✓			✓			
Display the directory's owner and permissions	✓	✓	✓	✓			
Delete the directory	✓				✓		
Change the directory's permissions	✓					✓	
Take ownership of the directory	✓						✓

Here's what the individual permissions mean for files:

	All	Read (R)	Write (W)	Execute (X)	Delete (D)	Change Permissions (P)	Take Ownership (O)
Display the file's owner and permissions	✓	✓	✓	✓			
Display the file's data	✓	✓					
Display the file's attributes	✓	✓					
Change the file's attributes	✓		✓				
Change data in and append data to the file	✓		✓				
Run the file if executable	✓			✓			
Delete the file	✓				✓		
Change the file's permissions	✓					✓	
Take ownership of the file	✓						✓

And what about **Not Specified**? That type of "permission" is only available when setting permissions for directories, and refers to the files within the directories. It means that the permissions for the user or group will be *removed* from the files in the directory when you close the Directory Permissions dialog box, and that when the user copies or creates files in this directory, no change will be made to the permissions. For instance, if you change the file permission to Not Specified for the user name JBrown, when you check one of the files in the directory you will find that no permissions have been specified for JBrown. Effectively you are removing permissions that have been set. That's not the same as setting No Access, by the way. If a user has No Access set on an object, it means he can't use it even if other members of his group *can* use it. If you *remove* permissions, though, the user may still be able to access the file, if he has permission to do so through a group of which he is a member.

Also, if you copy a file from one directory to another, it would normally "inherit" the permissions from the new directory. However, if you have set Not Specified for that user, File Manager *will not* change permissions—it will keep them as they were in the original directory.

When you look in the Directory Permissions dialog box (Figure 7.6), you can see that the list box shows the different people who have had permissions assigned. For each one, the entry shows the standard permissions. In parentheses after the standard permission you'll see the individual permissions. The first set of parentheses shows the permissions for the directory, while the second set of parentheses shows permissions for the files within that directory.

For instance, if you see **Full Control (All) (All)** it means that the user has been assigned the Full Control category, which provides All the permissions for the directory and All the permissions for the files in that directory.

Assigning Permissions

To assign permissions, begin by selecting a user or group from the list. If you don't see the one you want, click on the **Add** button to see the Add Users and Groups dialog box, shown in Figure 7.7. (This dialog box is used in various places throughout NT. We described it in detail in Chapter 5.) Select the groups you want to add, or click on the **Show Users** button and then select the users. Click on **Add** to place the names in the **Add Names** dialog box. You can also use the **Members** button to see the names of the members of the selected group, or use the **Search** button to enter a name for which you want to search.

Once you've got all the names you want, you can then select the **Type of Access** from the drop-down list box at the bottom of the dialog box. However, you won't be able to select one of the Special options, so you may want to wait until you return to the Directory Permissions dialog box to select an access type. Click on OK and the group or user you selected is added to the Permissions dialog box.

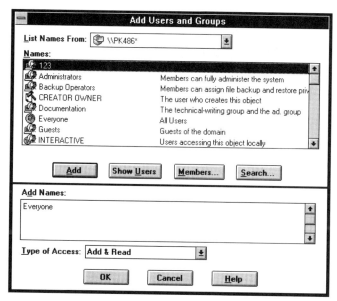

Figure 7.7 The Add Users and Groups dialog box

Now you can select the permission type you want—if you didn't do so in the Add dialog box—from the **Type of Access** drop-down list box in the Permissions dialog box. If you want to select individual permissions (rather than using the standard permissions), select **Special Directory Access** (for the directory itself), or **Special File Access** (for the files in the directory). Figure 7.8 shows the Special File Access dialog box, and the Special Directory Access dialog box is very similar, though it doesn't have the **Access Not Specified** option button.

You can select **Other** and then click on the check boxes you want. For instance, you might allow a user or group permission to Execute files in this directory, but not to Read. (Refer to the tables to figure out exactly what each permission means—it's not always obvious.) You could also select **Full Control**, allowing the user to do whatever he wants. The **Access Not Specified** option button, as we discussed earlier, tells File Manager to *remove* permissions from the files in the directory.

When you close the Special File Access or Special Directory Access dialog box, the changes are made to the selected group or user in the list box. Finally, notice the **Remove** button at the bottom of the dialog box. That lets you remove a user or group from the list. Simply select the listing and click on the button.

You are now ready to change the permissions. But remember the **Replace Permissions on Subdirectories** and **Replace Permissions on Existing Files** check boxes. Whatever choices you have made, they will have no effect on the subdirectories, or on the existing files, unless you have selected these check boxes. For instance, if you selected Access Not Specified in the Special File Access dialog box, you must also select Replace Permissions on Existing Files if you want to remove the permissions.

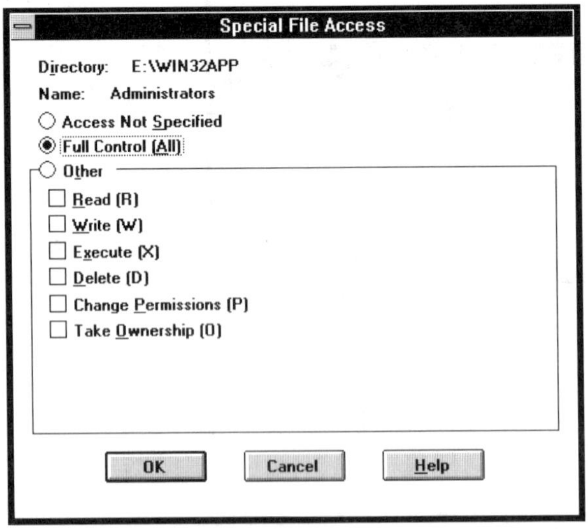

Figure 7.8 The Special File Access dialog box

A Few Guidelines

All these permissions can get quite confusing if you try to set up a complicated system. Here are a few things to remember:

- When you **copy** or **create** a new file, it takes new permissions, according to the target directory's settings (shown in the second set of parentheses in the Directory Permissions dialog box), *unless* **Not Specified** is set, in which case the permissions for that user or group on which Not specified is set will remain as they were before.

- When you **move** a file it retains its permissions—it doesn't take new permissions from the new directory.

- Permissions affect all areas of NT, not just File Manager. If you don't have the right to view the contents of a directory, you won't be able to use an application's File Open dialog box to access that directory, for instance.

- Users get all the permissions afforded them by all the groups of which they are members. You may think you have excluded a user from a particular right, not noticing that he's a member of a group that has that right.

- You can deny a user *all* permissions by assigning him No Access. Even if he's a member of a group with some permissions, once you've set No Access he can't do anything.

- Directory permissions affect the files inside. If a user has No Access to a directory, he can't get to files and subdirectories for which he has Full Access. If a user has Full Access to a particular file, but only Read permission for the directory itself, he won't be able to do much to the file—he can't rename it, for instance.

- Users can use the most permissive permissions available to their various groups, *unless* one of them is No Access. For instance, if a user has a Read permission through one of this group memberships, and a Change permission through another, he will, in effect, have the Change permission. However, if another group of which he is a member has No Access, the other permissions are overridden and he cannot use the directory or file.

- The user who creates a file or directory is the CREATOR OWNER. Only Administrators can take ownership away, unless the CREATOR OWNER gives another person the Take Ownership permission.

- When you move or copy files or directories to a drive formatted for another operating system (such as DOS' FAT or OS/2's HPFS), all permissions are lost. This security system only works on NTFS drives or Microsoft LAN Manager version 2.x servers.

- A variety of different messages are used to indicate that you've been denied access to a file or directory. Not all of these messages are clear—you may be told the file wasn't found, when really you don't have the right to read it—so if you've been denied the ability to carry out some kind of operation, check the permissions of all the files and directories involved.

Tip   Here's a quick way to set up an entire disk drive with common permissions. Select the root directory of the drive you want to modify (place the highlight on the drive letter at the top of the tree); select **Security|Permissions**; select the Replace Permissions on Subdirectories and Replace Permissions on Existing Files; set up the permissions as you want them, and then click on OK.

File and Directory Auditing

Windows NT lets you *audit* the use of any directory of file, so you have a record of who is using what, and who is trying to use what. Such a profile could give you an idea of how best to modify your security profile, to let users into areas they need, and keep them out of areas into which they shouldn't go.

Select the file or directory you want to check. You may be able to select several at once, though if the existing information is not the same for each you'll see a message asking if you plan to reset the data for all of them. If you want a security log of all files and directories on a disk, begin by selecting the root directory. Select **Security|Auditing** to see a dialog box like that shown in Figure 7.9. This is a Directory Auditing dialog box—if you selected a file, the dialog box you see won't have the check boxes at the top.

You've seen similar check boxes before, of course. Select **Replace Auditing on Subdirectories** and **Replace Auditing on Existing Files** if you want to modify not just the directory but the subdirectories and files within it. If you don't, NT will only audit attempted accesses in the directory and to any new files created in that

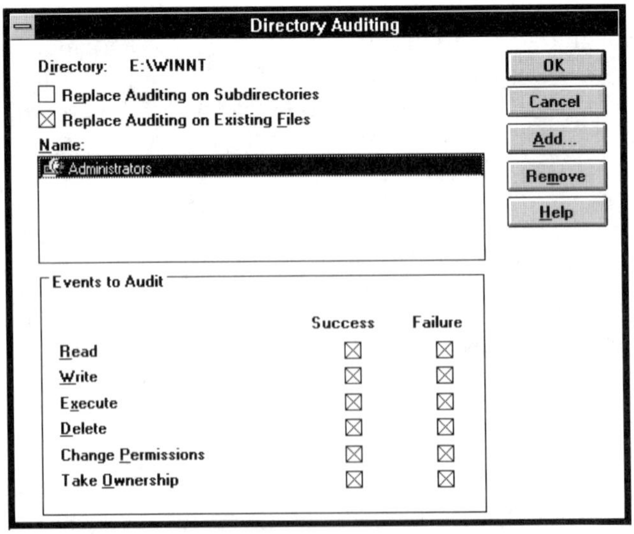

Figure 7.9 The Directory Auditing dialog box

directory. Next, click on the **Add** button and add the users or groups you want to keep an eye on.

Once you've added the users and groups, select them one by one and set the auditing profile by clicking on the check boxes. For each permission type—Read, Write, Execute, Delete, Change Permissions, and Take Ownership—you can request that an audit be kept for successful and failed attempts. When you click on OK, you have set the audit, and all the specified events will be logged in the SecEvent.EVT file in the WINNT\SYSTEM32\CONFIG directory. This Security report can be viewed in the Event Viewer—see Chapter 13 for more information.

Note The EventLog service must be running for this auditing to work correctly. See Chapter 13.

Deactivating File Access Security

Many users won't want to use file security. It really can be a headache at times, if you get your permissions mixed up. To make all the files and directories available to all users, log on as an administrator, select the root directory of the NTFS disk volume, select **Security|Permissions**, and then assign Full Control to Everyone. Make sure you select both check boxes so all subdirectories and files are affected. Another way to effectively deactivate all security measures throughout NT is to make sure that all accounts are assigned to the Administrators user group in User Manager. See Chapter 5 for more information. However, even Administrators can be locked out of files and directories—they can modify the permissions and get in, of course, but a user would have to understand *how* (by setting new permissions, and taking ownership first if necessary).

Sharing Data on a Network

There's a good chance that if you are running Windows NT, you are connected to a local area network. Windows NT's network features are one of its most important strengths. Built into the operating system is a security system that lets you assign or deny rights to your data. You can determine just who can access your work, and what they can do with it once they get to it.

Sharing Directories

 By default, NT sets up all your disks and the \WINNT directory as special administrative or default shared directories. If you look at the root directory of each disk, you'll see a small icon with a hand, offering the "file folder" that represents the directory. These administrative shares are all identified with $ signs, as we'll see in a moment. But Administrators and Power Users can remove these shares, locking out the Administrators temporarily. When the system is shut down and restarted the shares will be restored. You can also assign new shares, so nonadministrative users can use your directories and files.

To let another user access a directory or even an individual file, select the directory or file in File Manager's tree or directory panel, and then click on the Share Directory button (or select **Disk|Share As**). The New Share dialog box appears (see Figure 7.10).

If you selected an existing share—for example, the root directory of one of the disks—the **Share Name** will show the existing share name as a disk name with a $ after it (as in F$), or ADMIN$ for the WINNT directory. You can click on the **New Share** button to open another, identical dialog box, so that you can create a new share, one that can be used by others. You *cannot* modify one of the administrative ($) shares, so you can't simply change permissions to allow other users access.

If you selected a new directory, the directory's name will appear in the **Share Name** text box. This is the name other users will see when accessing the directory—you can change this name to whatever you want. The directory will still retain the same name in your File Manager, but other users will see the new name. For instance, you might rename a directory in which you are storing some word processing files, DOCUMENTAT'N, to make it clear to other users where they should look. However, users on some DOS-based workstations may not be able to use this directory, because the name is too long. If you want to make sure all workstations can use the directory, stick with 8-character names. If you only have NT and Windows for Workgroups workstations, you can use 12-character names. You can also include spaces in the names, though again, some DOS-based workstations won't be able to access them if you do so.

You won't normally want to change the Path. This shows the path to the directory you selected before opening this dialog box, though you could, if you wish, now set up sharing for a different directory by typing the path in this box. You can also type a **Comment**. This will appear in the Connect Network Drive dialog box—next to the directory name—when another user tries to connect to this directory. Even Windows for Workgroups workstations will see this comment. You might type something like, "These are the X1 Rev 3 Documents,"

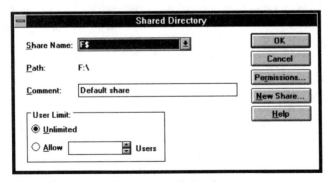

Figure 7.10 The New Share dialog box

anything that will clearly identify the contents of the directory. You can type up to 48 characters, though you may wish to limit yourself to 40 or less, because the extra characters may not appear in the dialog box anyway.

The **User Limit** area lets you define how many users may access this directory at any time. You will probably leave this set on **Unlimited**, but in some cases you may need to enter a number into the **Allow** incrementer, to define the maximum number of users who can connect to the directory.

The **Permissions** button displays the Access Through Share Permissions dialog box. This works much like the permissions boxes you've already seen. By default it will be set up with Everyone having Full Access. If you want to be more restrictive, click on the **Remove** button to get rid of the Everyone line, then use the **Add** button to add particular users or groups.

Your permissions choices are **No Access** (so you can deny a particular user access even though other members in his group have access), **Read**, **Change**, and **Full Control**. Here's what these mean:

	No Access	Read	Change	Full Control
Display subdirectory names and filenames		✓	✓	✓
Display file data and attributes		✓	✓	✓
Run program files		✓	✓	✓
Go to the directories' subdirectories		✓	✓	✓
Create subdirectories and change files			✓	✓
Change data in and append data to files			✓	✓
Change file attributes			✓	✓
Delete subdirectories and files			✓	✓

These are overridden, however, by your file and directory permissions on the NTFS disk drives. For instance, if you allow a user full access to a particular shared directory, and that directory contains files that are restricted to one user, other users will not be able to work with them.

Note You won't be able to select users to whom you can assign permissions from Windows for Workgroups computers. In order to let Windows for Workgroups users access data on an NT machine, set permissions for the Everyone group.

Checking on File Use

If a file is in use and you want to get to it—or you simply want to know who is using it—you can use the Properties dialog box. Hold the Alt key and double-click on the filename (or simply select the file and then select **File|Properties**) to display the dialog box, and then click on **Open By**. We looked at this dialog box earlier in this chapter—see Figure 7.4.

Note For your NT computer to share data over the network, the Server service must be started. See Chapter 15 for more information about networking.

Ending Network Sharing

 When you need to stop sharing a file or network, select **Disk|Stop Sharing**, or click on the third toolbar button. You'll see the dialog box in Figure 7.11, listing all the shared objects. On the left side of the list is the share name, which is followed by the disk letter and path. Simply select the ones you want to remove— drag across the entries, or press Ctrl and click on them—and then click on OK.

Note You must be an Administrator or Power User to end directory sharing. And ending a share can cause users to lose data.

Accessing Data on a Network

When you let other computers share data, your computer is operating as a *server*. Your computer can also operate at the same time as a *workstation*, using data stored on other computers.

 To connect to a network drive, select **Disk|Connect Network Drive**, or click on the first button in the toolbar. You'll see the dialog box in Figure 7.12. At the top of this box you'll see in the **Drive** box, the drive letter that will be assigned to the network directory. By default, it displays the first available letter, but you can select another letter from the drop-down list box.

```
┌─────────────────────────────────────────────────────┐
│ ▬        Stop Sharing Directory                       │
│                                                       │
│ Shared Directories on \\PK486:        ┌──────────┐    │
│ ┌──────────────────────────────────┐  │   OK     │    │
│ │ 📁A$          A:\              ▲ │  └──────────┘    │
│ │ 📁ADMIN$      E:\winnt           │  ┌──────────┐    │
│ │ 📁B$          B:\                │  │  Cancel  │    │
│ │ 📁Bernouli    F:\                │  └──────────┘    │
│ │ 📁C$          C:\                │  ┌──────────┐    │
│ │ 📁D$          D:\                │  │  Help    │    │
│ │ 📁DiskE       E:\              ▼ │  └──────────┘    │
│ └──────────────────────────────────┘                 │
└─────────────────────────────────────────────────────┘
```

Figure 7.11 The Stop Sharing Directory dialog box

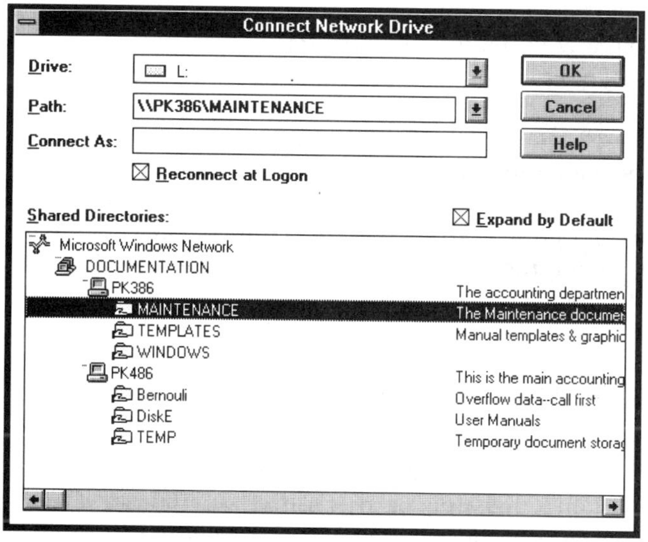

Figure 7.12 The Connect Network Drive dialog box

The **Shared Directories** list box initially shows the Microsoft Windows Network on the top line (or whatever type of network you are connected to), and if the **Expand by Default** check box is selected, the names of the available workgroups or domains, and the available computers within those workgroups and domains. If you double-click on one of the computers, the available directories will be displayed below the computer's name.

Notice that each computer may have a comment to the right of it. This comment comes from the Description line in the Server Properties dialog box if the computer is an NT machine (open this dialog box using the Control Panel's Server icon). If the computer is a Windows for Workgroups machine it's from the Comment in the Network Settings dialog box (also opened from the Control Panel). You can use the scroll bar at the bottom of the list to move along and view the entire comment. The comment to the right of each directory comes from the Shared Directory dialog box, and is entered when you set up the shared directory.

Select one of the share icons and the share path is placed in the **Path** text box near the top of the dialog box. You can also type the name of a computer and shared directory directly into the Path box (*computername**directoryname*), or type the name of a computer (*computername*) and click on OK to see a list of that computer's shares. The drop-down list box attached to this also contains other directories to which you have connected before, so you can select from one of these also.

The **Connect As** text box lets you enter another username with which to log onto the other computer. And the **Reconnect at Logon** simply tells NT that you want this network drive to be a "permanent" fixture, that you want NT to automatically reconnect to it the next time you log on. This check box is selected by default, so if you only want a temporary connection remember to disconnect it. (If, when you log on, one of the network directories is not available, you'll see a message asking if you want to continue attempting to connect to that drive each time you log on.)

 When you double-click on one of the directories, or select it and click on OK, the directory will be added to File Manager's drive bar, using the network-drive icon. By default a new window will open, displaying the contents of the network drive. You can turn this option off by deselecting **Options|Open New Window on Connect**. With this option turned off the drive icon is added to the toolbar, but File Manager doesn't open a new window.

Disconnecting a Network Drive

You disconnect a network drive in much the same way that you stop sharing one of your directories. Select **Drive|Disconnect Network Drive** or click on the second toolbar button. You'll see a dialog box listing the network drives. Simply select the ones you want to remove—drag across the entries, or press Ctrl and click on them—and then click on OK.

Note For your NT computer to access data over the network, the Workstations service must be started. See Chapter 15 for more information about networking.

Associating Document Files

In Windows 3.1 you can associate file extensions with executable files. This is used for "drag-and-drop" operations, and to allow you to run a program by "running" its document files. Windows NT also lets you associate extensions with executable files, but allows you to define much more information.

Select the file type that you want to associate with a particular application. You might select .LOG and .ME files and associate them with Notepad, for instance. Select **File|Associate** to see the dialog box in Figure 7.13. The **Files with Extension** drop-down list box contains all the associated extensions. You can select another if you wish, or type one in. The highlighted line in the **Associate With** box shows the "file type" of the extension in the Files with Extension box, and the application with which that type is associated. For instance, if TXT is in the Files with Extension box, you'll see that the file type is Text File, and the associated application is NOTEPAD.EXE. To simply associate the file with an existing application, select the application from the list and click on OK.

To create a new file type, click on **New Type**. You'll see the New File Type dialog box (Figure 7.14). In the **File Type** box enter a name to describe this sort of file. From the **Action** drop-down list box select the action that is associated with this file association—it's usually Open, but might be Print. Next enter the

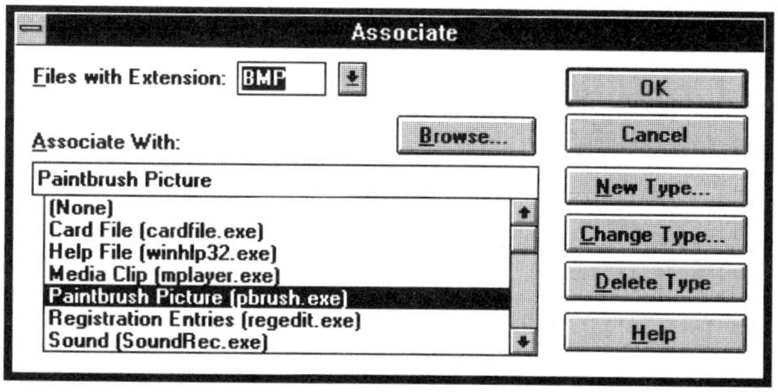

Figure 7.13 The Associate dialog box

Command, the application file associated with the file type. You can use the **Browse** button to search for the application. Finally, place %1 at the end of the command—this represents the name of the file selected in File Manager when the command is run.

The **Uses DDE** area contains advanced information about how the application operates when using Dynamic Data Exchange. It is usually entered by an application's installation program when it associates its own file types. The **DDE Message** is the command used when the application is already running; **DDE Message, Application Not Running** is the command used when the application has not started; **Application** is the application string used to begin a DDE conversation with the application; and **Topic** is the topic string used to begin a DDE conversation with the application.

At the bottom you can define what extensions you want to associate with the new file type. Type the extension in the **New Extension** box, then click on **Add** to put it in the list.

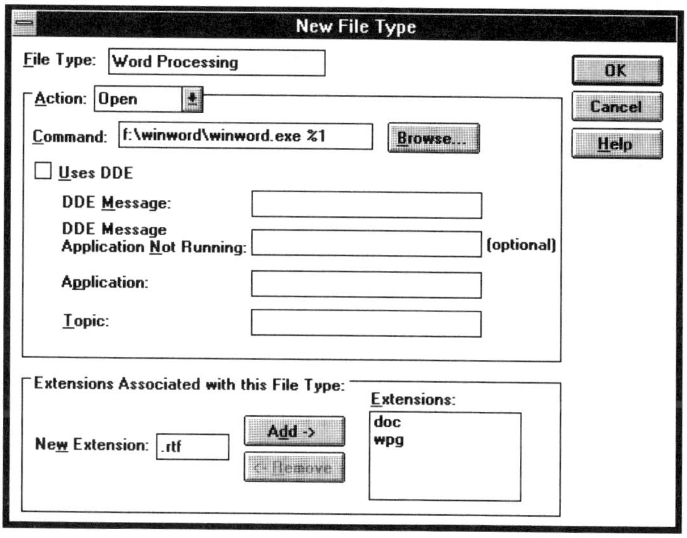

Figure 7.14 The New File Type dialog box

The Associate dialog box also has a **Change Type** button—this simply displays a selected type's data so you can modify it. You can also use the **Remove Type** to delete a type from the list. To "break" an association, select the extension in the **Files with Extension** box, click on the **(None)** entry, and click on OK.

A Few More Features

There are a few more things you might notice about Windows NT's File Manager. First, **floppy disks** can only be formatted in DOS's FAT format, not NTFS. And you can use the **Disk|Format Disk** command to format your floppies and other types of removable media, such as Bernoulli drives.

You may also notice the effect of NT's **multitasking** in File Manager. Most noticeable is when you are formatting disks. Unlike Windows 3.1, you can continue working in File Manager while NT formats a disk. The dialog box even has a Hide button—click on the button to remove the dialog box entirely, and it will format the disk in the background. You can also work while a search goes on in the background. After you begin the search you'll see a dialog box with a Hide button. Click on this button and then carry on working—you can even open another dialog box, such as the Associate dialog box. When the search is finished the Search Results window will appear below that dialog box.

There's an extra confirmation option. Select **Options|Confirmation** and you'll see the Confirmation dialog box you may be familiar with from Windows 3.1. At the bottom of the list is **Modifying System, Hidden, Read Only files**. Select this one to turn off the messages that appear when you modify those types of files. Windows 3.1 wouldn't let you do this, which many users found irritating.

The **Font** (Options|Font) dialog box has a couple of new options. At the bottom of the dialog box you'll find two check boxes: **Display Lowercase for FAT Drives** and **Display Lowercase for All Drives**. You may want to select different options, one for FAT and one for other types of drives, to differentiate quickly between the two. However, when you select Display Lowercase for All Drives, you are allowing the NTFS drives to display their correct case. In other words, if some filenames are lowercase they will display lowercase when you select this option, and the other files will display as uppercase. If you *deselect* this option, *all* files on the NTFS will be shown as lowercase.

There are a couple of new Window menu options: **Tile Horizontally** and **Tile Vertically**. These replace the Tile option. Actually, both are in Windows 3.1; you just have to know which key to press while you select the Tile option (pressing Shift would tile vertically). In many cases these options are exactly the same, depending on how many windows you have open.

Finally, you should note that .CMD files are executable in Windows NT, along with the other types that are executable in Windows 3.1: .EXE, .BAT, .PIF, and .COM.

File Manager's Menu Options

Here's a summary of File Manager's menu options (options marked by an * are new menu options):

File|Open (Enter)	Starts the selected application. If the file is not executable, File Manager checks the files associated executable file, runs the program, and loads the file. If a directory is selected, File Manager expands or collapses one level of subdirectories.
File|Move (F7)	Lets you move a file or directory.
File|Copy (F8)	Lets you copy the selected file or directory, to the same or another directory, or to the Clipboard.
File|Delete (Del)	Deletes the selected file or directory.
File|Delete	Lets you rename the selected file or directory.
File|Properties (Alt-Enter)	Lets you set a file's attributes (Read-Only, Hidden, Archive, and System), and displays information about the file.
File|Run	Lets you start an application, and load a file into its associated application.
File|Print	Lets you print a file, if that file is associated with an application.
File|Associate	Associates a file extension with an application, so you can use commands such as File|Open, File|Run, and File|Print on a document file.
File|Create Directory	Lets you create a new directory.
File|Search	Lets you search your hard disk or floppy disk for a specific file or file type.
File|Select Files	Lets you select multiple files at once by entering a file criteria.
File|Exit	Closes File Manager.
Disk|Copy Disk	Does a DOS DISKCOPY, copying information from one floppy disk to another.
Disk|Label Disk	Lets you add, modify, or remove a disk volume label.
Disk|Format Disk	Lets you format a floppy disk or other form of removable disk (such as a Bernoulli drive). The only format available is FAT.
***Disk|Connect Network Drive**	Lets you connect to a directory on another computer.
***Disk|Disconnect Network Drive**	Disconnects from a directory on another computer.

* Disk|Share As	Lets you define a directory as a shared directory on the network.
* Disk|Stop Sharing	Lets you end directory sharing.
Disk|Select Drive	Lets you select the drive you want to display in the current directory window.
Tree|Expand One Level (+)	Displays a directory's first-level subdirectories.
Tree|Expand Branch (*)	Displays all the subdirectories at all levels of the selected directory.
Tree|Expand All (Ctrl-*)	Expands the entire directory tree, displaying all the directories and subdirectories on the tree.
Tree|Collapse Branch (–)	Collapses the tree below the selected directory, so its subdirectories are not displayed.
Tree|Indicate Expandable Branches	Places a special mark on directory icons that have subdirectories. When the directory is not expanded, a + appears on the icon. When it is expanded, a – is shown instead.
View|Tree and Directory	Places two panels in the current directory window: The one on the left shows the directory tree, the one on the right shows the files in the selected directories.
View|Tree Only	Displays only one panel in the current directory window, showing the directory tree (no files).
View|Directory Only	Displays only one panel in the current directory window, showing a single directory.
View|Split	Displays a black vertical bar, used to place the border between the two panels in the directory window.
View|Name	Makes the file list display only filenames.
View|All File Details	Makes the file list include all information about each file: size, date, time, and attributes.
View|Partial Details	Lets you specify what information you wish to see about each file.
View|Sort by Name	Makes the file list place the files in alphabetical order, by name.
View|Sort by Size	Makes the file list place the files in order according to size.
View|Sort by Type	Makes the file list place the files in alphabetical order, by file extension.
View|Sort by Date	Makes the file list place the files in chronological order.
View|By File Type	Lets you select what type of files should be included in the list.

Options|Confirmation	Lets you decide which commands should display a confirmation dialog box before carrying out the operation.
Options|Font	Lets you select a different font and style for the File Manager.
*__Options|Customize Toolbar__	Lets you remove and add toolbar buttons.
*__Options|Toolbar__	Lets you remove the toolbar from below the menu bar.
Options|Drivebar	Lets you remove the drivebar from below the toolbar.
Options|Status Bar	Lets you remove the status bar from the bottom of the File Manager.
*__Options|Open New Window on Connect__	Makes File Manager open a new window each time you connect to a network directory.
Options|Minimize on Use	Makes the File Manager change to an icon when you start an application from its file list.
Options|Save Settings on Exit	Makes File Manager save its settings when you close it.
*__Security|Permissions__	Lets you assign permissions for files and directories, to define who can use your data and how.
*__Security|Auditing__	Lets you add information about file and directory use to a security log.
*__Security|Owner__	Lets you take ownership of files and directories, so you can control them.
Window|New Window	Opens a new directory window, so you can view another disk or another directory.
Window|Cascade (Shift-F5)	Places the open directory windows one on top of the other. The lowest in the stack is in the top-left corner of the File Manager window, and each subsequent document window is offset toward the bottom-right corner.
*__Window|Tile Horizontally__	Places the open directory windows so none are hidden, and each has equal space.
*__Window|Tile Vertically (Shift-F4)__	Places the open directory windows so none are hidden, and each has equal space.
Window|Arrange Icons	Lines the directory-window icons up tidily at the bottom of the File Manager window.
Window|Refresh (F5)	Searches the current drive and redisplays the file and directory information.
Window|1. *pathname*	Makes the named directory window the active one.

8

Print Manager

Microsoft totally revamped the interface used for printing when they designed Windows NT. In Windows 3.0 and previous versions, printer configuration was carried out using the Printers dialog box accessed from the Control Panel. While there was a Print Manager, its abilities were quite limited. In Windows 3.1, Microsoft added the ability to configure printers directly from Print Manager, without needing to open the Control Panel—Print Manager would access the Control Panel's Printers dialog box directly. In NT, Microsoft got rid of the Control Panel's Printers dialog box entirely, placing all printing control and configuration in the Print Manager, and added yet more features. (You can still get to the printer-control functions from Control Panel, but in NT, using the Control Panel's Printers icon opens Print Manager.)

That raises an important question. In Windows 3.1 you can use the Control Panel to turn off Print Manager, so print jobs all bypass Print Manager and go straight to the port without spooling. How does one disable Print Manager in NT? The answer is, you can't. Instead, you can use the Printer Details dialog box to tell NT to disable Print Manager's spooling for specific ports or print jobs, a much better system than in Windows 3.1. We'll explain how to do that in a moment.

Print Manager

Printers

Open Print Manager by double-clicking on the Print Manager icon in Program Manager's Main group, or by double-clicking on the Printers icon in the Control Panel. You'll see a window similar to that in Figure 8.1. You can see that the Print Manager window is quite different from that in Windows 3.1. Most importantly, each printer profile has its own **printer window**, which can be maximized, minimized, or moved to any position. You can tile or cascade these windows using the Window menu. When you maximize a window, its title appears in brackets in the Print Manager title bar. You can't remove these printer windows

133

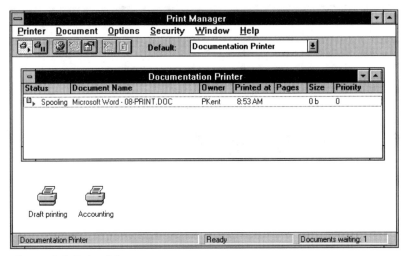

Figure 8.1 Print Manager

from Print Manager without deleting a printer profile. If you want, move them out of the way, or minimize them—they'll appear as printer icons at the bottom of the Print Manager window. Or Maximize the one you want to work with, and use **Ctrl-Tab** or the **Window** menu to move from one window to another.

Notice the columns in each printer window, and the **dividers** between these columns. If you place the mouse pointer over the line dividing two of these columns, the pointer changes to a horizontal, two-headed arrow. You can now drag the column divider to modify the column sizes. You can remove columns by moving a divider to the left until it touches the next divider—to get it back, point at the divider, hold Ctrl, and drag to the right. You can also drag a column or several columns off the window, removing that data from the window. For instance, if you are the only person using your computer or this printer profile, you may want to get rid of the Owner column—drag the divider to the right of Owner until it meets the divider on the left of Owner—and if you use long document names you may wish to enlarge that column. When you drag a column divider, the columns to the right move with it—you are sizing the column to the immediate left. So if you move a column off the window to the right, you can get it back by moving the rightmost column back to the left.

Notice also the **toolbar** under the Print Manager's title bar. The toolbar has the following buttons:

Printer|Resume

Printer|Pause

Printer|Connect to Printer

Printer|Remove Printer Connection

Printer|Properties

DocumentlRemove Document

 DocumentlDetails

There's also a **Default** drop-down list box which contains a list of all the available printer profiles, all the printer profiles that have been "created" with the PrinterlCreate Printer command. The printer displayed in this box is the one that applications will use as the default printer profile, that is, the one that will be used unless you use the applications' Print Setup dialog boxes to select another.

There are three different categories of printers: a local unshared printer, a local shared printer, and a network printer. These are the icons used to denote the three types of printers when the windows are minimized:

 Local unshared printer

 Local shared printer

 Networked printer

"Creating" Printers

In order to add printer profiles to Windows NT, you must be an Administrator or Power User. If you are using LAN Manager or Windows NT Advanced Server, Print Operators and Server Operators can also create printers. Windows NT lets you create printer profiles. Each of these creations is really a description of how NT should handle a print job: which port to send it to, which driver to use, whether to spool the print job, whether to print a separator sheet after the print job, and so on. We've used the term *profile* because, unlike in Windows 3.1, you don't simply select a printer driver: The driver printer is just one aspect in a printer profile, and a profile may even specify *several* printers.

This system allows you to provide a printer (profile) name for each different print configuration, even if you have only one printer, or even if you have none. If you want to print on a printer you don't have connected to your computer, you could create a printer profile that will let you create print files, which you can then take to a print-service bureau or another computer. Or, you can create several profiles for one actual printer, each one using different fonts or different halftone settings. You can even create a profile that sends the print job to several printers at once, to a printer "pool." You could create different profiles for different graphics resolutions, using one for draft printouts and another for the final job. Or perhaps you'll want almost identical profiles, the only difference being that one profile prints one copy, while the other automatically prints two copies (or five, or ten, or any other number you choose). Or create one shared profile for a printer, to be used by other network users, and a nonshared profile, to be used from your computer alone.

Begin by selecting **PrinterlCreate Printer**, and you'll see the dialog box in Figure 8.2. Enter a **Printer Name**. This is *not* necessarily the model name of the

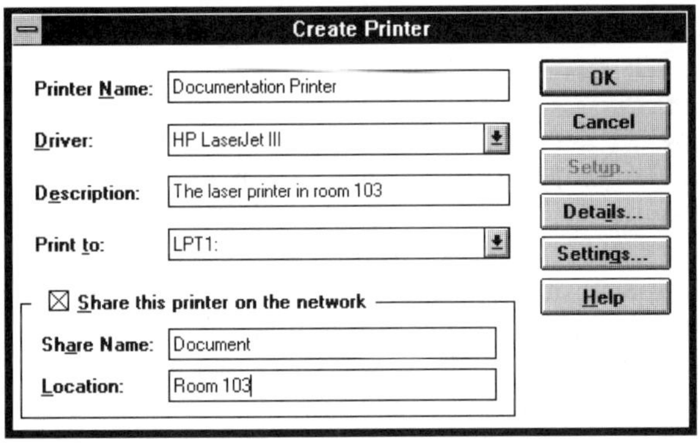

Figure 8.2 The Create Printer dialog box

printer—a LaserJet III or Canon LBP-8sx, for instance. It might be something like *Accounting Department Printer, Fast Printer,* or *Color Printer, 10 Copies,* or any text you want, up to 32 characters. This is the name that users will see when they are selecting a printer in an application, by using the File|Print Setup command.

In the **Driver** drop-down list box, select the print driver you want to use. If you have a driver from the manufacturer, select **Other** from the end of the list. (You'll see a dialog box telling you to insert the disk with the driver into a floppy drive.) You may also be able to use a different driver if your printer "emulates" another printer. For instance, many printers emulate the HP range of printers. If you don't have a suitable driver for your printer, you could then select a driver specified in the printer's documentation.

You can enter another 64 characters describing the printer profile in the **Description** text box. This information will appear in the Printer Properties dialog box (displayed by selecting Printer|Properties), and can be seen by some network users when connecting to the printer.

Now select a port from the **Print To** drop-down list box. This lists four serial and three parallel ports, although your computer may not have the hardware for all these. It also shows FILE which, as in Windows 3.1, lets you create a *print file* instead of sending the work to a printer. You can only select one port here—you'll be able to select more ports in the Printer Details dialog box. Other selections may appear in this drop-down list box—some printing systems may add to the list when you install them.

In some cases you will need to select the **Network Printer** option at the bottom of the list: if the **physical port** to which you want to connect is not listed, if you want to connect to a **LAN Manager 2.x server**, or if you want to connect to a **Hewlett-Packard Network Port.** When you select Network Printer, the Print Destinations dialog box appears. You can select Local Port, LAN Manager Print Share, or, in some cases, Hewlett-Packard Network Port (if it has been installed previously). You will then be able to enter the name of the local port, select the LAN Manager server, or choose the Hewlett Packard port.

Tip   You can enter more print-file names in this way: Select Network Printer, select Local Port, and then type another name—such as PRINTFIL—and click on OK.

Next, decide if you want this printer to be available on the network—if so, click on the **Share this printer on the network** check box. NT will automatically add the Printer Name to the **Share Name** text box, modifying it so that it can be read by MS-DOS workstations (though you can change this if you wish so network users will see a different name). You can also add a **Location**, a description of the printer's location that will be seen when network users connect.

You can now click on OK to install the printer—Print Manager will ask you to insert the correct Setup disk so it can copy the driver, if it's not already on the system. Or you can set up the printer details and port settings first. There's another button, **Setup**, which lets you set up the printer driver. At this stage the Setup button is not yet available, because you haven't yet loaded the driver (unless, of course, you selected the Other option at the bottom of the Driver list and loaded the driver). You can come back to this dialog box after the driver has loaded to set up its options—you'll use the Printer|Properties command, as we'll explain later.

Printer Details

Click on the **Details** button to see the Printer Details dialog box (Figure 8.3). You can use the **Available From** and **To** incrementers to set the times between which the printer may be used. By default it's set to 24 hours a day (12:00 am to 12:00 am), but some printers may not be available at all times. Some may be turned off in the evenings, for instance, or in a locked office. Users can still send print jobs to the printer, but they'll be stored in a print buffer until they can be printed during the scheduled times. So restricting times lets you set up an automated system for printing large documents at night—create two printer profiles for the same physical printer. Use one for large documents you don't need right away,

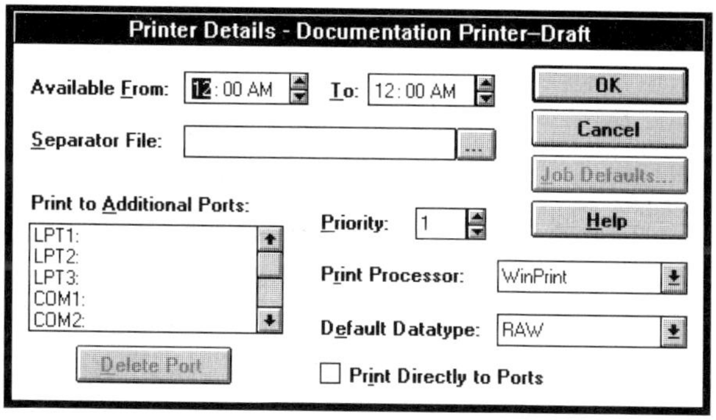

Figure 8.3 The Printer Details dialog box

and restrict the times to after work. Use the other profile for smaller documents that you need immediately, and restrict times to work hours.

If you want to print a separator page after each print job—to stop different print jobs from getting mixed up, and to identify the person who owns the print job, or even to switch printers between PCL and PostScript mode—select a separator file (a .SEP file) using the **Separator File** box. Click on the button at the end of this box to see a typical File Open dialog box and find the file you want to use. NT comes with several separator files, but you can create your own—you'll find the existing ones in the \WINNT\SYSTEM32 directory. You won't be able to find the default separator file, though, because it's not a real file (it's built into the program). You must type DEFAULT.SEP into the Separator File text box to use this one. (We are going to look at separator files in more detail a little later in this chapter.)

Now select a printer **Priority**. This determines which print jobs print first, if you have two or more printer profiles for the same printer. You can enter any priority, from 1 to 99. For instance, if you have a printer connected to your computer you could create two profiles. One will be set to priority of 1, and will be used only from your computer. The other is set to 2, and may be used by other network users. This ensures that your print jobs always print first, before those sent by network users.

You can create a **printer "pool"** using the **Print to Additional Ports** list box. A pool is a group of identical printers that may be used interchangeably. If you create a pool, Print Manager simply sends the print job to the first available printer in the pool. This list box displays all the available ports, other than the one you selected in the Create Printer dialog box as the Print To port. Click once on each port that you want to include (each port that is connected to a compatible printer). You may remove a port from the list by selecting it and clicking on the **Delete** button. (If the port you need is not listed, create the port using the Network Printer option in the Print To list box in the Create Printer dialog box, as we explained earlier.)

You will probably never need to change the **Print Processor** or **Default Datatype** entries. However, some special printing applications that you install may require different selections from these drop-down list boxes. Only change these settings if told to do so by a product's documentation or technical support service.

The **Print Directly to the Selected Ports** check box is where you turn off print spooling. This is the "reverse equivalent" of the **Use Print Manager** check box in Windows 3.1's Printer dialog box. When this check box is *selected*, this print profile bypasses Print Manager's spooling option, and sends the print job directly to the printer. (In Windows 3.1, of course, the Use Print Manager check box must be *cleared* to bypass spooling.) When the check box is *not* selected the print job is sent to a temporary file quickly, then "spooled" to the printer. Printing directly to the ports is faster than spooling, but will hold up your application—you can't use it until it's finished printing.

There are a couple of important differences between the way Windows 3.1 and Windows NT handle this option, though. First, Windows 3.1 makes you turn off the entire Print Manager—all print jobs, whichever print driver is in use, will bypass Print Manager. In Windows NT, though, you can make some printer profiles bypass Print Manager, and others not. This is especially useful if you are using an add-on printing product which needs to bypass Print Manager.

The other important difference is that Print Manager still has *some* control over print jobs. It will still put print jobs in a queue if the printer isn't ready, for instance, and you'll still see the print job in Print Manager's window.

Changing Job Defaults

Now click on the **Job Defaults** button. You'll see the Document Properties dialog box, as shown in Figure 8.4. You can select the **Form** here, the paper size—we'll look at forms in more detail later. You will also select the **Orientation** in this box—either **Landscape** or **Portrait**. And you can determine how many **Copies** the print jobs will usually make. These settings are the ones most print jobs will use when printing with this profile. Other features may be available, depending on the type of printer—some will let you select two-sided printing, for instance. This dialog box is available from an application's Print Setup dialog box (by clicking on the Setup button), so users can quickly change the settings before printing a job.

Click on the **Options** button to see the Advanced Document Properties dialog box (see Figure 8.5). This box lets you select the **Graphics Resolution**, and, if the printer is capable of printing in color, **Color** or **Monochrome**. You can also turn off **Scan for Rules**, a feature used by some printers to speed up processing of files containing lots of horizontal and vertical lines. This feature is on by default, but it may interfere with some printers, so you may need to turn it off. Also, **Download TrueType Fonts** is on by default—this sends the TrueType fonts to the printer to be stored in its memory. Turning it off sends the fonts as graphics. These advanced options may vary depending on the type of print driver selected, so check the Help screens for more information.

Close the Advanced Document Properties dialog box to return to the Document Properties dialog box. Click on the **Halftone** button and you'll see the Halftone Color Adjustment dialog box.

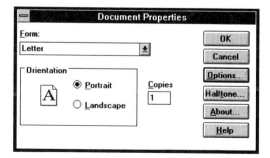

Figure 8.4 The Document Properties dialog box

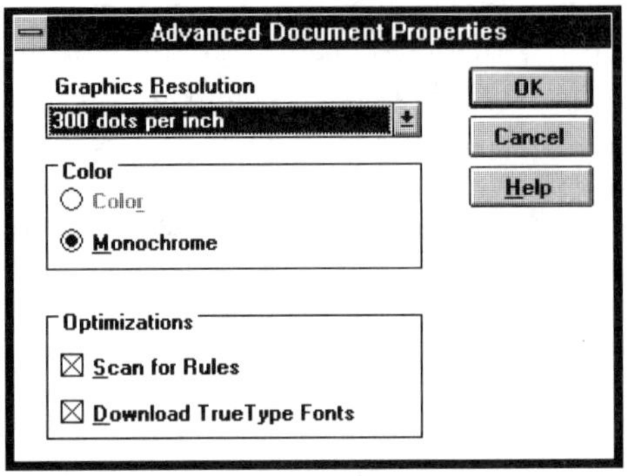

**Figure 8.5   The Advanced Document Properties
          dialog box**

Working with Halftones

Figure 8.6 shows the Halftone Color Adjustment dialog box. A halftone is a graphic in which different shades of gray or colors are simulated by mixing dots of black and white or of a limited range of colors. Black and white photographs in newspapers are halftones. The Halftone Color Adjustment dialog box lets you adjust the way in which your printer prints colors, and even lets you modify and save a bitmap graphic. If you are using a black and white printer, the sample will be in gray; if color, the sample will be in color.

The check boxes at the bottom of the dialog box control the halftone sample, which initially shows a palette containing your display adapter's different tones (if you have a 256-color driver, and are working with a black and white printer, you'll see 256 shades of gray). To remove or restore the halftone box, use the **View** check box. The **Maximize** box makes the sample box enlarge, filling the screen, but with the dialog box itself still visible. Once the sample is maximized, clicking the **right mouse button** will toggle the dialog box itself off and on.

As you'll see in a moment, you can actually select a bitmap that you want to print, and display that in the sample box. The **Palette** check box then toggles the display between the actual picture and the palette of possible grays or colors contained in the picture. For instance, if the bitmap is a 256-color image, you will see 256 squares, showing all possible colors. Of course, your monitor may not be able to display all 256 colors, depending on what video mode you are using, in which case many of these boxes will appear the same. The **Scale** check box displays the picture in it's original proportions. You can flip the picture using the **Flip X** and **Flip Y** check boxes.

Immediately above these check boxes is the **Picture** drop-down list box, which lets you select **Reference Colors**, **RGB Test Colors**, and the **NTSC Color Bar**. To the right of the drop-down list box is a series of numbers describing the currently selected image—the original bitmap size in pixels, the number of colors in the palette, and the current size of the image in pixels. For instance, the RGB Test Colors bitmap is **36x33, 256**, which means its original image size is 36 pixels wide

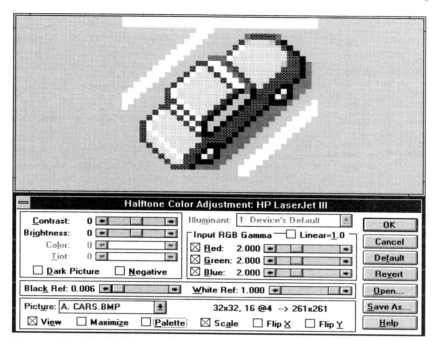

Figure 8.6   The Halftone Color Adjustment dialog box

by 33 pixels tall, and it has a 256-color palette. To the right of these numbers are the current pixel dimensions.

If you open a bitmap, its name will be displayed here also. Open a bitmap using the **Open** button. You'll see a Select a Test Picture dialog box, from which you can open a .BMP, .GIF, or .DIB file.

Now, onto the color controls. In the top left part of this dialog box are four sliders—**Contrast**, **Brightness**, **Color**, and **Tint**. The last two are only enabled if you are working in color. By default each of these is set to 0, but you can select any setting from –100 (on the left of the slider) to +100. As you change these settings you'll notice the bitmap changes. **Contrast** adjusts the variation in brightness between different parts of the picture. Adjusting **Brightness** changes the overall brightness of the image, from quite dark (–100) to a bright, washed out picture (+100). **Color** adjusts the amount of color saturation, –100 is no color saturation (just grays), while +100 provides very bright colors. The **Tint** slider adjusts the picture's hue—move to the left to add red, to the right to add green. (The Tint slider is disabled if you move the Color slider to –100.) The **Dark Picture** check box darkens it overall, to adjust for overexposure, and the **Negative** check box flips the colors, to create a negative image.

You can also adjust the lighting, by selecting from the **Illuminant** drop-down list box. The options simulate the different types of lighting and prints with which photographs are produced—you can select Tungsten Lamp, NTSC Daylight, Cool White Light, and so on. Each time you select one you will see the bitmap change.

The **Input RGB Gamma** settings let you adjust for unbalanced brightness, adjusting the levels of Red, Green, and Blue separately. Clear a check box and then adjust that slider, or select all three check boxes to link them together—when one moves the other two move also.

The **Black Ref** and **White Ref** sliders set the range between the darkest and lightest areas in the bitmap. You can increase the range by reducing both values.

The **Revert** button returns the bitmap to the settings it had when you opened the dialog box. The **Default** button returns all the settings to their default settings. When you've adjusted a bitmap's settings you can actually save a new file, using the **Save** button. If you save a color graphic with which you were working in gray, the new file will also be in gray.

When you close this dialog button using the **OK** button, you are setting the default halftone conditions for this printer. These settings can also be changed from within an application, using the Print Setup command. If you do so, you will only be changing the settings *for that application*, not for other applications using the printer.

Printer Settings

Now close the Halftone Color Adjustment, Document Properties, and Print Details dialog boxes, to return to the Create Printer dialog box (Figure 8.2). Click on the **Settings** button to configure the port to which you have connected the printer. You'll see either the Configure LPT Port dialog box (if the port you selected in the Create Printer dialog box is a parallel port), or the Ports dialog box (if you selected a serial port). If you selected a different sort of port—such as FILE—this button probably won't do anything, though other boxes may be used by some printing systems.

The **Configure LPT Port** dialog box lets you set up the **Transmission Retry** timeout. This is the time NT will wait when the printer pauses. If a printer can't accept anymore information it tells NT to stop transmitting, processes what it has, and tells NT to begin again. If a printer pauses more than 45 seconds (or 90 seconds for a PostScript printer), NT displays a message telling you there's a problem. You probably won't need to change this timeout unless you are using a PostScript printer or a printer on a network. Don't modify these when you first create a printer profile. Instead, change them if you run into problems—if NT displays warning messages when the printer is really okay.

If you specified one of the serial ports (COM ports), you'll see a dialog box showing a list of the ports. Select the port you want to configure and click on the **Settings** button in this dialog box. You'll see the Settings for COM*n* dialog box. You should set these options to match the printer this profile is using (check the printer's documentation). The **Advanced** button in this dialog box probably won't lead anywhere—it will just display a message box telling you that there are no user-configurable parameters for the port.

Loading the Printer Driver

Now, let's return to the Create Printer dialog box. Having finished setting up everything, click on OK. Print Manager will try to load the print driver. First it looks on your system, in the \WINNT\SYSTEM32\SPOOL\DRIVERS\W32X86 directory. If it can't find the drivers there, it displays a dialog box telling you to enter the path to the NT distribution disks. Enter the drive letter of the CD-ROM drive or the floppy drive.

When you click on OK, Print Manager looks for the drivers. If you are using a CD, it will be able to find them. If you are using floppies it won't, so it will tell you which of the Setup disks to place in the disk drive. Do so and click on OK to continue. After loading the driver, Print Manager displays the Printer Setup dialog box.

Incidentally, RISC- and x86-based computers use different printer drivers. If you have both types of machines on a network and share printers across the network, you will need both types of drivers. You can load the drivers at the workstations themselves, or on the x86-based server.

Entering Printer Setup Information

The Printer Setup dialog box is displayed automatically when you load a print driver. (You can also see it by opening the Printer Properties dialog box. Select **Printer|Properties**, or click on the fifth toolbar button, then click on the Setup button. The Printer Properties dialog box is the same as the Create Printer dialog box.)

Figure 8.7 shows an example, the Printer Properties dialog box associated with the HP LaserJet III. These boxes vary depending on the printer you select, so check the Help window for more information.

In the example, you can set the **Source** (the paper tray) and the form supplied by that source. That is, select each source (Upper Paper Tray, Manual Paper Feed, Envelope, and so on, and for each one select a form from the **Name** drop-down

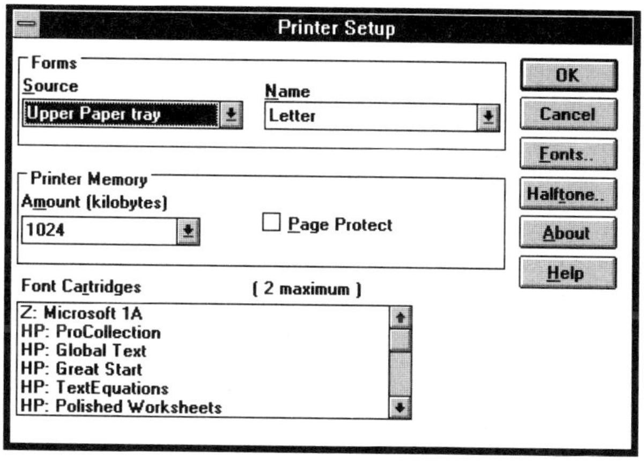

Figure 8.7 The Printer Setup dialog box for an HP III

list box (see later for more information about forms), the amount of **Printer Memory** and the **Page Protect** feature, and the **Font Cartridges** installed. There are also a couple of important buttons—the **Fonts** button, which lets you install and download soft fonts to the printer, and the **Halftone** button, used to determine the manner in which the printer produces halftones. Refer to your printer documentation for information about your printer's features, and to the driver's help system for information about the driver itself.

When you've finished setting up the print driver, click on the **OK** button and all the dialog boxes are removed. NT adds the new printer window to Print Manager. This printer profile is now ready to use.

Creating Separator Files

As you saw earlier, you can print separator files with each print job—these separator files are selected in the Printer Details dialog box (click on Details in the Printer Properties dialog box). Each file either prints a single page or switches a printer's print mode. NT comes with the following standard separator files:

DEFAULT.SEP	Prints an identifier page on a PCL printer. (This file cannot be edited).
PSLANMAN.SEP	Prints an identifier page on a PostScript printer.
PCL.SEP	Switches a printer from PostScript mode to PCL printing.
PSCRIPT.SEP	Switches a printer from PCL mode to PostScript mode.

The first character in the file is the *escape character*, which is used elsewhere in the file to prefix *escape codes*. The following list shows the escape codes you can use. We are going to assume that the escape character is @, though you can substitute another character by placing it as the first character in the file.

@N	Prints the username of the person who submitted the job.
@I	Prints the job number.
@D	Prints the date the job was printed. The date uses the Short Date Format in the Control Panel's International dialog box.
@T	Prints the time the job was printed. The time uses the Time Format in the Control Panel's International dialog box. The time is in 12-hour format, with leading zeros.
@L*xxxx*	Prints all the characters (xxxx) up until the next escape code. If these include nonprintable codes, they are sent to the printer verbatim. However, in block-character mode (see below), nonprintable characters will be represented by their image in the standard ASCII character set. For example, ASCII 0x01 is a happy face. To print the escape character itself, include it in the text as a double-escape (i.e. @@). This will be treated as a single normal character.

@Hxx   Prints the character represented by the hexadecimal ASCII code, *xx*. In block-character mode, nonprintable characters will be represented by an image, as in @L*xxx*.

@B@S   Enter single-width block-character mode. Any of the first five escape codes in this table will print in 8 x 8 block characters rather than as single characters. For example, if you use @N, the username will be printed with each character expanded to eight characters high and eight wide. If there's a carriage return in the @L text, printing continues in block-character mode on the next available line. Printing will continue in block-character mode until the @U code.

@B@M   Enter double-width block-character mode. Same as @B@S, but the characters are printed in blocks 16 characters high and 8 wide.

@U   Turns off block-character printing.

@n   Skip *n* lines from 0–9. 0 means moving to the next line. This escape code is the same in both-character and normal mode—it doesn't skip *n* 8-character-high lines; it simply prints *n* + 1 carriage returns and linefeeds.

@Wnn   Sets the width of the separator page to *nn* characters. The default width is 80, the maximum width is 256. Characters beyond this width are not printed. This can be used to restrict text to a certain number of characters. The new width takes effect starting on the current line.

@Fpathname Prints the contents of the file specified by *pathname*, starting on the next empty line. The contents of the file is printed without any processing.

@E   Sends a form-feed character, ASCII 0x0c, to the printer. This is not the same as entering @H0c, because @E sends the form-feed character as a single character even if you are in block-character mode. @H0c would send a block representation of the character.

Each new line in your separator file is sent as carriage return and a linefeed, so the receiving printer should not be in a mode that would translate this into two lines. And any text in the file that does not appear as part of one of the codes is not sent to the printer. You can't just enter a line or two of text and hope it's printed—it must be preceded by @L.

For instance, you might enter this into your separator file:

```
@
@B@S
@N
@U
```

```
@2

@D     @T
```

The first line simply identifies the escape character. The second line turns on single-width block-character mode. The next line prints the username—because it's in block-character mode each letter in the name will be printed eight characters high, as shown below. The next line leaves two blank lines, and the last line prints the date and time. You can see what the printed page will look like below:

```
PPPPP   KKK   KK                           t
  PP  PP  KK  KK                          tt
  PP  PP  KK KK    eeee    nnnnn   ttttt
  PPPPP    KKKK   ee  ee   nn nn    tt
  PP       KK KK  eeeee    nn nn    tt
  PP       KK  KK ee       nn nn    tt t
PPPP      KKK  KK  eeee    nn nn     tt
```

```
5/11/1993 6:45:04 PM
```

If you want to create your own separator file, create it in Notepad or another ASCII editor. Save it with the .SEP extension, in ASCII format. Then use the Printer Details dialog box to select it. You can also modify three of the existing .SEP files if you wish.

Working with Forms

Each printer's Printer Setup dialog box lets you assign a particular form to a particular paper source. Where does Printer Setup get this list of forms? From the Forms dialog box (select **Printer|Forms**—see Figure 8.8). This dialog box lets you view the forms that are available to applications running on this computer, and to create new ones. The list box displays all the forms currently available. Select a form and you'll see the information about that form in the lower part of the box—the **Name**, **Width**, **Height**, and the **Print Area Margins**. If you want to change the units used, select the **Metric** (for centimeters) or **English** (for inches) option button.

NT comes with over 40 form sizes already created—you can't rename or modify them. You can create your own, though. Simply type a new name into the **Name** text box, enter the new width, height, and margins, and click on the **Add** button. The **Delete** button lets you remove any of the new forms you add (it won't let you delete one of the standard set). Select the form you want to remove and click the button.

Not all forms are available on all printers, of course. If the form is too big for your printer, it won't appear in the Printer Setup's Name list. But any new forms you create that *do* fit the printer will appear at the *end* of this list (not in alphabetical order).

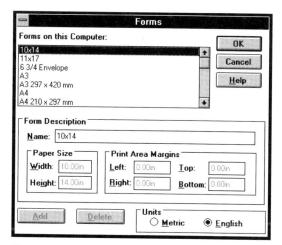

Figure 8.8 The Forms dialog box

Not only does the Forms feature let you assign different page sizes, but it also lets you create different margins for different purposes. If you print onto pre-printed stationery, you could create a Letterhead form, allowing enough space at the top of the form for the company logo, or a Sales form, with a large border down one side for illustrations, for instance.

Printer Security

Print Manager controls printer use in the same way that File Manager controls file and directory use. The **Security** menu has the same three options—**Permissions**, **Auditing**, and **Owner**. These features let you control who may use the printer, and also lets you set up security auditing, so you can keep a log of every person using it.

Setting Permissions

Select a printer and then select Permissions to see the Printer Permissions dialog box. You will use this to define who may use the printer, and how. By default the Administrators and Power Users have Full Control. Everyone may Print with the printer, and CREATOR OWNERs may Manage Documents (the documents they sent to the printer). You can, of course, provide Manage Documents or Full Control permissions to any user you wish. Here's a list of permissions and their default assignments:

	No Access	Print	Manage Documents	Full Control
Print		✓		✓
Control document settings			✓	✓
Pause, resume, restart, and delete print jobs			✓	✓
Change print order				✓
Pause, resume, and purge the printer				✓
Change printer properties				✓
Delete printer				✓
Change printer permissions				✓

The Printer Permissions dialog box works in the same way as the Permissions dialog box in File Manager. See Chapter 7 for more information.

Taking Ownership

As in File Manager, you can use the **Security|Owner** command to take ownership of a printer. This probably isn't as useful in Print Manager, though. Anyone who has Full Control—by default Administrators and Power Users—can take ownership. And even if the Full Control permission is removed from the Administrators group, they can still take ownership and reinstate Full Control.

Auditing Printing

Print Manager also lets you audit printer use, in the same way that File Manager lets you audit file and directory use. Select the printer you want to audit, then select the **Security|Auditing** command to see the Printer Auditing dialog box. Use the Add button to select the people you want to monitor—adding them to the Name list box. Then select each one in turn, and select the auditing options:

Print	Printing documents.
Full Control	Changing print-job settings; pausing, restarting, moving, and deleting print jobs; sharing the printer; changing printer properties; deleting the printer; changing printer permissions.
Delete	Deleting print jobs.
Change Permissions	Changing printer permissions.
Take Ownership	Taking ownership.

For each one, you can select Success and Failure. The audit information is saved in the SecEvent.EVT file, in the WINNT\SYSTEM32\CONFIG directory. This Security report can be viewed in the Event Viewer—see Chapter 13 for more information.

Note The EventLog service must be running for this auditing to work correctly. See Chapter 13.

Networking Printers

Printers are regarded as "resources" in the same way files and directories are resources. You can share printers with other users, or connect to printers on other computers. Print Manager handles these functions in a similar way to File Manager, so if you need a detailed discussion of sharing and connecting, you might want to read Chapter 7.

Connecting to a Printer

To connect to a printer somewhere else on the network, select **Printer|Connect to Printer** to see the Connect to Printer dialog box. This works in the same way as the box used to connect to a network directory in File Manager. You'll see the networks, and if the **Expand by Default** check box is selected (it is, by default), you'll see the workgroups or domains and the associated computers. Double-click on a computer icon to see the available printers. Select a printer to see the description, status, and number of documents waiting displayed in the **Printer Information** area at the bottom of the dialog box. Then double-click on the printer you want to use. If that printer is on an NT machine, then the correct drivers are, presumably, already installed. If it's *not*, you'll be asked to install the driver. You'll need the NT installation disk or disks—just follow the instructions.

 To remove a network printer window from Printer Manager, select the printer's window and then select **Printer|Remove Printer**. Or click on the fourth toolbar button.

Note For your NT computer to access data over the network, the Workstations service must be started. See Chapter 15 for more information about networking.

Sharing Printers

Sharing printers is done in the Create Printer or Printer Properties dialog box (see Figure 8.2). Simply select the **Share this printer on the network** check box, then enter a **Share Name** and a **Location**. When another user tries to get to this printer, he'll see the Share Name next to the printer icon in the Connect to Printer dialog box, the Location on the same line, and the printer's Description—also entered in this dialog box—in the Description line at the bottom of the Connect to Printer dialog box.

Note For your NT computer to share a printer over the network, the Server service must be started. See Chapter 15 for more information about networking.

Using Server Viewer

Administrators and Power Users can administer printers on other computers, using a service called Server Viewer. Select **Printer|Server Viewer**, and you'll see a dialog box listing the workgroup or domain. Double-click on the computer with the printers that you want to administer—this must be an NT workstation. Print Manager will open a Server window—as shown in Figure 8.9—which lists all the printers on that machine.

You can create new printers, remove existing printers, and change a printer's properties, using the normal toolbar buttons and menu commands. And if you double-click on any of the printers in the list, Print Manager will open a printer window, so you can manipulate the print jobs in the same way you can work with print jobs on your own machine.

You can **close** the Server Viewer using its Control menu.

Printing

Printing documents is much the same as with Windows 3.1. Select the correct printer from the application's Print Setup dialog box, then use the application's

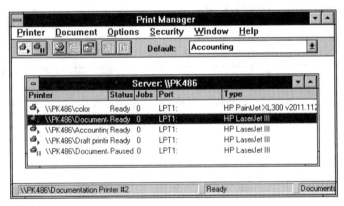

Figure 8.9 The Server Viewer window

Print option to send the data to the printer. The Print Manager window will not automatically appear when printing, as it does in Windows 3.1. Closing NT, or—if Print Manager is open—closing Print Manager, will *not* destroy the print queue (as it does in Windows 3.1). The files will remain on the hard disk, ready to print when you start NT the next time.

If you want to manipulate print jobs in some way, you must be an Administrator or Power User. Other users can only manipulate their own print jobs (but see the discussion of permissions earlier—you can increase or decrease permissions if you wish). You may want to move print jobs around in the print queue, for instance, or pause a printer. If a printer is being repaired or having paper or toner replaced, you could pause the printer, continue sending various print jobs to that printer, and then resume the printer when it's ready to accept print jobs again.

Begin by displaying the printer's window. Here are the operations you can carry out in the printer window:

Operation	Mouse/Keyboard	Toolbar	Menu
Stop the printer	Deselect the document first (press Spacebar or click the right mouse button).		Printer|Pause
Resume printing	Deselect the document first (press Spacebar or click the right mouse button).		Printer|Resume
Stop a document from printing	Select the document first.		Document|Pause
Resume printing the document	Select the document first.		Document|Resume
Change print order	Drag the document up or down the list, or select it and use Ctrl-Up Arrow or Ctrl-Down Arrow.		
Restart a document from the beginning (if the Print Directly to Ports option is not in use)	Select the document first.		Document|Restart
Remove a single waiting document from the print queue	Select the document and press Delete.		Document|Remove Document
Remove all waiting documents from the print queue	Select the window or icon first.		Printer|Purge Printer

---

Note   Pausing the document at the front of the queue stops all documents.

Let's take a look at a printer window and the information it contains (see Figure 8.10). These are the columns in the window:

Status   The status of the print job. You may see Paused (you used the Document Pause command), Printing (the document is being printed), Paper Out (the document can't print because the printer is out of paper), Spooling (the document is being sent to Print Manager by the application). If the column is blank, the document is printing or waiting to print.

Document Name   The name of the application and the document file from which this print job comes.

Owner   The username of the person who sent the print job to the printer. This is important if other network users have access to the printer, or if Windows NT was shut down before all the print jobs were finished, on a machine used by more than one person (when the next person logs on, the print jobs will continue).

Printed At   The time at which the print job was created by the application.

Pages   The number of document pages.

Size   The size of the .SPL file, the spool file created when the application tried to print. These files are usually stored in the \WINNT\SYSTEM32\SPOOL\PRINTERS directory.

Priority   The priority assigned to the print job. By default all documents have a priority of 0. You can change a print job's priority in the Document Details dialog box (see below).

   If you want more information about a print job, select it and then click on the last button in the toolbar or select **Document|Details**—or simply **double-click** on the listing. You'll see the dialog box shown in Figure 8.11. Several of the fields in this box are the same as the columns in the printer window, of course. These are the others:

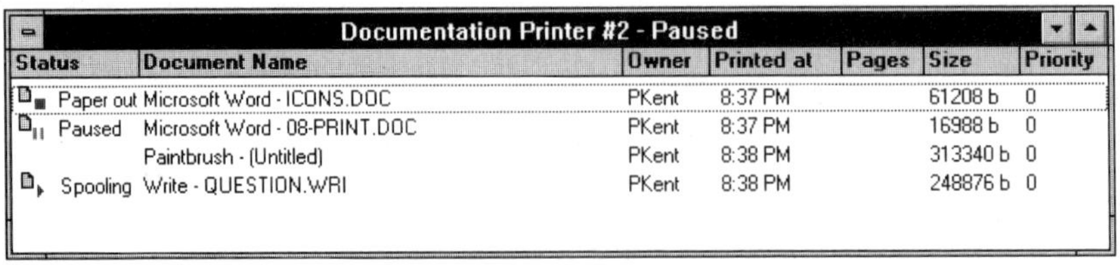

Status	Document Name	Owner	Printed at	Pages	Size	Priority
Paper out	Microsoft Word · ICONS.DOC	PKent	8:37 PM		61208 b	0
Paused	Microsoft Word · 08-PRINT.DOC	PKent	8:37 PM		16988 b	0
	Paintbrush · (Untitled)	PKent	8:38 PM		313340 b	0
Spooling	Write · QUESTION.WRI	PKent	8:38 PM		248876 b	0

Documentation Printer #2 - Paused

Figure 8.10 A print window, showing print jobs

Printed On	The name of the printer profile, the same as the name that appears in the printer window's title bar.
Processor	The printing processor used to print the document. This is set in the Printer Properties dialog box, and will rarely need changing.
Datatype	The datatype used to print the document. Also set in the Printer Properties dialog box, and also rarely needs changing.
Notify	The user to be notified about changes in printing status. This user can be different from the owner.
Priority	By default all print jobs have the same priority. You can increase the priority to make the print job print sooner. Earlier in the chapter we explained that each print profile has a priority, also. The document priority overrides the profile priority, so a high-priority document on a low-priority profile prints sooner than a low-priority document on a high-priority profile.
Start Time	The Available From time set in the Printer Details box for that printer profile. This is not document specific, of course, but affects all documents on that printer, and shows whether the document can be printed now, or must wait until later. You can change the time, to specify when this particular print job will print.
Until Time	The Available To time set in the Printer Details box for that printer profile. Again, you can modify it if you wish, for this specific print job.

Tip   To see a record of who printed what, and when and how, see the Event Log. See Chapter 13 for more information.

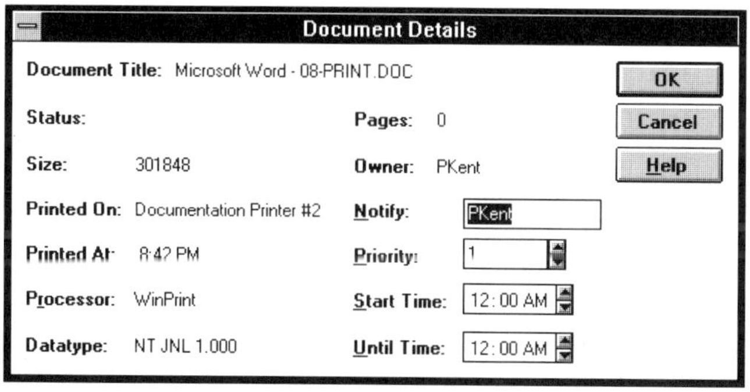

Figure 8.11 The Document Details dialog box

Modifying Printer Profiles

 You can, of course, change a printer profile whenever you wish. Select the printer window for the profile you want to change, and then select **Printer|Properties** or click on the fifth toolbar icon. You'll see another dialog box called the Printer Properties dialog box—this is exactly the same as the Create Printer dialog box (Figure 8.2), and everything works in the same way that it does for that dialog box. Clicking on the **Setup** button displays the other Printer Properties dialog box, the one used to configure the print driver (see Figure 8.7).

 To remove a printer profile entirely, select it and use the **Printer|Remove Printer** command. You can also use this method to **disconnect** from a network printer—or click on the fourth toolbar button instead.

The Menu Options

Here's a quick summary of the Print Manager menu options:

Printer|Connect to Printer	Lets you select a network printer.
Printer|Create Printer	Lets you add a printer "profile" to the Print Manager window. This is where you install print drivers and set up the printer.
Printer|Remove Printer	Removes the selected printer profile from the Print Manager window—if it's a local printer you are deleting the printer profile. If it's a network printer, you are simply disconnecting.
Printer|Properties	Displays the profile for the selected printer.
Printer|Forms	Lets you create forms—specific page sizes and margins—that are available for use by printers.
Printer|Pause	Stops the selected printer working.
Printer|Resume	Lets the selected printer continue working.
Printer|Purge Printer	Removes all print jobs from the selected printer.
Printer|Server Viewer	Lets you connect to another networked computer and manage all that computer's printers and print jobs.
Printer|Exit	Closes Print Manager. Even when closed, Print Manager remains active. Unlike Windows 3.1, NT's Print Manager doesn't automatically open when you print.
Document|Remove Document (Del)	Removes the selected document from the print queue, canceling the print operation.
Document|Details	Displays information about the selected document.

Document|Pause	Temporarily stops the selected document printing.
Document|Resume	Resumes printing the selected document.
Document|Restart	Restarts printing a document from the beginning.
Options|Toolbar	Turns the toolbar (below the title bar) on and off.
Options|Status Bar	Turns the status bar (at the bottom of the window) on and off.
Options|Save Settings on Exit	Saves the toolbar and status bar settings and window position.
Security|Permissions	Lets you define who can use the selected printer and how.
Security|Auditing	Lets you set up auditing for the selected printer, to keep a log of who is using the printer and how.
Security|Owner	Lets you assume ownership of the printer.
Window|Cascade (Shift-F5)	Cascades the printer windows inside Print Manager, laying them one on top of the other with title bars visible.
Window|Tile Horizontally	Places the printer windows so they are all visible, and all take an equal amount of space. They are placed one above the other.
Window|Tile Vertically (Shift-F4)	As with Tile Horizontally, but the windows are placed next to each other.
Window|Arrange Icons	Tidies up the icons at the bottom of the Print Manager window.
Window|Refresh	Updates the display in the selected window.
Window|*printername*	The Window menu lists each of the printer windows. Select one to make that window active.

9

Command Prompt

Command
Prompt

Windows NT has an unusual command prompt—a multi-operating-system command prompt. You can use Windows NT, MS-DOS, OS/2, and TCP/IP commands at the prompt. Although the icon is the same as the Windows 3.1 icon—a replica of the MS-DOS logo—this is *not* an MS-DOS command prompt. Yes, it looks very like much like it—you'll see the familiar drive letter and > sign, for instance—but when you open a Command Prompt window the MS-DOS subsystem has not yet started. NT has "co-opted" many MS-DOS commands and runs them without starting the MS-DOS subsystem. The Windows NT commands were originally based on the DOS 5.0 command set, not 6.0. That doesn't matter, though, because there was little difference between the DOS 6.0 "kernel" and that of 5.0. DOS 6.0 was an upgrade to 5.0, adding a few commands and capabilities. Some of these commands are already in NT (such as file backup and the ability to configure different startup options) and some will, or may be, added later (such as disk compression, virus protection, and deleted-file recovery). The core of 6.0's code, though, is the same as that of 5.0.

If you open the Command Prompt window, then use several familiar MS-DOS commands—COPY, DEL, MKDIR, CD, and so on—NT runs these commands itself, without invoking the MS-DOS subsystem. These are no longer really MS-DOS commands; they are now NT commands. And NT has added a few simple—and not so simple—commands. There's now a MOVE command, to move files (in MS-DOS 5.0 and earlier you must COPY and then DEL, though 6.0 also has a MOVE command). There's a PUSHD command, which saves the name of the current directory, and then moves you to the specified directory. You use this in place of the old CD command. For instance, you can use PUSHD C:\TEMP to change the current directory to the C:\TEMP directory. Later you can use the POPD command to return directly to the directory you were in when you used PUSHD.

So, what exactly can you do from this command prompt? You can:

- Start Windows NT, MS-DOS, Windows 3.1, Version 1.x character-based OS/2, and POSIX programs.
- Issue Windows NT commands.
- Issue Windows NT network commands, which have evolved from LAN Manager 2.1 commands.
- Cut and paste information between applications from different operating systems.

As we discussed earlier in this book, when you run a non-NT program a special *subsystem* opens and manages the program. When you first open the Command Prompt you are still in NT proper—none of the non-NT subsystems has started yet. It's not until you actually run one of those other programs that the subsystem starts—that's discussed in Chapter 10.

Command Types

NT runs several different categories of commands:

Native	Commands that use NT's 32-bit operating system. Many of the commands that have evolved from MS-DOS are now native commands.
Network	A subset of the native commands, these are used to configure and monitor a network.
Special Purpose	A subset of the native commands, there are three special purpose commands that may be removed from NT in later versions: ACLCONV, PORTUAS, DISK-PERF, which convert OS/2 and LAN Manager account files to an NTFS format, and manage disk-performance monitoring.
Subsystem	Commands that operate in one of the non-NT subsystems. These are older, 16-bit commands, commands that are only needed in the other operating systems, and commands that no longer run—because their functions have been taken over by NT—but which are accepted by NT in order to maintain compatibility with programs that use them.
Configuration	Commands that are used to configure the MS-DOS and OS/2 subsystems. They are added to the CONFIG.NT (MS-DOS) and CONFIG.SYS (OS/2) files. (See Chapter 10 for more information about these files.)

TCP/IP Utility   Commands used to manage connections to TCP/IP hosts, machines using operating systems such as UNIX. TCP/IP is a popular networking protocol used on many wide-area networks.

This may sound complicated, but it's not, because you don't need to know what type a command is when you want to use it. NT figures all that out for you. Just enter the command at the command-line prompt and press Enter—or enter the configuration command in the appropriate file—and NT runs it.

The NT Command Set

Windows NT's command set is based on MS-DOS 5.0 and LAN Manager 2.1—it contains most of these system's commands, with a few additions, many modifications, and a few commands left out (generally because they are no longer needed).

Note Some commands are only available if you are an Administrator. If you are not an Administrator and find you are unable to use a command, check the help file to see if you are using one of the Administrator commands.

NT also accepts certain OS/2 commands, and has a set of TCP/IP utility commands. For a short description of all the NT commands, see the end of this chapter. But let's start by looking at the changes to the two major command sets, the MS-DOS and LAN Manager commands. We'll start with what may be thought of as the DOS 5.0 command set. (Remember, these are really NT commands—it doesn't need to run the MS-DOS subsystem to use these commands. You might think of them as DOS 5.0 commands because they have "evolved" from that operating system.)

Note For detailed information about each command, see NT's Help system. Double-click on the Windows NT Help icon in the Main program group, then click on
Windows NT
Help   the "Access the Command Reference Help" entry.

New and Modified Commands from DOS 5.0

AT	New: Starts programs and batch files at the specified time.
CMD	New: CMD.EXE replaces COMMAND.COM.
CONVERT	New: Converts a file system from FAT or HPFS to NTFS.
DEL	Modified: Additional functions.

DIR	Modified: Additional functions. Can display DOS and NTFS names.
DISKCOMP	Modified: Switches /1 and /8 not supported.
DISKCOPY	Modified: Switch /1 not supported.
ECHOCONFIG	New: Displays messages during the processing of the MS-DOS subsystem CONFIG.NT and AUTOEXEC.NT files.
EMM	New: EMM.SYS (used in CONFIG.NT) replaces EMM386.EXE.
ENDLOCAL	New: Returns the environment variables back to the state previous to the SETLOCAL command.
FINDSTR	New: Like FIND, but also searches for specific text patterns using regular expressions.
FORMAT	Modified: 2.8 MB drives and 20.8 floptical drives supported; switches /B, /S, and /U not supported. Will format FAT, HPFS, and NTFS.
KEYB	Modified: KEYBOARD.SYS no longer used.
LABEL	Modified: ^ and & can be used in volume labels.
LOADFIX	New: Starts a program, loading it above the first 64K of conventional memory.
MODE	Modified: Many changes.
MORE	Modified: Many new functions.
MOVE	New: Moves files between directories.
PATH	Modified: Uses the %PATH% parameter to append the current path to the new one you are defining.
POPD	New: Changes to the directory saved by PUSHD.
PRINT	Modified: Switches /B, /U, /M, /S, /Q, /C, /T, and /P not supported.
PUSHD	New: Saves the name of the current directory, then moves to the specified directory. The stored name can be used by POPD.
RECOVER	Modified: The command can recover only *single* files. It can no longer recover all files on a named disk.
SETLOCAL	New: Lets you modify environment variables temporarily while running a batch file.
SORT	Modified: No need to set a TEMP environment variable before redirecting output. File size is unlimited.
START	New: Opens another command prompt window and, if specified, runs a program or command (in which case it runs the CONFIG.NT and AUTOEXEC.NT files first).
TITLE	New: Changes the title of the command prompt window.
XCOPY	Modified: Ten new functions.

WINVER	New: Displays the Windows NT version number.
&&	New: Ensures that the following command runs only if the preceding command was successful.
||	New: Ensures that the following command runs only if the preceding command failed.
&	New: Separates multiple commands.
( )	New: Groups commands.
^	New: An escape character which allows input of non-DOS symbols in a command.

DOS 5.0 Commands Not Available in Windows NT

ASSIGN	Not supported.
CTTY	Not supported.
DOSSHELL	Unnecessary with the Windows NT interface.
EXPAND	Unnecessary (only used for MS-DOS 5.0 installation disks).
FASTOPEN	Replaced by Windows NT inherent caching. It is only accepted to remain compatible with files created for MS-DOS.
FDISK	Replaced by Disk Manager.
JOIN	Not supported.
MIRROR	Not supported.
SYS	Not supported, because Windows NT will not fit on a standard 1.2 MB or 1.44 MB floppy disk.
UNDELETE	Not supported.
UNFORMAT	Not supported.

DOS 6.0 Commands Not Available in Windows NT

A number of commands that were added to DOS 6.0 are not available in Windows NT:

CHOICE	Not supported.
DBLSPACE	Not supported.
DEFRAG	Not supported.
DELTREE	Use RMDIR /S instead.
FASTHELP	Use HELP or the Windows NT Help icon instead.
INCLUDE	Not supported.
INTERLNK	Not supported.
INTERSRV	Not supported.
MEMMAKER	NT automatically optimizes MS-DOS subsystem memory use.
MENUCOLOR	Not supported.

MENUDEFAULT	Not supported.
MENUITEM	Not supported.
MSAV	Not supported.
MSBACKUP	For tape drives use the Backup utility (in the Administrative Tool group). For disk drives use BACKUP or XCOPY.
MSCDEX	Not supported. NT provides access to CD-ROM drives for the MS-DOS subsystem through NT CD-ROM-drive drivers. If no NT driver is available for your CD-ROM drive, you cannot use it, even for non-NT programs.
MSD	Not supported.
NUMLOCK	Not supported.
POWER	Not supported.
SMARTDRV	NT provides caching for the MS-DOS subsystem.
SUBMENU	Not supported.
VSAFE	Not supported.

NT's network commands have "evolved" from LAN Manager 2.1. As with the DOS commands, NT has retained and modified some commands, excluded some, and added others. The following table shows the new and modified commands.

New and Modified Commands from LAN Manager 2.1

AT	New: Lets you remotely schedule events.
NET ACCOUNTS	Modified: You cannot set server roles; this is controlled by Windows NT security.
NET COMPUTER	New: Lets you add or delete computers from a domain.
NET CONFIG	Modified: The functions controlled by this command are now inherent to Windows NT, so commands such as NET CONFIG PEER are not required.
NET CONFIG SERVER	Modified: Switches /AUTODISCONNECT, /SRVCOMMENT, and /HIDDEN can be configured. The switch /SRVHIDDEN is replaced by /HIDDEN.
NET CONFIG WORKSTATION	Modified: Switches /CHARCOUNT, /CHARTIME, and /CHARWAIT can be configured.
NET CONTINUE	Modified: Still available for some services (see NET PAUSE), but not for printing: Print Manager controls printing.

NET GROUP	Modified: Only used for members of a domain.
NET LOCALGROUP	New: Manages local groups.
NET PAUSE	Modified: You can pause Alerter, Messenger, Netlogon, Replicator, Server, Telnet, and Workstation. Print Manager is used to pause printers.
NET PRINT	Controls print jobs and queues—but use Print Manager to manage printers.
NET SEND	Modified: You can send messages, but not files. Windows NT Mail, however, lets you send files attached to messages.
NET SHARE	Modified: Creates, deletes, and displays shared resources. But remote administration is automatic, and you can use File Manager to carry out much of NET SHARE's work. Use Print Manager to share printers. Comm queues are not supported in this release.
NET START	Modified: You can start Alerter, Eventlog, Messenger, Netlogon, Replicator, Server, Snmp, Tcpip, Nbt, Telnet, and Workstation. These services can be started automatically (configured in Control Panel's Services dialog box).
NET START ALERTER	New: Starts a service that sends alert messages to other computers.
NET START EVENTLOG	New: A service that logs system, security, and application occurrences.
NET START MESSENGER	New: Starts a service that lets the workstation receive messages.
NET START NETLOGON	Modified: Starts Net Logon, which verifies log-on requests.
NET START REPLICATOR	Modified: Starts directory replication, copying directories between machines. But you can use the Control Panel's Server dialog box to configure the replicator, and the Services dialog box to start it.
NET START SERVER	Modified: Starts the server service. But you can use Control Panel's Services dialog box to start this service.
NET START SNMP	Modified: New logging options.
NET START TCPIP	New: Starts the TCP/IP service.

NET START TELNET	New: Starts the Telnet service.
NET START WORKSTATION	Modified: Starts the Workstation service. But you can also start the service using Control Panel's Services dialog box.
NET STATISTICS	Modified: Displays a statistics log for the workstation or server. The statistics log cannot be cleared.
NET STOP	Modified: You can stop Alerter, Messenger, Netlogon, Replicator, Server, Snmp, Telnet, and Workstation. But you can also use the Control Panel's Services dialog box.
NET USE	Modified: The /PERSISTENT switch has only yes and no values. Comm queues are not supported.
NET USER	Modified: Switches /LOGONSERVER, /MAXSTORAGE, /OPERATOR, and /PRIVILEGE are not supported.
NET VIEW	Modified: A new switch—/DOMAIN—lets you view domains and computers in a specified domain.

LAN Manager 2.1 Commands Not Available in Windows NT

NET	Use the Control Panel's Server dialog box and other administrative tools.
NET ADMIN	Use the Control Panel's Server dialog box and other administrative tools.
NET ACCESS	Use File Manager.
NET AUDIT	Use the Event Viewer.
NET COMM	Communication-device queues not supported.
NET CONFIG PEER	Unnecessary.
NET CONSOLE	Use Windows NT's security features.
NET COPY	Use File Manager.
NET DEVICE	Use Print Manager.
NET ERROR	Use the Event Viewer.
NET FORWARD	Not supported.
NET LOG	Not supported.
NET LOGOFF	Unnecessary: It's built into Windows NT.
NET LOGON	Unnecessary: It's built into Windows NT.
NET MOVE	Use File Manager.

NET PASSWORD	Press Ctrl-Alt-Del or use User Manager.
NET RUN	Not supported: No remote execution in Windows NT.
NET SEPARATOR	Use Print Manager.
NET START NETPOPUP	Unnecessary: Network messages are processed automatically.
NET START NETRUN	Not supported.
NET START NVALERT	Not supported.
NET START PEER	Not necessary: Peer functionality is built into Windows NT.
NET START REMOTEBOOT	Not supported.
NET STATUS	Use NET CONFIG SERVER and NET SHARE.
NET START TIMESOURCE	Not necessary: Included in the server service.
NET VERSION	Use Program Manager's Help|About.
NET WHO	Use Server Manager.

Using the Command Prompt Window

Command
Prompt

You can open the Command Prompt window by double-clicking on the icon in the Main program group, or by running the program CMD.EXE (which replaces DOS's COMMAND.COM). The window is closed by typing **EXIT** and pressing Enter, or by using the **Control menu|Close** command (or by **double-clicking** on the Control menu). If the window ever locks up, you can close it by selecting **Control menu|Settings** and clicking on the **Terminate** button, or by using the **End** button in the **Task List** dialog box. (Press Ctrl-Esc, select the Command Prompt entry, and click on End.)

NTFS Limitations

NTFS uses a very different filename system from MS-DOS, the operating system for which most of these commands were originally designed. A few modifications have been made to get around incompatibilities. Some commands have new parameters to help them handle the new filenames. For instance, the **DIR** command displays a directory listing—it's been redesigned, though, so the filenames are on the right (they're on the left in DOS). By default the listing will include the full filenames, which may be very long names with unusual characters if the directory is on an NTFS partition. If you use the /X switch after the command, though, the listing will include both the NTFS and the DOS names. (NT provides all files with long NTFS names with a short DOS name also.)

You may find this useful—some commands don't like the NTFS names because they can't recognize some of the characters used in the names. Microsoft came up with a way around this problem, but it's only a partial fix. The new command symbol ^ lets you enter these special characters. Let's say, for instance, you want to copy the file named MAP&DALLAS.DOC. The COPY command won't let you do this directly, because it doesn't like the & in the middle of the name. But if you type COPY MAP^&DALLAS.DOC FILENAME, it will be able to copy the file.

This system won't work with the extended-character set—the characters that appear after the first three rows in the Character Map—but there again you'd probably never need it to. On the other hand, it also won't work with spaces, and NTFS allows spaces in names, nor will it work with certain other characters that are also valid, such as +. If you are going to work at the command line with files, you'll probably want to use their shorter, DOS-style filenames.

Using Doskey

MS-DOS 5.0 has a program called Doskey. It's a TSR (terminate-and-stay resident) program. Once started (and you do have to start it yourself in MS-DOS), you can use it to recall the commands you have typed, edit the command line, and create macros.

Windows NT uses a slightly modified form of this program, and you don't have to start it—it's always available. You can still use the DOSKEY command, though, to customize it or display information about it.

Note Doskey is really a misnomer—remember that the Command Prompt is not an MS-DOS command line, it's the NT command line. Doskey works on all NT commands, not just on commands entered after starting the MS-DOS subsystems.

Doskey is based on two command buffers. The first is a list of all the commands you have used since you started the Command Prompt (each Command Prompt maintains its own, separate Doskey buffers). Each command is numbered as it is entered into the list, so the first one is command 1, the second is command 2, and so on. You can view a list of these commands (press **F7**), and reuse the commands—in many cases it may be quicker to recall a command from the list than retype it.

There's also another buffer, called the *template*, which contains the last command you used—though you can use the **F5** command to enter an earlier command into this template. You can use Doskey to enter selected portions of this command onto the command line.

Windows NT's version of Doskey differs from MS-DOS 5.0's in that it is always available—there's no need to start it—and that while the MS-DOS 5.0 version uses the command line for all prompts and command displays, the NT version uses a pop-up box that appears on top of the Command Prompt window.

These are the keystrokes used by Doskey for recalling and editing commands:

Insert	Toggles insert/overwrite mode. (Overwrite mode is the default.)
Enter	Executes command *and* returns to overwrite mode.
Left Arrow	Moves the cursor one character to the left.
Right Arrow	Moves the cursor one character to the right.
Ctrl-Left Arrow	Moves the cursor one word to the left.
Ctrl-Right Arrow	Moves the cursor one word to the right.
Home	Moves the cursor to the beginning of the line.
End	Moves the cursor to the end of the line.
Esc	Clears the command line.
Up Arrow	Enters the previous command in the list onto the command line.
Down Arrow	Enters the next command in the list onto the command line.
Page Up	Enters the first command in the list onto the command line.
Page Down	Enters the most recent command in the list onto the command line.
F1 or Right Arrow	Enters the last command (the one in the template), one character at a time.
F2	Displays a popup box—type the character in the command (held in the template) up to which you want to insert. (See the explanation of these function keys below this table.)
F3	Copies the remainder of the last command to the command line.
F4	Displays a popup—type the character in the last command *from which* you want to insert.
F5	Clears the command line, enters the previous command into the line, and places that command into the last-command template (the template from which the command entered by F1, F2, etc. comes).
F6	Places an end-of-file character (^Z) at the cursor position.
F7	Displays a popup list—use the arrow keys to move to the command you want and press Enter to run that command.
Alt-F7	Deletes all commands from memory.
F8	Type the first character or first few characters of the command you want to use (one you've used already in this session), then press F8 to display a matching command. Continue pressing F8 to move through all matching commands.

F9   Displays a popup asking you for a command number.
                                When you enter the number and press Enter, the com-
                                mand is entered onto the command line. (You can use F7
                                to find command numbers.)

If you often work with the command line (you're probably a programmer if
you do), these Doskey commands can help you work more quickly. You may already be familiar with them from MS-DOS 5.0. They work in a very similar manner, with a few slight differences.

The simplest method for using Doskey is to use the four keys that will recall
the commands you have used in the Command Prompt session. Pressing **Up
Arrow** displays the last command you used. **Page Up** will display the first command you used after opening the Command Prompt window. **Page Down** displays
the most recently used command, and **Down Arrow** moves to the next command
in the stored list. Pressing **Esc** clears the command line.

You can also press **F7** to see a list of the commands you've used. Figure 9.1
shows the popup that appears when you press F7. You can move the highlight
with the arrow keys (as well as Home, End, PgUp and PgDn), then press Enter to
run the command. Or use this list to find a command number. You can run a
command by pressing **F9**. A popup appears—type the command number, press
Enter to place the command onto the command line, then edit the command if
necessary, and press Enter to run it. You can clear the command buffer by pressing **Alt-F7**.

There's another way to find the command you want. Type the first character or
several characters of the command you want to recall, then press **F8**. Doskey will
complete the command. If it isn't the one you want, press F8 again, until the command you need appears.

Once you've recalled a command, use the editing keys to change it. If you are
copying files, for instance, you might want to change filenames or paths. Use the

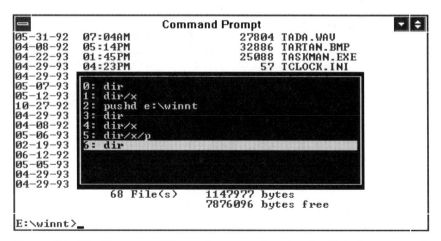

Figure 9.1 The Command Prompt popup, showing the list of commands

arrow keys, Ctrl-arrow keys, Home and End to move along the command line. Then type your changes. By default Doskey is in overtype mode, so when you type you will replace the characters on the command line. Press **Ins** to change to insert mode. When you press Enter, to execute the command, Doskey goes back to overtype mode. (By the way, the cursor does not have to be at the end of the line when you press Enter.) You can use the DOSKEY command to change the default mode to Insert. (We'll look at the DOSKEY command in a moment.)

The command *template* stores the last command you typed. The simplest way to use this template, and the one most familiar to DOS users, is to press the **F1** or **Right Arrow** key. Each time you press, Doskey enters one character from the command. Hold it down, and it enters each character, one after another. You can stop at any time to modify the command. Then press **F3** and Doskey enters the rest of the command.

You can get more sophisticated with the template. Press **F2** and a popup box appears asking you to *Enter char to copy up to.* For instance, lets say you are copying several files to another directory. The first command you use is COPY E:\WINNT\SYSTEM32\FILE.DOC C:\TEMP. You now want to copy another file, but this time from the WINNT directory. Press F2, then type S. Doskey types COPY E:\WINNT\ for you—it enters all the characters up to, but not including, the one you typed.

The **F4** key does the opposite—you enter the starting character in the popup box, press Enter, and Doskey enters everything *from* that character (and including that character) to the end of the command. Of course both the F2 and F4 methods have a serious limitation—if the character is duplicated in the command, the command may not do what you want (depending on that character's position).

The **F5** key copies the previous command from the list into the command line, *and* at the same time places that command in the template (so you can work on it with the template commands—F2, F4, etc.).

Creating Macros

It's surprisingly easy to create your own command-line commands. Doskey calls them macros, but once created they work just like any other command. For example, type this at the command prompt:

```
DOSKEY WIND=CD C:\WINDOWS
```

Press Enter, and you have just created a command called WIND. Each time you run WIND, the command line changes to the C:\WINDOWS directory (assuming you are in the C: drive). This command is only temporary, though. To save your macros, type:

```
DOSKEY /MACROS >MACRO
```

The last entry, MACRO, is the name of a file—you can use any name you wish. Each time you use this /MACROS switch, you overwrite the file, placing all the currently active macros in that file. The macro file is created in the current directory. To make sure you know where your macro files are, you may want to include a pathname with the filename—something like this:

```
DOSKEY /MACROS >E:\WINNT\SYSTEM31\MACRO
```

To use one of these macros in a subsequent Command Prompt session, you'll have to load the macro file. Use this command:

```
DOSKEY /MACROFILE=MACRO
```

Of course you'll have to use the pathname if you are not in the directory in which you created the macro file. Now you can create more macros, then use the `DOSKEY /MACROS >MACRO` command to add them—and the existing ones you opened earlier—to the MACRO file.

The macro we created is very simple, but what about adding more complicated commands. For instance, what about changing to the C: drive and *then* changing to the WINDOWS directory? A **$T** is used to separate commands. The command would look like this:

```
DOSKEY WIND=C:$TCD C:\WINDOWS
```

You can string several commands together in this way. These are the special characters you may use:

$G	Redirects the output of the macro to a file instead of the screen.
GG	Appends the output of the macro to a file, instead of replacing it.
$L	Reads input from a device or file instead of from the keyboard.
$B	"Pipes" the output from a macro to a command.
$T	Separates commands while creating macros.
$$	Enters a single $ character.
$1 to $9	The macro equivalent of the %1 to %9 values in batch files. These are parameters that may be included with the macro when run.
$*	Everything you type on the command line after the macro name is substituted for the $* in the macro.

Doskey lets you create macros with names that are the **same as existing NT** command names. Each time you type the name and press Enter, the macro runs, not the NT command. If you want to run the NT command instead, type a space in front of the command name.

You can **remove macros** at any time by pressing **Alt-F10**. However, this not only removes the macros from memory but also destroys the macro file, so you can't use it again.

How about making your Doskey macros available every time you open the Command Prompt, without having to load them manually? Open the Command Prompt program icon, and enter this in the Command Line text box:

```
CMD.EXE /K "DOSKEY.EXE /MACROFILE=FILENAME"
```

When you double-click on the icon, NT will run the DOSKEY command and open the Command Prompt—you won't notice anything different happening, but once you're into the command line you'll find that your macros are available. You can also get CMD.EXE to run a command and then close the Command Prompt window automatically, and to run multiple commands—see the online help for more information.

Modifying Doskey

While Doskey is automatically turned on in NT, the DOSKEY command is still present. Of course as you've just seen, you can use it to create macros, and some of the parameters are leftovers from MS-DOS—you'll probably never need them. But there are also several parameters you may want to work with:

/reinstall	Installs a new copy of the Doskey program, and clears the buffer.
/listsize=size	The maximum number of commands in the buffer.
/macros	Displays a list of all Doskey macros. Use a redirection symbol (/macros >filename) to create a macro file. You can also specify the particular executable for which you want to see a list of macros (see /exename, below): /macros:all means all the executables, /macro:exename lists them just for the specified executable.
/m	The same as /macros.
/history	Displays a list of the commands you've used since the beginning of the session. You can also see a list by pressing F7. Use a redirection symbol (/macros >filename) to create a file containing the commands.
/h	The same as /history.
/insert	Places the command line in insert mode by default. (If you don't use this parameter, the command line's default is overstrike.)
/exename=exename	Specifies the executable to use. You can create macros for a specific executable file, such as FTP.EXE, or a command interpreter other than CMD.EXE.
/macrofile=filename	Opens a macro file.

macroname=[*text*]	Creates a macro. The text is the actual command or commands. If you don't enter any text, the macro named *macroname* is cleared.

For more information about Doskey and macros, double-click on the Windows NT Help icon the Main program group, then click on the "Access the Command Reference Help" entry and find DOSKEY in the index.

Modifying the Command Prompt Window

When you start a new command interpreter—by running CMD.EXE from a File|Run menu option, by double-clicking on the Command Prompt icon, or by using the START command to open a new window from an existing Command Prompt window—the command prompt will open in a window rather than using the full screen. You can change it to full screen by pressing **Alt-Enter**. As you'll see in a moment, you can also change the default settings so it *always* opens full screen. There are also a number of other options that you can use to modify the Command Prompt window. The bottom half of the Control menu contains these special commands:

Edit|Mark	Lets you use the keyboard to mark text so you can copy it to the Clipboard.
Edit|Copy (Enter)	Copies the marked text to the Clipboard.
Edit|Paste	Pastes text from the Clipboard to the Command Prompt or application.
Edit|Scroll	Lets you use the arrow keys to scroll through an application.
Settings	Changes between full-screen and window mode, turns on QuickEdit, and lets you close the Command Prompt window if it has locked up.
Fonts	Lets you select the font you want to use—and, therefore, modify the window size, which is partly dependent on the font size.
Screen Size and Position	Increases the number of characters and lines the window can display in its width and height.
Screen Colors	Lets you change the window and popup colors.

Changing Fonts

You can modify the font used in the Command Prompt window—and also the size of the window—using the Control menu's Font option. The Font Selection dialog box (see Figure 9.2) is almost identical to the one you're used to from Windows 3.1.

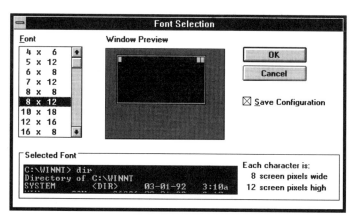

Figure 9.2 The Font Selection dialog box

Select a font from the **Font** list box and the **Window Preview** changes to show you how the Command Prompt window will appear on your screen. This depends on where you had the window before you opened the Font Selection dialog box. If the window was right next to the screen's right edge, or even slightly offscreen, as you modify the size the Control menu stays in the same position and the right and bottom edges of the sample window move. So you may need to close the Font Selection box, move the window to the top left of the screen, and try again.

The **Save Configuration** check box is not selected, so if you want to make sure that the settings are used the next time you open the Command Prompt, check this box before you close the dialog box. (And make sure you read the section below about creating different Command Prompt windows).

Display Options and Terminating

Select the **Control|Settings** command to see the Settings dialog box (Figure 9.3). This is similar to the one you've probably seen in Windows 3.1, though it doesn't include the multitasking options (NT handles all that itself). You can set the **Display Options**, deciding whether you want the command prompt in a **Window** or **Full Screen**. You can use this to change the settings for the current session, but if you want to make sure that the command prompt *always* appears full screen (the default is in a window), select Full Screen and then select the **Save configuration** check box.

You can also click on the **Terminate** button to close the Command Prompt if it has locked up for some reason. Remember, though, that it's usually safer to close from within the window itself, by using the application's close command, or by typing EXIT at the command prompt.

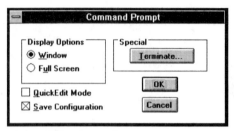

**Figure 9.3 The Command Prompt's
Settings dialog box**

Changing Screen Size and Position

Select **Control|Screen Size and Position** to see the dialog box in Figure 9.4. In Windows 3.1 you can only change the window's size using the Fonts dialog box—changing the font selection automatically adjusts the window's size (though there's also a WIN.INI command that lets you adjust the number of lines). Windows NT also lets you adjust the width and height of the window, the number of text columns that will appear and the number of lines that will be held in the display buffer.

Select a value from the **Width** incrementer. If you select a number of columns that can be displayed within your screen, when you close the dialog box the window will adjust to the appropriate size. If you select a very large number, though, NT leaves the dialog box the same size and adds a horizontal scroll bar.

You can also add lines by entering a value in the **Height** incrementer. NT will increase the size of the window and, if necessary, add a vertical scroll bar. Actually you may find it adds the scroll bar even when there's plenty of room for all lines to be shown *without* a scroll bar—you may have to click on the maximize button a couple of times to get the window to expand to its full size without a scroll bar.

If you want to save these new settings, make sure the **Save Screen Buffer Size** check box is selected. You can also select the **Save Window Size and Position** check box. If you size the window using the Maximize and Restore commands, or by dragging the border, this new size will be saved when you close this dialog box. (So, to save a window's position and size after moving or sizing it, select Control menu|Screen Size and Position, then click on OK.)

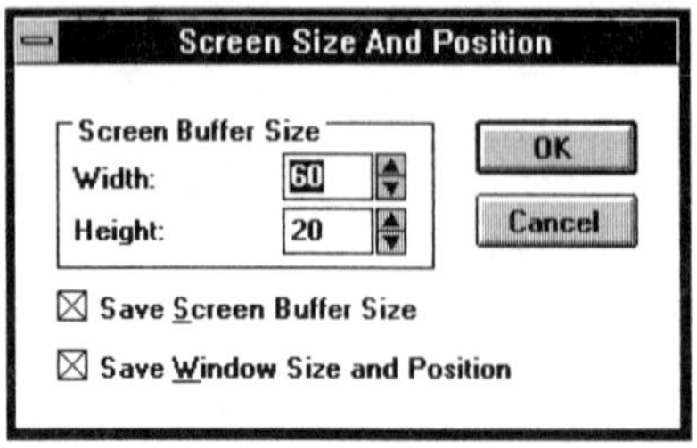

**Figure 9.4 The Screen Size and
Position dialog box**

Selecting Screen Colors

Windows NT even lets you modify the color of the Command Prompt window. Select **Control|Screen Colors** to see the Screen Colors dialog box (Figure 9.5). There are four different settings: Screen Text, Screen Background, Popup Text, and Popup Background. The Screen Text and Background are obvious, of course—they are the colors of the text in the Command Prompt window, and of the background on which the text is displayed (which is normally black). The Popup colors are the colors used in the Doskey popup boxes. For instance, when you press F7 to see the commands you've used since opening the Command Prompt window, you'll see a popup box containing a list.

To modify a color, select the option button of the item you want to change, and then click on the color in the color bar. You'll notice that the sample boxes at the bottom of the dialog box will change. When you've got all the colors you want, make sure **Save Configuration** is selected so that the Command Prompt window will always use those colors.

Changing the Display Mode

As in Windows 3.1 you can run the Command Prompt in a window or full screen. The quickest way to change between them is by pressing **Alt-Enter**. You can also open the Settings dialog box (**Control menu|Settings**), select the **Display Option** you want, and click on OK. (You can use the **Save Configuration** check box to save the settings, by the way, so that the Command Prompt window always opens the way you want it.)

If you are in Full Screen mode, pressing **Alt-Spacebar** displays the Command Prompt window as an icon, with its Control menu open. You can then select the Settings option to change to Window mode. (Selecting Restore or Maximize returns you to Full Screen.)

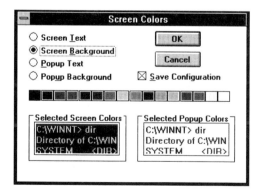

Figure 9.5 The Screen Colors dialog box

Creating a Home Directory

When you open the Command Prompt window it opens into the \USERS\DE-FAULT directory on your NT disk. You can create a *home directory*, though, so the Command Prompt always opens in the directory you want.

A home directory is similar to the *working directory* that you can define in an application's program icon. But the home directory affects *all* applications. For instance, when you type a filename—without a drive letter and path—into the Program Item Properties dialog box, NT will assume that file is in your home directory.

To set the home directory, open User Manager, double-click on the user for whom you want to modify the home directory, click on the Profile button, and then enter the directory path into the **Home Directory** area of the User Environment Profile dialog box. (Only an Administrator can get to this dialog box.) You can enter a local directory or one on another computer. For more information, see Chapter 5.

Creating Different Command Prompt Windows

Settings for a Command Prompt window are saved in the system registry (see Chapter 11 for more information about the registry and the Registry Editor). If you look in the Registry Editor you can find the settings by looking in the window titled HKEY_CURRENT_USER on Local Machine. Right at the top—the first "directory," or *key*—is Console. This section contains directories that store information about programs that run at the Command Prompt. Each key is named the same as the title of the window that appears when you run the program. So you'll see that one of the directories is called Command Prompt.

This is important because it means that you can configure different Command Prompt windows differently. Start the Command Prompt window using Program Manager's Command Prompt icon, change and save the settings, and you've created one Command Prompt window. Start the Command Prompt window by typing CMD and pressing Enter in Program Manager's Run dialog box (File|Run), and you'll start a different Command Prompt window which can be configured differently. Create another icon that runs CMD.EXE, but put a different title in the Program Item Properties' Description text box, and you'll create another Command Prompt window. You can set up each Command Prompt window differently. Just create new icons with different titles, then use the Control menu options to set each one up differently.

Copying Data Between Windows

As in Windows 3.1, you can use the Control menu commands to copy data to and from the Clipboard, allowing you to copy data between different subsystems. NT has the same methods used by Windows 3.1, plus one nice improvement. As before, you can use the **Control menu|Edit** options to **Mark**, **Copy**, and **Paste** data. Select Mark, then move the highlight with the arrow keys and press Enter to copy to the Clipboard. Use Paste to paste data from the Clipboard.

NT also has **QuickEdit**. By default it's turned on (you can turn it off—if you want to save memory—in the Settings dialog box). This lets you use the mouse to highlight text when the Command Prompt is in Window mode—press the mouse button and drag the pointer across the text you want to copy—then press Enter to copy it into the Clipboard.

The Help System

There are two places you can find information about commands—in the normal Windows Help system (double-click on the Windows NT Help icon the Main program group, then click on the "Access the Command Reference Help" entry), and at the command line itself. The command line provides lists of commands, and instructions for each command, though it is not available for TCP/IP and OS/2 commands. Type these commands to view help:

`help`	Lists all the native commands, with one-line descriptions of each.
`commandname /?`	Describes the specified command and its switches and parameters.
`help commandname`	This does the same as the previous help command in this list. In fact you might want to forget this one, because it only includes native commands, and *won't* provide information for MS-DOS subsystem commands such as EDIT.
`net help`	Lists all the network commands, with one-line descriptions of each.
`net help syntax`	Explains the syntax used for network commands.
`net commandname /help`	Describes the specified network command and its switches and parameters.
`net help commandname`	Describes the specified network command and its switches and parameters.
`net help commandname \options`	Displays a summary of the options available for the command.
`net help services`	Lists the network services for which help is available.
`net help net start servicename`	Describes the specified start-service command.

Error Messages

Windows NT has an error-message system that is a real improvement over that used by MS-DOS. When an error occurs, you may see a short error message, followed by an error code. For instance, you might see:

```
A service specific error occurred: 2481.
More help is available by typing NET HELPMSG 3547.
```

Type whatever you are told to—in this case NET HELPMSG 3547—and press Enter. You'll see an expanded message. Unfortunately this message is often of little use. Message 3547, for instance, says:

```
A service specific error occurred: ***.
EXPLANATION
A service specific error occurred.
ACTION
Refer to the help or documentation for that service to
determine the problem.
```

This really doesn't tell you anything worth knowing, though you may find some messages are more helpful. (Some are less helpful, though, being downright confusing, such as the one—2185—which tells you to check the spelling "using the Services option is (sic) the Server Manager tool," which, perhaps, means in Control Panel.)

Notice, however, that there are *two* message numbers in the previous example. Although it says type "NET HELPMSG 3547," on the previous line there's the number 2481. Try typing 2481 and you'll see this:

```
The UPS service is not correctly configured.
```

This may be a little more useful. At this point you could go to Control Panel and open the UPS dialog box and check the configuration. These messages are sometimes more helpful. For instance, if you type NET START NETLOGON, you might see an error and, again, two numbers. One is the useless 3547 message, but the other, 3095, will show you this:

```
This Windows NT machine is configured as a member of a
workgroup, not as a member of a domain. The Netlogon
service does not need to run in this configuration.
```

This seems a lot more helpful. With luck, we may see these error messages improve over time, until they become a truly useful feature of NT.

The Command List

The following table shows all the NT commands, including those used by MS-DOS, OS/2, and TCP/IP networks.

Note For detailed information about each command, see NT's Help system. Double-click on the Windows NT Help icon the Main program group, then click on the "Access the Command Reference Help" entry.

Windows NT Help

ACLCONV	Converts OS/2 LAN Manager permissions (recorded by the OS/2 BACKACC utility) to NTFS format.
APPEND	Appends directories to the current directory so that files may be opened as if they were in the current directory.
ARP TCP/IP	Command: Displays and modifies the IP-to-Ethernet or token-ring address-translation tables used by address-resolution protocol.
AT	Uses the Schedule service to start programs at a specified time.
ATTRIB	Displays and changes the read-only, hidden, system, and archive attributes assigned to files.
BACKUP	Backs up (archives) files onto floppy disks or a hard disk. To run NT's Backup utility, for backing up on tape, you would run NTBACKUP.EXE.
BREAK	Used in CONFIG.SYS or at the command line. Extends the ability to use Ctrl-C to stop a procedure to functions such as disk read and write operations and screen write operations.
BUFFERS	This command is not used by NT or the MS-DOS subsystem. It is accepted, however, to maintain compatibility with MS-DOS 5.0 files.
CALL	Calls another batch program, without stopping the parent batch program.
CD	An abbreviation of CHDIR.
CHCP	Displays or changes the active code page used by NT for the console. Used for customizing for international use.

CHDIR	Changes the current directory or displays the name of the current directory.
CHKDSK	Displays a report on a disk, and displays and corrects errors. Works on NTFS, FAT, and HPFS file systems.
CLS	Clears the command prompt window, removing everything but the command prompt and cursor.
CMD	New: Replaces DOS 5.0's COMMAND.COM. Starts the NT command interpreter, which displays the command prompt. You can change the environment used by the new command interpreter without changing that used by the parent interpreter.
CODEPAGE	OS/2 Command: Determines the codepage used by OS/2 programs—codepages define language support. This is a CONFIG.SYS command, and cannot be used at the command prompt itself.
COMP	Compares two files or sets of files.
CONVERT	Converts a disk partition from FAT or HPFS to NTFS.
COPY	Copies files.
COUNTRY	Configures the MS-DOS subsystem to recognize the correct language used by NT, so it can recognize the correct character set and punctuation.
DATE	Displays or changes the system date.
DEBUG	Starts the MS-DOS debug program, used to test executable files.
DEL	Deletes files.
DEVICE	Used in CONFIG.NT to load device drivers into memory.
DEVICEHIGH	Used in CONFIG.NT to load device drivers into upper memory.
DEVINFO	OS/2 Command: Prepares an OS/2 device to use code pages. This is a CONFIG.SYS command, and cannot be used at the command prompt.
DIR	Displays a directory listing. Use the /X switch to include both the NTFS and FAT filenames.

DISKCOMP	Compares the data on two floppy disks.
DISKCOPY	Copies data between floppy disks.
DISKPERF	Controls the disk-performance counters, which are used by Performance Monitor.
DOS	Used in CONFIG.NT to make MS-DOS create a link to the upper memory area, or partly load into the high memory area.
DOSKEY	Lets you create Doskey macros and modify the way in which Doskey works.
DRIVPARM	This command is not used by NT or the MS-DOS subsystem. It is accepted, however, to maintain compatibility with MS-DOS 5.0 files.
ECHO	Turns the display of a batch program's commands on and off. Also used to display a message.
ECHOCONFIG	New: Displays CONFIG.NT and AUTO-EXEC.NT messages when you start an MS-DOS program in a new Command Prompt window (it only runs once in each Command Prompt window). The command is placed in CONFIG.NT.
EDIT	Starts the MS-DOS ASCII editor.
EDLIN	Starts the MS-DOS Edlin ASCII editor, a Command Prompt editor.
EMM	New: A device driver which uses extended memory to simulate expanded memory and provides an MS-DOS subsystem with access to the upper memory area.
ENDLOCAL	Returns the environment variables to normal, after you used the SETLOCAL command.
ERASE	Deletes files.
EXE2BIN	Converts executable files to binary files.
EXIT	Closes the command interpreter, returning to the program that started it or closing the Command Prompt window.
FASTOPEN	NT doesn't use this command, but accepts it to remain compatible with MS-DOS files.
FC	Compares two files.
FCBS	Used in CONFIG.NT to set the number of file-control blocks that the MS-DOS subsystem can have open.

FILES	Used in CONFIG.NT to set the number of files that the MS-DOS subsystem can have open at the same time.
FIND	Searches files and directories for a string of text.
FINDSTR	New: Searches files and directories for a string of text. Unlike FIND, FINDSTR uses patterns of text.
FINGER	TCP/IP Command: Displays information about a user on a remote system.
FOR	Runs a command for each file in a set.
FORCEDOS	Forces NT to open the MS-DOS subsystem and run a program—used if NT can't recognize the program as a DOS program.
FORMAT	Formats floppy and hard disks. Floppy disks can only be formatted with the FAT system; hard disks may be formatted with NTFS, FAT, or HPFS.
FTP	TCP/IP Command: Transfers files between your computer and a File Transfer Protocol (FTP) node.
GOTO	Makes MS-DOS move to the labeled line in a batch program.
GRAFTABL	Displays extended characters in graphics mode—used if a monitor is unable to display extended characters.
GRAPHICS	Lets NT print the contents of the screen while using a CGA, EGA, or VGA adapter.
HELP	Displays information about a specified command.
HOSTNAME	TCP/IP Command: Displays the name of the current host.
IF	Used in batch programs to perform conditional processing.
INSTALL	Used in CONFIG.NT to load a memory resident program.
KEYB	Configures a keyboard for another language.
LABEL	Changes a disk's volume name.
LASTDRIVE	Used in CONFIG.NT to set the maximum number of hard drives that may be accessed.
LH	An abbreviation of LOADHIGH.

LIBPATH	OS/2 Command: The OS/2 path that may be searched for dynamic link libraries. This is a CONFIG.SYS command, and cannot be used at the command prompt.
LOADFIX	Starts a program and loads it above the first 64K of conventional memory.
LOADHIGH	Loads a program into upper memory.
MD	An abbreviation of MKDIR.
MEM	Displays information about the MS-DOS subsystem's memory use.
MKDIR	Creates a new directory.
MODE	Configures devices such as serial and parallel ports, code pages, the keyboard typematic rate, and display adapters.
MORE	Displays one screen of information at a time—used when viewing long files or when using commands (such as MEM) which display a lot of data (e.g., MEM |MORE).
MOVE	New: Moves files between directories.
NBTSTAT	TCP/IP Command: Displays information about the current TCP/IP connections over NBT (NetBIOS over TCP/IP).
NETSTAT	TCP/IP Command: Displays information about the current TCP/IP connections.
NET ACCOUNTS	Changes account parameters—passwords and logon requirements.
NET COMPUTER	Only available on advanced servers, this command adds computers to and deletes computers from domains.
NET CONFIG	Displays a list of configurable network services or the settings for a particular service, and lets you modify those settings.
NET CONFIG SERVER	Displays and changes Server-service settings.
NET CONFIG WORKSTATION	Displays and changes Workstation-service settings.
NET CONTINUE	Restarts services suspended by the NET PAUSE command—alerter, messenger, netlogon, replicator, server, telnet, or workstation.

NET FILE	Lists the open shared files on a server and the number of file locks, and closes shared files and removes file locks.
NET GROUP	Only for use with LAN Manager for Windows NT domains: Displays, adds, and modifies global groups.
NET HELP	Lists the commands for which help is available, or displays help for a specified command.
NET HELPMSG	Displays information about a Windows NT message.
NET LOCALGROUP	Displays the name of the server and of its local groups, and adds or modifies local groups.
NET NAME	Displays, adds, and deletes messaging names (aliases).
NET PAUSE	Pauses alerter, messenger, netlogon, replicator, server, telnet, or workstation.
NET PRINT	Lists and controls print jobs and queues.
NET SEND	Lets you send messages to other computers.
NET SESS	An abbreviation of NET SESSION.
NET SESSION	Lists and disconnects sessions between the server and other workstations.
NET SHARE	Lets you display and control shared resources, such as directories and printer ports.
NET START	Starts alerter, messenger, netlogon, replicator, server, telnet, or workstation.
NET START ALERTER	Starts alerter, a service that sends alert messages over the network.
NET START BROWSER	Starts the computer-browser service, which lets you monitor network connections.
NET START "COMPUTER BROWSER"	See NET START BROWSER.
NET START "DIRECTORY REPLICATOR"	See NET START REPLICATOR.
NET START EVENTLOG	Starts event log, a service that logs security, system, and application events.
NET START LOCATOR	Starts the RPC (Remote Procedure Call) Locator service, which is used by "distributed applications." The applications "server side" can "register" with the Locator, which can then provide the information to the "client side."

NET START MESSENGER	Starts messenger, a service that lets the workstation receive network messages, such as alerts.
NET START NBT	See NET START "TCPIP NET BIOS PROTOCOL".
NET START NETLOGON	Starts Netlogon, a service that controls domain logons on a network. May also be entered as NET START "NET LOGON".
NET START REPLICATOR	Starts replicator, a service that copies files between servers, ensuring that the files are the same in each location.
NET START RPCSS	Starts the Remote Procedure Call service. (See NET START LOCATOR.)
NET START SCHEDULE	Starts the Schedule service, a service which lets you use the AT command to start a program at a specified time.
NET START SERVER	Starts server, a service that lets a computer share resources on the network.
NET START SNMP	Starts SNMP (Simple Network Management Protocol), a service that lets a server report its status to a management system on a TCP/IP (Transport Control Protocol/Internet Protocol) network.
NET START TCPIP	New: Starts the TCP/IP service, to allow access to a Transport Control Protocol/Internet Protocol network.
NET START "TCPIP NET BIOS PROTOCOL"	Starts the NBT service (NetBIOS over TCP/IP).
NET START TELNET	Starts the Telnet service, to allow access to a Telnet network.
NET START WORK	An abbreviation of NET START WORKSTATION.
NET START WORKSTATION	Starts the Workstation service, allowing the computer to access network resources.
NET STATS	An abbreviation of NET STATISTICS.
NET STATISTICS	Displays performance information for a particular service.
NET STOP	Stops alerter, messenger, netlogon, replicator, server, telnet, or workstation.
NET TIME	Displays a server or domain time or synchronizes the computer's time with the server or domain.

NET USE	Connects to or disconnects from a network resource.
NET USER	Displays account information or adds and modifies user accounts.
NET VIEW	Lists servers and shared resources.
NLSFUNC	Used in CONFIG.NT or from the command line to load National Language Support information.
PATH	Defines in which directories NT should search for executable files.
PAUSE	Pauses a batch program and displays a message.
PING	TCP/IP Command: Checks the status of a remote host by sending "echo packets" and waiting for a response.
POPD	Moves to the directory stored by the PUSHD command, then clears the name from its buffer (so POPD can only be used once after each PUSHD).
PORTUAS	Merges information from a LAN Manager 2.x account database into a Windows NT user accounts database.
PRINT	Prints a text file, in the "background" if necessary.
PROMPT	Changes the format of the command prompt.
PROTSHELL	OS/2 Command: NT doesn't use this command, but it is accepted to maintain compatibility with OS/2 files.
PUSHD	Saves the name of the current directory, then moves to the specified directory. The stored name can be used by POPD.
QBASIC	Loads Windows NT QBASIC, a program that lets you program in BASIC, and which reads and interprets BASIC files.
RCP	TCP/IP Command: Copies files between computers.
RD	An abbreviation of RMDIR.
RECOVER	Recovers data from a defective disk.
REM	Used in CONFIG.NT or in batch files to include "remark" lines, informational lines that are ignored by Windows NT.
REN	An abbreviation of RENAME.

RENAME	Renames files.
REPLACE	Replaces files in one directory with files with the same names from another directory.
RESTORE	Restores files backed up using the BACKUP command.
REXEC	TCP/IP Command: Similar to RSH, in that it provides the remote execution of commands on hosts, but with password authentication.
RMDIR	Removes a directory.
ROUTE	TCP/IP Command: Prints, adds, deletes, and modifies routes in a network routing table.
RSH	TCP/IP Command: Remote Shell, connects to the host and executes a specified command.
SET	Displays, sets, or removes environment variables. This controls the MS-DOS subsystem, and is often used in AUTOEXEC.NT.
SETLOCAL	Lets you modify environment variables temporarily while running a batch file.
SETVER	Sets the version number reported by the MS-DOS subsystem to DOS programs. Used to "fool" programs into thinking they can run with the current version of DOS.
SHARE	NT doesn't use this command, but accepts it to remain compatible with MS-DOS files.
SHELL	Used in CONFIG.NT to specify the command interpreter that should be used for the NT Command Prompt window.
SHIFT	Used in batch files to change the position of the replaceable parameters %0 through %9, and to work with more than 10 parameters.
SORT	A filter, reading and rearranging data.
STACKS	Used in CONFIG.NT to specify the number of stacks—areas of memory—used to handle hardware interrupts.
START	New: Opens a new Command Prompt window.
SUBST	Allows you to assign a drive letter to a path, so you can access the directory at the end of the path using the drive letter.
SWITCHES	Used in CONFIG.NT to make an enhanced keyboard operate like a standard keyboard.

TELNET	TCP/IP Command: Starts terminal emulation using the Telnet service.
TFTP	TCP/IP Command: Transfers files using the Trivial File Transfer Protocol between workstations.
TIME	Displays or changes the system time.
TITLE	New: Changes the title in the Command Prompt window's title bar.
TREE	Displays the directory structure of the specified path or disk.
TYPE	Displays the contents of a text file on the screen.
VER	Displays the Windows NT version number at the command prompt. (See also WINVER.)
VERIFY	Tells NT whether or not it should verify all write operations, to ensure that no data is written to bad sectors.
VOL	Displays a disk's volume label (name) and serial number.
WINVER	New: Opens a dialog box which displays the Windows NT version number.
XCOPY	Copies entire directories, including all files and subdirectories.

OS/2 CONFIG.SYS Commands

These are the commands used in the OS/2 CONFIG.SYS file:

CODEPAGE	Determines the codepage used by OS/2 programs (codepages define language support).
DEVINFO	Prepares an OS/2 device to use code pages.
LIBPATH	The OS/2 path that may be searched for dynamic link libraries.
PROTSHELL	NT doesn't use this command, but it is accepted to maintain compatibility with OS/2 files.

TCP/IP Utility Commands

These are the TCP/IP networking utility commands:

ARP	Displays and modifies the IP-to-Ethernet or token-ring address-translation tables used by address-resolution protocol.

FINGER	Displays information about a user on a remote system.
FTP	Transfers files between your computer and a File Transfer Protocol (FTP) node.
HOSTNAME	Displays the name of the current host.
NBTSTAT	Displays information about the current TCP/IP connections over NBT (NetBIOS over TCP/IP).
NETSTAT	Displays information about the current TCP/IP connections.
PING	Checks the status of a remote host by sending "echo packets" and waiting for a response.
RCP	Copies files between computers.
REXEC	Similar to RSH, in that it provides the remote execution of commands on hosts, but with password authentication.
ROUTE	Prints, adds, deletes, and modifies routes in a network routing table.
RSH	Remote Shell, connects to the host and executes a specified command.
TELNET	Starts terminal emulation using the Telnet service.
TFTP	Transfers files using the Trivial File Transfer Protocol between workstations.

Command Symbols

NT has several symbols that help you work with the result or input of a command, and execute commands according to certain conditions.

>	Redirects output. You might send the output of a command to a text file, for instance, or to the printer.
>>	Redirects output, and appends it to the existing data. You might send the output of a command to a text file, adding it to the text already in the file.
<	Redirects input, taking the information needed for the command from a file instead of the keyboard. You could sort a text file, for instance, and display it on the screen, by typing SORT < FILENAME.TXT.
|	Pipes the output to another command—DIR |MORE, for instance, sends the output from the DIR command to the MORE command, which sends it to the monitor one screenful at a time.
||	New: Ensures that the following command runs only if the preceding command failed.
&&	New: Ensures that the following command runs only if the preceding command was successful.

        &   New: Separates multiple commands.

        ( )   New: Groups commands.

        ^   New: An escape character which lets you input special symbols—symbols not recognized by MS-DOS—in the command text. NT allows most characters in file and directory names, for instance, but you must place the ^ in front of the special character to enter them into a command. This method won't work with all special characters.

Note Windows NT's Command Prompt is based on the MS-DOS command line. For detailed information about how to work with the Command Prompt, read the on-line help and also refer to the MS-DOS documentation—DOS 5.0 or later. You'll find instructions on using batch files, redirecting and piping data, working with directories, and so on.

10

Working with Non-NT Programs

Windows NT runs a variety of different programs—32-bit Windows programs, of course, but also 16-bit Windows (Windows 3.1), MS-DOS, 16-bit OS/2, and POSIX programs. When Windows NT runs these programs it uses various different *subsystems* to manage them, but this is done invisibly. You can start the different types of programs in the standard ways—from a Program Manager icon, Program Manager's File|Run command, a File Manager icon, File Manager's File|Run command, and the command prompt. NT figures out what the program is, and how it must be managed.

There is a catch, though. In some cases Windows NT *won't* be able to run your programs. If you have programs which directly address hardware, instead of going through the operating system, they won't run in NT without the addition of special device drivers. For instance, some MS-DOS games and multimedia applications directly address the video hardware, instead of going through DOS. The MS-DOS subsystem would normally interface between the program and the hardware, but in the case of one of these programs it couldn't do so, because the program is not using normal DOS procedures to get to the video.

Other programs that won't run are those that access the disk drives directly, those that use proprietary disk-drive drivers—such as programs which compress data onto a disk drive—and programs that directly access other types of hardware, such as FAX and scanner cards. If you think one of your programs may be one of these "incompatible" programs, check with the program's manufacturer for an NT driver or a software upgrade.

Running Windows 3.1 Programs

Windows NT uses the new configuration-registry system to store information about its operating "environment." (Read Chapter 11 for more information about this system.) Windows 3.1, however, uses the SYSTEM.INI and WIN.INI files to store configuration information, and when you run Windows 3.1 programs in Windows NT these files will be used to provide the environment necessary to run those programs. These programs can write information into the WIN.INI and SYSTEM.INI files, just as they would if you were running the programs in Windows 3.1. The .INI files are not used by NT programs or NT itself.

The NT installation program encourages you to install NT in the Windows 3.1 directory. There are good reasons *not* to do so (as we discussed in Chapter 2), but if you *did* do so, NT set up a system by which it coordinates the two versions of Windows. When you open NT it loads the information from the .INI files into its configuration registry, so any changes to your system environment are reflected in the configuration registry data. If you make changes while running Windows NT, the changes are entered into the configuration registry and then, when you close NT, the relevant changes are written to the .INI files. The next time you open Windows 3.1, the "environment" will reflect these changes.

There are other .INI files used by Windows 3.1, though they are of less importance than SYSTEM.INI and WIN.INI. They tell their associated programs how to run, and these .INI files may be required by Windows 3.1 programs—though many will still run without this information. NT won't keep track of the information, though.

Will all Windows 3.1 applications run? We've already said that in some cases, when an application accesses hardware directly, it won't run without special drivers. There may be cases of other applications that don't run correctly, though. While Microsoft planned for NT to run Windows 3.1 applications fully, and within 10% of their normal speed, immediately before the release of Windows NT there were still a few Windows 3.1 applications that would *not* run correctly in NT. While Microsoft fixed many of the problems for the released version, you may still find an application or two that won't work properly. However, most of your Windows 3.1 programs should work correctly.

There's actually nothing for you to do to "configure" the environment in which your Windows 3.1 programs will run. Windows NT will handle it all for you.

Running MS-DOS Applications

If you have a computer with both MS-DOS and Windows NT, when you boot NT, it will read your DOS system's AUTOEXEC.BAT file and store the path and environment settings. It takes this information and places it in the CONFIG.NT and AUTOEXEC.NT files. When you start an MS-DOS program, NT looks at these files for operating information. These files are in the WINNT\SYSTEM32 directory.

Of course, much of the information in CONFIG.SYS and AUTOEXEC.BAT is not transferable to Windows NT. It will *not* take device drivers, for instance, so in order for you to use a piece of hardware—a CD-ROM drive or sound board, for instance—in an MS-DOS program running in Windows NT, it's no good having a device driver for MS-DOS; you must have one for NT.

Here's what AUTOEXEC.NT will probably look like:

```
@echo off
REM Windows NT DOS subsystem initialization file
REM
REM The normal c:\autoexec.bat for DOS initialization is
not used.
REM The file, autoexec.nt, is used to replace c:\auto-
exec.bat unless
REM another is specified in a PIF file.
REM
REM The display during DOS subsystem initialization is in-
active. To
REM activate the display during DOS initialization add the
command
REM "EchoConfig" to config.nt
REM Install network redirector (load before dosx.exe)
lh %SystemRoot%\system32\redir
REM Install DPMI support
lh %SystemRoot%\system32\dosx
```

As you can see there are only three commands in this file: @echo off (which turns off "echoing" of the both the subsequent commands and remarks to the screen and the echo off command itself); lh redir (which loads REDIR—network redirector—high. This program lets DOS programs use the network.); and lh dosx (which loads DOSX, a 16-bit DPMI host—a DOS "extender" which is used for Expanded Memory management).

When you boot NT, it takes the path and environment information from AUTOEXEC.BAT and combines it with the information in AUTOEXEC.NT and CONFIG.NT to set up the DOS environment.

Note In rare cases NT may not recognize a program as an MS-DOS program. You can use the FORCEDOS command to force NT to open the MS-DOS subsystem and then run the program. Use this format: FORCEDOS [/D *directory*] *filename parameters*, where the *directory* is the program's current directory, *filename* is the name of the program you want to start (and the path, if necessary), and *parameters* are the parameters the program requires, if any.

The CONFIG.NT Commands

These are the MS-DOS configuration commands that you can use in CONFIG.NT. Any others will be ignored.

COUNTRY   Tells NT which language to use.

DEVICE   Loads a driver, such as HIMEM.SYS or ANSI.SYS.

DOS   Describes how to use upper memory.

ECHOCONFIG   Tells NT to display the CONFIG.NT and AUTOEXEC.NT commands when it starts a DOS application.

FCBS   Defines the number of file-control blocks that can be open at the same time.

Using PIFs (Program Information Files)

As in Windows 3.1, you can control the manner in which an MS-DOS program runs in Windows NT by using a PIF (a program information file). Your existing PIFs will work in Windows NT, though it will ignore some options.

Double-click on the icon in the Main program group to open the PIF Editor. PIF Editor As you can see in Figure 10.1, NT's PIF Editor is much the same as Windows 3.1's. Even though NT will ignore many of the options in the PIF, it still lets you set them, so the PIF can be used in both NT and Windows 3.1.

Note We're only interested in NT-specific options here. If you'd like to see a detailed description of how PIFs work in Windows 3.1, see *Peter Norton's User's Guide to Windows 3.1*.

These are the options used by Windows NT:

Program Filename

Enter the name of the program you want to run. If the program is not in the WINDOWS directory, include the pathname. If the program is a .EXE or .COM file, you don't need to include the extension, but if you don't, when you save the file Windows displays a message saying you have the wrong extension. You must include an extension if it is a DOS batch (.BAT) file. Incidentally, if you want to run a program file that doesn't have a .EXE, .COM, or .BAT extension, you can build a DOS .BAT file (a *batch* file), and run it with a DOS command within that file, then create a PIF that calls the batch file.

Window Title

You can modify the name in the windows' title bar and the icon's label. This entry has no effect if you open the application by double-clicking on the icon. It only

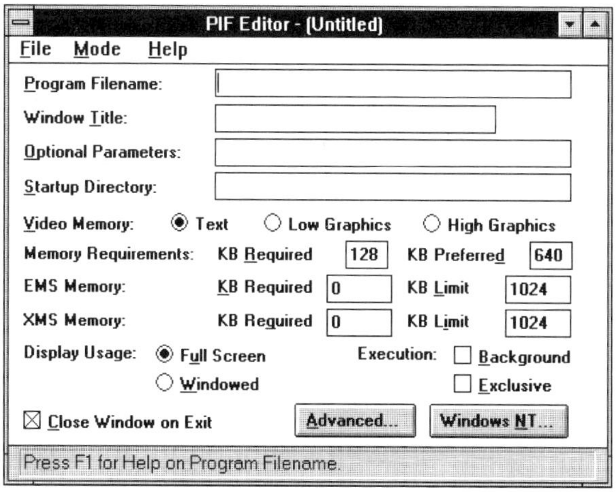

Figure 10.1 The PIF Editor

works if you double-click on the file in File Manager, or use File|Run in either File Manager or Program Manager. When you double-click on the icon, though, the entry in the Description line of the Program Item Properties dialog box is used. There is always an entry in this line, so your entry in the PIF file is always overridden. Make the entry in the Program Item Properties dialog box the same as in the PIF file, so Windows always uses your special title. If you don't enter anything in this text box, Windows just uses the program name.

Optional Parameters

Many programs have *switches* or *optional parameters* that you use when you start them. These may be instructions or filenames. For instance, the display-monitor test program DisplayMate uses the optional parameter c to set the menu colors to white and black. You would enter /c in the text box. You can enter up to 62 characters—see your application's documentation for information. By the way, if you use the File|Run command in File Manager or Program Manager, these parameters are not used.

Of course, this entry is optional; you only use it if the application you are going to run needs it. If you would like to be able to enter the parameters each time you open the application, simply type ? in this text box. When you use the PIF to start the application, Windows will display a dialog box in which you can type the parameters and continue.

Startup Directory

You can enter the pathname of the directory you want to be current when Windows opens the application. For instance, let's say you have a word processor that stores its document files in a directory called C:\WORD\DATA. When you start the program and then use its command for opening a document, you will find you are in the C:\WINDOWS directory. But if you enter C:\WORD\DATA in the Start-up Directory text box, you will be in the correct directory.

There are two things to remember when using this option. First, if you start the program by double-clicking on the icon, the Startup Directory entry is over-ridden by the Working Directory entry in the icon's Program Items Properties dialog box. Second, many applications let you enter a default directory into their setup information, so the Startup Directory is irrelevant.

Note You can use DOS environment variables in any of the preceding text boxes. For instance, if you include `set abc=c:\temp` in your AUTOEXEC.NT file, you can place C:\TEMP in the Start-up Directory by entering `%abc%`. The environment variable must be set before you enter Windows. See the SET command in your DOS documentation or the Windows NT Help system for more information.

EMS Memory and XMS Memory

Some DOS applications require EMS (Expanded) or XMS (Extended) memory. NT can simulate the memory when needed. In both cases the **KB Required** setting is the minimum amount required to make the application start. This can usually be left at 0, even if the application needs that type of memory for some procedures; few applications require it to actually run.

The **KB Limit** is the maximum amount of virtual expanded or extended memory that NT will provide to the application. Some applications will take all the expanded memory they can, even if they are not going to use it, so entering a number here stops the application from stealing memory, making it unavailable to other applications. If you enter –1 the application can use all that is available, though you will probably never need this setting. If you enter 0 it won't get any.

Note that for both XMS and EMS the KB Limit is set to 1024 by default. That doesn't matter if the application doesn't try to use that sort of memory. But if you are running an application that can use expanded memory but doesn't need to, set the value to 0 so it won't waste memory.

Display Usage

You can make Windows run a DOS application **Full Screen**—that is, so you can't see any window components—or **Windowed**, in a window with borders, title bar, scroll bars, and so on. A window will use more memory, but you will have a few of the usual advantages; you will be able to size and move the window, and use the Control menu. You will also be able to copy and paste text. Whatever you select here, you can change once the application is running by pressing Alt-Enter.

There's a slight difference between Windows 3.1 and NT here—if you have NT running on a RISC-based computer, the display option is ignored, because MS-DOS applications can only be run in windows, not full screen. And on IBM-compatible PCs you won't be able to run graphical applications in a window—they will only run full screen, and if a text-based program switches to graphics mode while running in a window, NT will automatically switch to full screen.

The following are the PIF **Advanced Options**, viewed by clicking on the Advanced button.

Reserve Shortcut Keys

Many DOS applications use shortcut key combinations that NT uses for various procedures. NT will normally take precedence. That is, if you use a shortcut key combination that both Windows and the application use, Windows uses it, not the application. You can tell Windows to ignore the combination—and let the application use it instead—by selecting the appropriate check box. These are the combinations, with the way Windows uses them:

Alt-Tab   Switches to the last-used application

Alt-Esc   Switches to the next application in sequence

Ctrl-Esc   Displays the Task List dialog box. If the application is full screen, Windows displays the last-used application, with the Task List dialog box above it.

PrtSc   If the application is in a window, this copies a picture of the full screen into the Clipboard. If it is running full screen, this copies a "text" picture into the clipboard.

Alt-PrtSc   If the application is in a window, this copies a picture of the window into the Clipboard. If it is running full screen, this copies a "text" picture into the clipboard.

Alt-Space   Opens the Control menu. If the application is full screen, it changes to a window first.

Alt-Enter   Toggles the application between full screen and a window.

Some of these keystrokes you simply don't need, so you can save some memory by disabling them. If you are going to run the application in a window, you don't really need the commands used to open the Control menu or swap to other applications; you can use your mouse to do that. Also, you won't need Alt-Enter because you can use the Control menu to swap to full screen—though without Alt-Enter you won't be able to swap back. Of course if you only want to run full screen or in a Window, you won't need Alt-Enter anyway. And you could disable two of the swapping commands (Alt-Tab, Alt-Esc, or Ctrl-Esc), and just use one of them. Then you won't need Alt-Spacebar either, because you can use the remaining swapping command and then open the Control menu with the mouse. Also, if you don't plan to take "snapshots" of the screen or window, you won't need the PrtSc or Alt-PrtSc commands.

Remember that reserving a shortcut for an application restricts its use while the DOS application is minimized and the icon selected. For instance, if you have reserved Alt-Tab, you won't be able to use Alt-Tab to move from the icon to another application.

Application Shortcut Key

You can assign a shortcut key to an application, so that you can quickly swap directly to that application. The Advanced Options dialog box's Application Shortcut Key is very similar to that in Program Manager, with some important differences. First, you have a different choice of keystroke combinations. Here are the rules:

- The combination must include Alt, Shift, or Ctrl.
- You can combine Alt, Ctrl, and Shift.
- You cannot use Esc, Enter, Tab, Spacebar, Print Screen, or Backspace.
- Unlike the Program Item Properties shortcut (which only allow three- and four-key shortcuts), you can create two-key shortcuts.
- Place the cursor in the box and then press the combination (don't type it). For instance, press Ctrl-1, don't actually type C t r l - 1.

Another important difference is that this keystroke combination cannot be used to actually open the application, only to switch to it from another application. (If you set a shortcut in the icon's Program Item Properties dialog box, you can start the application by displaying Program Manager and pressing the shortcut.) Finally, any shortcut you enter here will be overridden by the shortcut in the Program Item Properties dialog box—as long as you start the application using the icon. If you start the application using the File|Run command, or by double-clicking on the filename in File Manager, Windows lets you use the shortcut you entered in the PIF. Remember though, if you accidentally use the icon's shortcut while in Program Manager, you will open the application again, unless you place the same shortcut in both places.

Note   Remember that the shortcut you enter here overrides all other application shortcuts. For instance, if you use the shortcut Alt-E, it will no longer open an application's Edit menu. Rather, it will switch between applications.

Defining Custom Startup Files

Windows NT does provide an additional option in its PIF Editor. Click on the **Windows NT** button to see the dialog box in Figure 10.2. This dialog box tells NT which AUTOEXEC and CONFIG files should be run, to configure the MS-DOS

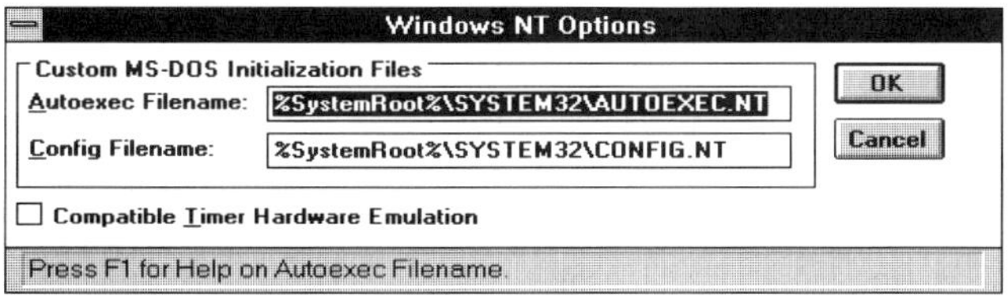

Figure 10.2 The PIF Editor's Windows NT Options dialog box

environment, before running the MS-DOS program itself. You can see that by default NT will run E:\WINNT\ SYSTEM32\ AUTOEXEC.NT and E:\WINNT \SYSTEM32\CONFIG.NT, but you can replace these files with different ones, and customize the MS-DOS environment for each program you run. You could load a TSR, for instance, or modify the path before running a program.

You can call these files whatever you want—they don't have to be .NT, .BAT, or .SYS files. You might name then after the application to which they are related. Start by editing your AUTOEXEC.NT and CONFIG.NT files (in the WINNT \SYSTEM32 directory), and save them with new names. Then enter the names in the Windows NT Options dialog box.

These files will not always be used when you run the MS-DOS program, though. NT only runs AUTOEXEC.NT and CONFIG.NT or their equivalents at one specific time—the first time an MS-DOS program runs in a Command Prompt window. If you exit that program, and then run another, NT will *not* run AUTOEXEC.NT and CONFIG.NT or their equivalents, or whatever you happen to have placed in the PIF Editor's Windows NT Options dialog box.

If you need those files to run, you'll have to open another window. You can do that by starting the MS-DOS program from Program Manager or File Manager, by opening another Command Prompt window and running the program in that, or by using the START command from the current Command Prompt window. For instance, to run QBASIC you would type START QBASIC. NT will open another Command Prompt window, run the AUTOEXEC.NT and CONFIG.NT files (or equivalents), and then run QBASIC in the new window.

Compatible Timer Hardware Emulation

In the Windows NT Options dialog box (Figure 10.2) you'll notice that there's a check box at the bottom called Compatible Timer Hardware Emulation. Don't touch this when you first create a PIF for an application—it can slow the application down or stop it from calculating time correctly—but if you find that the application starts but doesn't run correctly, go back to the PIF and select this check box. This will reduce the rate at which the DOS application sends timing signals, and may allow it to run correctly. Few applications will require this, though you may find some games that do.

Running OS/2 Programs

NT contains a certain amount of support for OS/2 programs, but it's by no means perfect. First, only IBM-compatible computers can run an OS/2 subsystem. On a RISC machine an OS/2 program will only run if it's also MS-DOS-compatible, in which case it can run in the MS-DOS subsystem. And even on an IBM-compatible machine, OS/2 support is limited—to 16-bit character-based programs.

When you try to start an OS/2 application, NT looks in the configuration registry for information. If it can't find any, it looks on the hard disk for OS/2's CONFIG.SYS configuration file. If it can't find that, it adds default information to the configuration registry. If it can find it, it copies the LIBPATH information to the configuration registry, along with %SYSTEMROOT%\SYSTEM32 \OS2\DLL, the path to the NT OS/2 directory.

Note Because you may have installed NT in a directory other than WINNT, and it may not be on drive C:, NT uses the term %SYSTEMROOT% to mean the root directory of the NT system-file directory branch.

Modifying the OS/2 Configuration

If you have Administrator privileges in NT, you can change the OS/2 configuration by editing OS/2's CONFIG.SYS file with an OS/2 text editor. When you open the file while working in NT, NT will place the information from the configuration registry into the text editor. When you make your changes and save the file, NT takes the new information and places it into the configuration registry. These will take effect the next time you log onto NT.

In order to modify the PATH information used by OS/2 you should use the Control Panel's System dialog box to enter a PATH statement into the User Environment Variable box.

The OS/2 CONFIG.SYS Commands

These are the OS/2 configuration commands that you can use in CONFIG.NT. Any others will be ignored.

PROTSHELL The command interpreter. This is set by NT to PROTSHELL=C:\OS2\PMSHELL.EXE C:\OS2\OS2.INI C:\OS2\OS2SYS.INI %SYSTEMROOT%\SYSTEM32\CMD.EXE.

DEVICENAME An NT device driver used by an OS/2 program. Not all OS/2 drivers will run in Windows NT, of course: They must be NT-compatible OS/2 drivers.

LIBPATH	The location of OS/2 dynamic link libraries.
SET	Sets environment variables. Some set commands are ignored: set path, set compspec, set video_devices, set vio_ibmvga, set vio_vga, and set prompt.
COUNTRY	Enters a country code to define information such as time, date, and currency formats.
CODEPAGE	Defines the codepage your system will use, according to the language you are using.
DEVINFO=KBD	Information used by the keyboard to interact with a particular codepage.

Starting Programs

You can start non-NT programs in the same way you start Windows NT programs. You are already familiar with some of these methods, but there are a few differences between Windows 3.1 and NT that you need to be aware of.

Here are the ways in which you can start applications:

- Create a Program Manager **icon**, and use the icon to start the application.
- In Program Manager select **File|Run**, type the file path, filename, extension, and parameters, and press Enter. If you are starting an MS-DOS program you can type the PIF name.
- In File Manager, use the **File|Run** command in the same way you would in Program Manager.
- In File Manager, **double-click** on the executable file or the .PIF.
- At the Command Prompt, **type** the executable filename or .PIF name—and path if necessary—and press **Enter**.
- At the Command Prompt, type **start** followed by the executable filename or .PIF name with the path if necessary, and press **Enter**. This starts the application in a separate window.

The last two options in this list are the new ones. While you could start MS-DOS programs from the DOS prompt in Windows 3.1, in Windows NT you can start *any* program from the Command Prompt, including NT programs. And the new command, START, lets you start a program in a separate window. This is probably a concession to programmers. While real people rarely open Command Prompt windows (or DOS Prompt windows in Windows 3.1), most programmers seem to have a prompt window on their screen as a permanent fixture, carrying out most commands from the prompt and ignoring Program Manager and File Manager. This new START command lets them do virtually everything from the prompt now—they don't have to leave the window to open new windows.

There's another advantage to using the START command to start an MS-DOS program—it creates a new environment. If you open the Command Prompt window, then run an MS-DOS program, NT runs the AUTOEXEC.NT and CONFIG.NT, establishing the environment. When you exit that application and open another, NT doesn't re-run AUTOEXEC.NT and CONFIG.NT, so the second application will run in the same environment as the first.

If you want the second application to run in its own environment—using the startup files specified in the PIF's Windows NT Options dialog box—you should either run the program from Program Manager or File Manager, or run the program at the Command Prompt using the START command. When you close the application that is running in a window opened with the START command, the window itself will close, as it would if you start the program from Program Manager or File Manager.

Cutting and Pasting with the Command Prompt Window

Windows 3.1 lets you copy and paste between applications running in the Command Prompt window and the Clipboard. Windows NT expands a little on these capabilities, by adding something called **QuickEdit Mode**. To turn this mode on, select **Control Menu|Settings** in the Command Prompt window. Then click on the **QuickEdit Mode** check box. (If you want this feature available every time you open the Command Prompt window, you should also select the **Save Configuration** check box.) Then click on OK.

Now, with the application running in a window, you can highlight text with your mouse. Simply point, hold the mouse button down, and drag the pointer across the text you want to grab. Then press Enter, and the text is copied into the Clipboard.

11

System Configuration

Microsoft has provided Windows NT with a new method for managing system hardware and software configuration. As a way to avoid the confusion of different configuration files on each system, Windows NT has the Configuration Registry, a single database that stores information about the operating system, your applications, and your computer's hardware. As NT is a multiple-user system, with the ability to provide each user with different rights and privileges, the registry provides a way to store user-specific information, not only data related to the machine as a whole.

The registry is structured in a directory tree-like format—in fact the Registry Editor looks a little like File Manager, with icons in a "tree" on the left, and configuration entries on the right. There are four trees, each one in its own document window in the Registry Editor. These trees contain information about the computer hardware, information used to maintain compatibility with Windows 3.1, information related to all the users on the computer, and information related to the user who is currently logged in.

While Microsoft's documentation occasionally claims that all modifications can be made from "graphical elements such as Control Panel and Windows NT Setup," this is not entirely true. There are still options that can only be modified in the configuration registry itself, and nowhere else, and to do this you can use the Registry Editor.

System Security

The Registry Editor is not fully available to all users. Some areas are off limits to all but the Administrators. However, users still have access to areas where they can do damage (see Chapter 3 for information about recovering from configuration

203

problems). By default, most users can get into the Registry Editor and make changes, changes that could have serious results to their own configurations, at least.

To block users from getting into the configuration registry, use File Manager to deny access to the REGEDT32.EXE file for everyone but administrators (see Chapter 7). Registry Editor also has a Security system, similar to that in File Manager, that lets you deny users access to certain keys. Use the Security|Permissions command.

The Configuration Structure

Your system configuration is contained in several *hives*, or sections. Each hive is related to a file on your hard disk, stored in the \WINNT\SYSTEM32\CONFIG directory. Here are the initial hives and corresponding files:

HKEY_LOCAL_MACHINE\SYSTEM	SYSTEM.ALT
HKEY_LOCAL_MACHINE\SOFTWARE	SOFTWARE.LOG
HKEY_LOCAL_MACHINE\SECURITY	SECURITY.LOG
HKEY_LOCAL_MACHINE\SAM	SAM.LOG
HKEY_USERS\DEFAULT	DEFAULT.LOG

User-profile hives are created when a user logs onto the system. The related files are stored in the same directory, and are named *USERNAMEnnn* and *USER-NAMEnnn*.LOG.

It is from the hives that the information you will view in Registry Editor is taken.

Configuration Registry Editor

Registry Editor is a special application designed to let you view and modify information in the Configuration Register, which you might think of as an advanced .INI file. Although the Editor looks like File Manager (and has many of the same features), this is simply a convenient way to find your way around the configuration files.

Regedt32

You can run Registry Editor from the command line—type REGEDT32 and press Enter—or add its icon to Program Manager. You may want to add its icon to the Main program group if you think you will work with Registry Editor often, but most users will probably never touch it. (Most changes to the configuration can be made using NT's tools—Windows NT Setup, Control Panel, User Manager, and so on.) To create the icon, simply type REGEDT32 in the Command Line text box of the Program Item Properties dialog box.

When you run Registry Editor, it takes information from the configuration registry hives and places it in the four windows (see Figure 11.1). Each window contains a configuration *tree*. Inside each tree are a number of *keys* and *subkeys*,

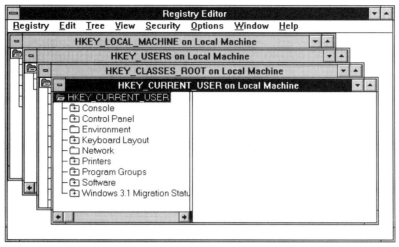

Figure 11.1 The Registry Editor

which use the same icons as the directories and subdirectories in File Manager. To the right of the tree is one or more *value entries* inside the selected key.

Each value entry is made up of three parts: the *name, type,* and *data.* For instance, in the HKEY_LOCAL_MACHINE tree, in the HARDWARE\DESCRIPTION\System subkey, you might find the value "SystemBiosDate : REG_SZ : 01/15/88." The value name is SystemBiosDate, the value type is REG_SZ, and the data is 01/15/88.

These are the four configuration trees you will see:

HKEY_USERS	Information about all the computer's users and their *profiles,* information about how each user has set up program groups, window sizes and positions, and Control Panel settings such as colors and the mouse setup.
HKEY_CURRENT_USER	Information about the user currently logged on. This information is taken from the HKEY_USERS tree.
HKEY_LOCAL_MACHINE	Information about the computer's hardware and software that is common to all users.
HKEY_CLASSES_ROOT	Information about file associations, used for starting applications, DDE (Dynamic Data Exchange), and OLE (Object Linking and Embedding). This information comes from the HKEY_LOCAL_ MACHINE tree, and duplicates information from the Registration Info Editor, a Windows 3.1 application also available in NT.

HKEY_USERS

The HKEY_USERS window shows two keys, user profiles for the computer. A profile describes the Windows NT "environment" in which a user will work: the colors that will be used, the mouse and keyboard setup, the screen saver, the applications with which file extensions have been associated, and so on. The first is the default profile, which all users have when they first log onto the computer. The second profile is that of the user currently logged on (that's you). This second profile shows information specific to you, such as the five personal program groups provided to you when you first logged on, and any new ones you have created. It also shows modifications you have made to the color scheme, changed mouse options, and so on.

HKEY_CURRENT_USER

The HKEY_CURRENT_USER window duplicates the second profile shown in the HKEY_USERS window. It shows the profile information for the user who is logged on. Changes made here are also seen in the HKEY_USERS windows.

HKEY_LOCAL_MACHINE

The HKEY_LOCAL_MACHINE window shows information about the computer itself, and information about the software that is common to all users. The Hardware section, for instance, provides data used by Windows NT to interface with the hardware. The Software section contains information about common program groups you have added to Program Manager. There are five keys in this tree:

HARDWARE	Each time Windows NT boots, information about the machine's hardware is compiled—the type of processor, SCSI adapters and devices, communications ports, the type of pointer you are using, and so on.
SAM	This subkey contains security information about user and group accounts. If the system is a Windows NT Advanced Server, it contains network domain information.
SECURITY	This subkey contains all the computer's security information (including the SAM tree), such as user privileges.
SOFTWARE	Information about all the software on the system, including file-extension associations, Object Linking and Embedding properties, and software names and version numbers.
SYSTEM	This subkey controls the manner in which NT boots the computer and operates.

HKEY_CLASSES_ROOT

Regedit

The HKEY_CLASSES_ROOT tree is used solely for compatibility with Windows 3.1 applications. Windows 3.1 has an application called the Registration Info Editor. This application is available in Windows NT, and you can even create an icon to get to it, if you wish. The data held in both HKEY_CLASSES_ROOT and the Registration Info Editor tells NT which files are associated with which applications. NT uses this information for OLE, drag-and-drop (dragging a file icon to Print Manager, for instance, to print a file), and to start applications from File Manager or Program Manager by "running" a document file. This information is much the same as the file-extension association information that is stored in the [Extensions] section of WIN.INI in Windows 3.1.

The first part of HKEY_CLASSES_ROOT lists the different file extensions that have been associated with applications. For each extension the configuration registry holds an abbreviated application name—MFile or calfile, for example. Lower down the tree, these abbreviations are explained—for each abbreviation the configuration registry holds the command used to open the application and to print with the application using drag-and-drop. This information is also displayed in the Software\Classes section of the HKEY_LOCAL_MACHINE.

Working with Registry Editor

Will you ever need to change anything in the Registry Editor? For most users, the answer is probably no. There are a few simple things they may want to change (see the table later in this chapter), but most changes to NT's configuration can—and should—be made elsewhere.

However, advanced users may want or need to work in Registry Editor, particularly software developers. And in some cases, even average users may need to modify something at the behest of technical support personnel.

Should you wish to modify configuration registry entries, how do you work with the Registy Editor? You can add or delete keys, modify, add, or delete values, even load and save configuration data in files. (See the Menu Options at the end of this chapter for a complete list of all the available commands.)

Note Some of the following commands will not be available if the **Options|Read Only Mode** command has been selected. Also, the security permissions may not allow you to modify some keys and values—only Administrators have full access.

If you ever need to add a new subkey, select the key to which you want to add it, and select **Edit|Add Key**. (You can't add subkeys to the HKEY_USERS or HKEY_LOCAL_MACHINE trees—you must use the Registry|Load Hives command to do this.) You'll see a dialog box in which you can type the subkey's name and the default *class* for the value entries that will be added to the key. These are the classes:

REG_SZ	A string of data (various characters, often readable text).
REG_BINARY	Binary data (a binary number).
REG_MULTI_SZ	Multiple-line string of data.
REG_EXPAND_SZ	Expandable string, a string containing a variable that is replaced by something else when called by an application.
REG_DWORD	DWORD data, a number 4 bytes long.

To add a value, select **Edit|Add Value**. This time you'll enter the value name and select the data type from a drop-down list box. When you click on OK the appropriate editor appears—the String Editor for REG_SZ and REG_EX-PAND_SZ, the Multi-String Editor for REG_MULTI_SZ, the DWORD Editor REG_DWORD, and the Binary Editor for REG_BINARY. You can enter the actual data and click on OK to add it to the configuration.

Keys and values can also be deleted, of course. Select the item and press **Del**, or select **Edit|Delete**. You'll be asked to confirm the operation. To edit a value, **double-click** on it, or click on it and select **Edit|Binary**, **Edit|String**, **Edit|DWORD**, or **Edit|Multi String**, according to the type of data (although all types can be viewed in all of the edit boxes). You can also select any value and use the **View|Display Binary Data** command to see the value in binary data.

Here are a few things you might want to change in Registry Editor:

Value name	Purpose	Path to the key
IconTitleFaceName	The font used for the icon titles in Program Manager.	HKEY_CURRENT_USER \Control Panel\Desktop and HKEY_USERS\Default \Control Panel\Desktop.
IconTitleSize	The size of the font used for the icon titles in Program Manager.	HKEY_CURRENT_USER \Control Panel\Desktop and HKEY_USERS\Default \Control Panel\Desktop.
NoRun=1	Disables Program Manager's File|Run command.	HKEY_USERS\Default \Software\Microsoft\Windows NT\CurrentVersion\Program Manager\Restrictions and HKEY_USERS\usernumber \Software\Microsoft\Windows NT\CurrentVersion\Program Manager\Restrictions.

Value name	Purpose	Path to the key
NoClose=1	Stops the user from closing NT by using Control|Close, Alt-F4, File|Logoff, or by double-clicking on the Control menu.	HKEY_USERS\Default \Software\Microsoft\Windows NT \CurrentVersion\Program Manager\Restrictions and HKEY_USERS \usernumber \Software\Microsoft\Windows NT \CurrentVersion\Program Manager\Restrictions.
EditLevel=1	The user cannot create, delete, or rename Program Manager groups.	"
EditLevel=2	Same as Level 1, plus restricts actions carried out on program items. Disables File|New, File|Move, File|Copy, and File|Delete.	"
EditLevel=3	Same as Level 2, plus disables the Command Line in the Program Item Properties dialog box, so the user can view icon information, but not create new ones.	"
EditLevel=4	Same as Level 3, plus disables all areas in the Program Item Properties dialog box, so the user can still view the information but not change it.	"
NoFileMenu=1	Removes the File menu entirely.	"
NoSaveSettings=1	Disables the Options|Save Settings on Exit and Options|Save Settings Now commands.	"

Advanced Operations

Registry Editor also lets you load and unload data to and from the HKEY_USERS and HKEY_LOCAL_MACHINE trees, and to save keys from any of the trees. To save a key, select it and then choose the **Registry\|Save Key** command. Enter a file-name in the Save Key dialog box and click on OK.

This key can be loaded into any key in the HKEY_USERS or HKEY_LOCAL_ MACHINE trees. Select the key into which you want to place it and use the **Registry|Load Hive** command. (Once saved, the key is regarded as a *hive*, a file containing configuration data.) You can also unload the hive with the **Registry|Unload Hive** command.

The **Registry|Restore** data lets you copy the data from a hive—a saved key— onto another existing key, destroying the original data. You can also use the **Registry|Restore Volatile** command to overwrite the existing data, with the difference being that when you restart your computer the changes will be lost.

The **Registry|Select Computer** command lets you view configuration data from another computer. **Registry|Close** closes all the windows associated with the selected one. **Registry|Open Local** opens the windows for the local machine (to replace them if you had closed them earlier).

For more information about the configuration registry, get a copy of the Windows NT Resource Guide. And scan through the following menu-options table, to see what other features are available.

The Menu Options

Here's a summary of Registry Editor's menu options:

Registry|Open Local	Opens the windows for the local machine.
Registry|Close	Closes all four windows associated with the selected document window in Registry Editor.
Registry|Load Hive	Loads information from a hive. You can use this to load a key saved with the Registry|Save Key command.
Registry|Unload Hive	Unloads the Hive information.
Registry|Restore	Restores a hive on top of the existing registry information—this data will remain, even after you restart your computer.
Registry|Restore Volatile	Restores a hive on top of the existing registry information, but when you restart your computer the information is lost.
Registry|Save Key	Lets you save the data from the selected key and all its subkeys in a file. That file can be loaded into the hive later using Load Hive, or restored using Restore or Restore Volatile.
Registry|Select Computer	Lets you open the configuration registry on another networked machine.
Registry|Print Subtree	Prints the data in the selected key and its subkeys.
Registry|Printer Setup	Lets you select and set up a printer.

Registry|Save Subtree As	Saves the selected key and its subkeys, and all values, in a text file.
Registry|Exit	Closes Registry Editor.
Edit|Add Key	Lets you create a subkey in the selected key.
Edit|Add Value	Lets you add a value to the selected key.
Edit|Delete (Del)	Deletes the selected key and its subkey, or the selected value.
Edit|Binary	Displays the selected value in the Binary Editor.
Edit|String	Displays the selected value in the String Editor.
Edit|DWORD	Displays the selected value in the DWORD Editor.
Edit|Multi String	Displays the selected value in the Multi String Editor.
Tree|Expand One Level (+)	Displays a directory's first-level subdirectories.
Tree|Expand Branch (*)	Displays the subdirectories at all levels of the selected directory.
Tree|Expand All (Ctrl-*)	Expands the entire directory tree, displaying all the directories and subdirectories on the tree.
Tree|Collapse Branch (-)	Collapses the tree below the selected directory, so its subdirectories are not displayed.
View|Tree and Data	Displays both the tree and the data panels in the selected window.
View|Tree Only	Displays only the tree panel in the selected window.
View|Data Only	Displays only the data panel in the selected window.
View|Split	Lets you split the selected window into the Tree and Data panels, and adjust the split position.
View|Display Binary Data	Displays the selected value in binary.
View|Refresh All (Shift-F6)	Refreshes all the tree windows, updating them with changes that have occurred since you opened Registry Editor. If Options|Auto-Refresh is selected, this command is disabled.
View|Refresh Active (F6)	Refreshes the active window, updating it with changes that have occurred since you opened Registry Editor. If Options|Auto-Refresh is selected, this command is disabled.
View|Find Key	Searches the selected key's subkeys for a specific key.

Security\Permissions   Lets you assign permissions for keys, so you can deny—or allow—access to certain areas.

Security\Auditing   Lets you audit the user of the Registry Editor, so you can see who is changing what.

Security\Owner   Lets a user take ownership of a particular key.

Options\Font   Lets you select the font you wish to use in the Registry Editor.

Options\Auto Refresh   Makes Registry Editor update its trees with changes in the configuration registry as they occur (other processes may be making changes while you are viewing the data).

Options\Read Only Mode   A safety feature which stops changes being written into the configuration registry.

Options\Confirm on Delete   Makes a confirmation dialog box appear when you try to delete a key or value.

Options\Save Settings on Exit Saves the Option menu settings and the window positions when you close Registry Editor.

Window\Cascade (Shift-F5)   Places the open windows one on top of the other. The lowest in the stack is placed in the top-left corner of the Registry Editor window, and each subsequent document window is offset toward the bottom-right corner.

Window\Tile (Shift-F4)   Places the open document windows so none are hidden, and each has equal space.

Window\Arrange Icons   Lines the document window icons up tidily at the bottom of the Registry Editor window.

Window\1. *pathname*   Makes the named document window the active one.

12

Performance Monitor

Performance Monitor provides a system for measuring, warning, reporting, and recording the performance and behavior of your computer and network, and other computers on the network. You can view this information in "real time"—as it happens—or use the Log window to record the data, and then view it later. This information can be used for troubleshooting or planning—by determining what system resources are overused, perhaps, and need to be augmented.

On opening Performance Monitor for the first time, you may find a great temptation to close it and never open it again. You might look at the hundreds of obscure and confusing parameters and decide there's nothing in it for you. But don't close it too soon—while many of Performance Monitor's capabilities are way beyond anything the average user will ever need, there are a few things it can do for everyone.

You can, for instance, monitor your paging file for a few days. You can measure how much is in use, sampling it every 10 minutes or so during the day, and record the maximum amount used. You can then decide whether you need to increase the paging file's size—and increase system speed—or decrease its size and save valuable disk space.

You can also monitor your hard disks, and get Performance Monitor to send an *alert* message when you get low on disk space. You might monitor network use to see how much traffic is occurring, and when the busy times are, and then adjust resources accordingly. You might check disk-drive and partition use on a server, to see which volumes are used most heavily, and move files and directories accordingly, spreading resources across more networked machines.

Many of the parameters that Performance Monitor lets you check will be unintelligible to most users—parameters such as *asynchronous pin reads per second* (cache), *piggybacked ACK queued per second* (NetBEUI), and *paged pool frees per second* (memory). You can monitor system performance at such a depth that only hardware and software developers will ever use some of these parameters. But take a close look and you'll find a few things that might be useful to the ordinary user.

Note While most operations in Performance Monitor can be carried out without a mouse, some important operations—such as selecting an item in the legend—cannot.

Starting Performance Monitor

Before you open Performance Monitor, decide whether you need to monitor disk performance, on your computer or another. If you do, then you'll need to use the **DISKPERF** command. Open the Command Prompt window, then type DISKPERF and press Enter. You'll see a message telling you if Disk Performance counters are "set to start." You'll probably see a message saying that they're not—the default.

If that's the case, type this:

```
DISKPERF -Y \\computername
```

If you want to monitor your own machine, you can omit the \\computername parameter. Otherwise enter the network name of the computer. Then press Enter, and after the command executes, reboot your computer.

Note You must be an Administrator to use the DISKPERF command, although anyone can use Performance Monitor.

Performance Monitor

When you log back into NT you can start Performance Monitor. Double-click on the icon in the Administrative Tools program group. You'll see a window similar to that shown in Figure 12.1 (without the data, of course).

Performance Monitor has four separate windows, only one of which can be viewed at any time (although you can run more than one "instance" of Performance Monitor, that is, you can open it two or more times, so you have two or more Performance Monitor windows open). You can change windows using the View menu, or with the first four icons on the toolbar:

 Chart window   Displays the monitored data in a graph or histogram. When using current data the chart will show up to 100 samples—you can define the sample interval. When using data recorded earlier, the chart shows all the data you select, regardless of the total time.

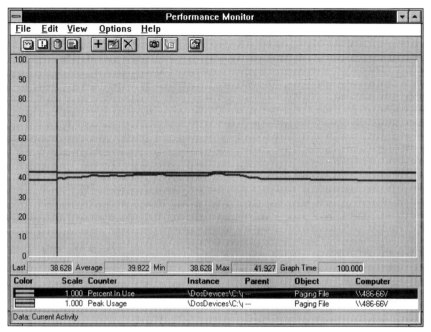

Figure 12.1 Performance Monitor, with the Chart window displayed

	Alert window	Displays alerts, lines entered into a table when a value for a monitored parameter crosses a preset boundary. The list can contain up to 1,000 entries.
	Log window	Lets you define what data you want to record, and in which file it should be saved. This data can be used in the Chart, Alert, and Report windows later.
	Report window	Displays a text report, showing the most recent value for each of the selected parameters. When using data recorded earlier, the report shows the average values over that period.

Figure 12.1 shows an example of one of these windows, the Chart window. You'll see the others later in this chapter.

Performance Monitor uses six types of files:

.PMC   chart settings file

.PMA   alert settings file

.PML   log settings file

.PMR   report settings file

.PMW   workspace settings file, containing data from all four settings groups, chart, alert, log, and report

.LOG   log file, containing data saved from a previous monitoring session

The first five files tell Performance Monitor which items should be monitored and what format to use—which colors, line thicknesses, and so on. You can either save—and restore—settings for each section separately, maintaining different files for the chart, alert, log, and report, or you can save them all together in a .PMW file.

The .LOG files, on the other hand, contain the actual performance data. These files are created using the Options|Log command in the Log window, and are opened by the Options|Data From command.

Performance
Monitor

When you first open Performance Monitor, it will use the default settings, with no monitoring in progress. You will define what and how you want to monitor. Later you can add the name of the monitoring file you want to use—a .PMW file—to the Command Line box in the icon's Program Item Properties dialog box, so Performance Monitor always opens with the same setup.

Once you've set the various parameters, Performance Monitor begins monitoring, and stores data temporarily—up to 1,000 alerts and 100 chart samples, for instance. But when you close Performance Monitor, you lose the settings and all this data—unless you choose to save them. Save settings with the File|Save commands, and save data with the Options|Log command. These procedures are described later in this chapter.

Creating a Chart

Figure 12.1 shows the Chart window. If you don't see a window similar to this, click on the first button in the toolbar to change to the chart window (or select **View|Chart** or press **Ctrl-C**). The chart displays 100 samples—the sampling rate is once every second, though you could change that to a faster or slower rate. Old data—after the 101st sample—simply disappears off the graph—and you can't get it back. You *can* store data, however, and restore it to the chart, using the Log window. We'll explain how later in this chapter.

Begin creating a chart by clicking on the fifth toolbar button, or by selecting **Edit|Add to Chart** (**Ctrl-I**). The Add to Chart dialog box pops up (see Figure 12.2). Start by deciding which **Computer** you want to monitor. By default the machine on which you are working is displayed in the Computer text box, but you can click on the button at the end of this text box to select another computer on the network. (You can monitor more than one computer at a time—select a computer, select the objects you want to monitor, then select another computer, and repeat.) Now select the item you want to monitor from the **Object** drop-down list box. The options you have available depend on your system's configuration. You'll see options such as these:

Cache	The disk-cache performance—parameters such as the percentage of copy-read hits and data flushes per second.
Logical Disk	The disk partitions—parameters such as disk writes per second and the amount of free space.

Memory	The system memory—parameters such as mapped pages per second and committed bytes.
NetBEUI	The NetBEUI network protocol—parameters such as canceled connections and disconnects.
Objects	Program objects—parameters such as threads, mutexes, and semaphores.
Paging File	The PAGEFILE.SYS file—peak usage and percent in use.
PhysicalDisk	The disk drives (as opposed to partitions)—parameters such as percentage disk read time and disk reads per second.
Process	Program processes—parameters such as percentage privileged time and page faults per second.
Processor	The CPU operations—parameters such as percentage privileged time and interrupts per second.
Redirector	The system which redirects I/O requests across the network—parameters such as hung sessions and bytes per second.
Server	Network processes—parameters such as sessions forced off and total files opened.
System	The operating system—parameters such as system time up and write operations per second.
Thread	Program threads—parameters such as context switches per second and base priority.

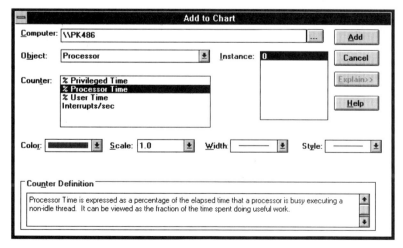

Figure 12.2 The Add to Chart dialog box, after clicking on the Explain button

Note If you don't find a long list of objects—perhaps the Object list box is empty or contains just a few—you may be displaying data from a log file. Close the dialog box, select Options|Data From, and make sure that Current Activity is selected.

Once you've selected from the Object drop-down list box, look at the **Instance** list box. In some cases you can select the particular "instance" (or item) on which you want the "object" (or process), monitored. For example, if you selected Logical Disk, you will now see your disk volumes listed in the Instance list box—you can select which partition you want monitored. If you selected Physical Disk, you will see the disks listed in the Interval list box—you'll just see 0 if you only have one disk, but if you have more than one you'll see each one numbered. If you selected Process in the Object drop-down list box, you will see the different programs and procedures you can monitor.

Now select what you want to measure from the **Counter** list box. For an explanation of each item in this box, click on the **Explain** button, to expand the dialog box. The **Counter Definition** explains the highlighted item in the Counter list box. There are literally hundreds of different parameters—counters—that you can monitor. You may want to spend a few minutes selecting each object, then reading the options in the Counter list. (A simple way to do this is press the Down Arrow to move through the Counter list.) You can read each definition to try to figure out what each one is, and decide which might be useful for you.

Quite frankly, much of this is stuff that not even the average system administrator will want to monitor, let alone the average user. Few people will want to monitor Mutexes or Semaphores (objects), Peak Virtual Pages or Write Bytes/sec (process), or the % Privileged Time for a particular thread, though some programmers and performance testers may find these options useful. Perhaps an ordinary user may want to monitor Logical Disk and Physical Disk, or perhaps Paging File (to determine the best size), though it's doubtful whether many will bother. Some system administrators will find the Server options useful.

Now that you've selected the item you want to monitor, you must decide what it will look like on the chart. Select the line's color from the **Color** drop-down list box. From the **Scale** drop-down list box you can select a ratio from 0.000001:1 and 10000.0:1. If you select 10 (meaning 10:1), a value of 50 will be shown on the graph as 500. The default vertical scale only goes up to 100, but you'll see in a moment how to modify that. You can also select a line **Width**, though if you use any but the thinnest width you won't be able to select a line **Style** (dotted and dashed lines). You may have to experiment a little—you'll find, for example, that some colors are simply not very distinct on thin lines. If so, you may have to select a brighter color, a thicker line, or a different line style.

Now click on the **Add** button to add the item to the chart. The dialog box remains open, so you can select and configure more items, and the color in the Color dialog box automatically changes, selecting the next color in sequence. Even though the dialog box remains open, monitoring begins immediately.

Note There's a shortcut to adding items. Select several at once by dragging the mouse pointer across them in the Counter or Instance list, by holding down Ctrl while you click on them, or by holding down Shift while you press the down arrow. Then simply click on the Add button. All the items will be added to the chart with the line style, and Performance Monitor will give each one a different color.

Configure the other items you want to see in your chart, and when you've finished click on **Done** to close the box. You'll now see a **legend**, the items listed at the bottom of the chart (see Figure 12.1). The columns show the line color and style, the **Scale**, **Counter**, **Instance**, **Object**, and **Computer**, all of which you've just seen in the Add to Chart dialog box. Some items may also have something in the **Parent** column—for instance, if you are monitoring a logical disk drive (a disk partition), the Parent column shows the disk number on which that partition is found.

There's a useful little feature called **chart highlighting**. Press **Ctrl-H**, and the parameter that is selected in the legend will appear on the chart as a thick white line. Click on another entry in the legend and that parameter will become white, the first one returning to its original color. Turn off the highlighting by pressing Ctrl-H again. This feature is especially useful if you have several parameters close together on the chart.

Modifying the Chart

 You can modify the manner in which a counter is displayed by **double-clicking** on it in the legend, or by selecting it and clicking on the sixth toolbar icon, or by selecting **Edit|Edit Chart Line**. You'll see the Edit Chart Line dialog box, which is the same as the Add to Chart dialog box, except that much of it is disabled—all you can do is change the color, scale, width, and style.

 To remove a chart line, select it in the legend and then click on the X toolbar button or select **Edit|Delete From Chart**. Of course if you want to change a line to show a different item, you'll have to delete it and add a new one using the Add to Chart dialog box.

Click on one of these items to view more data or edit it. The text boxes immediately above the legend show the selected item's **Last**, **Average**, **Minimum**, and **Maximum** values. You can also see the **Graph Time**, which is the length of the horizontal axis—the number of seconds shown on the graph, from the left side to the right. As the graph updates, the red vertical line moves across the graph—if the Graph Time says 10, it means it takes 10 seconds to move all the way across the graph. (At very fast updates—speeds above one update every tenth of a second—the Graph Time will be incorrect.)

The chart always displays 100 intervals—that is, it fits 100 readings between the left and right margins. For example, if the Time Interval is 5 seconds, the chart is 500 seconds wide—and the Graph Time in the Value Bar will show 500. The vertical red line which shows the current reading will take 500 seconds to travel all the way along the chart—at which point it starts again, covering the old readings.

You can adjust this setting by selecting **Options|Chart**, by pressing **Ctrl-O**, or by clicking on the last button on the toolbar. You'll see the Chart Options dialog box (see Figure 12.3). Modifying the **Time Interval** changes how often you will see an update on the chart. Its default (1.00) means that you'll see an update every second. You can enter any value, from 0 (which actually provides about 10 updates every second) up to 100,000,000 seconds (that's 190 years—should be enough). Just remember that it's in seconds, so for long intervals you'll have to convert from minutes or hours (or days?) to seconds. These are instantaneous samples, by the way. If you select an interval of one day, you won't get an average over the day—you'll get a "snapshot" once a day.

Notice also that you can turn the **Periodic Update** off by selecting **Manual Update**. Do this if you want to take samples yourself, using the **Options|Update Now** command (**Ctrl-U**) or by clicking on the camera button in the toolbar.

The **Vertical Maximum** adjusts the vertical scale, of course. Again, you can enter any value you want. There will usually be 20 vertical intervals, so if you have a maximum of 100, the values will be 5, 10, 15, and so on, up to 100. If you use a maximum of 75, though, the values will be 3.8, 7.5, 11.3, and so on. The most sensible value will depend, of course, on what you are measuring. You'll want to adjust it so the scale is small enough to show plenty of detail, but not so small that the lines go off scale.

The check boxes modify the chart features. You can remove the **Legend** (which also removes the value bar, containing the Last, Average, Min, Max, and Graph Time), or you can remove the **Value Bar** alone. You can also remove the **Vertical Labels** (the numbers on the vertical axis). You can also *add* **Vertical Grid** and **Horizontal Grid** lines. Finally, the Gallery options let you choose a **Histogram**—a bar chart—instead of the default Graph. The Histogram has a bar for each item, showing only the most recent value, as you can see in Figure 12.4.

To start over again and create a new chart—clearing all the parameters from the legend—select **File|New Chart**. Or use **Edit|Clear Display** to remove the lines from the chart, but continue monitoring the selected parameters.

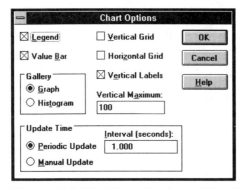

Figure 12.3 The Chart Options dialog box

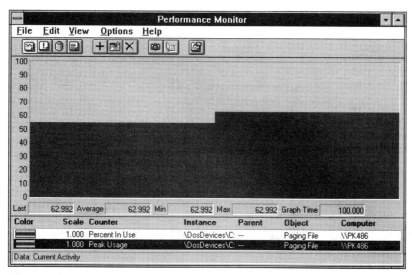

Figure 12.4 A histogram in the Chart window

Working with Alerts

Now let's look at the Alert window. Click on the second toolbar button, select **View|Alert**, or press **Ctrl-A** to see the window (Figure 12.5). In the middle is a list box showing the alerts—events that have exceeded a limit you set. At the bottom of the window you can see the legend, which is very similar to that in the Chart window. The only difference is that instead of Scale you'll see Value, which is the alert limit you set. The character preceding the value shows if it was an upper or lower limit. For instance, if you see >50.0000%, it means that an alert appears whenever the item exceeds 50%. If it said <50.0000%, the alert would appear when the item's value dropped below 50%.

To add an alert item, select **Edit|Add To Alert** (**Ctrl-I**) or click on the fifth toolbar icon. You'll see the Add to Alert dialog box (Figure 12.6), which is very similar to the Add to Chart dialog box. The major differences are that you can only select a color, not a line style (you may want to pick the color to match the one used in the Chart, if you are monitoring this parameter there), and that you will enter **Alert If** parameters. Enter the value which should act as a trigger for an alert. For instance, if you want to know when the network is becoming overloaded, you might select Server from the Object drop-down list box, Sessions from the Counter list box, and then enter, say, 20 into the Alert If text box, making sure that the **Over** option button is selected. Or you can have Performance Monitor create an alert if some value falls **Under** a certain value. You could select LogicalDisk, Free Megabytes, and enter a value that will act as a trigger if the amount of free space on that volume falls too low.

You can also tell Performance Monitor to **Run Program on Alert**—to start a program when an alert occurs. Enter the program's name—and path, if necessary—

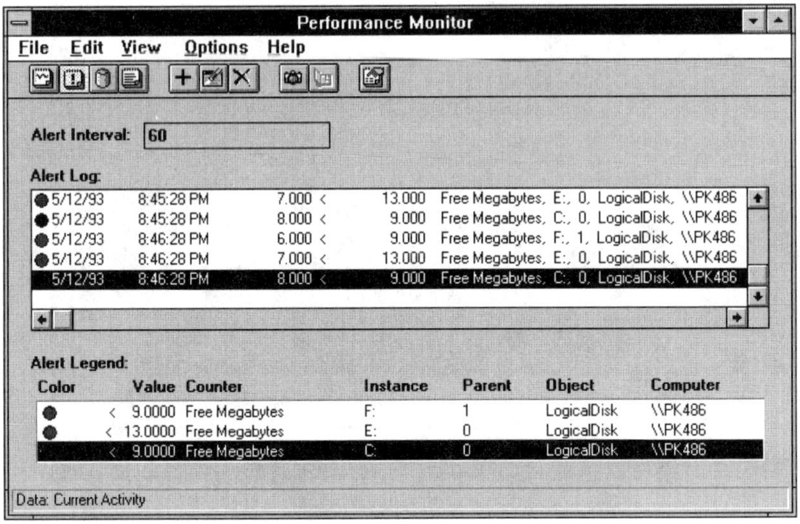

Figure 12.5 Performance Monitor's Alert window

into the text box. Then select either **First Time** (to make the program run the first time the alert occurs) or **Every Time** (to make the program run every time it occurs). Performance Monitor will pass the alert information to that program. You can use this to run anything you want—you might run CMD when you receive a Logical Disk error (so you can run CHKDSK), or the Control Panel's Server dialog box when you receive a Server alert (enter CONTROL.EXE SERVER). When you close the dialog box, you'll see the legend now contains the alert information, and the alerts will begin appearing in the list—assuming limits are being crossed—with the oldest at the top of the list, the newest at the bottom.

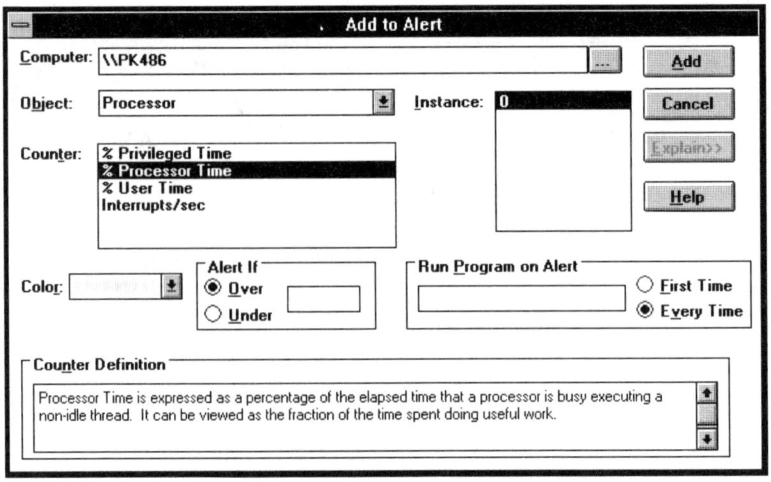

Figure 12.6 The Add to Alert dialog box, after clicking on the Explain button

Just below the toolbar you can see the **Alert Interval** text box. (This is a "relic" of an early version of Performance Monitor—you can't actually change the interval here. You'll do that in the Alert Options dialog box, which we'll look at in a moment.) By default, the sampling interval is 5 seconds. Each time Performance Monitor samples the data, it checks to see if any of the parameters have crossed the limits you set. If they haven't, then nothing is added to the list. If a parameter *has* crossed a limit, an entry is added to the list. The entry has a color—the color selected when you added the alert, which is a quick way to identify the entry, and perhaps to correlate it with the chart. It also shows the date and time, the parameter value, the limit you set (preceded by > to mean an "Over" limit or < to mean an "Under" limit), the counter, the instance, the parent, the object, and the computer.

 You can also check a parameter's status at any time using the **Options|Update Now** command (**Ctrl-U**), or by clicking on the camera toolbar button. Up to 1,000 alerts can be added to the list, then they start to "drop off the bottom." You can clear the list with **Edit|Clear Display**, and both clear the list and remove the alert settings with **File|New Alert Settings**.

 Everything else works in much the same way as the Chart window. You can edit the alert items (select the item and then use the **Edit|Edit Alert Entry** command or the sixth toolbar button). You can delete items with the **Edit|Delete Alert** command or the seventh toolbar button, and you can use the camera button or **Options|Update Now** (**Ctrl-U**) to make manual updates. You can also load data from a log file—we'll look at that procedure later in this chapter.

Customizing Alerts

 There are a few ways to customize the Alert window. Select **Options|Alert** (**Ctrl-O**) command or click the last toolbar button to see the Alert Options dialog box (Figure 12.7). You can set the **Alert Interval** in seconds from 0 seconds up to anything you want (again, like the Chart window, the limit is 190 years). You must enter full seconds, no decimals.

Of course, you can also turn off the **Periodic Update** and turn **Manual Update** on. You can also turn on **Switch to Alert View**, which makes Performance Monitor display the Alert window whenever an alert arrives. Of course this doesn't help if the application is minimized or behind another window. So there's another way to receive a message.

The **Send network message** option tells Performance Monitor to send a message, either to your computer, or to another on the network, using the Server's Messenger system. In order to use this, Messenger must be started. You can use the Services dialog box to start it, and to set it up so that it starts automatically when NT boots—see Chapter 6. It may have started already, of course—open the Control Panel's Services dialog box and look for Messenger.

When you choose **Send network message**, you must then enter the computer name into the **Net Name** dialog box. Don't enter the customary \\ before the name, though, or you won't get the message. For instance, type 486-66V, not \\486-66V.

```
┌─────────────────────────────────────────────┐
│ ▬                 Alert Options               │
├─────────────────────────────────────────────┤
│  ☐ Switch to Alert View          ┌─────────┐ │
│                                  │   OK    │ │
│  ┌─Network Alert─────────────┐   └─────────┘ │
│  │ ☒ Send network message    │   ┌─────────┐ │
│  │ Net Name:                 │   │ Cancel  │ │
│  │ ┌───────────────────────┐ │   └─────────┘ │
│  │ │ 486-66V               │ │   ┌─────────┐ │
│  │ └───────────────────────┘ │   │  Help   │ │
│  └───────────────────────────┘   └─────────┘ │
│  ┌─Update Time───────────────────────────┐   │
│  │                Interval (seconds):     │   │
│  │ ◉ Periodic Update  ┌──────────────┐    │   │
│  │                    │ 60           │    │   │
│  │ ○ Manual Update    └──────────────┘    │   │
│  └────────────────────────────────────────┘  │
└─────────────────────────────────────────────┘
```

Figure 12.7 The Alert Options dialog box

When an alert is generated related to this parameter, a message box will appear on the named computer. It won't go away either—it's set to "always on top"—until you click on OK. Figure 12.8 shows an example. One of these messages will appear for each alert, so if the limits are crossed frequently, or if you have a short sample interval, you'll see a lot of these messages.

Remember, these options are set for the entire Alert window, not for each parameter. So you will get a message for all alerts that are generated, regardless of their importance.

Even if you don't use either of these indications, there's one more alert indicator; Performance Monitor automatically places a small icon—an exclamation mark in a circle—on the status bar of the Chart, Log, and Report windows. Next to the icon is a number indicating how many alerts have been received. (Changing the Alert Options will clear this indicator until the next alert arrives.)

The Report Window

Select **View|Report**, press **Ctrl-R**, or click on the fourth toolbar icon to see the Report window (Figure 12.9). This window displays a text report, showing the most recent values for the selected items (if monitoring current activity) or the average data (if using information from a .LOG file). You can export this data to a database or spreadsheet if you wish.

You add items to the report in the same way you would for the chart—using **Edit|Add to Report** (**Ctrl-I**) or the + toolbar button—though of course you won't be entering line colors and styles, you'll just be selecting computers, objects,

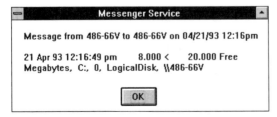

Figure 12.8 An alert message, sent via Messenger Service

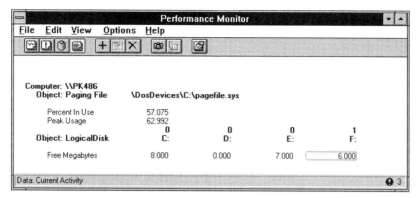

Figure 12.9 The Performance Monitor's Report window

counters, and instances. You can use the **Explain** button to remind you what each one is. When you add parameters, Performance Monitor places them in the window's workspace, starting at the top and working its way down, one selection above another. If necessary a vertical scroll bar will be added, so you can move through the report. If you add several instances of one counter—for example, you might add the LogicalDisk object, select the Free Megabytes counter, then select all of your disk drives—each instance will appear in a separate column. If you enter enough columns, a horizontal scroll bar will be added, so you can move to the right to view the hidden columns.

  You have only one report option that you can modify, the sample interval. Select **Options|Report** (**Ctrl-O**) or click on the last toolbar button. Select **Manual Update** if you want to take "snapshots" of the data with the camera toolbar button (or **Options|Update Now**, or **Ctrl-U**). Or select **Periodic Update** and enter or select a value, in seconds, in the **Interval** drop-down list box.

  You can delete items in the same way as in a chart, but you can't edit them. Click on a value and select **Edit|Delete from Report**, or click on the X toolbar icon to remove the entry from the report. Select **Edit|Clear Display** to remove the values from all the parameters, but leave the parameters in the report, ready for the next sample. To start over completely, select **File|New Report Settings**. This will remove all parameters from the workspace.

Recording Data in the Log Window

  If you want to actually record data in a file—not just display it—you'll have to use the Log window. This window is the only one that can record data—the others can then read the data recorded here, and create their own information—charts, alerts, or reports. You might want to record data, then create the charts, alerts, and reports later, or even export the data to a database. Click on the third toolbar icon—yes, it's supposed to look like a wooden log—or select **View|Log** (**Ctrl-L**) to see the Log window (Figure 12.10).

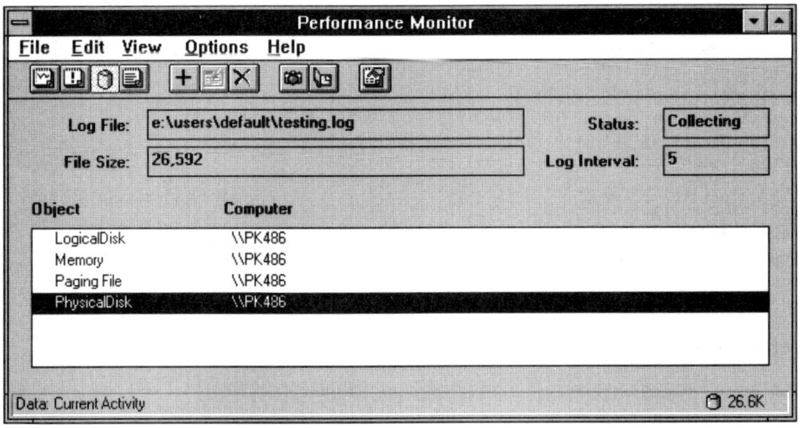

Performance Monitor

File   Edit   View   Options   Help

| Log File: | e:\users\default\testing.log | | Status: | Collecting |
| File Size: | 26,592 | | Log Interval: | 5 |

Object	Computer
LogicalDisk	\\PK486
Memory	\\PK486
Paging File	\\PK486
PhysicalDisk	\\PK486

Data: Current Activity   26.6K

Figure 12.10   The Log window

The Log window doesn't display any sample information, it simply lets you determine what you want to be recorded, and displays your settings. Begin by clicking on the fifth toolbar button, or by selecting **Edit|Add to Log** (**Ctrl-I**). You'll see the Add To Log dialog box (Figure 12.11). Begin by selecting the computer you want to monitor, then the objects for that computer. Your options are very limited here—you don't specify Counters and Instances, you simply select the **Objects** you want to monitor. These are the same objects you saw in the Chart and ALERT windows (see the list earlier in this chapter). You are, in effect, telling Performance Monitor to store all the information from the selected objects, so later you can use the Chart, Alert, and Report windows to extract more detailed information.

Select objects by dragging the mouse pointer across the names or by holding Ctrl down while you click on the ones you want. Then click on the **Add** button to add those items to the Log window. Click on **Done** to close the box.

Now you need to define where to store the information, and how often to sample. Select **Options|Log** (**Ctrl-O**), or click on the last toolbar button to use the Log Options dialog box. This box lets you select a directory in which you want to place the .LOG file, enter a filename, and enter an **Update Time**, or log interval. Enter any interval you want, or select **Manual Update**.

Note   If you don't enter a file extension, Performance Monitor will save the file without one.

If you are ready to begin the monitoring, click on the Start Log button to close the dialog box and begin logging immediately. Or, you can close the dialog box and return to start logging later. When you close the dialog box, notice that the text boxes at the top of the window have changed. **Log File** now shows the path

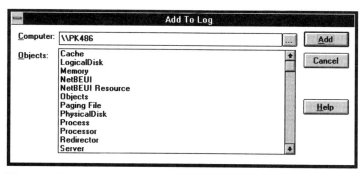

Figure 12.11 The Add To Log dialog box

and filename of the file that is storing the information and **Log Interval** shows the sampling interval you selected. If you have begun logging, **Status** shows Current—if you haven't, it shows Closed. **File Size** shows the current size of the log file—if you are logging a lot of objects, with a short sampling interval, the file can get very large, very quickly.

Note   Until you have selected some objects to log, the Start Log button in the Log Options dialog box is disabled.

Once the logging begins, you won't see a lot happening. You'll notice the File Size incrementing, and you'll also see a picture of a log in the bottom right corner, with a number indicating the file size in MB. But that's it. You are collecting information for future use, not displaying it in any manner.

When you are ready to stop logging, open the Log Options dialog box and click on the **Stop Log** button. You can also use this to simply *pause* logging. You can close the dialog box, then return later and click on **Start Log** to append data to the same log file.

If you want to log different objects, select the **File|New Log Settings**. This clears the objects from the list, but the same path and filename remains in the Log File text box—you can append to this log file, or open another.

Entering Bookmarks

You can enter bookmarks into a log file, so that you can identify events when you come to use the information later. You will be able to use the bookmarks to identify the beginning and end of a significant event.

 While logging, click on the ninth toolbar button or select **Options|Bookmark** (**Ctrl-B**). A small dialog box appears, into which you can type up to 51 characters. Click on OK to place the bookmark in the file.

Using Saved Data

You can use the data in the .LOG file to create a chart, alert list, or report. You can then export that data to another application if you want—a spreadsheet, database, or word processor. To use data in a .LOG file, go to the appropriate window and select **Options|Data From**. You'll see a dialog box that lets you select **Current Activity** (to use "real-time" sampling) or **Log File**. Select Log File and click on the button at the end of the text box. When the Open Input Log File dialog box opens, select the log file, then close both dialog boxes.

Note   If Performance Monitor is creating a file when you select a log file in the Chart, Alert, or Report windows, logging will stop. And selecting Log File in one window stops the monitoring of current activity in the other windows.

Now select the parameters you want to view, using the usual **Edit|Add to Chart** method. The data is added to the chart, alert list, or report. All the data in the file is used, but if you want to specify the time span, select **Edit|Time Window** (**Ctrl-E**) to see the Input Log File Timeframe dialog box (see Figure 12.12). This box lets you define the starting and ending times (and dates) for the data that you want to select. The large gray strip near the top of the dialog box is actually a scroll bar, with a large scroll box at each end. You can drag the boxes along the bar to set the starting and finishing times. If you are working in a chart, you can see gray lines on the chart moving as you move the scroll boxes, showing you which part of the chart you are selecting. (While you can set a time *before* you select parameters if you wish, selecting the parameters *first* will let you see the gray lines on the chart.) Also, if you drag the *middle* of the gray bar, you will be dragging the entire time interval, shifting the start and finish times to the left and right as you move the bar left and right.

  If you set any **Bookmarks** in the log file, you'll see them listed in the bottom half of the dialog box, along with notes showing when you started logging after a

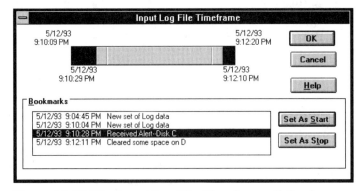

Figure 12.12 The Input Log File Timeframe dialog box

pause. You can select one of these entries at the beginning of an event and click on **Set As Start**, then click on the one at the end and click on **Set As Stop**. This will automatically select the correct times and dates for you. Now close this dialog box, and create your chart, alert list, or report as normal, adding parameters using the Edit|Add To command or the + toolbar button.

If you are creating an **alert list** you can also select the sample interval—click on the last toolbar button and enter the **Interval**. This will affect how many entries will appear in the alert list.

Performance Monitor creates the chart, alert list, or report for you, using the parameters and time scale you selected. It doesn't use a sample interval for the chart or report this time, because it has all the data it needs. In the case of the **chart** it forces all the data into the confines of the chart. For instance, if you selected a two hour time span in the Input Log File Timeframe dialog box, the Graph Time shown in the Values Bar will be 7200 seconds. So the interval used when you created the .LOG file is not relevant now—if you created the file with the interval set to five seconds, there's 1,440 samples in two hours, but all of them are used to create the chart. When you use logged data in a **report**, the report will show the average values over the selected time.

When you use log data like this, logging in the Log window is going to stop. You won't be able to log more data, but you will be able to *relog* data—which we'll explain next. When you want to return to monitoring current data, use the **Options| Data From** command and select the **Current Activity** option button—then go back to the Log window and start over again.

Splitting Log Files (Relogging)

You can extract information from a log file, and place that information in another .LOG file. This is known as *relogging*, and can be used to create smaller, more specific files that you can then export or use to create charts, alerts, and reports, or to add data to a single large archive file.

Start by going to the Log window. If the file that contains the information is *not* displayed in the Log File text box at the top of the window, select **Options|Data From** and find the file you need. Then use the **Edit|Add to Log** (**Ctrl-I**) command or the + toolbar button to open the Add to Log dialog box and select the objects you want to place in the new file. Of course the list will only include those objects that were originally recorded in the file you selected.

When you close the Add to Log dialog box, select **Edit|Time Window** (**Ctrl-E**) and in the Input Log File Timeframe dialog box use the scroll bar or the bookmarks to select a starting and finishing point, as we explained earlier.

 Now, having selected the objects and the time range from which you want to extract information, use the last toolbar button, or the **Options|Log** (**Ctrl-O**) command to open the Log Options dialog box. You'll notice that the Start Log button has been replaced by the **Relog file** button. (This button is disabled until you've selected the objects you want to extract and entered a filename.)

You can either enter a new filename—to create a smaller file containing only the information you are extracting—or name an existing .LOG file to append the information to the end of the file. (You might do this if you are exporting the data to a spreadsheet or database.) When you've selected the file, click on the **Relog file** button and the new file will be created, or the data appended.

Saving and Reusing Settings

If you want to monitor the same data each time you open Performance Monitor, or if you have several different sets of data you monitor periodically, you should create settings files. There are two ways to do this: You can create individual settings files for each window—one for the chart, one for the report, and so on—or you can create a *workspace* settings file, which combines all four windows' settings into one file. The first method is the most flexible, of course, letting you "mix-'n-match" different settings, while the second method is easiest.

To save a window's settings in a separate file—.PMC for a chart, .PMA for an alert list, .PML for a log, and .PMR for a report—open that window and then use the **File|Save Settings** (**Shift-F12**) command to enter a filename. Of course, you can also use the **File|Save As** (**F12**) command to save settings modified from an existing file in a new one.

To save all four windows' settings in a single .PMW file, use the **File|Save Workspace** (**Ctrl-W**) command to enter a filename. This command works as a Save As command—you must *always* select or enter a filename; Performance Monitor won't automatically assume you want to save the settings in the same file, so it will give you the chance to specify another file.

Now, to use any of these settings you can use the **File|Open** (**Ctrl-F12**) command. If you want to open an individual window's settings file, open that window then select the command. That window's settings-file extension will be selected automatically in the File Open dialog box. If you want to open a workspace file, though, you can do so from any of the four windows. Use the **File|Open** command, but then select the **Workspace Files (*.pmw)** entry from the **List Files of Type** drop-down list box in the File Open dialog box.

Of course, you can open a workspace settings file automatically when you open Performance Monitor. Add the name of the .PMW file (include the extension) after PERFMON.EXE in the Program Manager icon's Program Item Properties dialog box. You can't do this with any of the other settings' file types, though. However, if you want to be able to open Performance Monitor with several different settings' profiles, create a separate .PMW file for each configuration, then create an icon for each one.

Exporting Data

You are not limited to using NT's performance data in Performance Monitor. You can create ASCII text files—comma or tab delimited—and then import them into a database, spreadsheet, or word processor.

Each window's data is exported separately. (In the case of the Log window, only the header information—computer name, filename, interval, and the objects in the file—are exported, so to export "real" data you must use one of the other windows.)

First, set up the window from which you want to export. If you want to export logged data, use the Options|Data From command. Add the objects to your chart, alert list, or report. Then use **File|Export** command to see the Export As dialog box. Enter a filename. Microsoft recommends the .CSV extension for files containing comma-delimited text (columns of data separated by commas) and .TSV for files with tab-delimited text. But it really doesn't matter—whatever you select, the export file will be an ASCII file.

Select one of the **Column Delimiter** option buttons, **Tab** or **Comma**. Then click on OK and the file will be saved. You can now open this file in any database, spreadsheet, word processor, or any other kind of application that accepts ASCII files. You could export to a spreadsheet and use the data to create more sophisticated charts, for example, or include the data in a memo you are creating in a word processor.

Tip   A quick way to export a chart, a small alert list, or report is to press Alt-Print Screen, then place the cursor in the other application where you want to position the data and press Ctrl-V. A picture of the window will be pasted into the application. Or you can paste the picture into Paintbrush and edit out the pieces you don't want, then copy and paste to another application.

Customizing the Window

You've seen how to customize each separate window—using the Options dialog boxes—but you can also customize the Performance Monitor window as a whole. Once you've begun monitoring, you may want to remove some of the window components to make more room for the data. You can remove the menu and title bars (press **Ctrl-M** or select **Options|Menu and Title**). There's a quick way to do this—press **Enter** to toggle the menu and title bars on and off, or **double-click** in the workspace—in the middle of the chart or report, for instance, or on the blank gray area near the alert list's and log's text boxes (below the toolbar). Of course, you'll have to use one of these methods to turn the menu and title bars back on once you've removed them. You can still move the window, even when the title bar has gone—just point to the workspace and drag.

You can also remove the toolbar (**Ctrl-T** or **Options|Toolbar**) and status bar (**Ctrl-S** or **Options|Status Bar**). The **Options|Always on Top** (**Ctrl-P**) makes the Performance Monitor window stay above the active window, so it's always visible. Of course, if it's maximized, you won't be able to work in any other application, so you'll have to resize or minimize it (the icon will remain on top).

The Menus and Toolbar

The following is a summary of the Performance Monitor menu options:

File|New *item* Settings

Clears the window of its current settings, removing all parameters, so you can create a new chart, alert, log, or report.

File|Open (Ctrl-F12)

Opens an existing chart, alert, log, or report settings file, or a workspace file that combines all four settings.

File|Save Settings (Shift-F12)

Saves the settings in a .PMC, .PMA, .PML, or .PMR command, so you can use the File| Open command to reuse the settings later.

File|Save Settings As (F12)

Saves the settings in file with a new name.

File|Save Workspace (Ctrl-W)

Saves a .PMW file, which stores all four settings—chart, alert, log, and report—so you can use the File|Open command to reuse the settings later.

File|Exit (Alt-F4)

Closes Performance Monitor.

Edit|Add To *item* (Ctrl-I)

Lets you add a monitoring parameter to a chart, alert, log, or report.

Edit|Edit Chart Line/Alert Entry

Lets you modify the item selected in the legend.

Edit|Time Window (Ctrl-E)

When using data from a log file, lets you select the time span from which the data should come. (This option is disabled until you select a log file using Options|Data From.)

Edit|Clear Display

Lets you clear the data from the chart, alert list, or report, so the monitoring can start again.

Edit|Delete From *item*

Removes the parameter selected in the legend from the chart, alert list, report, or log.

View|Chart (Ctrl-C)

Displays the performance chart, so you can create a line graph or histogram.

View|Alert (Ctrl-A)

Displays the alert window, so you can display a list of alerts, parameters that cross upper and lower limits that you set.

View|Log (Ctrl-L)

Displays the Log window, so you can save sampling data in a .LOG file for later use.

View|Report (Ctrl-R)

Displays the Report window, so you can display a text report of the most recent parameter values.

Options|Chart	Lets you modify options related to the chart, alert window, log, or report.
Options|Menu & Title (Ctrl-M)	Removes the menu bar and title bar. Double-click on the display area (outside text boxes) to replace the bars.
Options|Toolbar (Ctrl-T)	Removes and replaces the toolbar.
Options|Status Bar (Ctrl-S)	Removes and replaces the status bar.
Options|Always on Top (Ctrl-P)	Turns the Always On Top feature on and off. When on, the window or minimized icon is always visible, even if another application is active.
Options|Data From	Lets you use data from a .LOG file to create a chart, alert list, or report.
Options|Update Now (Ctrl-U)	Immediately updates the chart, alert window, log, or report, without waiting for a scheduled update.
Options|Bookmark	Lets you enter a bookmark comment into a log. This command is only available when logging is in progress.

These are the toolbar buttons and the commands they replace:

View\|Chart

View\|Alert

View\|Log

View\|Report

Edit\|Add to *item*

Edit\|Edit Chart Line

Edit\|Delete From *item*

Options\|Update Now

Options\|Bookmark

Options\|Chart/Alert/Log/Report

13

Event Viewer

Windows NT has a system called *event logging* to keep track of important *system, security,* and *application* events. A separate log is created for each type of event, and these logs may be viewed in the Event Viewer application.

System events | Significant events logged by Windows NT system components, such as failures during startup, warnings about disk capacity running low, and print jobs being deleted or purged from a printer.

Security | Events such as logons and logoffs, computer shutdowns, changes to file, print, and security settings, and the use of specific user rights.

Application | Events such as error messages recorded by 32-bit applications running under Windows NT.

When you start NT, the event logging service (EventLog) begins automatically. (You can change this setting so that it will only begin when you manually start it. Use the Control Panel's Services dialog box—see Chapter 6.) System and application events will be logged with no further interaction from you. Security events may be logged if they have been set up correctly in File Manager, User Manager, Print Manager, ClipBook Viewer, and Registry Editor.

Note The Event Viewer can be opened by any user, but only an Administrator can view the Security log information, clear logs of the current data, or save the data in an archive file.

You can use the Event Viewer for a variety of purposes. You'll use it when the system automatically sends you warning messages after booting your computer—you may get messages telling you that your disk drives are almost full, for example. You could set security auditing on a printer so you can see a log of who is using what printer and when. This information can help you configure your network printers correctly. Or you might want to monitor the use of a particular directory to see who is getting into it and when, or watch Registry Editor so you'll know if anyone tries to change the configuration data.

Setting Up Logging

Windows NT doesn't log everything automatically. You have to set things to run correctly first. There are two main procedures—first, make sure that the EventLog service is running, and then turn on security auditing in the applications in which you want to use it.

Services

By default, the EventLog is started automatically when you boot your computer. Go into the Control Panel and open the Services dialog box. Find EventLog in the list of services and look in the Status column to see if it has started. If not, you can start it using the Start button. You can also use the Startup button to open a dialog box that will define what happens to the EventLog when you boot NT—whether it should be automatically started, left turned off but available for a manual start, or disabled (so no user or other service may start EventLog).

Once the EventLog service is running, System logging is automatic. Application logging is also automatic, but it is up to your various programs to use this facility—NT makes it available, but not all programs will bother to place messages in the log (non-NT programs won't use it, of course).

Security logging is not turned on automatically; you must turn it on in the applications you want to log. These are the security events you can log, and how you must turn them on:

User activities, such as logging on and off and using user privileges; turn on using the Policies|Audit command in User Manager. See Chapter 5.

Note   None of the following items will be logged *unless* you use the Policies| Audit command in User Manager to turn on the File and Object Access auditing first.

File and directory access—Turn on the File and Object Access auditing, then go to File Manager and use the Security|Auditing command to specify the type of auditing. See Chapter 7.

Printer use—Turn on the File and Object Access auditing, then go to Print Manager and use the Security|Auditing command to specify the type of auditing.

ClipBook page access—Turn on the File and Object Access auditing, then go to ClipBook Viewer and use the Security|Auditing command to specify the type of auditing.

Configuration Registry changes—Turn on the File and Object Access auditing, then go to Registry Editor and use the Security|Auditing command to specify the type of auditing.

What Will Be Logged?

So exactly what events will be logged? You have no control over **system events**. These are defined internally by NT. Nor have you direct control over **application events**, at least not through Windows NT. Any NT application may be programmed to use NT's event log, so it's up to each program's publisher to decide what will be logged and whether you will have any control over this logging (through the application itself). Some of NT's own applications use application logging, but they don't provide control over what is logged.

You can define the *types* of **security events**, though, with User Manager, File Manager, Print Manager, Registry Editor, and ClipBook Viewer. User Manager simply sets up Auditing, defining which sorts of security auditing should be carried out. In the other applications, though, you specify procedures related to each application, and define *who*—which groups or users—will be audited, and even what object—which file or directory, printer, configuration-registry *key*, or ClipBook *page*. In each case, you select the object you want to monitor, then open the Auditing dialog box (Security|Auditing), and add the names of groups and users to the dialog box. Then, for each group or user, define exactly what you want to audit. (See Chapter 5 for more information about adding groups and users to the Auditing dialog box.)

Note By default, only Administrators have the right to set up auditing. However, other users may be assigned the **Manage auditing and security log** right in User Manager.

User Manager

User Manager

Open User Manager from the Administrative Tools program group in Program Manager. Then select the **Policies|Audit** command to see the Audit Policy dialog box (Figure 13.1).

You can turn off security auditing by selecting the **Do Not Audit Any Events** option button (this is the default). To select the events you want to audit, click on the **Audit These Events** option button and then select from the list. For each event, you can log **Success** and **Failure**. These are the events:

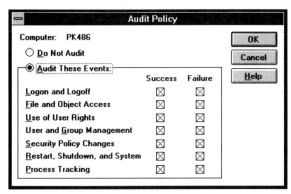

Figure 13.1 User Manager's Audit Policy dialog box

Logon and Logoff	A user tried to log on or off the computer, or make a network connection.
File and Object Access	A user tried to access a directory or file for which auditing has been set in File Manager, access a printer for which auditing is set in Print Manager, or carry out a procedure in ClipBook Viewer or Registry Editor for which auditing is set.
Use of User Rights	A user has tried to use a right assigned in User Manager (excluding logging on and off, which are covered by the first option).
User and Group Management	A user tried to change the computer's user accounts or groups, or change a password.
Security Policy Changes	A user tried to change the User Rights or Security Audit policy in User Manager.
Restart, Shutdown, and System	A user tried to restart or shut down the system, or an event occurred that affects system security or the security log.
Process Tracking	Detailed system-process auditing—events such as programs and processes starting and finishing, and indirect object accesses. This information will only be of use to system developers or for system troubleshooting.

File Manager

File Manager

To control file-security event logging, open File Manager from the Main program group in Program Manager, select the directory or files that you want to watch, and then select the **Security|Auditing** command to see the Directory Auditing dialog box. You can only audit NTFS file partitions, so if you installed NT in an

HPFS or FAT partition, or if you have some non-NTFS partitions, you won't be able to audit those partitions.

These are the events that you can audit (and again, you can monitor both successful and failed attempts):

Read	A user tried to access a directory or read a file (open or copy it).
Write	A user tried to write to a directory or modify a file.
Execute	A user tried to execute a program file.
Delete	A user tried to delete a file or directory.
Change Permissions	A user tried to use the Security|Permissions command to modify a group's or user's file and directory privileges.
Take Ownership	A user tried to take ownership of a file or directory, using the Security|Owner command.

Note Remember that the selections you make here have no effect unless you select File and Object Access in User Manager's Audit Policy dialog box.

Print Manager

Print Manager

To control printer event logging, open Print Manager from the Main program group in Program Manager, select the printer you want to monitor, and then select the **Security\|Auditing** command to see the Printer Auditing dialog box. These are the events that you can monitor:

Print	Printing documents.
Full Control	Changing print-job settings; pausing, restarting, moving, and deleting print jobs; sharing the printer; changing printer properties; deleting the printer; changing printer permissions.
Delete	Deleting print jobs.
Change Permissions	Changing printer permissions.
Take Ownership	Taking ownership.

ClipBook Viewer

ClipBook Viewer

To control ClipBook event logging, open ClipBook Viewer from the Main program group in Program Manager, select the Local ClipBook page you want to monitor, and then select **Security\|Auditing**. These are the events you can monitor:

Read	Copy from the Clipbook page.
Delete	Delete the Clipbook page.
Change Permissions	Change permissions for the page.
Change Audit Types	Change auditing choices for the page.

Registry Editor

Regedt32

Registry Editor lets you monitor who is working in the various configuration registry *keys.* These are the events you can monitor:

Query Value	View a value.
Set Value	Modify a value.
Create Subkey	Create a new subkey.
Enumerate Subkeys	Identify subkeys.
Notify	Notification events.
Create Link	Create symbolic links in subkeys.
Delete	Delete keys.

Note Remember that the selections you make in File Manager, Print Manager, Clip-Book Viewer, and Registry Editor have no effect unless you select File and Object Access in User Manager's Audit Policy dialog box.

Using Event Viewer

If you leave EventLog with its default Services setting, it starts automatically and begins logging during the boot process. It monitors boot up and logon and watches for any problems—devices unable to start, for instance, perhaps because of missing or faulty hardware, a service that hasn't started, or missing files. It also looks for things to warn you about—such as hard disk drives that are almost full. You may even see a message telling you that the Security log is full or that a service failed to start.

You won't necessarily see a message for all events that are logged. If your system appears to be having some kind of problem after booting, open the Event Viewer to see if any messages in there give you an idea of what is going on. For instance, the Event Log may contain messages warning you that your disk drives are almost full, but you won't see a dialog box telling you this.

Also, some of the messages that do appear are not very clear. For instance, if one of your floppy disk drives is not connected correctly, you might get the message "User configuration data does not contain all required information" entered into Event Log.

Date	Time	Source	Category	Event	User	Computer
5/13/93	9:45:59 AM	Serial	None	25	N/A	PK486
5/13/93	9:45:58 AM	EventLog	None	6005	N/A	PK486
5/13/93	9:44:34 AM	EventLog	None	6006	N/A	PK486
5/13/93	9:41:36 AM	Srv	None	2013	N/A	PK486
5/13/93	9:41:36 AM	Srv	None	2013	N/A	PK486
5/13/93	9:41:36 AM	Srv	None	2013	N/A	PK486
5/13/93	9:41:35 AM	Srv	None	2013	N/A	PK486
5/13/93	9:36:28 AM	Serial	None	25	N/A	PK486
5/13/93	9:36:27 AM	EventLog	None	6005	N/A	PK486
5/13/93	9:32:45 AM	EventLog	None	6006	N/A	PK486
5/13/93	7:15:56 AM	Srv	None	2013	N/A	PK486
5/13/93	7:15:56 AM	Srv	None	2013	N/A	PK486
5/13/93	7:15:56 AM	Srv	None	2013	N/A	PK486
5/13/93	7:15:55 AM	Srv	None	2013	N/A	PK486

Event Viewer - System Log on \\PK486

Log   View   Options   Help

Figure 13.2 The Event Viewer window, showing the System Log

Event Viewer

Start the Event Viewer by double-clicking on the Event Viewer icon in Program Manager's Administrative Tools program group. When you first open Event Viewer it will automatically display the system log (see Figure 13.2), but you can select another log if you wish using **Log|Security** or **Log|Application**. (If you are not an Administrator, you won't be able to view the Security log.) Notice that the title bar shows which log is currently displayed (along with the name of the computer with which that log is associated). It's important to understand that the three logs are *separate* logs, because most of the menu commands affect only one log at a time, and if you want to store log data for later use you will have to save each set of data independently.

These are the columns of data that appear in this window:

Date   The date on which the event occurred.

Time   The time at which the event occurred.

Source   The source of the event, the software system that sent the information. This may be the name of an application or the name of a software component such as a device driver. In the case of the Security log, this entry will simply say Security. You can see a list of all the possible sources by selecting the particular log, selecting the View|Filter Events command, and opening the Source dropdown list box.

Category   The type of event that took place. This column usually says None in the System log. In the Security log it might say Object Access, File Access, Logon, Logoff, user of User Rights, or User and Group Management.

Event ID   An ID number provided to a type of event. While this is of no interest to most users, it may be required by a technical support representative, or may be used by software-developers.

User   The name of the user who was working when the event occurred. N/A often appears in the System log, in particular for events that occur during system boot (because there's no user). You may also see SYSTEM in the User column, even when a user *was* involved—when someone deleted a printer, for instance.

Computer   The name of the computer being logged. As you'll see in a moment, you can monitor events on other network computers.

In the left column, next to each event's data, you'll see a small icon that provides a quick indication of the type of event or message. The following examples are from the event *description*, displayed in the Event Detail dialog box, which we'll look at in a moment:

❶ Information Significant but successful events that occur infrequently. For example, "New cartridge has been inserted. From device: \Device\Tape0."

① Warning Warnings of possible future problems. For example, "The F: disk is at or near capacity. You may need to delete some files."

⊛ Error Existing problems. For example, "The following boot or system start driver(s) failed to load: Cdfs_Rec Fat_Rec Ntfs_Rec Scsiflop Sgikbmou."

🔑 Success Audit A successful attempt at a security-audit procedure. For example, "Object Open:

            Object Server: Security
            Object Type: File
            Object Name: E:\TEMP\scs10.tmp"

🔒 Failure Audit An unsuccessful attempt at a security-audit procedure. For example, "Logon Failure: Reason: An unexpected error occurred during logon User Name: billb."

This data is the information stored in the event logs at the time that you opened Event Viewer. The Viewer is not automatically updated with new information while the window is open, unless you select another log. If you want to display new log events, events which occurred since you opened the window, select **View|Refresh** or press **F5**.

Many Event Log messages will be of no interest to many users—messages telling you that a printer is out of paper, for instance, or that a particular document printed, though they may be useful for auditing printer use. Other messages are very useful, though, even to the normal user who doesn't want to track the minutiae of system operation. It's useful to know when your drives are getting close to full, or that certain drivers that you require are not loading for some reason, or that one service could not start because another one hadn't yet started.

Once you've found an event you want to look at, **double-click** on it, or select it and press **Enter**, or select it and choose the **View|Detail** command. You'll see the Event Detail dialog box (see Figure 13.3). The information at the top of this dialog box is the same as the information you saw in the Event Viewer window, with the addition of the **Type** field, which is used instead of the icons we looked at a moment ago (Information, Warning, and so on). In addition, you can see a **Description** of the event. This will often give a more detailed, useful description of what is going on. It's here that you'll see the messages telling you that your hard disk is almost full, that a service failed to start, or that someone opened a file.

In some cases you'll see related **Data**—hexadecimal program code. You can display this data in **Bytes** (each line shows a byte of data) or **Words** (each line shows Dword data, information structured into 4-byte pieces). Again, this information is of no direct use to the average NT user, but may be useful to system developers or even occasionally requested by technical-support personnel.

Finally, notice that this dialog box has **Previous** and **Next** buttons. Click on Previous to display the data from the event above the current one in this list, or click on Next to display data from the event below the current one. These buttons provide a quick way to read the event messages that occurred during a boot, for instance. They refer to the previous or next *in the list*, not chronologically, so if you have selected View|Newest First (explained in a moment), Previous moves to the event immediately *after* the current one (up the list), while Next moves to the event that occurred immediately *before* the current one.

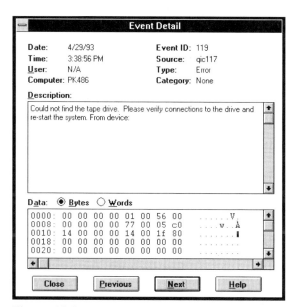

Figure 13.3 The Event Detail dialog box

Arranging the Data

You have several options for modifying the manner in which the data is displayed in the window. By default the first option on the View menu (**View|All Events**) is selected, but you can select specific event types. Begin by selecting the **View|Filter Events** option to display the Filter dialog box (Figure 13.4).

Your first options are related to the date of the events. By default the **View From** area is set to **First Event**, and the **View Through** area is set to **Last Event**— meaning that all events from the oldest in the log through to the most recent are displayed. But you can enter View From and View Through dates and times using the incrementer boxes, to specify the interval in which you are interested. There is no need to select the **Events On** option buttons, since they are selected automatically as soon as you change the dates and times.

You can also select the **Types** of events you want to see by selecting the check boxes. The types are indicated in the log by the icons we saw earlier: Information, Warning, Error, Success Audit, and Failure Audit. Use the **Source** drop-down list box to select the systems from which you want to see messages, and select from the **Category** drop-down list box—though in some cases you won't have any options except All in this list box.

You can also enter the **User** name, **Computer**, and even **Event ID**, if you wish, to further define the logged events you want to see. Notice the **Clear** button in this dialog box. You can use this to set everything back to the defaults, which is the equivalent of selecting View|All Events.

Having defined which events will be displayed, you can now select the order. They are always displayed chronologically, but you can have the most recent at the top (**View|Newest First**) or at the bottom (**View|Oldest First**).

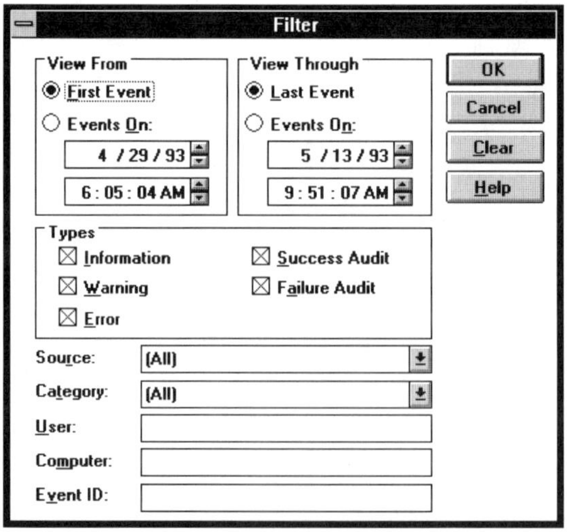

Figure 13.4 The Filter dialog box

You can search through the displayed events for a particular event using the **View|Find** command (**F3**). This displays a dialog box similar to the Filter dialog box, except that there are no date settings. You can select in which direction you want to search by using the **Up** and **Down** option buttons, and there is a **Description** field. This field lets you search for information saved in the Event Detail dialog box's Description text box.

Setting Event Viewer Preferences

To configure Event Viewer's "preferences," select **Log|Log Settings**. You'll see the dialog box shown in Figure 13.5. Remember, we told you that each log is a separate entity, and you can define settings for each one individually. Begin by selecting the log you want to change from the **Change Settings For** drop-down list box. Next, select the **Maximum Log Size**, in Kbytes. This defines how many events can be stored. The default is 512 Kbytes, which will store well over 2000 events. That's a lot for the System and Application logs, although the Security log can easily fill up in a day or two, depending on what you are logging and what is being done on the computer. If you enter a size that is *smaller* than the file currently used to save log data, that setting has no effect until you have cleared the log—Event Viewer won't automatically throw out data to reduce the file size.

Now you can define the **Event Log Wrapping**, which determines how—or if—the data in the log should be overwritten. If you select **Overwrite Events As Needed**, as soon as the logging system runs out of space in the event-log file, the oldest events will be overwritten by the newest—and you won't be informed. If you select **Overwrite Events Older Than**, you can enter the number of days you want to store the events for. If the log fills up it can remove log events older than this age, but no younger. So if the log fills up very quickly—sooner than the events age beyond the limit—it won't be able to overwrite any events. The system will display a message telling you that the log is full, and you will have to clear it.

The **Do Not Overwrite Events (Clear Log Manually)** option is similar—if the log fills up you will be informed, so that you can save the data and clear the log.

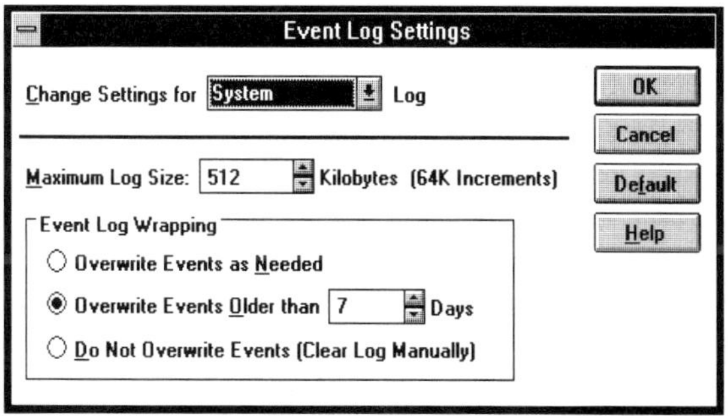

Figure 13.5 The Event Log Settings dialog box

Saving Data

The current log data is saved in three files: AppEvent.EVT, SecEvent.EVT, and SysEvent.EVT. These files are stored in the WINNT\SYSTEM32\CONFIG directory. As you've just seen, these log files can be filled with data, at which point you'll have to decide what to do with the information. You can save log data for future use if you wish. Select **Log|Save As**. You'll see a normal File Save dialog box—select a directory and enter a name for the file.

Note   Remember, you are saving data only from the log currently displayed in the window. If the title bar says "Event Viewer - Security Log" when you use the Log|Save As command, you are only saving the Security log data. If you need to save the system and application data, you must display each log and use the Log|Save As command each time.

You have three formats to choose from (see the **Save File as Type** drop-down list box)—you can save the file as an **.EVT** file, which you can open in Event Viewer later. Or select one of the **ASCII .TXT** options—Text Files or Comma Delimited Text Files. The first file type uses tabs to line up the data so you can import it into a word processor. The second file type uses commas to separate "fields" so you can import it into a database or spreadsheet. The first type is *not* a "tab-delimited file," though, because the tabs are used to line up data in columns, not to differentiate fields—tabs appear *within* fields as well as between.

Exporting an ASCII file lets you include event data in other documents—memos, email, reports—and create charts and databases. The Data information that is seen in the Event Detail dialog box is discarded when you create an ASCII file. The fields in the ASCII file are in this order: Date, Time, Source, Type, Category, Event ID, User, Computer, Description.

To open data from an archived log file in Event Viewer, select **Log|Open**. Use the Open dialog box in the normal way to select and open the file. You will then see a dialog box with three option buttons, asking you what the log-file type is, System, Security, or Application. Event Viewer needs this information so that it can enter the correct Description into the Event Details dialog box. Most of this description isn't saved with each entry in the Event Log, rather it is displayed as and when it is needed, depending on the Event code. So if Event Viewer thinks a Security log is, say, an Application log, it won't know which description to use (it would display a message telling you that the description can't be found).

Just click on the option button and click on OK to open the file. You'll notice that the title bar changes to show the name of the file you've just opened. You'll also notice, if you open the Log menu, that there is no longer a check mark against any of the three log types. To remove this archived file and display one of the three current log files, just select one from the Log menu. (To replace the log file you'll have to use the Log|Open command again.)

Clearing Logs

If you don't use the overwrite options we looked at earlier, or if you use the Over-write Events Older Than option but the log fills up before the events age beyond the limit, eventually you will be forced to clear the logs. You must log in as an Administrator to do this.

First, display the log you want to clear, and select the **Log|Clear All Events** command. You'll see a message box asking if you want to save the log first. Click on Yes and the Save As dialog box appears, letting you save the data in an .EVT or .TXT file. Click on No, however, and you'll see another message box warning you that you will permanently lose all the information in the event log. Click on Yes to continue—and discard the data—or on No to cancel the operation.

Again, using the Clear All Events command only clears events in the displayed log. To clear data in all three you must select each one in turn.

Logging Another Computer

You can log events on a computer somewhere else on the network. (That computer must have the EventLog service running.) Select **Log|Select Computer** to see a typical Select Computer dialog box. You can select the computer from the list, or type its name in the Computer text box—make sure you precede the name with \\.

The Menu Options

These are Event Viewer's menu options:

Log|System	Displays the system events in the Event Viewer window.
Log|Security	Displays the security events in the Event Viewer window.
Log|Application	Displays the application events in the Event Viewer window.
Log|Open	Opens an archived event-log file.
Log|Save As	Lets you save the current information in an archive file.
Log|Clear All Events	Removes all events from the displayed log. You will have the chance of saving the data first.
Log|Log Settings	Determines how the log will operate—the size of the log file, whether or not to over-write logged events, and, if overwriting, how long to save events before doing so.

Log|Select Computer	Lets you select another computer on the network to log.
Log|Exit	Closes Event Viewer.
View|All Events	Displays all the events logged.
View|Filter Events	Lets you select the events logged by entering various filtering criteria.
View|Newest First	Displays the events with the newest at the top of the window, the oldest at the bottom.
View|Oldest First	Displays the events with the oldest at the top of the window, the newest at the bottom.
View|Find (F3)	Lets you search for a specific event.
View|Detail (Enter)	Displays detailed information about the selected event.
View|Refresh (F5)	Updates the log immediately. (Otherwise the window only displays information logged up to the time that you opened Event Viewer or selected another log.)
Options|Low Speed Connection	Select if watching events on a network to which you are connected by a low-speed method, such as a modem.
Options|Save Settings on Exit	Saves the window size and position; the View|Filter and View|Find criteria; the chronological order (Newest First or Oldest First), the type of log displayed (system, security, or application), and the Low Speed Connection setting.

14

Disk Administrator

Disk Administrator is NT's version of disk-management tools such as DOS's FDISK. It has a few tools that are not present in DOS, however, such as the ability to create *stripe sets*, to assign drive letters to drives and partitions, and the ability to save and restore a description of your disk configuration.

Note You can only use Disk Administrator if you are an administrator.

Disk Administrator

Open Disk Administrator by double-clicking on the icon in the Administrative Tools program group. The first time you run this, and every time you run it after changing your disk configuration, you'll see a dialog box telling you that Disk Administrator has to update your system configuration. Click on OK and within a moment or two you'll see the Disk Administrator. Figure 14.1 shows the Disk Administrator window. You'll notice that each of your disks is listed, starting with Disk 0 at the top of the window. For each disk, Disk Administrator shows each disk partition in a separate box, the size of which indicates the relative size of the partitions (though you can change this with the Options|Region Displays command).

Notice also that each drive partition has a color and pattern in a bar at the top of its block. This is to help you quickly identify the type of partition, and the legend near the bottom of the Disk Administrator window will show you what each color and pattern indicates (again, you can change these, using the Options|Colors and Patterns command). Within each partition you'll see the assigned drive letter, the volume label, if any, the file-system type (NTFS, FAT, or HPFS), and the size of the partition. Finally, there's a status bar at the bottom, which shows information about the selected partition.

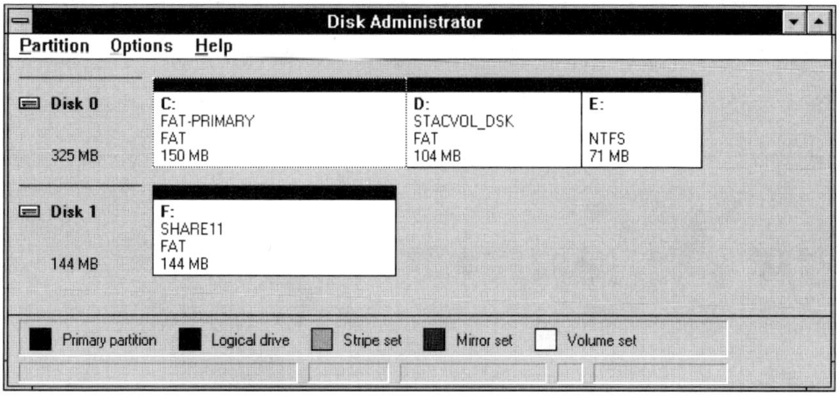

Figure 14.1 The Disk Administrator window

Deleting a Partition

To delete a disk partition, select the partition and then select **Partition|Delete**. Disk Administrator will warn you that you are going to lose all your data. Click on OK and the partition is removed—the box in Disk Administrator will now be shown with gray crosshatching, and the words Free Space appear above the disk size, inside the box.

Configuring a Disk

When you want to set up a disk for use with NT—perhaps a new disk or a disk on which you have removed all the partitions—you can create either primary or extended partitions. A *primary* partition is one that may be marked as the disk volume that will be used by the operating system, and is given a disk letter. The primary partition stores the operating system's system files, and can be used as a boot drive, the drive that will start the operating system. An *extended* partition is an area that may be subdivided into *logical disk drives*. The extended partition itself won't have a disk-drive letter, but the logical drives within it will. NT will always reserve at least one MB for a primary partition, though, so if you create only extended partitions you will lose that MB.

You can create four primary partitions, or three primary partitions and an extended partition, or one extended partition. You can't create more than one extended partition, and if you plan to use this disk as a FAT disk (the MS-DOS file system), you should only create one partition—DOS doesn't like disks with multiple primary partitions.

Note   You can only create *one* partition on a removable disk, such as a Bernoulli disk.

Creating a Primary Partition

To create a primary partition, click on the gray crosshatched area that represents the unformatted disk drive., and select **Partition|Create**. You'll see the dialog box shown in Figure 14.2. This shows you the smallest and largest size partition you can create, and the incrementer box will show the largest size. If you only want one partition on the drive, click on OK and you'll use all the space for the primary partition. Otherwise, enter a different size into the incrementer and click on OK.

Disk Administrator will indicate the size of the drive you are creating by removing the gray crosshatch, giving the disk a drive letter, and putting a bar across the top of the box using the Primary Partition color. You haven't actually done anything to the disk, yet—that won't happen until you close Disk Administrator.

Creating an Extended Partition

If you want more than one partition on your disk, you'll probably want to create an extended partition with the rest of the disk space. (You can't create extended partitions on removable-disk drives.) You could create more primary partitions if you are going to make this an NTFS disk, but not if it will be a FAT disk.

To create an extended partition, click on the gray crosshatched area and select **Partition|Create Extended**. You'll see the same dialog box you used when creating a primary partition. Select the partition size and click on OK.

Note You can only create one extended partition, so you'll probably want to use all the remaining free space. If you don't, you won't be able to use the remaining free space unless you create a *primary* partition in it.

When you create the primary partition you may wonder for a moment if anything has happened. The disk space looks the same as free space—visually, the only difference is that Disk Administrator has swapped the crosshatching. Extended

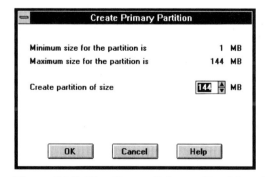

Figure 14.2 The Create Primary Partition dialog box

partitions are shown with diagonal lines running from top left to bottom right, while free space runs from top right to bottom left.

Creating Logical Drives

Now that you have an extended partition, you can add logical drives. Select the partition and select **Partition|Create**. Again, you'll see the same dialog box. Select the size of the drive and click on OK. You can add several logical drives. You may want to create several to help you organize your program and data files, in the same way you use directories and subdirectories within a drive to organize files.

Creating and Extending Volume Sets

A *volume set* is a *logical* disk drive made up of free space on one or more disk drives—up to 32 separate drives. NT can combine this free space into what appears to be a single drive. MS-DOS won't be able to recognize this drive, but NT will. (A disk drive or partition is known as a *volume.* Several joined together are, therefore, a volume *set.*)

Begin by clicking on the first area of free space that you want to include in the volume set. Then press and hold the **Ctrl** key, and click on the next area. Keep holding Ctrl while you click on each area of free space in turn. Now that you have all the areas selected, choose the **Partition|Create Volume Set** command. Enter the size of the volume set you want—or better yet, accept the maximum size— and click on OK. If you enter a value less than the full size, NT will have to apportion the remaining free space equally among the drives.

NT will assign a disk-drive letter to this volume set—each part of the volume, on the various disks, will have the same drive letter. To indicate the components of a volume set, Disk Administrator uses a bright yellow band. Your applications and File Manager will see the volume as a single drive, and will use it as such.

You can *extend* a volume set—add more free space to the disk—or even take a normal disk partition and add free space to it, thereby creating a volume set. Select the areas of free space, and the existing partition if necessary, and then select **Partition|Extend Volume Set**. (You can't include the *system partition*—the primary partition that contains the boot files—in a volume set.)

How, then, to remove a volume set? You would have to select the volume set and use the **Partition|Delete** command. Of course, you will lose data when you use this command, so you should back up all your files first.

Creating Stripe Sets

A *stripe set* is similar to a volume set, but has very particular requirements. While volume sets can use more than one partition on a single disk, a stripe set must get its blocks of free space from *different* disks. And each partition will be created about the same size—if you enter a value that cannot be equally divided, Disk Administrator will modify it, selecting a close value that can be divided. Stripe sets work in a very different way, also. Volume sets are used as you might imagine—think of each component part of a volume set being placed on top of the last component. As you place data in the volume set, the components at the bottom are filled first—the more data you place in the volume-set "disk," the "higher" up the set you go. But stripe sets *don't* work like this at all.

As the name might suggest, NT will write data in "stripes" across the various component partitions. The first stripe is on one partition, the next on another partition, and so on, through the entire set and back to the original. So rather than storing data in contiguous blocks, NT will spread it across the stripe set, storing a bit here, a bit there. As with volume sets, MS-DOS programs will not be able to read data on a stripe set.

Stripe sets are created in the same way that you create volume sets, except that you select the **Partition|Create Stripe Set**. Stripe sets are also removed using the Partition|Delete command.

Completing Your Changes

All the changes you make while working in Disk Administrator are simply plans—you haven't yet actually done anything to the disks you worked on. When you close Disk Administrator you'll see a message asking if you want to save the changes. Then you'll see a dialog box telling you that you must restart NT. You won't have any options—there's only an OK button in this box. However, you can go and work in other applications and click on the OK button later—the dialog box will remain "on top," but you can push it off to one side if you wish.

Formatting the Disk

You still haven't finished yet. When you reboot NT you must then format the new partitions. Open the Command Prompt window by double-clicking on the icon in the Main program group. At the prompt, type:

```
Format driveletter:system /V:label
```

For instance, to format an NTFS volume with the label NTFS2 and the drive letter F:, type `Format F:NTFS /V:NTFS2` and press Enter.

The format may be NTFS, FAT, or HPFS. The label is the volume label that appears in File Manager's document window, in brackets, when the contents of the drive is displayed. You can see more information about this command by typing `format /?` and pressing Enter, or by using the Command Reference (double-click on the Windows NT Help icon in Program Manager, then on the Command Reference button in the Contents page).

If you have been working on a removable disk, you can use File Manager's Disk|Format Disk command to format it in FAT. Just select the command, select the disk drive, and click OK.

Assigning Drive Letters

Disk Administrator lets you override the default drive letters and assign your own "static" letters. This forces NT to reserve that drive letter for the selected drive, and not to reassign it to another drive when you add or remove drives.

As in MS-DOS, NT normally selects drive letters for each drive. The first two drives, A: and B:, are your floppy drives. The first primary partition in the first disk drive is C:, the next primary partition is O:, and so on. After all the primary partitions have been given drive letters, the logical drives are given letters in sequence also, followed by removable-media drives (such as CD-ROM drives, Floptical, and Bernoulli drives) and network drives.

Using the **Partition|Drive Letter** command overrides these assignments, and forces NT to use the letter you assign. (You can only assign drive letters to fixed hard disks, not to removable hard disks.) Click on the volume box and then click select Partition|Drive Letter. You'll see a dialog box with two options. You can select **Assign drive letter** and then select the letter you want to use from the drop-down list box—any letter from C to Z, or you can select **Do not assign drive letter**. If you select this second option you are not disabling the disk drive—instead, you are telling NT to select the drive letter for you. (When you close the dialog box the volume box won't show a drive letter, but after rebooting NT will assign a letter.)

You are limited to 24 disk volumes (you can have more volumes, but NT won't be able to use them). This limit includes network drives.

Marking a Volume as Active

On IBM-compatible PCs, one volume must be marked as *active*. This volume is the one which contains the files needed to boot the operating system, so it must be a primary partition. Usually volume C will be the active volume—look closely and you'll see a small asterisk in the color bar of the C-volume box. (With the default color this asterisk is difficult to see.)

You could use another operating system by marking its system partition as active. Select the volume and then select **Partition|Mark Active**.

Saving and Restoring Configurations

You can save—and later restore—information about your disk drives. This information is stored on a floppy disk, another Emergency Repair disk, if you like. (The Emergency Repair disk was created when you installed NT.)

Select **Partition|Configuration|Save**. You'll see a message telling you to place the disk in drive A:, and telling you that this procedure will save information about drive letters, volume sets, and mirrors. Place the disk in the drive and click on OK, and NT saves the data.

If you ever have a problem you can restore the data from the floppy, using the **Partition|Configuration|Restore** command. After restoring the data from the disk (only one set of data can be stored on a floppy disk, in a file called SYSTEM.), Disk Administrator will tell you to shut down the system.

You can also restore a configuration from another NT installation on your hard disk. Use the **Partition|Configuration|Search** command.

Customizing Disk Administrator

You have a couple of ways to customize Disk Administrator. First, you might want to change the colors. In particular, you might want to change the color used for the primary partition, because it's so dark that you can't see the asterisk used to denote the active partition.

Change colors by selecting **Options|Colors and Patterns**. You'll see the dialog box in Figure 14.3. For each type of "drive"—primary partition, logical drive, stripe set, mirror set, and volume set—you can select a **Color** and **Pattern**. Pick the drive type from the drop-down list box, select the color and pattern, then select the next drive type. Click on OK when you've finished.

You can also modify the way in which Disk Administrator assigns space to the boxes used to denote volume size. Select **Options|Region Display**. You'll see the dialog box in Figure 14.4. Select which disk you want to modify from the drop-down list box, then click on one of the option buttons. You can **Size regions based on actual size**—so the volume boxes look proportionally correct (a 100 MB drive will appear to be twice the size of a 50 MB drive). You can **Size all regions equally**—so that each volume box is the same size, regardless of the disk size. Or you can **Let Disk Administrator decide how to size regions**—in many cases this option looks the same as the Size regions based on actual size option,

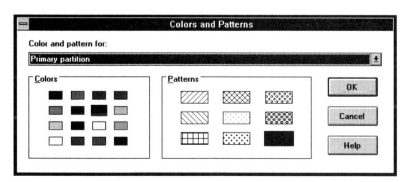

Figure 14.3 The Colors and Patterns dialog box

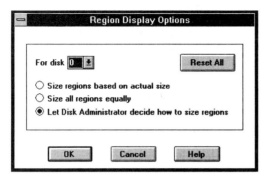

Figure 14.4 The Region Display Options dialog box

but if you have several disks with great variation in size (on 10 MB and one 300 MB, for instance), Disk Administrator may decide not to size them proportionally. The **Reset All** button tells Disk Administrator to determine sizing for *all* the disks.

You can also use the **Options|Status Bar** and **Options|Legend** to turn those two window components on and off. The Status bar is redundant anyway, it shows the same information that can be seen in the selected volume box. The legend, just above the status bar, shows the colors and patterns used to denote the different disk volume types, and you may not need this.

Mirror Sets and Windows NT Advanced Server

Microsoft is selling a product called Windows NT Advanced Server, a "superset" of NT features designed for advanced networking. The Disk Administrator in Windows NT Advanced Server has another feature—*disk mirroring*. This is a procedure in which you set up one disk as a mirror of another. Whenever an application writes a file on one disk, the mirror disk is updated at the same time. This is sometimes used in networks as an additional security measure—if the original disk is damaged, and the data unreachable, the mirror disk is still available.

This will probably never concern you, unless you use NT Advanced Server. NT won't recognize mirror sets initially, but you can modify the disks that were originally combined into mirror sets by NT Advanced Server. Should you ever have to take a disk from an NT Advanced Server to an NT workstation, first save the configuration data on a floppy disk in NT Advanced Server. Then restore the configuration using NT Disk Administrator's **Partition|Configuration|Restore** command. You can then assign the individual drive letters, or delete the volumes and repartition.

NT Advanced Server supports *parity striping,* also known as *RAID5.* This is a more advanced form of striping than that available in NT itself. As in NT, partitions on different disk drives are used to create one "logical" drive. But in parity striping parity checks are used so that if one area fails, the logical drive can automatically recover.

The Menu Options

These are the Disk Administrator menu options:

Partition|Create	Lets you create a *primary* partition from unused space on a disk drive, or create a *logical* drive from the selected extended partition.
Partition|Create Extended	Lets you create an extended partition.
Partition|Delete	Lets you delete a disk partition, as long as it is not the active partition on disk 0, or the partition containing the Windows NT program files.
Partition|Create Volume Set	Combines areas of free space on one or more disks to create a single "logical" drive.
Partition|Extend Volume Set	Adds areas of free space to an existing volume set, or combines a disk partition with free space to create a volume set.
Partition|Create Stripe Set	Combines areas of free space on two or more disks to create a single "logical" drive. Data on a stripe set is spread across the component areas in stripes.
Partition|Mark Active	Marks the selected primary partition as the active volume, the one containing the files needed to boot the operating system.
Partition|Drive Letter	Lets you select a partition's drive letter, overriding NT's selection.
Partition|Configuration|Save	Saves the disk-configuration information on a floppy disk.
Partition|Configuration|Restore	Restores the disk-configuration information from a floppy disk.
Partition|Configuration|Search	Searches your hard disk for another NT installation, and restores the disk configuration from that installation.
Partition|Exit	Closes Disk Administrator.
Options|Status Bar	Turns the status bar at the bottom of the window on and off.
Options|Legend	Turns the legend, just above the status bar, on and off.
Options|Colors and Patterns	Lets you select colors and patterns for the different types of drives and partitions.
Options|Region Displays	Lets you adjust the size of the blocks denoting logical drives.

15

Managing Your Network

Windows NT has many built-in networking features, unlike other operating systems. Network software has to be "imposed" on DOS, for instance, often leading to conflicts with other programs. NT's networking software is an inherent part of the operating system, so it works smoothly and without causing problems with your applications. Microsoft intended NT to work with many different networks, and to do so easily.

NT's networking can be seen as two different sets of features: as *server* features, and as *workstation* features. Server features are those that make your computer's resources available to other computers—disk space, existing files and programs, printers, and so on. Workstation features are those that let you use other computers' resources. You can set up an NT machine as a dedicated server. That is, the sole purpose of the computer is to provide resources to other machines, in what is known as a *dedicated-server network*. Or you can use your computer as a workstation, using other computer's resources, but not letting other computers access yours. Or you can combine the two functions, using resources on other machines and letting other machines use yours. This form of networking is sometimes called *distributed networking*. NT is also designed to integrate with another Microsoft Product, Windows NT Advanced Server, in a system known as *domain-administered networking*. Such systems use one or more computers as domain *controllers*, controlling functions such as logging and the creation of user accounts for all the computers in their particular domains (groups). Once a user logs onto a domain, he can access resources throughout the domain, without having to log on to each computer individually.

Windows NT lets you define *which* resources will be available. You can set up your machine as a workstation, and only allow very minimal resource sharing, limiting other users to only those directories that they really need, for instance.

Note If you've been using Windows for Workgroups, you can use the same hardware in Windows NT. You'll install the EtherExpress-16 LAN driver that comes with Windows NT. You will also find that many of the features you are used to in Windows for Workgroups are also available in Windows NT.

You can connect a Windows NT workstation to other existing networks. If your company has a Microsoft LAN Manager or a Novell Netware network, for instance, you can connect an NT workstation to that network, even if the other workstations are not running NT.

Installing Your Network

Once you've installed a network-adapter card in your computer, you need to install the drivers and other software components that let your computer communicate on the network. You may have already done this during the NT installation procedure (see Chapter 3). To install network software later, use the Control Panel.

Network

Double-click on the Control Panel's Networks icon. In Windows 3.1 the Networks dialog box that appears when you click on the Networks icon varies depending on the network you are working with. In Windows NT, however, networking is integrated, so the **Networks Settings** dialog box is always the same.

Note Only Administrators can make changes to the network configuration.

At the top of the Networks dialog box (Figure 15.1) you'll see the **Computer Name**, the name by which your computer is identified on the network. You originally entered this when you installed NT, but you can change it now by clicking on the **Change** button and entering a new name into the Computer Name dialog box.

You'll also see the **Workgroup** or **Domain**. A *workgroup* is a grouping of users who have the same or similar user profile. Each user will have access to the same printers, servers, and other system resources. For example, one workgroup might be set up for the accounting department, another for documentation, and so on. If you want to connect to a Windows for Workgroups network, for instance, your computer must be a member of a workgroup. A *domain* is also a group of like users, but in domain-based networks—such as LAN Manager or Windows NT Advanced Server—the domain is much more significant than a simple workgroup. Computers in a domain share many more functions and characteristics than computers in a workgroup. A domain can be controlled from one computer, with all logons being monitored from that location, for example. In fact, a domain may even contain several workgroups. You can modify the workgroup or

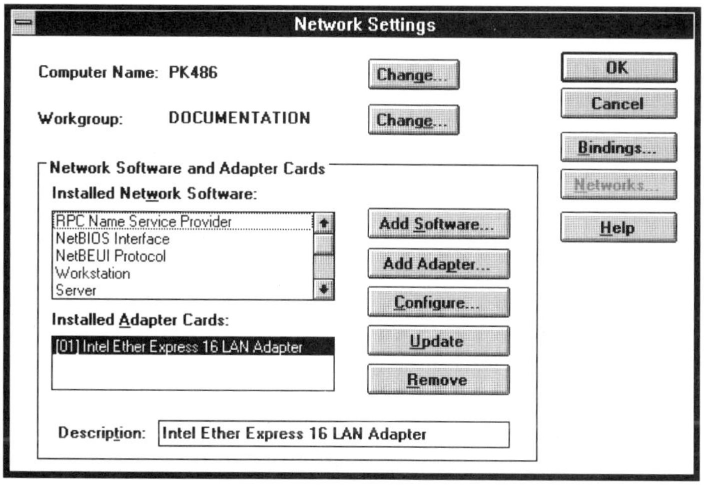

Figure 15.1 The Network Settings dialog box

domain name by clicking on the **Change** button. We'll come back to that, though, because in order to join a domain (though not a workgroup) you must load your network software first.

Installing Network Software

The **Network Software and Adapter Cards** area of this dialog box, is where you will install and configure the software required to operate on the network. On the left you can see the **Installed Network Software** and **Installed Adapter Cards**. The first is software that is required for NT to operate on the network, the second is software to interface NT with the particular network-adapter card that has been installed.

When you install an adapter card and connect to the network, come to this dialog box and click on the **Add Software** button. You'll see a dialog box with a drop-down list box, listing various network-software components, such as TCP/IP Protocol, DLC (Data Link Control) Protocol, FTP Server, and SNMP Service. Your network manufacturer should be able to tell you which components you will need. (The Other option, at the end of the list, lets you install software from a manufacturer's disk.)

If you are going to use Windows for Workgroups, for instance, you need the following software:

> Microsoft NetBEUI
>
> Windows Server
>
> Windows Workstation

Check the Installed Network Software list in the Network Settings dialog box—these components may already be installed.

Select the option you need, then click on OK. NT displays a dialog box telling you to enter the path to the NT distribution disks. Enter the drive letter of the CD-ROM drive or the floppy drive.

When you click on OK, NT looks for the drivers. If you are using a CD, it will be able to find them. If you are using floppies it won't, so it will tell you which of the Setup disks to place in the disk drive. Do so and click on OK to continue. You may have to use this dialog box several times to load each of the software components you need.

You'll use the same procedure to install the driver for the adapter card. Click on the **Add Adapter** button this time. You'll be able to select one of the dozen or so drivers included with NT, or select Other to install one provided by the manufacturer. Incidentally, if you are using a Windows for Workgroups adapter—the adapter that is provided in some of the Microsoft Windows for Workgroups kits—you'll use the Intel EtherExpress 16 LAN Adapter driver.

If you ever need to install an upgraded driver, select the item in the **Installed Network Software** or **Installed Adapter** list box, then click on the **Update** button. NT will ask where to look for the OEMSETUP.INF file—drivers provided by manufacturers must always come with this OEMSETUP.INF file, which lists the drivers on the disk and tells NT which files to install.

If you want to remove network software or an adapter card, select the item from the appropriate list, click on **Remove**, and follow the instructions in the dialog box that appears. Removing a component does not actually remove the files from your hard disk, it simply removes the information from the configuration register.

Modifying Network Search Order

NT lets you work with several networks at once. You can install all the necessary software, and then provide a "search order," the order in which NT will search the networks for a particular resource.

Click on the **Networks** button to see the Network Provider Search Order. You'll see a list of networks, in the order in which they will be accessed. If you want to move one, select it and then use the **Up** or **Down** button to shift its position.

Configuring Software Components

Some of the components you have installed may need configuration information. For instance, the following components can be configured:

RPC Name Service Provider	The name of the provider (Windows NT Locator or DCE Cell Directory Service), and, if using the second provider, the Network Address.
NetBIOS Interface	Network Route and Lana number.

NetBEUI Protocol	Memory allocation (minimize memory, balance, maximize throughput and connections).
Server	Memory allocation and Browser broadcasts to LAN Manager 2.x clients.
Adapter board	IRQ level, I/O Port Address, transceiver type, memory mapping, etc, depending on the type of adapter board.

You can normally forget about all of these except the adapter board settings, which must match the board you installed. (See the board's documentation.)

If you *do* need to change configuration data, select the item and then click on the **Configure** button.

Joining a Domain or Workgroup

To join a domain or workgroup, click on the **Change** button next to the Domain or Workgroup name at the top of the dialog box. You'll see the Domain/Workgroup Settings dialog box (Figure 15.2).

To join a workgroup, type the name of the group into the **Workgroup** text box. This can be an existing group or a name that will be used by a workgroup later—something such as *Documentation, Accounting, Managers,* or whatever you choose. The name can be up to 15 characters long, but mustn't include these characters:

, . " < > * + = \ | ?

The workgroup name is used by NT to connect to other computers. In File Manager, for instance, when you use the Connect Network Drive command, NT looks for workgroups of which your computer is a member. If it can't find a group with the same name, you may still be able to connect to another computer (depending on the network type), as long as you know the computer's name and the path of the shared directory.

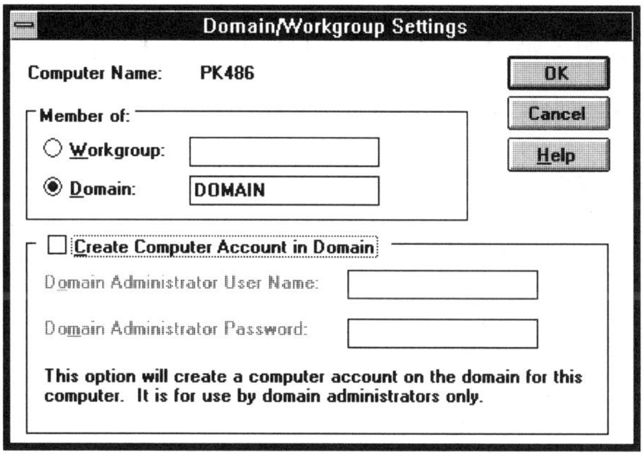

Figure 15.2 The Domain/Workgroup Settings dialog box

To join a network domain, you must either make sure that your computer has an account on an existing domain—because as soon as you close the dialog box Windows NT will try to link to that domain—or you must be a domain administrator.

The network administrator can give you the domain name and make sure your computer has an account. (Make sure the Computer Name at the top matches the account name your network administrator uses.) Select the **Domain Name** option button and type the name of the domain.

If you are the domain administrator you can use a Computer Name that has not yet been added to the domain. Then click on the **Create Computer Account in Domain** check box, and enter your **Administrator Name** and **Administrator Password**. When you click on OK the computer will be added to the domain.

Viewing Network Bindings

The **Bindings** button in the Networks dialog box lets you assign network bindings, to assign components to the various software *layers* used in networking. NT automatically binds all the network components to allow for use in any circumstance, but if your computer has more than one adapter installed, or if you very rarely use the network, you can "disconnect" or "unbind" the bindings to save memory. However, unless you've got a reasonable idea about what should be bound to what—or you are willing to live with the consequences—you shouldn't make any changes in this dialog box.

The Network Bindings dialog box (see Figure 15.3) shows the connections between levels. By default, the **Show Bindings for** drop-down list box displays <**All Components**>, though you can select the specific component in which you are interested. The table shows the actual bindings. For instance, you might see *Workstation->NetBEUI Protocol->Intel EtherExpress-16LAN Driver->[01]Intel EtherExpress-16LAN Adapter*. (This won't all fit in the table, so you have to use the horizontal scroll bar to move through the list.) The light bulb in the left column shows whether the binding is enabled or not—it *is* if the light bulb is yellow, with "glare dots" around it. If the bulb is gray, without the dots, it's disabled. If it's difficult to

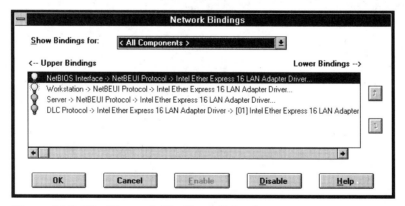

Figure 15.3 The Network Bindings dialog box

see this on your monitor, look at the buttons at the bottom of the dialog box. If the **Disable** button is available, the highlighted binding is, of course, enabled.

You can change the state with the **Disable** and **Enable** buttons, or you can **double-click** on the line in the list. But remember that disabling these will, of course, disable the network itself. When you close the Networks dialog box NT will tell you that you must restart, and when you log back on, the services you disabled will no longer be available. Of course this is a simple way to stop all other computers from accessing your resources—disable Windows Server, but leave Windows Workstation enabled, and you'll still be able to use the network, but everyone else will be locked out of your system.

If your computer has more than one network protocol, you can also modify the binding order. In the list box select the path you want to move, and then click on the buttons on the right side of the list box to move it up and down.

Acting as a Server

In order to make your computer act as a server—whether you want it to be a dedicated server, or to be used as both server and workstation—several conditions must be met. First, you must make sure that the **Server** has started. This will probably be set up to start automatically each time you start Windows NT, but you can quickly confirm that it has started.

Services

Go to the **Control Panel** and double-click on the **Services** icon. The Services dialog box (see Figure 15.4) will show you the status of each service. The word *Started* should appear in the Server status column. You can start the service by selecting it and clicking on **Start**. Notice also the **Startup** column; if this shows Manual for a service you want to start automatically, select that service and click on **Configure**. Then, in the Server Service dialog box, select **Automatic** to make

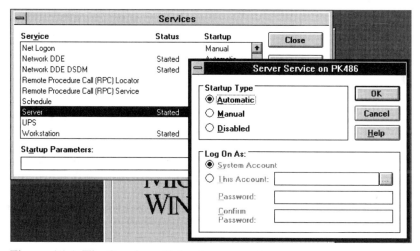

Figure 15.4 The Services dialog box

it start each time you log on. (Or you can select **Disabled**, so the service cannot be started and your machine cannot be accessed by other computers.)

Note Server can't start automatically unless you have at least 12 MB of memory.

Providing System Resources

File Manager

Once your network is running, the next step is to decide which resources you want to make available. To make **disk directories or files** available to other users, go to **File Manager** and use the **Disk|Share As** command. You can provide access to all the directories on a drive by selecting the drive letter in the directory tree and then using the Share As command. By default, *none* of your directories are available to other users except for domain administrators.

You can use the **Disk|Stop Sharing** command to deny access to a drive that you previously shared. Simply select that shared directory or drive, and then select the command. See Chapter 7 for more information about sharing data.

Print Manager

You can also share **printers** with other machines. In Print Manager, select the printer you want to share, and then select **Printer|Properties**. Then select the **Share this printer on the network** check box in the Printer Properties dialog box. See Chapter 8 for more information.

ClipBook
Viewer

You can also share **Clipboard data**, through the ClipBook Viewer. Select the *page* you want to share, then use the **File|Share** command. See Chapter 18 for more information.

Tip If you have trouble making network connections—perhaps when you try to access another computer's disk drive, NT can't find the computer—try turning the computers off and then on again. This sometimes resets the adapter card and lets things flow.

Controlling Server Connections

Server

The rather oddly-named Properties dialog box controls Server connections, and is displayed by double-clicking on the Control Panel's Server icon (see Figure 15.5). It helps you administer the way in which your computer acts as a network server. You can enter a description of your computer so other users will be able to identify it easily, monitor resource use (viewing information about how many other computers are using your computer's resources, and which resources are in use), close resources, and set up file replication and administrative alert messages. The Properties dialog box *doesn't* provide information about your computer's workstation sessions, resources on other computers being used by your computer.

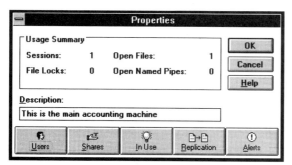

Figure 15.5 The Properties dialog box

When you double-click on the Server icon the Properties For dialog box pops up (Figure 15.5). The **Description** box is where you can enter the description of your machine seen by other users when they try to connect to a networked resource.

This dialog box provides an overview of what is going on:

Sessions   The number of computers accessing your computer's resources.

Open Files   The number of your computer's files opened by other computers.

File Locks   The number of file locks applied by network users to your resources.

Open Named Pipes   The number of open named pipes, systems that allow one process to communicate with a remote process.

Print Jobs   The number of print jobs pending on your computer that have been sent by other computers.

These entries are not continuously updated. Server updates them when you open the dialog box itself, and when you click on the buttons at the bottom— which open other dialog boxes. Nor are those dialog boxes continuously updated. So to be quite sure about what's going on, click on one of the buttons, then press Esc to update the contents of the Properties dialog box.

From this dialog box, you can carry out several operations by clicking the buttons:

Users   Shows you the names of the computers connected to yours, and the resources those computers are using.

Shares   Shows the shared resources on your computer, and the computers connected to each resource.

In Use   Shows the resources on your computer being used by other computers, but doesn't show you which other computers.

Replication Lets you define directory replication, a feature by which directories are automatically copied from or to other computers.

Alerts   Lets you define which other computers should automatically receive alert messages.

Viewing Resource Use

NT provides several ways to view information about who is using your computer, and what resources they have access to. Click on **Users** in the Properties For dialog box to see the User Sessions dialog box (Figure 15.6). The first panel, at the top of the box, shows information about the users connected to your computer, while the panel at the bottom shows the resources being used by the user selected in the top panel. This is the information in the top panel:

Connected Users   The username of the connected user.

Computer   The computer name of the connected user.

Opens   The number of resources being used by this user.

Time   The time since the user connected to your computer.

Idle   The time since the user last carried out an action on your computer. A user may have one of your files open, and may be working in it, but your computer won't recognize this work as an "action" until the user saves or closes the file.

Guest   Whether the user is a "guest" account (Yes or No).

Below this list box is **Connected Users**, which shows the number of users connected to your computer. The panel at the bottom provides information about the user highlighted in the top panel:

Resource   The resource in use—this may be:

    🗀   A directory or file

    🖨   A printer

    ▮   A named pipe

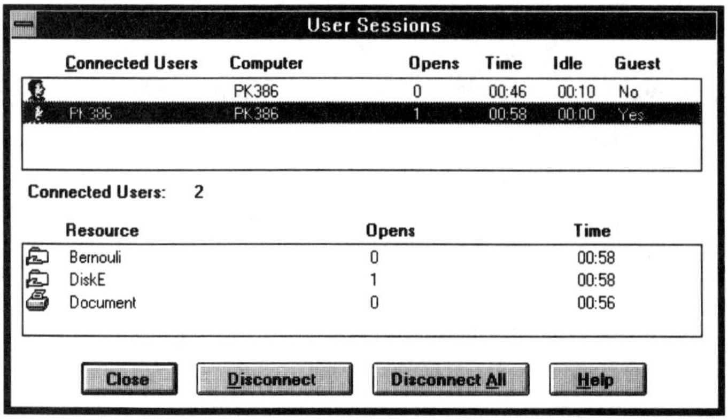

Figure 15.6 The User Sessions dialog box

> 🔮 An unknown type of resource or an administrative share
> (those directories, indicated with $, that NT automatically
> lets administrators connect to)

Opens   The number of resources opened by the user.

Time   The time since the user connected to this resource.

Note   It's possible for Server to miss some of the connections, so you may see less than
there actually are.

Notice that you can disconnect users from this dialog box. Select a user and
then click on **Disconnect**, or click on **Disconnect All** to shut them all down. This
may cause the users a problem, though it may not. Disconnecting a user does not
in itself stop that user from reconnecting, and in fact the computer may reconnect automatically. For instance, if the user is using a Windows for Workgroups
computer and you disconnect, when the user tries to save the file in which he is
working, Windows for Workgroups will try to *reconnect* to save the file. In order to
keep the user from reconnecting you must go to File Manager and use the
Disk|Stop Sharing command to restrict access to the directory.

Click on the **Shares** button in the Properties For dialog box to see the Shared
Resources dialog box (see Figure 15.7). This also shows how resources are being
used, though "from a different angle." The top box lists all the resources, and the
bottom box lists the users connected to the selected resource.

Sharename   The name of the resource—again, this may be a directory
                   or file, a printer, a named pipe, or a unknown resource, or
                   an administrative share.

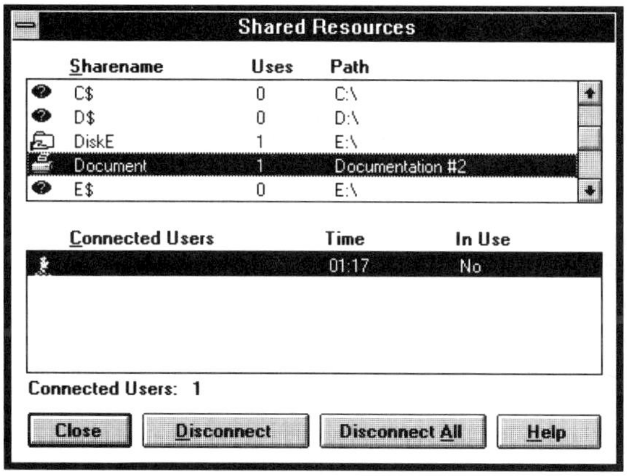

Figure 15.7 The Shared Resources dialog box

Uses   The number of users connected to the resource.

Path   The path to the shared resource. If the resource is a direc-
                        tory, this will show the disk and path in which that directory
                        is found. If it's a printer it will show the printer name.

The lower list box shows information about the users connected to the resource selected in the top box.

Connected Users   The names of the users connected to the resource selected
                        in the top box.

Time   The elapsed time since a user connected to the resource.

In Use   This column shows Yes if a user is actually using the re-
                        source. For instance, a user may be connected to a drive or
                        printer, but may not have opened any files or be printing
                        anything—in which case the entry will be No.

This dialog box also has **Disconnect** and **Disconnect All** buttons. However,
note that you are not disconnecting a user simply from the selected resource—he
will be disconnected from *all* resources to which he is connected. There is, however, a way to disconnect users from specific resources, while letting them continue working with other resources. Click on the **In Use** button in the Properties
For dialog box to see the Open Resources dialog box (Figure 15.8).

This dialog box shows a list of all the resources that are open. For each one, it
shows the user who is using it (**Opened By**); the permissions the user has on that
resource—Read or Write, for instance (**For**); the number of **Locks** on the
resource; and the **Path** to that resource.

This dialog box has a **Refresh** button—click on it to update the information
in the list box (remember that the other boxes are "snapshots" taken when the
box is opened). You can click on **Close Resource** or **Close All Resources** to disconnect users from a particular or all resources. If you close just one resource,
though, the users remain connected to the others.

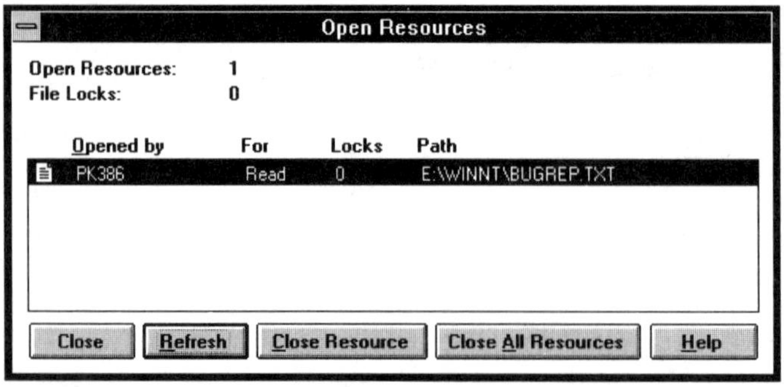

Figure 15.8 The Open Resources dialog box

Using Directory Replication

If you are on a Windows NT Advanced Server network you can use *directory replication*, a system in which a directory on one computer is automatically copied to another computer—or sometimes to another disk on the same computer, or even another directory on the same disk. Each time the data changes in the source directory (on the *export server*), those changes are copied to the target directory (on the *import computer*). Any Windows NT workstation can operate as an import computer. Only Windows NT Advanced Servers can operate as an export server.

We're not going to explain directory replication in detail, because it's not really a Windows NT feature—it's a Windows NT Advanced Server feature. Refer to the NT Advanced Server documentation for information about configuring the Replicator account that is required for using directory replication. Here's how you set up your computer as an import computer, though.

Click on the **Replication** button in the Server's Properties dialog box to see the Directory Replication dialog box (see Figure 15.9). Select the **Import Directory** option button. By default, the replicated directory will be stored in the \WINNT\SYSTEM32\REPL\IMPORT subdirectory. You can change this if you want, but NT has setup special permissions for this subdirectory, and changing it could cause problems.

By default, Replicator is already set up to import from the local domain, the domain of which your computer is a member. However, you can select a different domain if you wish. When you do this, though, the default directory importation will not be carried out, so if you want to import from both your *local* domain and *another* domain, you must add them both to the **From List**. Click on the **Add** button to select the computer from which you wish to import. You'll see the Select Domain dialog box—double-click on the domain or workgroup name to see a list of the computers in that group, then double-click on the computer's name to add it to the **From List** list box in the Directory Replication dialog box. This computer must be a Windows NT Advanced Server, and the *export* directory will be

Figure 15.9 The Directory Replication dialog box

defined there—all you have to do is select the computer, not the directory itself. You can also remove domains from this list with the **Remove** button.

Now click on the **OK** button, and NT will start the Directory Replicator service for you. (This service is set to start manually, so if you want it running all the time, you should go to the Services dialog box in Control Panel and set it to start Automatically when your computer boots.)

Now reopen the Directory Replication dialog box, and you'll notice that the **Manage** button is now enabled. Click on this button to see the Manage Imported Directories dialog box (see Figure 15.10). This shows you the **Sub-Directory** names, the names of the subdirectories which will be added. Click on the **Add** button to enter the name of a new subdirectory (or select a subdirectory and click on **Remove** to remove it from the list).

This dialog box also shows the number of **Locks** against the subdirectory. There could be more than one lock against a directory, and as long as a number other than 0 appears here, the directory cannot be imported.

The **Status** shows information about the importation. If it shows **OK**, this subdirectory is receiving regular, correct updates from the imported directory. If it shows **No Master**, it means that the subdirectory is *not* receiving regular updates for some reason. **No Sync** means that the imported directory in this subdirectory is not up to date, perhaps because of a communications failure, an open file that couldn't be copied, the import computer not having the correct access permissions, or some other kind of error. None of these statuses appear until replication has taken place, so if the field is blank, it means that replication has never occurred.

The **Last Update** field shows the last time replication occurred. If the directory is locked, the **Locked Since** field shows the time and date of the first lock applied against the directory. (This field is not updated until you close the dialog box.) Notice the **Add Lock** and **Remove Lock** buttons. Each time you click on one of these, a single lock is added or removed. You can do this to temporarily stop importation and restart it. Locks can be applied at either end, so you shouldn't remove locks applied by the other end.

You can add more subdirectories to the list, or remove them, using the **Add** and **Remove** buttons, but you won't normally need to do so, as this is controlled from the other end, the export server.

Figure 15.10 The Manage Imported Directories dialog box

Managing Alerts

Click on the **Alerts** button in the Properties dialog box to see the dialog box shown in Figure 15.11. The **Send Administrative Alerts To** list box shows the names of the computers to which your computer will send alerts—messages about resource use, UPS power signals, printer problems, and so on, indicating possible problems. You can add a name to this list by typing the computer name into the **New Computer or Username** text box and clicking on the **Add** button.

Tip   For some reason, this dialog box doesn't show a list of the available computers. To add several to the list, open File Manager, select Disk|Connect Network Drive to see a list of computers. If you click on a directory name, you can then copy the computer name (using Ctrl-C) from the Path text box.

In order for Alerts to work, the Alerter service must be running on your computer, and the Messenger service must be running on the receiving computers. The Messenger service is probably set up to start automatically, but the Alerter service may be set to start manually. Use the Control Panel's Services dialog box to change these settings if necessary.

Managing a Workstation

Using your computer as a workstation is much simpler than running it as a server. The Workstation service must be running, of course, but it's probably already set up to start automatically—use the Control Panel's Services to change it if necessary.

Once you have your networking software correctly installed, you can run your computer as a workstation from within various applications. In **File Manager** you can connect to another computer's shared directories and files. In ClipBook Viewer you can view and use shared ClipBook pages, data from the Clipboard. In Print Manager you can connect to another computer, and use its printer as if

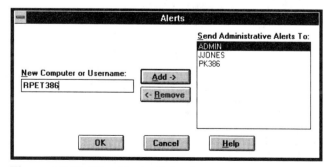

Figure 15.11 The Alerts dialog box

it were connected to your own computer. In Registry Editor you can connect to another computer and view its configuration data (if you're an Administrator).

In many applications, you'll even find a **Network** button in the File Open dialog box. When you want to open a file on another computer, click on this button to see the Connect Network Drive dialog box, select the computer and directory you want to use, and click on OK—that directory will be added to the Drives drop-down list box. In fact, if you've already connected to a drive—in File Manager or another application—you'll find that the directory already appears in the Drives drop-down list box. You won't have to add it each time you need to use it. (See Figure 15.12.)

More Network Utilities

Windows NT has several network utilities that you may be familiar with if you've used Windows for Workgroups. They provide several different ways in which network users can communicate with each other and share information:

Mail
: An email application, which lets you send text messages to other network users.

Schedule+
: A scheduling application which can be used off the network, or shared with other network users so you can coordinate meetings and other events.

Chat
: A sort of "real time" email system, in which you type a message and the characters appear in the other user's Chat window immediately—that user can then respond immediately, so you can "chat" to each other.

ClipBook Viewer
: An extended Clipboard, which lets network users share clipboard data. It can also be used to store Clipboard data for future use.

These programs are described in chapters 16 to 18.

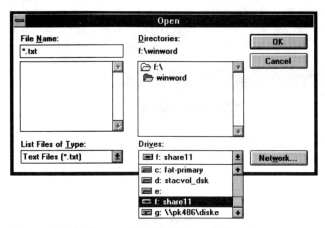

Figure 15.12 Notepad's File Open dialog box

16

Network Utilities—Mail

Windows NT Mail is an *email* (electronic mail) application. It lets you send and receive messages across a computer network. NT Mail was first released as Windows for Workgroup's MSMail, and it can be used on a Windows for Workgroups network to interface with Windows 3.1 workstations. Not only does it let you share text messages, you can even use it to share pictures and sounds, and can place entire files in messages—the recipient can extract the file from the message and use it in its original application.

Setting Up Mail

Mail requires a common *post office*. Someone in the workgroup must have a directory in which the post office has been established, and everyone else in the workgroup must have full access to that directory. This post office is used to store messages and let users retrieve them when they want them.

Mail

Start Mail by double-clicking on the Mail icon in the Main program group. The first time you open Mail you'll see a message telling you that you must either create a post office or connect to an existing one (Figure 16.1). If you are setting up the first terminal in a workgroup, you will have to create a post office—on subsequent terminals you will then connect to the existing post office (you can't have more than one post office per workgroup). You should do this from the computer you wish to use as the Mail Administrator, because the computer which creates the post office automatically becomes the administrator. Once the Mail system is running this computer will be able to change user names and passwords.

Figure 16.1 The Welcome to Mail dialog box

When you select the option to **Create a new Workgroup Postoffice**, you'll see a message box warning you that only one postoffice is needed for each workgroup, and that if you create a postoffice you will become the administrator. Click on OK and you'll then see a directories list box. Select the directory in which you want to save the postoffice. (NT will create a subdirectory named WGPO—with over 50 subdirectories of its own—in the selected directory.) You can even click on the **Network** button to select a drive on a different machine. Remember, though, you want to select a machine that will be on all the time that the mail service will be needed. The obvious choice is a dedicated server, though you can also put the postoffice on a workstation, also. Wherever you decide to put it, make sure you have full access to the drive and directory.

If you selected a network directory, when you click on OK Mail may seem to lock up for a minute or two. Mail is creating all the WGPO subdirectories, which takes a little time.

After selecting a directory, you will see the Administrator Account Details dialog box (Figure 16.2). This box shows information that other users can see when searching the Postoffice List directory (which you'll learn more about in a few moments). You can enter your **Name**, type your account name in the **Mailbox** field, type over the **Password** with a new one (or even remove the existing one entirely), enter your **Phone** numbers, your **Office** number and **Department** name, and a short **Note**. You *must* have a Name and Mailbox name—the password is optional, and the rest of the text boxes are simply for information. Fill in the information and click on OK, and you'll see a reminder to make the post office directory a shared one—you should probably go straight to File Manager and share it now (see Chapter 7 for information on sharing directories). Make sure you make it available to all network users who will be using the mail system, and that you provide read and write access. And make the actual WGPO directory a shared one—it's not good enough to simply share the disk or directory in which you placed the WGPO postoffice directory. You can change these Account Details later, using the Mail|Postoffice Manager and Mail|Change Password commands.

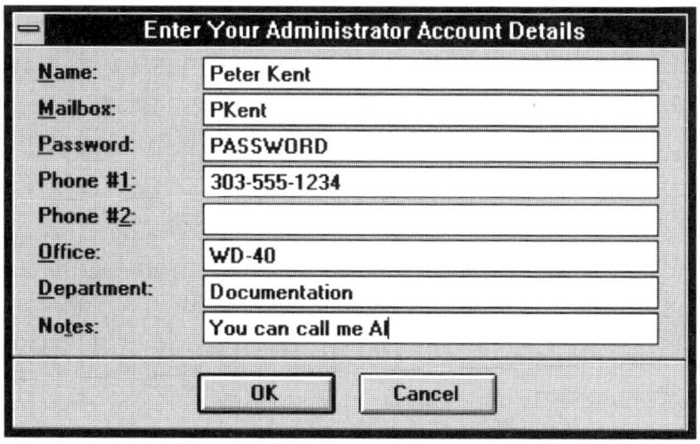

Figure 16.2 The Administrator Account Details dialog box

Note If you, as the administrator, forget your password, you are in real trouble. The only option is to delete the postoffice directories from your hard disk and create a new postoffice. The tip which appears under Opening Windows NT Mail later in this chapter—placing the password in the icon—is a way to avoid this problem. If another user forgets a password you will be able to create a new one.

Adding Mail Terminals

Once you have created a postoffice, you can then add other terminals to it. You will now select the **Connect to an existing post office.** You'll see a dialog box asking you for the network path of the post office. Type the name in this format:

```
\\computername\sharename
```

For instance, type \\PK386\WGPO. You can even connect to a postoffice on the same machine—if the postoffice was created on your machine from another computer. Enter your machine's computername and the WPGO directory's sharename. When you click on OK, Mail will connect to the postoffice. Then you'll see a dialog box asking if you have an account on the postoffice. The administrator can create accounts from his terminal, using the Mail|Postoffice Manager command (which we'll look at later). If you've done this, then all you have to do at each terminal is say Yes at this dialog box and then enter the mailbox name you assigned to the account.

If you haven't already created an account, click on the No button and you'll see another Account Details dialog box (in Figure 16.2). Enter the new account information and click on OK.

Tip If your company already has an email system, you can purchase an *extension* to Windows NT Mail, upgrading it to Mail 3.2. That system will allow you to interface with other systems. Contact Microsoft for more information.

It's possible for Mail to get a little confused about who is who. If you played around a little with Mail and Schedule, entering account information just to see what is what, when you actually come to create Mail accounts you may find that Mail won't let you. You might see a message telling you that your account information is incorrect. You will have to start over. Go to Registry Editor (see Chapter 11), and open the HKEY_USERS on Local Machine window. Find the second *key* below HKEY_USERS. This will start with an S and have a long number. That's the key that pertains to the current session. Then travel down the tree to the \Software\Microsoft\Mail\Microsoft Mail key. Then delete the Login and ServerPath values. This will let you start over again.

Adding Mail Accounts

The first release of MSMail was in Windows for Workgroups, in which it was assumed that each computer would have only one mail account (it *is* possible to add multiple accounts in Windows for Workgroups, though you have to play around in the MSMAIL.INI file to do so). Windows NT, of course, has the capability of multiple users on one machine—so you need to be able to create two or more Mail accounts on each machine.

NT Mail has been modified slightly from MSMail to allow you to do this easily. First, use the Mail|Postoffice Manager command (described later in this chapter) to create the accounts (assuming you are the administrator). Then create the first mail account on the machine that needs multiple accounts. When asked if you already have an account on the postoffice, you will click on Yes, and enter one of the account names. Because you'll have several users on one machine, you'll probably want to use passwords.

After creating that account, log off the computer and log back on with another account. When you start Mail you'll see the Sign In dialog box, displaying the username of the previous account. You can type over this with one of the other account names, enter the password, and click on OK to open that account. So each user can now open his own account in this manner—or anyone else's account, if he has the password.

Opening Windows NT Mail

Each time you open Windows NT Mail, you'll see a Mail Sign In dialog box asking for your password. If you didn't change your password when you first created your mail account your password is simply *password*. (You can change—or remove—your password using the **Mail|Change Password** command once you are in Mail.)

When you click on the OK button, Mail opens, displays the Inbox window (see Figure 16.3), and checks the post office for pending mail. Notice that you have three folders: **Deleted mail** (which will contain mail that you delete using the Edit|Delete command or Delete button on the toolbar), **Inbox** (mail that you have received), and **Sent mail** (messages that you sent). As you'll see later, you can

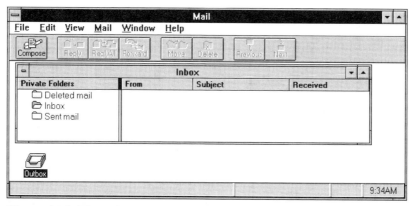

Figure 16.3 The Windows NT Inbox window

also create your own folders. By default, all messages you send are saved in the Sent mail folder, and all deleted messages are removed from the Deleted mail folder whenever you close the Mail application. As you'll learn later, you can change these defaults, and even decide whether to save individual messages as you send them.

The column headings in the Inbox window are actually buttons. Click on **Private Folders** to see the Shared Folders (and vice versa—you can also use the View|Shared/Private Folders command to toggle between the two types of folder). You'll learn more about folder types later. Click on **From** to sort the list of messages according to who they came from, click on **Subject** to sort them according to the subject, and click on **Received** to sort them into the order in which they were received. These are the same as the View|Shared Folders/Private Folders, View|Sort by Sender, View|Sort by Subject, and View|Sort by Date menu options. There's also a **View|Sort by Priority** option. As you'll see a little later, messages may be prioritized as High, Normal, or Low priority, and this option sorts the messages accordingly. And you can move the column divider by dragging it to the left or the right. You may want to do this if you have created your own folders and the names stretch further to the right. (If you need to use the keyboard to do this, use the View|Split command.)

Tip To open Mail automatically when you open NT, put the Mail icon in the Startup program group. You can bypass the Sign In dialog box by entering your account name and password in the Program Item Properties dialog box. For instance, enter **MSMAIL32.EXE PKent** *password*. It's no longer a completely secure password, but you've already entered a password to log onto NT, so the icon shouldn't be accessible to anyone else. (The Startup Group is a personal group.) You must have a password in order to use this method (it won't work with a blank password). There's one catch. If you are running Schedule+ already, you won't be able to open Mail using this method. So if you want to start both Schedule+ and

Mail from Startup, put the icon with the name and password *first*, and then the icon *without* the name and password.

Using the Address Book

Before we send a message, let's take a look at the Address Book. Select **Mail\Address Book** and the Address Book pops up (see Figure 16.4). Initially it shows the Post-office List, all the names associated with the postoffice to which you are connected. If you are on a large network, you may want to create your own address book—or books—to make it easier to find the people you need to communicate with.

 You already have a personal address book. To add someone to this, simply select the name and click on the second button from the left at the bottom of the dialog box. You can select several names at once if you want—drag the mouse pointer across them while holding the mouse button down, or press Ctrl and click once on each one you want.

Tip   By default, when you write a message to someone, Mail will automatically add their name to your Personal Address Book. See Selecting Mail Options, later in this chapter.

 You can see your **personal address book** by clicking on the second button from the top, next to the list of names. The title at the top changes to indicate which "Directory" (or address book) you are currently viewing.

 If you want to always see your personal address book whenever you open the Address Book, you must set it as the default. Click on the button at the top, and you'll see a list of all the different directories that are available—initially just the Personal Address Book and Postoffice List, though some mail add-on products

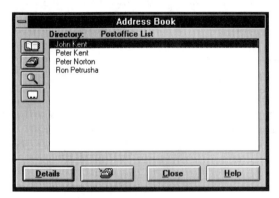

Figure 16.4 The Address Book, after selecting Mail\Address Book

can add more books. Select the Personal Address Book, and click on the **Set Default** button.

 If you have a large address book, you can find your way through it quickly by pressing letters on your keyboard. Each time you press a letter, the highlight moves to the next name that begins with that character. You can also **search** the list using the third button from the top, the magnifying glass. When you click on this you'll see a simple Name Finder dialog box. Type a few characters from the name you are looking for and click on OK, and the list changes to show just those names matching the characters. To return to a full address book, click on the top button.

 There's another way to add addresses to a phone book. Click on the fourth button down on the left side to see the New dialog box. This box will show Custom Entry. Click on OK, and you'll see a dialog box in which you can enter a person's **Name**, **E-mail Address**, **E-mail Type**, and a **Comment**. You must enter at least the first three items. Then click on the leftmost button in the dialog box to add the address to the address book. This entry is always added to your *personal* address book, even if the postoffice list was displayed in the Address Book dialog box. Actually this Custom option isn't a lot of use to you if you are using the standard Mail system. It's intended for use by a *gateway* to another email system.

Once you've found the name you're looking for, you can see more information about this person by clicking on the **Details** button (or double-click on the entry in the list). If it's a custom address, you see the same dialog box you saw when you entered the custom address, but otherwise you'll see a dialog box that shows the account details information. There's a button at the bottom of this dialog box that adds the person to your personal address book.

Finally, if you are in your personal address book, you can remove entries by selecting them and clicking on the **Remove** button. Of course you can't do this in the Postoffice List. If you want to remove someone from the postoffice list you'll have to use the Mail|Postoffice Manager command (assuming you're the mail-system administrator).

Sending Messages

To send a message to another user, click on the Compose button or select **Mail|Compose Note** (or press **Ctrl-N**). When the Send Note document window pops up, enter the **To** and **Cc** names. You can either type this name, or click on the **Address** button, and select the person from the Address Book—which will look different from the one we've just looked at, as you can see in Figure 16.5. (If you decide to *type* the names, click on **Check Names** when you've finished—if you made a mistake Mail will tell you.)

Tip   You can experiment with Mail by sending a message to yourself.

**Figure 16.5 The Address Book, after clicking on
Address in the Send Note window**

The four buttons on the left side are still the same, and you've also got a
Details button, a **Remove** button (if the personal address book is displayed), and
a **"to personal address book"** button if the postoffice list is displayed. But you've
got other options. The idea in this dialog box is to add names to the **To** and **Cc**
lists. Select one or more, then **drag** the selection into the desired list, or click on
the **To** or **Cc** button. Or **double-click** on an entry to move it to the To list (or to
the *last* list in which you've placed a name, so once you've added to the Cc list
double-clicking adds to that). Everyone in the To list will receive an "original" of
the message you are sending, while everyone in the Cc list receives a "copy." Of
course there's not a lot of difference in electronic mail, but the Cc copies will be
marked as such, so the recipient will know that he's getting a "copy," rather than
being a primary recipient of the message.

Tip You can place the cursor in the To and Cc fields, so you can type names, delete
names, or cut and paste them.

When you've got the names you want, click on OK to return to the Send Note
window. The To and Cc fields will be filled in. Move to the Subject field and type a
title for your message. Then move into the blank workspace below and type your
message (Figure 16.6). You can use the usual Edit-menu options—Undo, Cut,
Copy, Paste, and Delete. You can also copy text from a file using the select **Edit|
Insert from File** command. This is intended for use with plain ASCII text. If you
use a word processing document, the formatting codes will appear as "garbage"
characters.

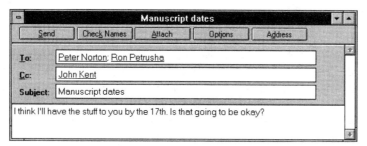

Figure 16.6 The Send Note window, showing the subject in the title bar

You're not limited to text, though, as you can also use the **Attach** button to place an attached file inside the message (as an OLE—Object Linking and Embedding—"package") or use the Edit menu to embed data. We'll look at those options in a moment.

Before you finally send the message, you can set certain options. Click on the **Options** button, then select **Return receipt** (if you want to know when the person receiving the message actually reads it) and **Save sent messages** (if you want a copy of the message placed in your Inbox's Sent Mail folder—this is the default).

You may also select a **Priority**. This has no effect on the speed at which the mail is delivered; rather, it affects the icon that is displayed at the beginning of the message listing in the inbox. The High-priority message has a red asterisk and a paper clip next to the envelope icon, while the Low-priority message has a gray arrow pointing downward.

Close the Options dialog box and you're ready to mail your letter. Just click on **Send** and away it goes. You'll notice the icon on the status bar at the bottom of the window change as the letter is mailed and Mail searches for the correct mailbox. If the Outbox is visible (it may be hidden below the Inbox), you'll see the message appear for a few seconds, then disappear as it's sent on.

Note To cancel out of the Send Note dialog box without sending a message, just double-click on the Control menu.

If a message **can't be delivered**—probably because you entered an invalid name—you will receive a message from the system itself. It will be from the "System Administrator" and its subject will be "Undeliverable Mail." If you open the message you will be able to read who the message should have gone to and when. This message will have a Send Again button. Click on it to go to the Send Note document window. The message will already be in the window, and all you have to do is enter a new To name. By the way, it's possible for a name to be invalid yet not be caught when you click on the Check Names button. If you entered a name into the Address Book manually, the Check Names function will think it's correct, even if it is not.

Embedding and Attaching Data

As we've already mentioned, Mail messages are not limited to text. You can send just about any kind of data. There are several ways to do this. To attach an entire file, click on the **Attach** button. You'll see a File Open-type dialog box. Find the file you want to attach and click on the Attach button in this dialog box to place a package in the document. You can continue attaching files—click on Close when you are finished. These files are *embedded*, not linked, though they appear to be linked in some ways (the icon titles refer to a filename).

You can also embed an object using the **Edit|Insert Object** command. This is a typical OLE Insert Object procedure, the same as you might use to insert an object into a word-processing document. You'll see a dialog box listing the OLE objects. Select the one you want—a Paintbrush picture, for instance, a Sound, a Media Clip—then click on OK. Create your object, then close the application and the object is saved in the Mail message.

There's yet another way to embed an object, by going the other way—create it in an application, copy it to the Clipboard, switch to the Mail document, then use the **Edit|Paste Special** command to drop it in place. You can also embed an object using the **Edit|Paste** command. If the object comes from an OLE *server* it may be automatically embedded, depending on the application from which it comes—a Paintbrush picture will be embedded, Word for Windows text won't. (The Edit|Paste Special command provides more options—it allows you to select the format type.) And if the data isn't from an OLE server, the Edit|Paste command simply places a copy in the document.

These methods are all OLE procedures that are the same in Windows 3.1. For a good description of all the different ways to use OLE, see *Peter Norton's User's Guide to Windows 3.1*.

Tip   You can extract attached files from messages and save them on your hard disk. This lets you use mail as a convenient way to swap files between users. See "Saving Messages and Attached Data," later in this chapter.

Reading and Replying

Mail

Mail

When you receive a message you'll hear a chime. If your Mail icon is on the desktop somewhere it will flash, then you'll see a couple of envelopes pop out of the letter box. If Mail wasn't open when the message was sent to you, the mail will arrive when you open the application and it connects to the postoffice—you'll see an icon on the status bar with an envelope sticking through the mail slot. The message files are copied from the postoffice to your hard disk. (They are saved in MSMAIL.MMF, in your WINNT directory.)

The mail will appear in the Inbox. To read it, simply **double-click** on it, or select it and press **Enter** or select **File|Open**. Another document window pops up, with your message inside (see Figure 16.7). The header shows the name of the person who sent it, the time and date that the message was sent, the people it was "copied" to (Cc:), and the subject of the message.

Urgent:
Today's
Meeting

If you minimize the message, you'll see an open-envelope icon at the bottom of the Mail window. You can leave several of these messages minimized like this, and they'll remain in this state even if you close Mail—the next time you open the application they'll still be there, in minimized form. (If a message arrives with nothing in the subject text box, the icon titles will simply say, Read Note.)

You can work with these messages in the same way you worked with your own, outgoing, messages. You can cut, copy, and paste text. You can paste or embed images, sounds, spreadsheet cells, and so on. This lets you add information to a message that you may want to forward or return.

Forward

To **Forward** a message, simply click on the Forward button on the toolbar, select **Mail|Forward**, or press **Ctrl-F**. (If the Outbox is visible, you can simply use the mouse to drag the entry from the Inbox onto the Outbox.) The FW: dialog box appears, which looks pretty much the same as the Send Note dialog box. Make any changes you want on the To, Cc, and Subject lines, add whatever you need to the message, click on the Send button, and away it goes.

Reply

Replying to a message is similar. Simply click on the Reply button in the toolbar, select **Mail|Reply**, or press **Ctrl-R**. You'll see the RE: dialog box, which, again, is the same as the Send Note dialog box. Make any changes you want and click on Send. This replies to the person who sent the message. If you want *everyone* to get a copy of your reply—other recipients of the original message and the copies—

ReplyAll

use the **ReplyAll** button on the toolbar, the **Mail|Reply to All** option, or press **Ctrl-A**. By the way, these replies and forwarded messages are treated in the same way as normal messages—by default they are saved in the Sent Mail folder (unless you change the setting in the Options dialog box while working in the message, or by using the Mail|Options command).

Previous

Next

You can move through the messages in your Inbox, displaying one after another, using the **Next** and **Previous** buttons on the toolbar. Or select **View|Next**, **View|Previous**, or press **Ctrl->** or **Ctrl-<**.

When you've finished with a message, you have several options. You can delete the message, placing it in the Deleted Mail folder: Click on the Delete toolbar

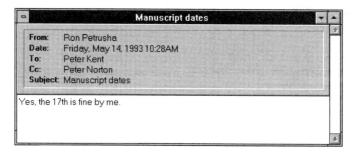

Figure 16.7 A received message

button or select **File|Delete**. Deleting a message while it is displayed automatically opens the *next* message in the Inbox.

 If you want to move the message to another folder, click on the **Move** button in the toolbar, select **File|Move**, or press **Ctrl-M**. You will see the Move Message dialog box (Figure 16.8). Select whether you want to move the message to a **Private** or **Shared** folder, and then select the folder from the **Move To** list. Or use the **New** button to create a new folder (you'll learn about creating folders in a moment). You can also copy a message to another folder, using the **File|Copy** command.

Organizing Messages

Mail provides a number of ways to help you handle messages. Once you've received a message you can leave it where it is, move it to another folder, or delete it. As we'll see in a moment, you can also save messages and folders in separate files, for future use.

When you first create Mail your Inbox has three folders: **Inbox**, **Sent Mail,** and **Deleted**. All messages that are received are placed in the Inbox folder, and remain there—even after you've read them—until you move them elsewhere or delete them. To view the contents of another folder, double-click on that folder, or select it and press Enter.

 You can delete a message by selecting it and pressing **Del**, by clicking on the Delete toolbar button, or by selecting **File|Delete**. Remember that you can select more than one message at a time—click on the first entry in the sequence and then hold Shift while you click on the last in the group, or hold Ctrl while you click on each one you want—so you can delete a whole group at once. "Deleting" a message doesn't actually remove it from the Inbox—it moves it to the Deleted Mail folder. By default this folder is emptied each time you close Mail, but you can turn this option off (use the Mail|Options command to see the Options dialog box) so that the mail will remain in the Deleted Mail folder. If you select an entry in the Deleted Mail folder and press **Del**, it really is removed.

The **Sent Mail** folder, by default, saves a copy of each message that you send to someone. Again, you can turn this option off, using the Mail|Options command.

Figure 16.8 The Move Message dialog box.

However, each time you send a message you can click on the Options button in the Send Note document window and change the Sent Mail setting—saving a message if you set the default to "don't save," or not saving a message if the default is "save."

You can, of course, **create your own folders**. First, decide whether you want it to be a **Private** or **Shared** folder. Private folders are stored on your hard disk, and available only to you. Shared folders are stored in the postoffice, and are available to all other members of the postoffice (though you can decide the type of access they will have). Next, decide whether you want the folder to be a sub-folder of an existing one. If so, you may want to select that folder now. (Remember, you can toggle between displaying the Shared and Private folders using the View|Shared/Private Folders command).

Now, select **File|New Folder**. Then click on the **Options** button in the New Folder dialog box (Figure 16.9). Start by giving the folder a name—Documentation Project, for instance, or Recent Memos. Now, select **Private** or **Shared** to define where the folder should be placed. If you already selected this option in the In-box before you selected the File|New Folder command, then this is already set correctly. And if you selected a folder in the Inbox, the folder is already selected in the **Subfolder Of** list box. You can, of course, select another folder into which to place your new folder, or you can select **Top Level Folder**, to create a folder that is not a subfolder of any other.

If you are creating a shared folder, you can also define the type of access that other users may have. Use the **Other Users Can** check boxes to define whether other users will be able to **Read**, **Write**, or **Delete** messages. (If the Delete option is off—but the Read option on—a user won't be able to move a message out of the folder, but will be able to copy it.) Finally, you may want to add a **Comment** line. Other users will be able to read this comment when they view the Folder Properties—this dialog box looks exactly the same as the New Folder dialog box, and is displayed by selecting the folder and pressing **Alt-Enter** or choosing **File|Folder Properties.** If you created the folder you can change the name, comment, and Other Users Can options in the Folder Properties dialog box, but if it's not your folder you won't be able to change anything—you'll only be able to view it.

Now that you've got your new folders, how can you use them? As you've already seen, you can move messages from your Inbox folder to any other folder while the message is open. You can also move one or more messages while working in the Inbox document window. Select the messages and **drag** them into another folder. Or, if you want to move the message from the Shared folders to the Private folders—or vice versa—click on the **Move** toolbar button, select **File|Move**, or press **Ctrl-M**. You can also use the **File|Copy** command to place a copy of the message in another folder. (You can also copy messages by holding down **Shift-Ctrl** and **dragging**.)

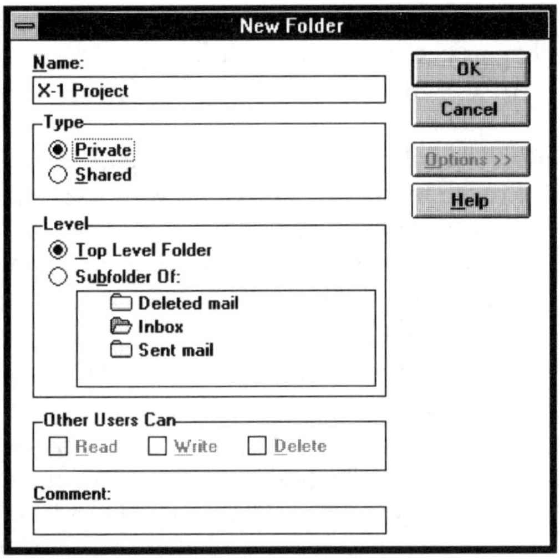

Figure 16.9 The New Folder dialog box

Tip You can move and copy folders in the same way you move and copy messages. You can only move or copy the ones you created (and only Private folders, not Shared), and moving a folder into the Deleted Mail folder will delete the folder and all its contents.

Notice also the + and – signs next to the folder names. (You won't see these signs unless you have subfolders.) Click on one of the signs—on the sign itself, not on the folder. When you click on a – sign, the subfolders disappear, and the sign turns into a +. Click on a + and the folders reappear, and the sign turns back into a –.

Saving Messages and Attached Data

If you use Mail very often, you can quickly find your folders cluttered and difficult to work with. Mail provides several ways to save information that you receive as messages. You can save messages as text files, save entire folders, including the messages, and extract attached files from messages.

To create a **text file** from the message, select the message in the Inbox then select **File|Save As**. You'll see a typical Save As dialog box. Select a directory, provide a name and click on OK. This file will be a .TXT file—all embedded graphics and other objects will be removed.

You can place **multiple messages** into one text file, using two methods. In the Inbox, select the messages you want and use the File|Save As command. All the messages will be placed together in one file. Or, when the Save As dialog box opens, select an existing text file. You'll see a small message box asking if you want to Append or Overwrite. Select Append and the message (or messages) will be added to the end of the file.

If you want to save files that have been attached to a message, open the message (you can't just select it, you must view it in a message window) and then select **File|Save Attachment**. You'll see a dialog box that shows all the attachments in the file (Figure 16.10). Select the directory into which you want to place them. If you want to save all the attachments—using their original names—you can click on the **Save All** button. But if you only want to save some of the files, or if you want to save them with different names, you'll have to do so individually. Click on the first file in the **Attached Files** list box, then change the name in the **File Name** text box, if you wish, and click on **Save**.

This procedure will only work for attached files. What if you have embedded objects you want to save? You can use the **Edit|Edit** *appname* Object command. When the object opens in its source application (assuming you have a copy of the source application on your hard disk), you can save it using the File|Save As command.

Mail also lets you **save entire folders**, messages and all, and retrieve them later. These messages are in normal Mail format—nothing is removed, so when you reload them later they will contain the graphics and embedded and attached files. You might create a folder called ARCHIVE1, for instance, copy old messages into it—messages you think you may need later, but don't want on the system right now—and then save the folder. Or simply archive data directly out of existing folders into copies with the same names.

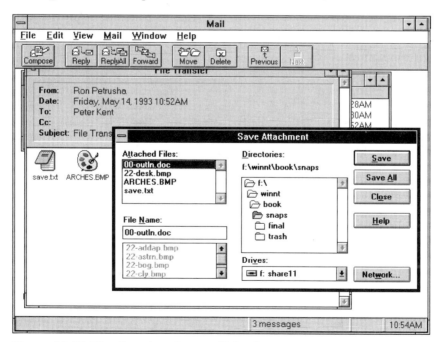

Figure 16.10 The Save Attachment dialog box

Tip   You can only save Private folders, not Shared ones even if they belong to you. If you want to save a Shared folder, create a corresponding Private folder first, and copy the Shared messages into it.

Select **File|Export Folders**. When the Export Folders dialog box appears, select a directory and enter a name, then click on OK. If you enter a new name, you'll be asked if you want to create a new .MMF file—just click on Yes. If you chose an existing .MMF file, Mail will add the messages to that file.

You'll see another Export Folders dialog box. You can now select **All Folders**, if you want to save all your Private folders. Or you can select one or more folders from the **Selected Folders** list box. Now click on the **Options** button. You'll see a small dialog box that lets you select **Messages Received or Modified** between particular dates (Figure 16.11). Enter the dates in the incrementer boxes and click on OK.

Now, you're ready to export. You can either click on the **Move** button—in which case the messages will be removed from the folders and placed in corresponding folders in the .MMF file—or **Copy**, which will place copies in the .MMF file and leave the originals in the Mail folders. In *neither* case will the folders themselves be removed from the Mail inbox. When you've finished, click on the **Close** button.

If you ever need to see your archived messages, you can quickly reload them using the **File|Import Folder**. You'll go through a similar procedure to start with—select the filename, then select the folders you want to import, and decide whether you want to move or copy the data from the archive file. If you are importing into folders of the same names, you will see a dialog box giving you several options: You can **Save latest version of all messages**, so if you have made changes to a message, only the most recent version is copied; you can **Save all**

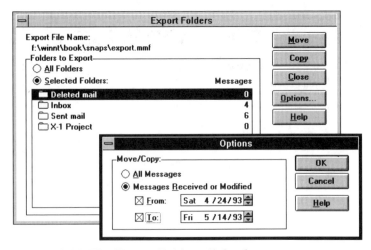

Figure 16.11 The Export Folders dialog box

messages, so all messages are copied, even if there are several versions of individual messages; or you can **Rename destination folder**, in which case you'll be able to enter a new folder name, and copy *all* messages into the new folder. There's also a **Don't prompt on remaining duplicate folders names** check box, to make the Import system use your selection for all subsequent folders. Once you've imported messages you can use them in exactly the same way you use your existing messages.

There's another way to "export" folders. Use the **Mail|Backup** command. This is a quick way to copy *everything* from all the folders in your Inbox to a .MMF file. You won't be able to select which folders should be saved. You can use this .MMF file in the same way you do the others, by using the File|Import Folder command to copy messages back into your Inbox.

Creating "Mailing Lists"

If you commonly send messages to a particular group of people—perhaps you manage a group and send memos to everyone in that group—you can create a *personal group*, then address messages to that group. Instead of entering each person's name each time you send a message, you will enter the group name, and Mail will figure it all out for you.

Select **Mail|Personal Groups**. When the Personal Groups dialog box appears, click on the **New** button. Type a name for your group into the New Group dialog box that appears, then click on Create to see an address book, which works in the same way as the address book we looked at earlier. The top list shows the Postoffice List or your Personal Address Book—click on the top button on the left side to select which list you want. Select the people you want to add to your personal group and click on the **Add** button. When you've got all you want, click on OK, and you've created your personal group.

Now, whenever you are sending a message, you can type the name of the personal group in the To field, or click on the Address button and select the group from the Address Book—it will appear in your Personal Address Book. You can come back and edit your group—to add or remove names—by using the Mail|Personal Groups command again, selecting the group, and clicking on the Edit button.

Searching for Messages

If you use Mail all the time you may find your inbox getting cluttered. Mail provides a search function to help you find your way through all those messages. Select the folder you want to search, then select **File|Message Finder**. You'll see the dialog box in Figure 16.12.

You can search for four types of information: the **From** name, the **Subject**, the **Recipients**, or the **Message Text**. The Recipients may be anyone to whom the message was sent or copied to (Cc). And the Message Text may be any text that appears anywhere inside the message. You can type just about any amount into

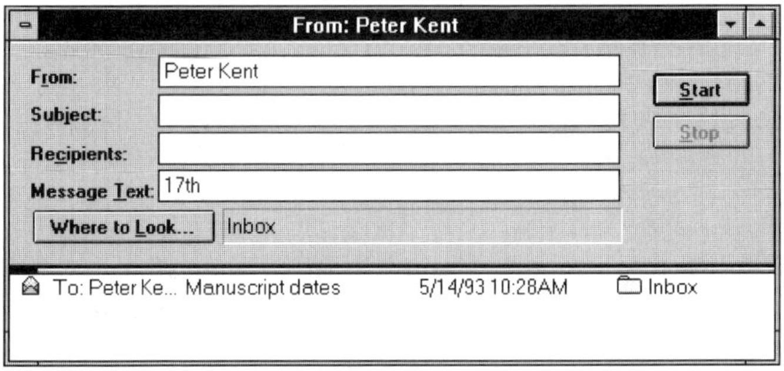

Figure 16.12 The Message Finder dialog box

the Message Text box—thousands of characters if you wish, far more than you would ever really need.

Notice that to the right of the **Where to Look** button, a text box shows you in which folders the search will be made. You can click on the button and then select the folders you want; either select **Look in all folders** or select a single folder. Unfortunately, you can only search Private folders, not Shared ones.

When you are ready to search, click on the **Start** button. Message Finder searches the specified folder and its subfolders and then lists all the messages that fit the criteria in the box below. (If there are a lot of matching messages you can drag the bar between the gray criteria area and the list upwards to make more room.) You can now read a message by double-clicking on it. Use the Previous and Next tool-bar buttons to move through them. You can also delete a message here, which will remove it from the message folder and place it in the Deleted Mail folder.

Printing Messages

Printing Mail messages is quite straightforward. The **File|Print Setup** command lets you select the printer you want to use, and works the same as in most other Windows applications. You can print a message while you are reading it, or you can select one or more messages from the Inbox. Choose the **File|Print** command or press **Ctrl-P**. The Print dialog box lets you select another printer (click on the **Setup** button), and select the **Print Quality**. These quality options will vary depending on the type of printer selected. The higher the quality, the slower the printing. You'll have to experiment, because you may find that some of the options don't seem to have much effect, or, in some cases, may produce an illegible or blank printout. The last option in this dialog box is **Print Multiple Notes on a Page**. By default the check box is selected, which means that Mail won't start a new page for each message (assuming you are printing more than one, of course). If you turn this off, the new setting is saved, so every time you print— even after closing Mail and returning—Mail will use your new choice.

The printed messages start with a header containing your name. This is followed by the first messages From and To names, the date the message was sent, and the message itself.

Selecting Mail Options

Select **Mail|Options** to modify Mail's operating options. You'll see the Options dialog box (Figure 16.13). By default all the check boxes are selected, and most are fairly obvious. The **Save copy of outgoing messages in Sent Mail folder** means that all messages you send will also be placed in the Sent Mail folder. As you've seen, each time you send a message you can use the Options button in the Send Note dialog box to change this setting.

The **Add recipients to Personal Address Book** option ensures that whenever you send a message, Mail will check to see if the names of the people it's going to are in your Personal Address Book. If not, Mail will add them for you. You can also specify how frequently Mail should **Check for new mail**. By default, every 10 minutes Mail will go and look in the postoffice to see if anything has arrived. You can set any time from 1 to 9999 minutes, however.

You can also define what should happen **When new mail arrives**. By default, mail will **Sound chime** and **Flash envelope**—the mouse pointer changes to an envelope for a moment or two when the mail arrives (so quickly you may not notice it), even if you are in another application.

You can turn off the default setting of **Empty Deleted Mail folder when exiting**. Turn this option off and your deleted messages will stay in the Deleted Mail folder until you delete them from that folder. The default automatically removes them each time you close Mail.

Finally, there's the **Server** button, which displays the dialog box shown in Figure 16.14. You can choose to store your MSMAIL.MMF (the message file) locally (the default), or in the Postoffice. Storing message files in the Postoffice itself would let you get to them from another computer.

The **Copy Inbox on Postoffice for Dial-in Access** is used if you dial into the network using RAS (Remote Access Service). If you select this check box, NT will copy the inbox messages to the calling computer, synchronizing the messages in the various locations.

There are many more options that can be set by entering lines in the MSMAIL32.INI file. You can select fonts, automatically compress your message

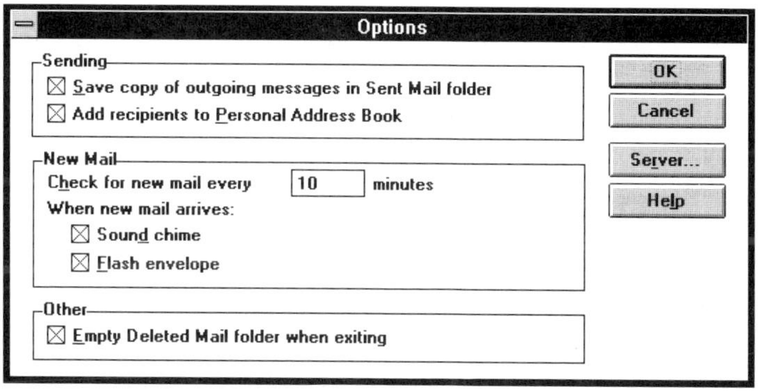

Figure 16.13 The Options dialog box

files, define how quickly mail should retrieve files when you start up, and so on. Some of these entries are easy to use, though some require more information—Microsoft publishes an MSMail technical reference. For more information, open Mail's Help system and search for Configuration File Entries.

Administering the Post Office

The **Mail|Postoffice Manager** command displays a dialog box that contains a list of the postoffice users. You can select a person from that list and click on the **Remove** button to remove them from the system. Or click on the **Details** button to see the same account-details dialog box you saw when you first created an account. You can then change the person's name, mailbox, password, and so on.

You can also use the Postoffice Manager's **Add User** button to add more users to the system. You'll see the same account-details box—just enter the new information. Finally, the Postoffice Manager lets you **compress** Shared folders. Click on the **Shared Folders** button to see the Shared Folders dialog box, which shows you the number of folders, the number of messages, and the disk space used by the messages. If there's an entry next to **Recoverable bytes in folders**, the **Compress** button will be enabled. Click on that button and Mail will compress the data into a smaller area. (When you delete messages, they're not immediately taken from the .MMF file, so compressing the file will "purge" it of deleted messages.) Only compress folders when other people are not using the folders. You may want to do this in the evening, for instance, when everyone's gone home.

As we mentioned earlier, if the administrator forgets his password, the whole system is in real trouble—the only option is to delete the postoffice files and recreate the postoffice. If another users forgets a password, though, the administrator can create a new one.

Also, all users may modify their passwords using the **Mail|Change Password** command. They will have to enter their current password, then enter the new password twice.

Moving and Renaming the Postoffice

You may eventually have to move or rename a postoffice. Perhaps you are installing a new, larger disk drive, or the machine with the postoffice has to be sent out for service. Whether renaming or moving, everyone on the system must close Mail and Schedule+ (use one of the File|Exit and Sign Out commands, as explained in

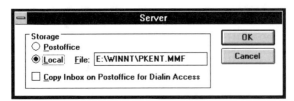

Figure 16.14 The Server dialog box

the next section). Then, in File Manager, select the WGPO directory (the postoffice) and move or rename it. (To rename it you will choose Disk|Share As and enter a new name.)

Go to Registry Editor (see Chapter 11), and open the HKEY_USERS on Local Machine window. Find the second *key* below HKEY_USERS. This will start with an S and have a long number. That's the key that pertains to the current session. Then travel down the tree to the \Software\Microsoft\Mail\Microsoft Mail key. Then change the ServerPath value to show the new information In some cases you may also have to change the ServerPassword, entering the new password for the shared directory.

Closing Mail

There are two ways to close Mail. You can exit Mail and "sign out" at the same time, or you can exit without signing out. Other NT applications may use the postoffice—Schedule+, for instance, uses the Mail system to share information. (Schedule+ and its associated "reminder" application, MSRMND32, are the only applications that come with NT that will work with the postoffice, though other applications may be available from third parties.) If you "sign out" of Mail, you will also close down Schedule+. If you exit without signing out, however, you will close Mail, but Schedule+ can continue running because you are still logged onto the Mail account.

To exit without signing out, select **File|Exit**, **double-click** on the Control menu, or press **Alt-F4**. To exit and sign out at the same time, select **File|Exit and Sign Out**.

Note Schedule+ has a facility called MSRMND32 that can remind you of appointments even when Schedule+ is closed. However, signing out of Mail will stop this feature from working. To ensure the reminders continue, exit without signing out. See Chapter 17 for more information.

The Menu Options

Here's a quick summary of the Mail menu options:

File|Open	Opens the selected message.
File|Move (Ctrl-M)	Moves the selected message to another folder.
File|Copy	Copies the selected message to another folder.
File|Delete (Ctrl-D)	Deletes the selected message, placing it in the Deleted Mail folder. If the message is in that folder, deleting it removes it from Mail entirely.

File|Save As	Saves the selected message as a .TXT file.
File|Save Attachment	Extracts attached files from the displayed message, and saves them in their original formats.
File|Message Finder	Searches the private folders for a particular message.
File|New Folder	Creates a new folder.
File|Folder Properties (Alt-Enter)	Modifies the selected folder's settings.
File|Export Folder	Archives messages from Mail to a .MMF file.
File|Import Folder	Loads messages from a .MMF file back into Mail.
File|Print (Ctrl-P)	Prints the selected messages.
File|Print Setup	Selects and configures a printer.
File|Exit (Alt-F4)	Closes Mail without signing off the Mail postoffice, so other applications using the Mail system—such as Schedule+ and MSRMND32—can continue running.
File|Exit and Sign Out	Closes Mail and signs off the Mail postoffice, so other applications using the Mail system—such as Schedule+ and MSRMND32—will also close.
Edit|Undo (Ctrl-Z)	Undoes the last operation.
Edit|Cut (Ctrl-X)	Removes the selected text from the message and places it in the Clipboard.
Edit|Copy (Ctrl-C)	Copies the selected text from the message and places it in the Clipboard.
Edit|Paste (Ctrl-V)	Places a copy of the data from the Clipboard in the message.
Edit|Paste Special	Embeds a copy of the data from the Clipboard in the message.
Edit|Delete (Del)	Deletes the selected text.
Edit|Select All	Selects the entire message text, or all the messages in the inbox.
Edit|Edit *appname* Object	Edits the selected OLE embedded object in the displayed message.
Edit|Insert Object	Inserts an embedded object into a message.
Edit|Insert from File	Inserts text from a file into a message.
View|Change Font	Available while a message is displayed—toggles between the two available fonts.
View|Next (Ctrl->)	Available while a message is displayed—displays the next message in the Inbox.

View|Previous (Ctrl-<)	Available while a message is displayed—displays the previous message in the Inbox.
View|Shared/Private Folders	Toggles between displaying the Shared and Private Folders in the Inbox document window.
View|New Messages	Checks the postoffice to see if any new messages have arrived.
View|Sort by Sender	Sorts the Inbox messages by Sender name.
View|Sort by Subject	Sorts the Inbox messages by Subject.
View|Sort by Date	Sorts the Inbox messages by date.
View|Sort by Priority	Sorts the Inbox messages by message priority.
View|Open Inbox (Ctrl-G)	Opens the Inbox folder if the Inbox document window is open.
View|Split	Lets you use the keyboard to adjust the column-division between panels in the Inbox document window.
View|Tool Bar (Ctrl-T)	Toggles the toolbar on and off.
View|Status Bar	Toggles the status bar on and off.
Mail|Compose Note (Ctrl-N)	Displays the Send Note dialog box so you can write a message.
Mail|Reply (Ctrl-R)	Displays the RE: dialog box so you can write a reply to the selected message.
Mail|Reply to All (Ctrl-A)	Displays the RE: dialog box so you can write a reply to the selected message, and send the reply to all the recipients of the original message.
Mail|Forward (Ctrl-F)	Displays the FW: dialog box so you can forward the selected message.
Mail|Address Book	Displays the Address Book.
Mail|Personal Groups	Lets you create groups of recipients—the group names can then be used in the To field of the Send Note dialog box.
Mail|Options	Lets you set up Mail's default options.
Mail|Change Password	Lets you change your password.
Mail|Backup	Creates a .MMF archive file, copying all the messages from all the folders in the Inbox.
Mail|Postoffice Manager	Lets you administer the postoffice, so you can add and remove users, change user details, and compress shared folders. This option is enabled only for the account that originally created the postoffice.

Window|New Window	Opens another Inbox document window, so you can have more than one folder open at a time.
Window|Cascade	Cascades the Inbox and Outbox document windows, so all the title bars are visible.
Window|Tile	Tiles the Inbox and Outbox document windows, so each has an equal amount of space.
Window|Arrange Icons	Tidies up the Inbox and Outbox icons at the bottom of the Mail window.
Window|*foldername*	Lets you select an Inbox or Outbox document window, or an open or minimized message window.

17

Network Utilities—
Schedule+

Schedule+ is a project-schedule planner that uses the Mail system to share data among a group of people. It helps workgroups organize their time. Using a series of Appointment Books, each person in the group can schedule meetings and other events by reviewing the times that other potential attendees have available. A group member can then select a block of time and "invite" the other people to the meeting by automatically sending a message across the Mail system.

Starting Schedule+

In order to use Schedule+ fully you must first create an account on Mail. See Chapter 16 for more information. You can work "offline" before creating a Mail account, but won't be able to use all the group-scheduling features.

Schedule+ Double-click on the Schedule+ icon in the Main program group to start. You'll see the Mail Sign In dialog box, the same one you see when you start Mail. Enter your Name and Password, and click on OK.

Note If Mail is already open, you won't need to enter your Sign In information—this dialog box *won't* appear, because you have already signed into the Mail system.

As with Mail, you can bypass this sign-in procedure by entering your account name and password in the icon's Program Item Properties dialog box. However, that will cause a problem if Mail is already open, because you will have signed on already. You may want to create two icons, one to use if Mail is already open, and one to use if it isn't.

As you can see from Figure 17.1, Schedule+ is based on an appointment calendar. On the left side of the window, though, you'll notice four tabs which are used to move between the three different sections—the Task List, Planner, and the Appointment Book. (The last tab—Today—jumps you straight to the current day's Appointment Book page.)

Notice also the **Notes** text box. You can enter information related to the day in here. This isn't a puny 100 or 200 characters, either. You can enter thousands of characters. You could save an entire document in here, and then copy it out of the Notes box and into a word processor on the day you needed it. When you open Schedule+ it automatically checks to see if there are any notes for the current day. If there are, it pops up a Daily Reminder dialog box, containing the Notes text. (You can turn off this feature using the Options|General Options command.)

We'll start by working with Appointments.

Working with Appointments

When the Schedule+ window opens, you'll see your Appointment calendar for the current day. The first entry at the top of the list will be set to 8:00, though you can scroll up or down the list using the scroll bar or the PgUp, PgDn, and arrow keys.

Figure 17.1 The Schedule+ window

If you look on the calendar in the top right side of the window you'll notice that today's date is highlighted. You can display a different date, though, by clicking on any number—the highlight will move to that number, but you'll now see that today's date is marked by a sort of "indentation." You can select a different month and year using the drop-down list boxes immediately above the calendar (you can pick any year from 1920 to 2019). Changing the date in this calendar changes the date on the line immediately above the appointment calendar. Whenever you want to return to the current day, simply click on the **Today** tab at the top left side of the window. And the bottom left side of the status bar always shows the current time and date.

Note If you don't have a mouse, select **Edit|Goto Date** or press **Ctrl-G** to display a dialog box from which you can select another date.

How, then, to enter appointments? You have a couple of options. You can use a dialog box to create an appointment and set all of its options. Or you can use the mouse or keyboard to create an appointment directly on the Appointment Book, and then use the Appointment menu to modify it.

The Appointment Dialog Box

Let's start with the dialog-box method of creating an appointment. Select **Edit|Add Appointment**, double-click on a blank entry in the Appointment Book, or press **Ctrl-N** to see the Appointment dialog box (Figure 17.2). If necessary, select the **Start** and **End** times and dates from the **When** incrementer boxes at the top. If you've already highlighted an area in the Appointment Book, these values have already been set, though you can modify them, of course. Notice the **Tentative** check box. If you select this, Schedule+ will assume the time and date you've selected are not set in stone. In fact, when someone else opens your Appointment Book (you'll learn all about that later) or views your busy time, the appointment

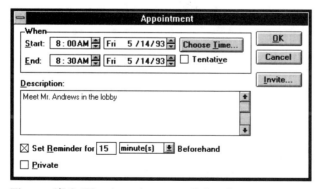

Figure 17.2 The Appointment dialog box

won't even appear, though when *you* look at your Appointment Book the appointment will appear in a gray box, rather than the usual white.

You can enter a **Description** of the appointment. This can be a lot more than a mere description, actually—you could copy and paste an entire itinerary or meeting schedule from another application, for instance. Other attendees will be able to view the information to see what you have in mind. The **Private** check box, however, keeps the description secret. Other users opening your Appointment Book won't be able to see the description if you select this check box.

Speaking of attendees, click on the **Invite** button to see your Mail Address Book (see Chapter 16 for more information about Mail), which works in the same way as in Mail. Select the people you want to invite, click on **Add**, then click on **OK**. Those names will appear in the **Attendees** list box. You can even select personal group names, so you can invite an entire group of people at once.

If you want a reminder to appear before the appointment, make sure the **Set Reminder for** check box is selected. Select a time period (minutes, hours, days, weeks, or months), then select a time value. If you schedule an event a long way in the future, you might want to set a reminder a week or month in advance, then reset it for a day or so in advance.

There's one more feature we must cover—you can display a calendar to help you select a time and date, and even ask Schedule+ to find the best time. Click on the **Choose Time** button to see the dialog box shown in Figure 17.3. (This is actually a slightly modified Planner—we'll be looking at the Planner again later in this chapter.) The people you plan to invite to this meeting will appear in the **Attendees** list box—though you can click on the **Change** button to see the Address Book again if needed.

The grid shows an 11-day period. You can select another period using the calendar and drop-down list boxes in the top right corner of the dialog box. The grid shows your busy time periods in blue, your free time periods in white, and

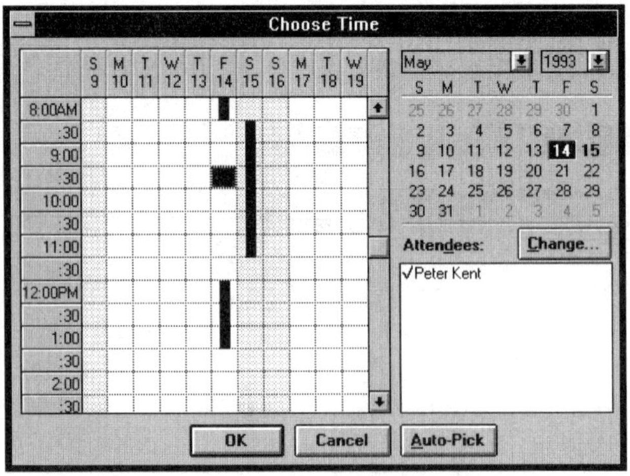

Figure 17.3 The Choose Time dialog box

"nonworking" periods in light gray. Invitees' busy periods are shown in dark gray. Schedule+ assumes that Saturday and Sunday are not working days, but you can set the workday's starting and ending time using the Options|General Options command. You can also change the colors using the Options|Display command. We'll explain both these procedures later in this chapter.

If you click on the **Auto-Pick** button, Schedule+ searches for the first time that everyone has free, and highlights that time. It will look for a block of time as long as the one you have defined by the **Start** and **End** incrementer boxes in the Appointment dialog box—so if you selected a Start time of 9:00 and an End time of 10:30, it looks for a free block that is an hour and a half long. Since the default appointment length is 30 minutes, if you didn't change these values it automatically searches for a half-hour free period. But you can quickly define another length of time. Simply drag the mouse vertically over several blocks (each one is 30 minutes). Then click on Auto-Pick, and Schedule+ will use the new length. Each time you click on Auto-Pick, Schedule+ searches for the next available time.

Of course you can also pick a free time yourself, by dragging the mouse over one of the white areas (remember, the white areas show periods during which all attendees will be free). Or use Tab until the highlight is on the grid, then use the arrow keys to move to a time, and Shift-arrow to select a block of time.

When you've finished, click on OK in the Choose Time and Appointments dialog boxes. If you entered other users into the Attendees list box, you will now see the Send Request dialog box (Figure 17.4). The **To** box will show the attendees, of course. The **Subject** text box will contain the Description text—you can use the End and arrow keys to move through the text. **When** shows the suggested time and date. If you want a response, select **Ask for Responses**—when the recipient of this message reads it, his Send Request check box will automatically be selected. (You'll see what that means in a moment.)

Finally, you can type a message into the blank area at the bottom, perhaps explaining why you've scheduled the meeting, or threatening a punishment if

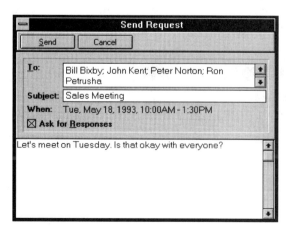

Figure 17.4 The Send Request dialog box

the invited person doesn't turn up. When everything's finished, click on the **Send** button and Schedule+ uses the Mail system to send a message to the invitees. It logs the appointment into your Appointment Book, placing a little "shaking hands" icon to indicate that you've invited everyone. You may also see a bell icon (if you set a reminder) and a key icon (if you made the description private). Now you can sit back and wait for everyone to explain why they won't be there.

Appointment Messages

Right now you've entered an appointment for yourself, but not for the people you invited. They will receive your invitations—the invitations are stored in Schedule+'s Messages document window—probably somewhere underneath the Appointment Book. The message window icon has a red triangle pointing at it if there are unread messages. Of course, you may not be able to see the icon, and if you don't read the messages the first time you open Schedule+ after they arrive, the red triangle won't be included next time. So keep an eye on your message box, and perhaps move your Appointment Book around so the message box is always open when you open Schedule+.

When an invitee double-clicks on one of these messages—or selects it and clicks on **Read**—he'll see a message like the one in Figure 17.5. If you selected the Ask for Responses check box when you sent the invitation, the **Send Response** check box is selected. If he doesn't want to respond using the network— perhaps he's having lunch with you in a few minutes anyway—he can clear this check box.

If the invitee decides that the scheduled appointment is okay, he will click on the **Accept** button. Schedule+ will add the appointment to his Appointment Book, and, if the Send Response check box is selected, will display the message box shown in Figure 17.6. Notice that there's a message at the bottom of the gray area saying "Yes, I will attend." The invitee can add a message above the line in the message area, and even modify the original message. When he clicks on **Send,** the acceptance message is returned to you, and will appear in your message box with a big blue check mark next to it.

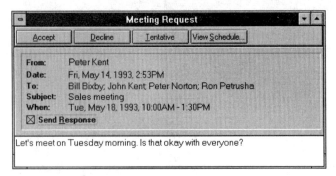

Figure 17.5 The Meeting Request message

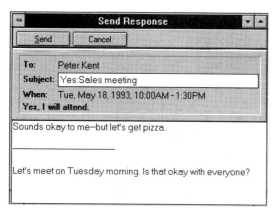

Figure 17.6 The Send Response dialog box

Of course, if the invitee doesn't like the time he can click on **Decline** in the Meeting Request box. You'll see the same Send Response dialog box, but this time the message will say "No, I won't attend." And there's also a **Tentative** button. The appointment appears in your book as a tentative one—it appears in gray, and isn't visible to other users—and the message in the Send Response box will say "I might attend."

If the invitee clicks on the **View Schedule** button he'll see his Appointment Book, with the date of the meeting displayed. He can check to see if he is free at the requested time—he may have scheduled something else since you checked his schedule.

Note Schedule+ messages also appear in your Mail Inbox, and can be responded to directly from there.

What if, after a day or two, you haven't received a response to a request for a meeting? You might try selecting the appointment and then selecting the **Appointments|Resend Mail** command. This will send the same invitation message. You can add to the message if you wish, and then click on Send. If that doesn't work, you might try Chat (see Chapter 18), or you can always use the phone—or perhaps even your feet (a system sometimes known as "sneakernet").

Entering Appointments Directly

The simplest way to create an appointment is to select a time period in the Appointment Book—you can **drag** the mouse down across the time slots, or use Shift-arrow—and then just begin typing. Your typed words appear in a little box sitting on top of the appointment calendar (Figure 17.7). You can use the mouse to drag the top of this box to move the appointment to a different time, or drag

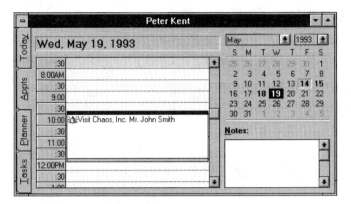

Figure 17.7 An appointment being entered into the Appointment Book

the bottom of the box to extend the time period covered. When you've entered all the information, just move somewhere else. Click on another time slot, for instance.

This is a quick and easy way to add a simple appointment. If you create one of these appointments for a future date, a "reminder" icon automatically appears preceding the text. This means you'll see a reminder box a few minutes before the appointment (by default, 15 minutes before, though you can change the default with the Options|General Options command.) But that's it: You haven't decided who else should attend, you haven't adjusted the reminder, you haven't set the appointment as private, and so on.

Tip   If you enter an appointment and the reminder icon doesn't appear, either it's turned off in the General Options dialog box, or you just entered an appointment on a day, or at a time earlier than the current time and date.

You can now add "features" to your appointment. If you **double-click** on the appointment, or select it and choose the **Edit|Edit Appt** or press **Ctrl-E**, you'll see the same Appointment dialog box we looked at earlier (Figure 17.2). But you can also add features individually. Select the appointment and select **Appointments| Tentative** (or press **Ctrl-Shift-T**) to make the appointment tentative (that is, it won't appear in the Appointment Book when another network user looks at it, and it will appear in gray when you look). To make the appointment description private—so other users can't read it—select **Appointments|Private** (or press **Ctrl-Shift-T**). To set a default reminder (defined in the General Options dialog box), select the appointment and choose the **Appointments|Reminder** command or press **Ctrl-Shift-R**.

The Reminder

When it's time for Schedule+ to remind you that you have an appointment, it will pop up a dialog box similar to that in Figure 17.8. Your appointment Description is shown in the text box—you can copy from this box into a word processor or other application, but you won't be able to modify it here. By default the **Don't notify me again** option button is selected. If you have placed a reminder a long time before the appointment, though, you may want to set another reminder—enter a time in the **Notify me again in** text box. Be careful here—this is not the same as the time you entered when you set up the appointment (which was the amount of time *before* the appointment, of course). If you see the reminder 4 hours before an appointment, and you enter 10 minutes in the **Notify me again in** text box, you'll see another reminder 3 hours and 50 minutes before the appointment, not 10 minutes before.

If you missed an appointment while Schedule+ was not running, you'll see a Reminder dialog box for that appointment when you next open Schedule+. But Schedule+ has a program called MSRMND32 that runs invisibly after you close Schedule+. MSRMND32 continues popping up reminders for you. However, it will only be able to do this if you have not signed off the mail system. For more information, see the discussion on how to close Schedule+ later in this chapter.

Msrmnd32

If you don't start Schedule+ every day, but still want to see your reminders, you could place the MSRMND32.EXE icon into your Startup group. You will see the Sign In dialog box each time you start NT, so you can sign into the Mail system. Then MSRMND32 will run invisibly. Or add your mail account name and password to the icon—type **MSRMND32** *accountname password* (MSRMND32 pkent wedyip, for instance). MSRMND32 will open automatically, without any interaction from you. Your account must have a password in order to use this method—it won't work on an account in which you left the password blank.

Remember that you have *three* applications that can log onto the mail system—Mail, Schedule+, and MSRMND32. Once any one of the three logs on, the other two don't need to. In fact, if you try to automate the logon, you *won't be able to log on*. For instance, if you have MSRMND32 log on to the mail system for you when you log on to NT—by putting the icon in Startup—you won't be able to use a Mail or Schedule+ icon that uses the same "*applicationname accountname password*" trick to

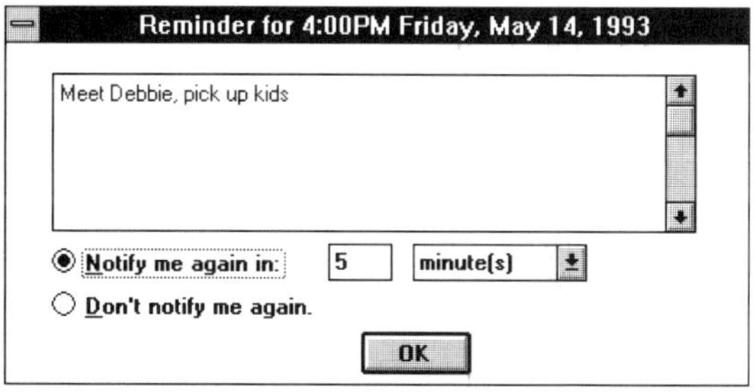

Reminder for 4:00PM Friday, May 14, 1993

Meet Debbie, pick up kids

⦿ **N**otify me again in: `5` `minute(s)` ▾
○ **D**on't notify me again.

[**OK**]

Figure 17.8 The Reminder dialog box

log on. You'll have to use the normal one that has nothing more than the application name in the icon's Command Line text box.

Deleting Appointments

Deleting an appointment is simple enough—just select it and then use the **Edit|Delete Appt** command or press **Ctrl-D**. The appointment is immediately removed from the book, unless it was an appointment to which you had invited other people. In this case you'll see a message box asking if you want to send cancellation notices out. Click on Yes and you'll see a dialog box similar to the one used when you sent invitations. You can enter a subject, type a message, and click on Send.

Recurring Appointments

The procedure for creating recurring appointments is very similar to that used for a one-time appointment. You might want to set recurring appointments for management meetings you hold each week, or a regular lunch date, or to remind you to go to the gym every Thursday lunch time—any event that occurs regularly, whether it be every day, week, two weeks, month, or year.

Start by creating an appointment at the time and date of the first event. Use the keyboard or mouse to block off a space in the Appointment Book, and, if you wish, type a description into the appointment. Then select **Appointments|New Recurring Appt** or press **Ctrl-R**. You'll see the dialog box in Figure 17.9. At the top of the dialog box, in the **This Appointment Occurs** area, you see how often the appointment occurs. Schedule+ initially assumes the appointment will occur every week at the same time and day. You can click on the **Change** button to modify this. You'll be able to select a different interval—Daily, Weekly, Bi-Weekly (every two weeks, not twice a week!), Monthly, or Yearly. You'll also be able to select a different day. And you can select a Duration, the time during which Schedule+ should continue scheduling this event—by default it assumes you want

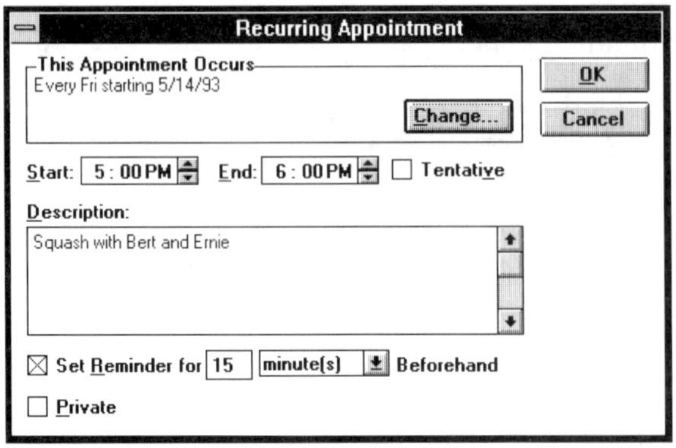

Figure 17.9 The Recurring Appointment dialog box

it to continue forever, but you might set a limit—the next year or six months, for instance.

The rest of the Recurring Appointment dialog box contains features found in the Appointment dialog box. You can change the **Start** and **End** times, make the appointment **Tentative**, enter a **Description**, make the description **Private**, and modify the **Reminder**. You *can't* use the Choose Time feature to find an available time slot, of course—it wouldn't be a recurring appointment if you could. Nor can you "Invite" other people to a regular event. Other people can only be invited to a specific event, though if you wish you can create a recurring appointment, then select each day in turn and use the Edit|Edit Appt command to Invite other people.

When you close the Recurring Appointment dialog box, you'll see that the appointment has a small "arrows in circle" icon. If you look on each day in the recurring schedule—each week, month, or whatever—you'll see that Schedule+ has set an appointment for you. Each of these will also have the same icon (though that icon will disappear if you modify the appointment with the Appointment dialog box).

Tip To convert an existing one-time appointment into a recurring one, simply select it and then press Ctrl-R. The new appointments will *not* contain the invitations that the original had.

What if you want a recurring appointment, but also want to invite other people? This is difficult to arrange, because you need to make sure everyone has that time free each week or month. First, arrange with everyone to keep that time available, then create a simple appointment using the Appointments|New Appointment command and invite all the other people. Then, when you've finished, select the appointment and use the **Edit|Copy Appt** command (**Ctrl-Y**). Now move to the next date on which you want this appointment, select the time, and select **Edit|Paste** (**Ctrl-V**). The new appointment will be pasted into this period. Double-click on the appointment to open the Appointment dialog box, and you'll see that the Attendee list is still there. Click on the OK button and you'll be able to send a message inviting the other people to that specific date.

If you ever need to see a list of recurring appointments, use the **Appointments|Edit Recurring Appts** command. You'll see a dialog box listing all the recurring appointments. You can select an appointment and click on the Edit or Delete buttons, or use the New button to add another recurring event to the list.

Using the Planner

The Planner provides a way to search your schedule for available time for appointments. Click on the **Planner** tab on the left side of the window or press **Alt-P** to see the Planner document window (Figure 17.10). You've seen most of the Planner

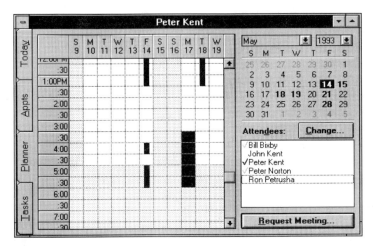

Figure 17.10 The Planner document window

already. It looks much the same as the Choose Time dialog box used to select a time for an appointment in the Appointment Book. The Choose Time box is, indeed, a mini-Planner, and its purpose is the same.

To find an available time for an event, begin by selecting the people you want to invite. Click on the **Change** button and use the Address Book to select the people. They'll be added to the Planner's **Attendees** list, and their appointment information will be added to the Planner's grid. As in the Choose Time dialog box, you'll be able to see where people have time available. You can use **Appointments\Auto-Pick** (**Ctrl-A**) to find the first available time slot. Use the command again to find the next available time slot, and so on. Of course, at this point Schedule+ doesn't know how much time you need for the appointment, so it searches for the first available 30-minute time slot. Just keep pressing Ctrl-A until you find a period that is long enough. Or use the mouse or keyboard to highlight any time slot that is of the length you need—Auto-Pick will then know how long of a period to search for.

When you've found a suitable time, just select **Appointments\New Appointments** (or press **Ctrl-N**), and use the procedure we looked at earlier to create an appointment. When you close the dialog box, Schedule+ will send a message inviting people to the meeting. The Planner also has a **Request Meeting** button. This lets you send a message to the people you want to invite. You can do this *before* scheduling a meeting, to discuss the possible time or the agenda.

By the way, by clicking on a name in the Attendees list you can turn off the check mark next to its name, and remove that person's information from the Planner. You might want to do this if you are scheduling several appointments, with different people. Instead of going to the Appointment Book each time to add or remove people, you could add them all to the list and then make sure only the ones you want to be invited have check marks when you make an appointment.

Tip   To go straight to a particular time and date in the Appointment Book, double-click on a square in the Planner's grid.

Using the Task List

The Task List is a sort of "to do" list, a way to record things you have to do and the date by which they must be done. Click on the **Tasks** tab on the left side of the window or press **Alt-T** to see the Task List (Figure 17.11). The quickest way to add a task is to type the description into the **New Task** text box at the top of the document window and press **Enter** (or click on **Add**). This will place a "priority 3" task in the list, but won't enter any **Due By** date.

You can also create a new task by selecting the **Tasks|New Task** command or by pressing **Ctrl-T**. You'll see the Task dialog box, as shown in Figure 17.12. Type the **Description**, then select a **Project** from the drop-down list box if necessary. Projects let you group tasks—we'll look at them in more detail in a moment. You can even create a new project by entering a new project name. You can edit an existing task by double-clicking on it, or by selecting it and choosing the **Edit|Edit Task** command (**Ctrl-E**), or you can select it and click on the **Edit** button at the bottom of the document window.

 You can now select a **Due Date**. You may also want to select a **Start Work** date and click on the **Set Reminder** check box. This causes a reminder box to appear a number of days (or weeks or months) before the task must be completed (and you'll see the "bell" icon on the entry in the Task List). You can also select a **Priority**, any number from 1 to 9 or a letter from A to Z. By default the tasks in the Task List will be sorted according to their priority levels, though you can use the Task

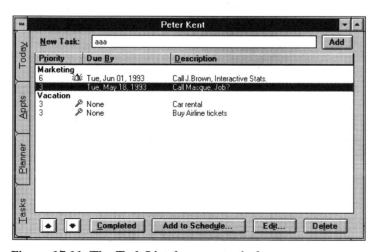

Figure 17.11 The Task List document window

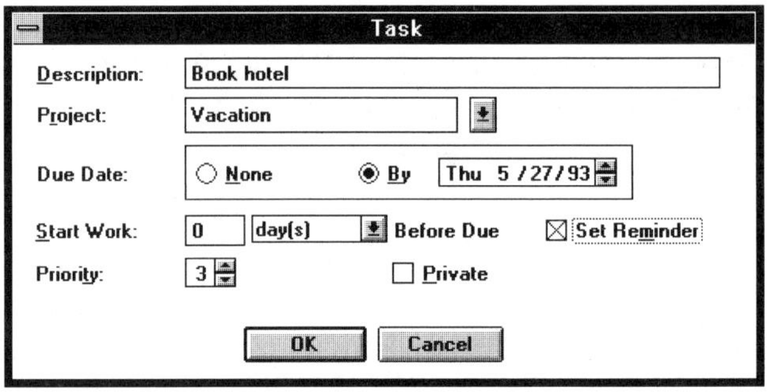

Figure 17.12 The Task dialog box

menu to select another sort method (by date or alphabetically by description). The priorities start with 1 through 9, and *then* go to A to Z. In other words, a task with a priority of 9 is higher than one with a priority of A. Of course you can choose to use only letters or only numbers if you wish.

The last option is the **Private** check box. Selecting this ensures that no other network user can see the description of this task. Private tasks have a key icon next to their names.

Using Projects

Projects let you group tasks together. For instance, if you have to give a speech in another town you could create a project, then assign various tasks to the project— write speech, prepare slides, make hotel reservations, and so on.

Select **Tasks|New Project** to see the Project dialog box. Then enter a **Name** and, if you want to make sure other network users can't view tasks assigned to this project, select the **Private** check box. Click on OK and the project will be added to the Task List. If it's a private task, you'll see a key icon. (You can edit a project name and its "private" status by double-clicking on it, or by selecting it and clicking on the Edit button at the bottom of the window.)

As you saw a moment ago, you can assign tasks to a project. If you've made the project private, all of its tasks will also be private. And the tasks will appear below the project name in the Task List. Tasks within a project will be sorted independently of other tasks.

Recurring Tasks

In the same way that you create recurring appointments, you can also create recurring tasks. You might have to prepare a weekly report, for instance, or deposit your payroll taxes each month, or call your mother once a week.

Select **Tasks|New Recurring Tasks** to see a dialog box similar to the Task dialog box. You can enter a description, select a project, enter a reminder and a "start work" date, select a priority and make the task private. The only difference is that to select a date you'll click on the **Change** button to see the Change Recurrence dialog box, the same box you see when setting a date for a recurring appointment. You'll select the frequency—daily, weekly, monthly, etc.—the actual day of the week or month on which it occurs, and, if you wish, a date on which to remove the task from the list.

When you enter a recurring task, you'll notice the familiar "arrows in a circle" icon on the line to indicate that the task recurs.

There's also a **Tasks|Edit Recurring Tasks** command. This displays a box similar to the one displayed by the Tasks|Edit Recurring Appointments command. You can use this box to view all the recurring tasks you've entered, and edit or delete them, as well as create new ones.

Selecting the View

You can view your tasks in several different ways. By default, the **Tasks|View by Project** option is selected. This means that the list will contain project headings; each heading is followed by the tasks assigned to the project. That means, of course, that the tasks are only sorted within projects, so a low-priority project may appear above a high-priority one if it is assigned to a project that appears earlier in the list. You can turn this view off by pressing **Ctrl-Shift-V**, or by selecting the menu option.

You can also modify the sorting order. By default the tasks are sorted according to priority, with the high-priority tasks near the top. When View by Project is turned on, of course, they are sorted *within* project groups. You can also sort according to due date (**Tasks|Sort by Due Date**) or alphabetically by description (**Tasks|Sort by Description**).

Tip   The quickest way to change the sort order is to click on the column headings at the top of the Task List. Clicking on **Due By**, for instance, sorts the entries by due date. Press **Ctrl** while clicking to sort in *reverse* order.

Working in the List

 While working in the list you can quickly change certain settings using the buttons at the bottom of the window. For instance, you can select an entry then click on the **up-** and **down-arrow** buttons to change the task's priority.

You can also **remove** tasks from the list, and there are two ways to do this. Selecting the task and clicking on **Delete** simply removes the task. But selecting it and clicking on **Completed** removes it from the list and places a note in the current day's Appointment Book Notes box indicating that the task was finished today.

If you need to edit a task, select it and click on the **Edit** button, or **double-click** on the entry, or select it and press **Enter**. And if you'd like to **move** a task from one project to another, just drag it up or down the list with the mouse. (If you don't have a mouse you'll have to edit the task, changing the entry in the Project text box.)

Missing Tasks

When you look in the list you might find that some tasks seem to be missing. If so, select **Tasks|Show All Tasks** to ensure that all tasks are included. (If you see Tasks|Show Active Tasks instead of Show All Tasks, all the tasks are already included—perhaps you accidentally deleted one.)

If the list is in "**Show Active Tasks**" mode, tasks which are inactive will not be shown. (Check the bottom right side of the status bar to see what mode the list is in.) An **inactive** task may be defined as a task which has a Start Work Before Due time set that has not yet been reached. For instance, if the task must be completed by May 30, and the task has Start Work 5 days Before Due set in the Task dialog box, the task will not appear in the list until May 25.

Assigning Time to Tasks

The Task List, Appointment Book, and Planner are all integrated in Schedule+. The **Add to Schedule** button at the bottom of the Task List displays the Choose Time dialog box. You've seen this before, of course, when scheduling appointments or working in the Planner. Simply find a time that is available to work on the task, then select it with the mouse or using the Shift-arrow key method. Click on OK, and Schedule+ automatically creates an "appointment" in your Appointment Book for you. The appointment will contain the task description and the project to which it belongs, if any. You can assign several time slots to a task, if you wish, by selecting several different times in the Choose Time dialog box (you'll have to open and close the box once for each appointment you want to set).

Letting Others Use Your Data

The whole idea of Schedule+ is to provide you with a group-scheduling system. Sure, you can use it even if you are not on a network, to keep track of your appointments and the tasks you need to complete. But Schedule+ is linked to the Mail system for a reason, so group members can find out when other members are available, and arrange meetings. So you have to decide who will have what rights to your data. Schedule+ provides several access levels—from none at all, to total access.

Select **Options|Set Access Privileges** to see the dialog box shown in Figure 17.13. Initially you'll see one entry in the **Users** list box—Default. And this will be set to **View**—we'll see what this means in a moment. You can assign the same privileges to everyone on the Mail network, if you like. Or you can use the **Add** button to see the Address Book and add more people to this list. By adding people

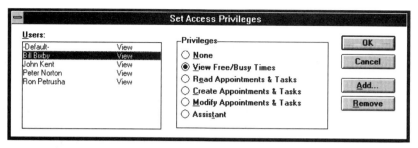

Figure 17.13 The Set Access Privileges dialog box

you can set specific access levels, letting some people do more than the default, and others do less. Also, if you want to assign someone as an *assistant*, you need to enter that person's name into the User's list.

In the **Privileges** area you can see the types of access that are available. Click on an entry in the Users list box, and then click on one of the Privileges option buttons to define that person's privileges:

None	The user cannot do *anything* with your Schedule+ data.
View Free/Busy Times	The user can *see* your free and busy times in Planner and the Choose Time dialog box, but can't see the appointments that you have scheduled, or add or modify anything. Nor can the user open your Appointment Book.
Read Appointments & Tasks	The user can also open your Appointment Book to read your appointments and tasks.
Create Appointments & Tasks	The user can also add new appointments and tasks.
Modify Appointments & Tasks	The user can also modify existing appointments and tasks.
Assistant	The highest access level. The user will also receive and send your Schedule+-related messages. (We'll explain this in a moment.)

Note Remember that regardless of these settings, you can hide information from other users by making appointment and task descriptions Private.

The default setting, View, is the best setting in most situations, so you may not need to change it. It lets other users see when you are available, but not see any detail.

Selecting an Assistant

If you assign someone assistant privileges, that person will be able to do *almost* anything in your schedule that you can. You'll still be able to enter private appointments and tasks that your assistant won't be able to see, but he'll be able to do everything else. And the real advantage to having an assistant is that you can have all your messages forwarded to the assistant's mail box, and the assistant can answer your mail for you. Select Options|General Options and then select the **Send Meeting Messages Only to my Assistant** check box. You won't see your messages at all. If you are setting up "resource" accounts, you will use this method to forward a resource's messages to the person administering the resource. More about that in a few moments.

Using Other People's Data

You've already seen how to use other people's data to some degree. When you "invite" a person to a meeting, Schedule+ automatically takes that person's busy- and free-time information and places it into the Planner or Choose Time dialog box. You can then create the appointment, and automatically enter the appointment into that person's Appointment Book (assuming you have the Create Appointments & Tasks privileges for that person's data).

You can also open another person's entire appointment book—select **File|Open Other's Appt. Book** and you'll see your Address Book. Now, select the people whose books you want to open, click on **Add**, then click on **OK**, and you'll see a document window open for each appointment book you have selected. (Of course, this assumes that you have the right privileges to open another appointment book. You must have the Create Appointments & Tasks privileges or higher.) Now you can work in the appointment books as if they were your own.

Setting up "Resources"

A *resource* account is one which is used to schedule the use of *something*, rather than of someone's time. That something might be a conference room, a slide projector, an auditorium, or some kind of service. Schedule+ lets you set up an account for each resource. People who want to use a particular resource can then "invite" the resource to the meeting, and then use Auto-Pick to select a time at which the resource is available.

You could do this in Windows for Workgroups' MS Mail, but the technique to do so was "hidden," because MS Mail didn't let you create multiple accounts on one computer very easily. However, NT Mail *does* let you create multiple accounts— see Chapter 16 for a description of how.

Using Postoffice Manager, create one Mail account for reach resource—the conference room, the auditorium, and so on. You can enter a full description in the user name text box, and a short name (such as Conf and Auditor) in the

Mailbox text box (the account name). You could add some kind of indicator to resource accounts—start each name with an asterisk, so they appear at the top of your Address Book and Postoffice Manager. When you've added all the resources, close the Postoffice Manager and close Mail—use the File|Exit and Sign Out, to make sure you are completely signed off the mail system (if another application, such as MSRMND32, is running, you won't be signed off if you don't use this command).

Now it's time to open Schedule+. When you see the Sign In box, type the Mailbox name of the first resource in the Name text box, enter its password, and click on OK. This will open the Appointment Book for that resource. Now select **Options|Set Access Privileges**, and define who may use this resources data and how. If you want to let users actually make appointments—reserve time—select the Create Appointments & Tasks option. But, if you prefer to let them see when the room is available, and then request a time, leave the setting at View Free/Busy Times. You might want to assign Assistant privileges to yourself, the administrator, or to another person, a secretary perhaps, who is in charge of assigning time for the resource. That way the assistant will be able to use the File|Open Other's Appt. Book command to get to a resource Appointment Book, and will never have to sign on using the resource's account name again.

When you close the Set Access Privileges dialog box, use the **Options|General Options** command, and then select the **Send Meeting Messages Only to my Assistant** check box. This will ensure that the assistant will receive all the requests to use the resource (the "invitation" messages). There's another check box, **This Account is for a Resource**, but you may not want to use it. If you select this, it effectively turns off the messaging system for this account. Users won't be able to send messages to the account (or the account's assistant) asking if they can book the resource for a particular time. They'll still be able to view the resource's busy and free times, and, according to the privileges you provide, even make and modify appointments, but they won't be able to send messages requesting the use of the resource.

Close Schedule+ again—use File|Exit and Sign Out. Then open it again but this time use the next resource's name. Continue like this until you have set up the access privileges for all the resources. Now the resource accounts can be used by Schedule+ users in the same way they use other people's accounts—they can check for free time, and "invite" the resources to meetings.

Online vs. Offline

In order to manage all the data sharing required for group scheduling, Schedule+ maintains *two* data files. First, there's a .CAL file on your hard disk (in the WINNT\SYSTEM32 directory). This is your *offline* file, and its named after your logon name—PKENT.CAL, for example. Then there's another .CAL file in the Mail postoffice, in the WGPO\CAL directory. This is your *online* file, and it's assigned a number by Schedule+. There's also a .POF file which maintains a list of all users' free and busy times—this is the file that Schedule+ reads when you want to invite other people to a meeting.

The online and offline files should match as much as possible, so Schedule+ updates the files now and again:

When you open Schedule+

When you close Schedule+

When you use the File|Work Online command

When you use the File|Work Offline command

When you use the File|Move Local File command

If you are offline, when another user modifies your online file

You can define in the General Options dialog box whether you want to work online or offline. By default, you will be working online, though if the postoffice is not available—perhaps that machine is not running—Schedule+ will ask if you want to work offline. Also, you can select the **Startup Offline** check box in the General Options dialog box, so that you will be working offline each time you start Schedule+. However, once working, you can always change which file you are working with by using the **File|Work Online** and **File|Work Offline** commands.

Of course it's possible for contradictory information to be entered. You might make an appointment offline, and then another user makes an appointment at the same time online. When the files are merged Schedule+ will enter *both* appointments, but Schedule+ won't warn you of the conflict.

Taking Your Data with You

Schedule+ provides a simple way to take your Schedule+ file with you, so you can use it on a business trip or at home. You can even use it on a Windows 3.1 machine, because the files are compatible with the Windows for Workgroups version of Schedule+.

Select **File|Move Local File**. You'll see a typical File dialog box. Select the floppy drive onto which you want to place the local file (the *offline* file), and click on OK. Schedule+ will actually move the file onto the disk—it will no longer be in the original directory.

Now you must load the .CAL file onto the other computer. First, you must have Schedule+ installed with the same account name (unless, of course, you want to change the .CAL filename each time you move it between computers). The first time you place the file onto the other computer you will use File Manager to move or copy the file into the correct directory (usually the WINDOWS directory on Windows 3.1 machines, or the WINNT\SYSTEM32 directory on NT machines). When you've finished working on the other machine you can then use the File|Move Local File to move the file back onto the floppy, and the File|Move Local File command at the original machine to move it back onto the hard disk. Now, for subsequent moves, you can use File|Move Local File instead of File Manager, because Schedule+ on the second machine will now know the local file is on a floppy.

Of course, if the second machine is connected to the network, you don't need to use a floppy—you can use the File|Move Local File command to move the .CAL file directly onto the other computer.

Tip   What if you lose the .CAL file when you take it? On your work machine, open Registry Editor (see Chapter 11). Select the HKEY_USERS on Local Machine window, then select the second key below HKEY_USERS. The second key will be named S- followed by a number. (This is the configuration data for the person currently logged on.) Now work your way down the "tree" to \Software\Microsoft \Schedule+\Microsoft Schedule+. Then change the Local Path= entry to Local Path=E:\WINNT*filename*.CAL. Now, when Schedule+ opens it will tell you it can't find the file, and then displays a File Open dialog box. Click on OK and Schedule+ will copy your online .CAL file on the postoffice into a new .CAL file on your hard disk.

If you try to work offline after you've put your local file on a floppy, Schedule+ will try to use that floppy. If it's not there, it will write the data onto the online file, and display a message telling you that the offline copy is not up to date. The next time you start Schedule+ with the floppy installed, the offline file will be updated with the changes.

Printing Reports

Schedule+'s **File|Print Setup** command provides a few options that are not common to most Print Setup dialog boxes (see Figure 17.14). Along with the usual features—selecting a printer, paper size, paper source, and the paper orientation— you can also enter the page **Margins**, and select the units of measurement used

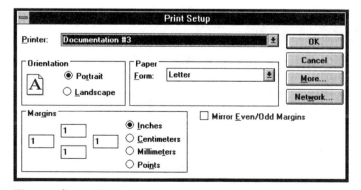

Figure 17.14 The Print Setup dialog box

for margins. Adjusting these margins will actually shrink the table size, so you can shrink a calendar down onto a smaller page, so it will fit into your "real" appointment book, for example. If you go too far, though, Schedule+ may be forced to remove or truncate text—you'll see a warning first. (You'll see in a moment how the Print dialog box also lets you select a paper format to shrink the page by actually shrinking the text size used.)

There's also a **Mirror Even/Odd Margins**. This won't make much difference using the standard margins and paper format, but if you use the Junior or Pocket paper formats (selected in the Print dialog box, as you'll see in a moment), or if you enter different left and right margin measurements, mirroring the printouts will provide a "gutter," so the "inside" of each page always has the larger margin. This will help you if you are binding these sheets into a "book," in a three-ring binder, for example, or stapled together. (We'll come back to these in a moment.) The **More** button in this dialog box lets you view the print driver's Advanced Document Properties dialog box.

When you are ready to print, select the **File|Print** command or press **Ctrl-P**. You'll see the dialog box shown in Figure 17.15. Begin by selecting the type of printout you want from the **Print** drop-down text box:

Daily View	Each page contains one day's data, in a similar format to that which you can see in the Appointment book, including notes.
Weekly View	A grid with seven columns and rows for each half hour during the work day, plus a row for appointments after the work day and one for daily notes.
Monthly View	A typical monthly calendar, with seven columns and five rows, one for each week.
Text View	A list of the appointments, but not in a grid format.
Tasks	A printout that looks the same as your task list.

Now, if you selected anything but Tasks, make sure you have the correct **Starting** date—it will already be set to the date currently displayed in the Appointment Book or Planner. Then select the **For** period, how many days, weeks, or months you want to print.

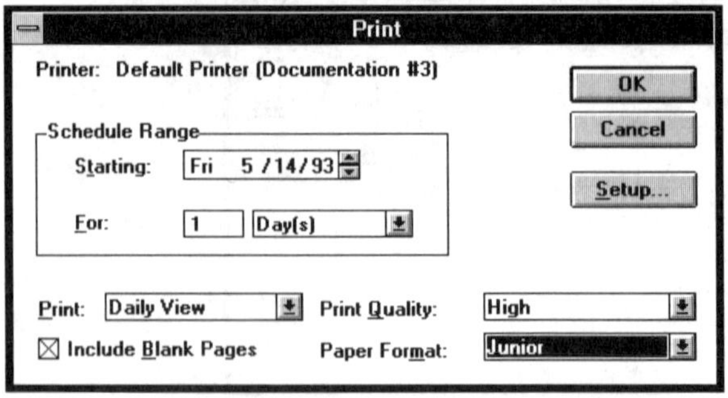

Figure 17.15 The Print dialog box

Select the **Print Quality** if you wish—this varies depending on the type of printer. On some printers the different options will make no difference, on others some may make your printout illegible. The **Paper Format** automatically adjusts the margins and the print size, so you can print appointment book pages of three different sizes—**Standard** makes the pages almost fill the sheet of paper, leaving 1 inch for each margin. **Junior** is a smaller image, about 5 by 8 inches. And **Pocket** is smaller still, about $3\frac{1}{2}$ by $6\frac{1}{2}$ inches. Experiment with these sizes, and find which is the most convenient—you may be able to fit one of the smaller ones into your day-runner-type book. You can further modify page settings by clicking on the **Setup** button to see the Print Setup dialog box again. When you select a Junior or Pocket paper format, Schedule+ automatically places the table in the top left corner of the paper—if you are putting this in a book, it is, in effect, placing the table on an *even* page—with the margin on the right side. You can change the margins around, if you like, so the left margin is larger than the right, making the page, in effect, an *odd* page. You can also select **Mirror Even/Odd Margins** so if you print several pages Schedule+ will move the largest margin from the left side to the right, then the left, and so on.

Finally, you may want to select **Include Blank Pages**. By default, this is turned off, because it makes Schedule+ skip pages that have no appointments. However, if you want the "blank" pages—perhaps you are printing a calendar to stick on your wall—you must turn the option on.

Archiving Schedule+ Data

Once you've passed the date of an appointment, you may want to remove it from Schedule+. You can go through each day, deleting each appointment, of course, but it's easier to just archive them. Select **File|Create Archive**. You'll see a dialog box asking for a date. Enter the date of the first day you want to *keep* in the **Archive Data Before** incrementer and click on OK. You'll then be able to select a directory into which Schedule+ will place an .ARC file.

When you click on OK you'll see a warning box—click on OK and all the data is removed from your Schedule+ .CAL file and placed in the .ARC file. You can now delete this file, if you want. Or you can keep it for future reference. In fact, you can use this file over and over—each time you use it, Schedule+ simply adds the new data to the existing data. To see the contents of the file, select **File|Open Archive** and then double-click on the filename. A new document window will open, with Archive: *filename*.ARC in the titlebar. Of course, your Current appointment Book remains active also, in another document window. You can close the archive document window using its Control menu, or simply let Schedule+ close it automatically when you exit the program.

Note   If you don't close the archive window before you close Schedule+, it will appear in the Schedule+ window next time, regardless of which mail account opens Schedule+. So if it contains confidential information, make sure you close it first!

Working with Other Scheduling Programs

If you need to export and import appointments to and from other time-scheduling programs, Schedule+ may be able to help. You could even merge appointments from one person's Schedule+ account to another's using these methods.

To copy your appointments into a format that other programs can use, select **File|Export Appointments**. (See Figure 17.16.) You have two **File Format** options: Schedule+ or Text. Use the first option if you want to merge a Schedule+ account with another, or if you have another application that can read that format. The Text format would let you export data to a word processor. If you select Schedule+ you'll have no **Schedule Range** options—you'll have to export **All** the data. If you selected Text, though, you can use the **From** and **To** incrementers to select the dates of the data you want to export. You can also choose whether to include the **Daily Notes** in the export. Then, when you click on OK you'll be asked to select a filename and directory into which to place the data (a .SCH or .TXT file).

Schedule+ can import three different formats. Select **File|Import Appointments** to see a File Open-type dialog box. From the **List Files of Type** drop-down list box select the format you want: **Schedule+ (*.SCH)**, **Win Calendar (*.CAL)**, or **WP Office (*.FIL)**. The Win Calendar format is the Windows 3.1 Calendar file format, so you can use those files if you used to work with that application.

Find the file you want to import and double-click on the filename. You'll see the Import Format dialog box (Figure 17.17). Confirm that the correct format is selected. Then decide if you want to **Add All Appointments**—this will try to add all appointments, including those set at the same time as existing ones. If you want to make sure you don't import duplicate appointments, select **Do Not Add Duplicate Appointments**. Or leave Add All Appointments selected, and select the **Ask About Conflicting Appointments** check box. With this selected, if Schedule+ finds an appointment in the import file at the same time as the existing one, it will ask you if you want to import it or not. If you click on Yes, Schedule+ will

Figure 17.16 The Export Appointments dialog box

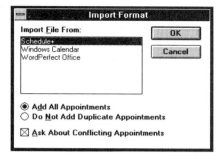

Figure 17.17 The Import Format dialog box

import it and place it *next* to the existing appointment in your Appointment Book. (That's also what the program will do for all the duplicates if you select Add All Appointments but *don't* select Ask About Conflicting Appointments.)

Adjusting Display Colors and Font

If you would like to modify the colors used by Schedule+ or the font, select Options|Display. You'll see the Display dialog box, shown in Figure 17.18. The drop-down list boxes contain the colors you can use for various components. The **Appointment Book Background** color is the color of the entry area in the Appointment Book—before you enter an appointment, of course. The **Planner Background** color is the one used for available time slots in the Planner and in the Choose Time dialog boxes. (By default, it's white.) The unavailable time slots are simply the background color darkened a little. By default, the "unavailable" color is gray, but if you change the background color to, say, light green, the "unavailable" color will be dark green.

The **User** color is the one used to show your own busy periods in the Planner and Choose Time dialog boxes—it's blue by default. And the **Others** color is used to show other peoples' busy periods—dark gray by default. Finally, the **Page**

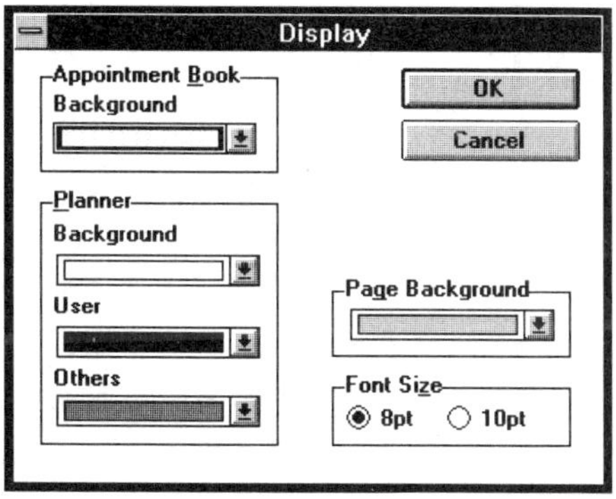

Figure 17.18 The Display dialog box

Background is the color of the unused areas of the Appointment Book, Planner, and Task List document windows—light gray by default.

You can also change the **Font Size** used for the column and row headings in the Appointment Book and Planner, and for the Appointment descriptions in the Appointment Book. It has no effect on other areas, such as the Task List text or the daily Notes.

Setting Default Options

To set Schedule's defaults, select **Options|General Options**. At the top of the General Options dialog box you will see **Startup Offline** (see Figure 17.19). Select this if you want to work in Schedule+ without logging onto the Mail system. You would want to select this if you are not on a network, for instance, or if you rarely use Schedule+ for group appointments. Once Schedule+ is running, you can always use the File|Work Online command to log on.

The **Set Reminders for Notes** check box tells Schedule+ that you want to see a reminder box appear when you open Schedule+ if you have entered anything in the Appointment Book's Notes for that day. You'll see a Daily Reminder dialog box with the note in a list box.

The **Set Reminders Automatically** option makes Schedule enter a reminder each time you create an appointment. By default that reminder will be 15 minutes before the appointment, though you can select another time interval. Of course, whatever you set here, you can configure each appointment's reminder individually when you create that appointment. If the **Sound Audible Alarm** check box is selected, each time a reminder box appears, your computer will play the Schedule+ Reminder sound. (You can modify this sound in the Control Panel's Sound dialog box—if you have a microphone attached to your sound

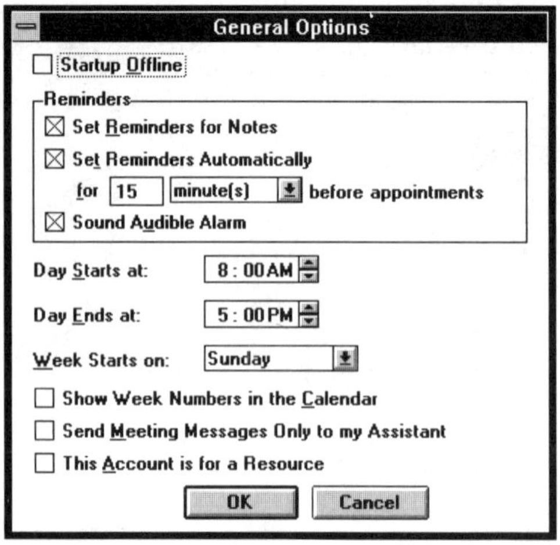

Figure 17.19 The General Options dialog box

board, or if you buy some custom sounds, you could use any sound you want—Big Ben, a voice telling you have a reminder, and so on.)

The **Day Starts At** time defines the first entry in your Appointment Book when you open Schedule+. It's initially set at 8:00 AM, so when you open the program you'll see 8:00 AM as the first time slot at the top of the Book. The Day Starts At option, combined with **Day Ends At**, also defines which areas of the Planner Schedule+ will color gray, and which will be white. These colors are intended to show which hours of the day are available for meetings and which are outside of work hours.

The **Week Starts on** option lets you decide which day should appear first in the Calendar in the top right corner of the Appointment Book and Planner, and in the left column of the Planner's grid. It's initially set to Sunday, though you might prefer Monday. You can pick any day of the week, though. And the **Show Week Numbers in the Calendar** simply adds a column on the left side of the calendar showing each week's "position" in the year. The first week of December, 1993, is week 48, for instance. This option also adds a command to the Edit menu—Go To Week, which lets you enter a week number to jump to that week.

If you have used the Options|Set Access Privileges command to assign another person as your assistant, the **Send Meeting Messages to my Assistant** check box is enabled. Select this if you want all "invitation" messages from other people to be forwarded—across the Mail system—to the person you designated as your assistant.

Finally, the **This Account is for a Resource** check box tells Schedule+ that the Appointment book is not used to schedule a *person's* appointments, but to schedule the use of a "resource" such as a conference room, an auditorium, multimedia equipment, and so on. (This was discussed earlier in this chapter.) You don't necessarily want to do this, as it turns off messaging to and from the resource account.

Close Schedule+ — But Continue Seeing Reminders

Schedule+ can be closed in the same way—and with the same results—that you close Mail. You can exit and "sign out" at the same time, or you can exit without signing out. If you "sign out" of Schedule+, you will also close down Mail. If you exit without signing out, though, you will close Schedule+, but Mail can continue running. To exit without signing out, select **File|Exit**, **double-click** on the Control menu, or press **Alt-F4**. To exit and sign out at the same time, select **File|Exit and Sign Out**.

Schedule+ has a neat feature that's sadly lacking from most appointment programs. In most cases, a program is no good to you once it's closed—it can't remind you of your appointments. But you can let Schedule+ run a program in the background—**MSRMND32**—that *will* keep track of your appointments. MSRMND32 is loaded automatically each time you open Schedule+. If you sign out of Schedule+, you will automatically *close* MSRMND32, and won't receive your reminders. This also applies to Mail, of course—if you sign out of mail you will also be closing MSRMND32 (and Schedule+ if it's still open). So if you want to continue seeing your reminders, just exit—don't exit and sign out.

The Schedule+ Menu Options

Here's a quick summary of the Schedule+ menu options:

File|Turn Off/On Reminders

Turns reminders on and off. When off, the appointment-reminder dialog box will not appear.

File|Work Offline/Online

Toggles between working online (on the .CAL file in the postoffice's WGPO\CAL directory) and offline (on the .CAL file in the WINNT directory).

File|Move Local File

Lets you move your Schedule+ data file (the .CAL file) to another directory or onto a floppy disk, perhaps so you can take it home with you.

File|Open Other's Appt. Book

Lets you open another person's appointment book, as long as you have the correct privilege.

File|Export Appointments

Creates a file containing all your Schedule+ data, in .SCH or .TXT format.

File|Import Appointments

Imports data from a Schedule+ .SCH export file, or a Windows 3.1 Calendar .CAL file, or a Word Perfect Office .FIL file.

File|Create Archive

Removes appointments and places them in an .ARC file.

File|Open Archive

Opens an .ARC archive file in a document window, so you can view old appointments.

File|Print (Ctrl-P)

Prints your appointments or tasks in several different formats.

File|Print Setup

Lets you select a printer and set up page margins.

File|Exit (Alt-F4)

Closes Schedule+ without signing off the Mail postoffice, so other applications using the Mail system—such as Mail itself—can continue running. MSRMND32 will also continue, so reminders continue appearing.

File|Exit and Sign Out

Closes Schedule+ and signs off the Mail postoffice, so other applications using the Mail system—such as Mail itself—will also close. Also, Schedule Reminders will not continue appearing.

Edit|Undo (Ctrl-Z)

Undoes the last operation. This might be Undo Edit (the last typing, for instance),

	or Undo Create (an appointment you just created).
Edit|Cut (Ctrl-X)	Removes the selected text and places it in the Clipboard.
Edit|Copy (Ctrl-C)	Places a copy of the selected text in the Clipboard.
Edit|Paste (Ctrl-V)	Places a copy of the contents of the Clipboard into an appointment or text box, or, if you have copied an appointment (Edit|Copy Appt.), places a copy of the appointment into the Appointment Book at the selected time.
Edit|Edit Appt (Ctrl-E)	Lets you change the selected appointments time, description, reminder, and attendees.
Edit|Task (Ctrl-E)	Lets you modify the task selected in the Task List.
Edit|Copy Appt (Ctrl-Y)	Copies an appointment, so you can use Edit|Paste to place it in another Appointment Book time slot.
Edit|Move Appt (Ctrl-O)	Quickly moves an appointment to another time and date.
Edit|Task (Ctrl-D)	Removes a task from the Task List.
Edit|Delete Appt (Ctrl-D)	Removes an appointment from the Appointment Book.
Edit|Find (Ctrl-F)	Searches the Appointment Book for an appointment containing the specified text.
Edit|Go To Date (Ctrl-G)	Displays a dialog box from which you can select a date for the Appointment Book or Planner. Selecting a date while in the Task List displays the Appointment Book.
Edit|Go To Week (Ctrl-W)	This command only appears if you selected the Show Week Numbers in the Calendar option in the General Options dialog box. It lets you enter a week number to move to that week. Selecting a week while in the Task List displays the Appointment Book.
Appointments|New Appointment (Ctrl-N)	Adds a new appointment to the Appointment Book.
Appointments|Auto-Pick (Ctrl-A)	Available in the Planner, it finds the next time that all the selected attendees are available.

Appointments|New Recurring Appt (Ctrl-R)	Creates a new appointment and schedules it on the same time and day at a regular interval.
Appointments|Edit Recurring Appts	Lets you view a list of recurring appointments and select one to edit.
Appointments|Tentative (Ctrl-Shift-T)	Sets the selected appointment as a tentative appointment, so it appears in gray in your Appointment Book, and doesn't appear when other users refer to your Appointment Book.
Appointments|Private (Ctrl-Shift-P)	Sets the selected appointment's description as private, so other users can't read it.
Appointments|Set Reminder (Ctrl-Shift-R)	Places a default reminder on the selected appointment. The default is 15 minutes before the appointment, though you can change the default in the General Options dialog box.
Appointments|Re-Send Mail	Sends another message to someone you invited to an appointment—used if the person hasn't responded to your first message.
Tasks|New Task (Ctrl-T)	Adds a new task to the list.
Tasks|New Project	Creates a project to which tasks may be assigned.
Tasks|New Recurring Task	Creates a task that will occur multiple times, at a regular interval.
Tasks|Edit Recurring Tasks	Lets you edit a recurring task.
Tasks|View by Project (Ctrl-Shift-V)	Displays tasks in the list underneath the projects to which they are assigned. Turning this off removes project headings from the list.
Tasks|Sort by Priority	Sorts the Task List entries according to their priority settings.
Tasks|Sort by Due Date	Sorts the Task List entries according to their dates.
Tasks|Sort by Description	Sorts the Task List entries into alphabetical order by description.
Tasks|Show Active Tasks/All Tasks	Toggles between showing all tasks in the list, and only those currently active (non-active tasks are those whose due dates and start-work dates have not been reached).

Options|Change Password	Lets you change the password used in Schedule+ and Mail.
Options|Set Access Privileges	Lets you assign access privileges to other people, defining who can do what with your Appointment Book.
Options|Display	Lets you modify the text size and colors used in the Schedule+ window.
Options|General Options	Lets you set up various operating characteristics, such as whether to start offline and whether to automatically set reminders on appointments and notes.
Options|Status Bar	Turns the status bar on and off.
Window|Cascade (Shift-F5)	Places the open document windows one on top of each other, so each title bar is visible.
Window|Tile (Shift-F4)	Places the open document windows so they all take up an equal amount of space.
Window|Arrange Icons	Tidies up the document-window icons at the bottom of the page.
Window|Messages	Displays the Messages document window.
Window|*name*	Displays the named document window— your Appointment Book, or perhaps someone else's, or an archived Appointment Book.

18

Network Utilities— Chat and ClipBook Viewer

Windows NT comes with another couple of utilities originally released in Windows for Workgroups—Chat and ClipBook Viewer. Chat is a sort of real-time message system, one in which your message appears on another computer as you type it. And ClipBook Viewer is an application which lets you share your Clipboard data with other computers, and save data for future use.

Chat

If you'd like to send a real-time message to someone on the network—a message the person will receive immediately and to which he or she can respond immediately, you can use Chat. Both Chat and Mail use text, of course, but we could use the analogy of making a telephone call. Mail is like calling someone and having to leave a voice-mail message. Chat is like calling someone and getting through. Chat is aptly named, because it lets you "talk" to the other person (though using text). As you type, the other person can see what you are typing, character by character, and can then type a response.

Open Chat by double-clicking on the Chat icon in the Accessories program group. As soon as the window opens, select **Conversation|Dial** or click on the dial button. A box appears listing the computers in your workgroup. Double-click on the computer with which you want to communicate, and the box disappears. The status bar in the bottom of the Chat window will show *Dialing computername*, and on the other computer Chat opens automatically. The Chat icon will be placed

on the desktop, and the handset will be wobbling from side to side. If the Chat
window is already open, the title bar will flash. And if system sounds are enabled
in the Control Panel's Sound dialog box, the receiving computer will also beep.

Tip You can assign any sound you want to Chat, using the Chat Incoming Ring and
Chat Outgoing Ring options in the Sound dialog box.

  When the other user responds—by selecting **Conversation|Answer** or by click-
ing on the second toolbar button—the status bar changes to show that you are
now connected (and any existing text from a previous call is cleared from the
window). You can now begin typing. The top panel of the window is the outgoing
text—the text you type. This will appear in the bottom panel on the other person's computer, and you will see his response in the bottom panel on your Chat
window (see Figure 18.1).

As you type, each character is transmitted immediately. The other user sees the
text instantaneously, in effect. If you delete characters, those characters are deleted on the other computer. You can even go back several lines and correct
something, and the correction will also appear in the other user's Chat window.
You will also find the Clipboard commands useful. You can cut and copy text into
the Clipboard, and paste it wherever you want. You can copy text from your word
processor and paste it into the Chat window, to transmit it to the other person.
You can copy incoming text and paste it back into the outgoing panel. You can
copy text from Chat into your word processor. And you can copy an entire mes-
sage—use **Edit|Select All**—hang up, call another person, and paste the previous
message into the outgoing panel. You can only paste text, though—Chat won't
accept any kind of picture.

You can also send special characters. You can get those characters from Character Map, or by using the Alt-0*code* method of typing extended-character-set
characters. There's one catch, though. You can only use one font at a time, and if

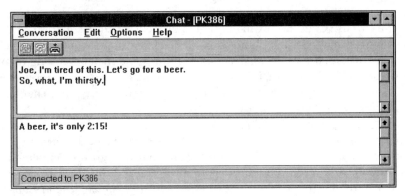

Figure 18.1 The Chat window, during a conversation

the person receiving the message isn't using the same font, it may turn into a different character (more on this in a moment).

 When you have finished your "conversation," select **Conversation|Hangup** or click on the third toolbar button. (Unlike a phone conversation, both ends are hung up at the same time.)

Take a look at the Preferences dialog box (**Options|Preferences**; see Figure 18.2). This box lets you decide what to do with the **Partner's Message**—use the **Partner's Font** or use your **Own Font**. By default, you will see the message in the partner's font, the font that the partner uses for his transmit panel. This ensures that you will see exactly what he or she sends. Notice also that this dialog box lets you move the transmit and receive panels from the default **Top and Bottom** to **Side by Side**.

You can select the font you want to use with the **Options|Font** command. The dialog box you will see is a typical font-selection box. Select the font name, style, size, and perhaps underline or strikeout. You can also select a font color. This font color will appear on the other computer, by the way, if that user has selected Use Partner's Font in the Preferences dialog box. These font settings, then, affect your transmit panel, but only affect your receive panel if you select Use Own Font in the Preferences dialog box.

Tip A workgroup will probably want to decide on a standard format for the font used in Chat. If everyone uses the same font, the Partner's Message options in the Preferences dialog box no longer matter.

You can change Chat's background color with the **Options|Background Color** command. You will see a typical Windows color-selection dialog box—you've got almost 50 colors to choose from, though you won't be able to create any custom colors. The Background Color is also affected by the Partner's Message setting in the Preferences dialog box. If the other user has selected Use Partner's Font, your background color will appear in his or her receive panel.

There are three more commands in the Options menu. You can turn off the **Status Bar**, the **Toolbar**, and the **Sound** you hear when someone calls you. Chat's a simple and fun application to use—and what's even better is that you can look like you're working even when you're shooting the breeze.

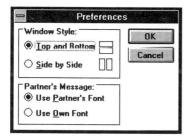

Figure 18.2   The Preferences dialog box

Note There's a bug in the way that Windows for Workgroups workstations connect to NT machines. You may find that it's impossible to connect if you try to use Chat, dialing from the Workgroups workstation to the NT machine—you'll be asked for a password, and won't be able to go any further. (The same problem will occur in ClipBook Viewer when you try to connect to an NT ClipBook from a Workgroups machine.) Probably the only way around the problem is to provide the Workgroups machine with an account on the NT machine, and then make sure the Workgroups computer logs onto the network using that account's name and password.

This problem will probably only occur in workgroups, not in NT Advanced Server domains.

ClipBook Viewer

ClipBook Viewer is an advanced Clipboard. In fact it contains the Clipboard within it, but lets you copy data from the Clipboard into a ClipBook page, and store multiple pages, so the data can be saved for future use by your computer or shared with other computers.

A major criticism of the Windows Clipboard has been that it can only contain a single item—one picture or one block of text. Each time you copy something to the Clipboard, the existing data is lost. Several add-on applications, both share-ware and commercially distributed, are available to get around this problem, automatically saving the existing data each time you copy to the Clipboard. The ClipBook can also save this data, though you must do it manually—it won't save it for you each time.

ClipBook
Viewer

When you first open ClipBook Viewer—by double-clicking on the icon in the Main program group—you will probably see an empty document window called **Local ClipBook**. The Viewer can be a little confusing at times, as it may open with the Local ClipBook document window either maximized or at least on top of the Clipboard icon. But if you minimize the Local ClipBook you'll be able to see the Clipboard icon.

Double-click on the Clipboard icon, and you will see the contents—the data that you pasted into the Clipboard from one of your applications. While the Clipboard is open you can carry out normal Clipboard operations, the ones you are used to seeing in Windows 3.1. You can save files in the .CLP format, or open existing .CLP files (replacing the contents of the Clipboard, of course). You can use **Edit|Delete** to clear the Clipboard contents. And you can use the **Display** menu to view the Clipboard data in various formats.

Copying to and from the ClipBook

 Other commands are now available, the most important of which is **Edit|Paste**, which pastes the Clipboard image into the Local ClipBook, the ClipBook on your machine (or click on the Paste button on the toolbar). A dialog box opens, into which you must type a **Page Name**. This is the name by which the image will be identified in the ClipBook. If you are just adding a few "pages" to the book, you might want to enter a number. If you are working with a lot of pages, though, you will probably want to enter a descriptive name that will help you find the data when you need it next. You can enter any character, including spaces, and you can use quite long names (though only about 47 characters will be displayed in the list of pages). You can also click on the **Share Item Now** check box in this dialog box if you want to begin sharing the data with another computer on the network—we'll come back to data sharing in a moment.

When you create a ClipBook page, ClipBook Viewer automatically creates a .CLP file in the WINNT directory. It assigns a code number to the file. These files can be opened directly into the Windows Clipboard—using the File|Open command—or copied or moved to other directories. If you move a file, the listing will still appear in the ClipBook, though you won't be able to view it.

 Your Local ClipBook provides a great way to save data for future use, getting around the one-item-only limitation of the Clipboard. Later, when you want to use the data again, you can copy from the ClipBook page back into the Clipboard, and paste from there into an application.

Open the Local ClipBook document window. To see a list of all the pages, select **View|Table of Contents** (or click on the toolbar button). To see the thumbnail view, select **View|Thumbnails**, or click on the Thumbnails button in the toolbar. Figure 18.3 shows the Local ClipBook in Thumbnails view.

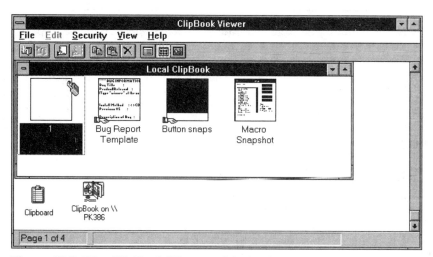

Figure 18.3 The ClipBook Viewer, with the ClipBook window showing thumbnails

Now select the page you want. To confirm you've got the right one, select **View|Full Page,** or click on the toolbar button, or simply double-click on the table of contents listing or thumbnail, and the image will appear in the document window. If you have got the one you need, select **Edit|Copy** or click on the Copy button in the toolbar, and the data is copied into the Clipboard. Double-clicking on the Full Page view returns you to the Table of Contents or Thumbnails, depending on which view you were in previously.

Tip   You *copy* from the ClipBook into the Clipboard, and *paste* from the Clipboard into the ClipBook, which is not always easy to keep straight. Remember that you paste from the Clipboard into applications, and copy from applications into the Clipboard. Or, to jog your memory, point at the fifth button on the toolbar and press and hold the mouse button—the status bar will describe what that operation does. Move the pointer off the button before releasing if you don't want to continue.

Sharing Your Data

When you want to share the contents of a Local ClipBook page, you have two options. You can either click on the **Share Item Now** check box when you paste the item from the Clipboard into the ClipBook (as we saw earlier in this chapter), or you can select the page from the Local ClipBook document window and then select **File|Share** (or click on the Share button in the toolbar). Either way, you'll see the dialog box in Figure 18.4.

Note   You can only share one page at a time—you can't select an entire ClipBook.

You are now presented with two **Sharing Options**. You can **Start Application on Connect**. This means that NT will automatically run the application that created the data in the other computer. If the object is not text or a bitmap, you should select this check box, so NT can start the source application when another user tries to use the object.

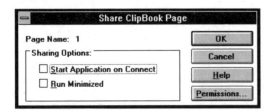

Figure 18.4 The Share ClipBook Page dialog box

The other option is to **Run Minimized**. If you selected Start Application on Connect, then you may want to select Run Minimized in order to keep that application out of the way when it opens.

If you want this ClipBook page available to anyone, just click on OK and you've finished. If you want to restrict access, though, click on the **Permissions** button. You'll see a typical permissions dialog box (as described in Chapter 7). These are the types of access that you can assign to different users:

No Access   Cannot use the ClipBook page in any way.

Read   Can copy from the ClipBook page into the Clipboard.

Read & Link   Can copy from the ClipBook page into the Clipboard, and create an OLE link with the data.

Change   Can Read and Link, and can also replace the ClipBook page with other data, or delete the page.

Full Control   Can carry out any operation with the data, and can assign permissions and take ownership.

By default, you will have Full Control, and Everyone will have Read & Link access.

When you close the Share ClipBook Page dialog box, the page will be ready for another computer to use it. You will see the hand icon that is used throughout NT to indicate that an object is being shared.

Note To stop sharing a page, select it and then select File|Stop Sharing or click on the fourth toolbar button.

Connecting to Another ClipBook

To connect to another computer's ClipBook, select **File|Connect**, or click on the first button in the toolbar. You'll see the Select Computer dialog box. Pick a computer from the list, and click on OK (or just double-click on the entry). The ClipBook will open in your ClipBook Viewer. If you are working with graphics, it may take a little while for the ClipBook to open. (In the case of a very complicated image, it may not come through at all—you may see a message saying there's a problem with the connection. Remove the message box and you could then see a message, in the ClipBook page window, saying that ClipBook doesn't have enough memory.)

Now you can use the **Edit|Copy** command (Ctrl-C) or click on the fifth toolbar button to copy the data from that ClipBook page into your Clipboard. And from there you can copy it to another application. You can also view it, using the View|Thumbnails, View|Table of Contents, and View|Full Page commands.

Note To disconnect a networked computer, use the File|Disconnect command, or click on the second toolbar icon.

OLE and ClipBook

ClipBook even supports Object Linking and Embedding. Embedding is simple. Just connect to the other computer's ClipBook, copy the data into your Clipboard, and embed into an application in the normal way. (In some cases you can embed by simply pasting—some applications automatically embed data when pasting from OLE servers. In other cases you will use the application's Paste Special option.)

Images are also linked in the same way as in Windows 3.1. Copy the image from the other computer's ClipBook to your Clipboard, then use the Paste Link or Paste Special command to link the data into your document.

Note There's a bug that may make it difficult for a Windows for Workgroups machine to access ClipBook data from an NT machine.

ClipBook Viewer Security

ClipBook Viewer has the same security commands as File Manager and Print Manager: Security|Permissions, Security|Auditing, and Security|Owner.

ClipBook's Menu Options and Toolbar

Here's a quick summary of the ClipBook's menu options and toolbar icons:

	File|Open	Opens a .CLP file in the Clipboard document window.
	File|Save As	Saves the contents of the Clipboard document window into a .CLP file.
	File|Share	Only enabled when the Local ClipBook document window is selected. This option lets you share a single ClipBook page with another computer.
	File|Stop Sharing	Only enabled when the Local ClipBook document window is selected. This option lets you stop sharing ClipBook pages.

🖼	**File|Connect**	Lets you connect to another computer's Clip-Book.
🖼	**File|Disconnect**	Only enabled when a ClipBook from another computer is selected. This option lets you disconnect from the ClipBook.
	File|Exit	Closes ClipBook Viewer.
🖼	**Edit|Copy (Ctrl-C)**	Copies the selected page from the Local Clip-Book or a network ClipBook into the Clip-board, from where it can be pasted into an application.
🖼	**Edit|Paste (Ctrl-V)**	Copies the contents of the Clipboard into the Local ClipBook.
🖼	**Edit|Delete (Del)**	Empties the Clipboard.
	Security|Permissions	Only enabled when the Local ClipBook is selected. Lets you define who can access the selected Local ClipBook page.
	Security|Auditing	Lets you set up security auditing, to see who is using what ClipBook page.
	Security|Owner	Only enabled when the Local ClipBook is selected. Lets a user on your computer take ownership of the selected page (if that user has the right to do so).
	View|Toolbar	Removes the toolbar.
	View|Status	Removes the status bar.
🖼	**View|Table of Contents**	Only enabled if a ClipBook is selected. Displays a list of the pages.
🖼	**View|Thumbnail**	Only enabled if a ClipBook is selected. Displays a "thumbnail" image of each ClipBook page.
🖼	**View|Full Page**	Only enabled if a ClipBook is selected. Displays the selected ClipBook page.
	View|Default Format	Only enabled if the Clipboard is selected. Makes the Clipboard display the data in its default format.
	View|*formats*	Only enabled if the Clipboard is selected. Lets you select another format in which to display the data. The options depend on the type of data and the application it comes from.
	Window|Cascade (Shift-F5)	Cascades the Clipboard and ClipBook document windows.

Window|Tile Horizontally   Tiles the Clipboard and ClipBook document
                                   windows one on top of each other.

Window|Tile Vertically   Tiles the Clipboard and ClipBook document
(Shift-F4)   windows side by side.

Window|Arrange Icons   Arranges the document window icons at the
                                   bottom of the ClipBook window.

Window|Refresh (F5)   Refreshes the selected ClipBook, to make sure
                                   it is displaying all available pages.

19

Tape Backup

Windows NT has a built-in tape-backup utility. You can back up any files that NT can read—NTFS files, of course, but also DOS's FAT and OS/2's HPFS. You can even back up data from network drives. You can carry out several different kinds of backup—you can do full backups, backing up everything on a drive, or select the particular files and directories you want. You can do normal backups (setting the files' archive bits) or copy backups (duplicating the files, not changing archive bits). You can also do differential, incremental, and daily backups, which we'll explain in detail later. Plus, of course, you can restore data from your tapes back onto your hard drives. You can even do unattended backups, though you have to jump through one or two hoops to do so.

Everyone can use Backup, but only Administrators and those given Backup privileges in User Manager have full Backup and Restore rights. Those users can back up and restore regardless of the access privileges set in File Manager. You can find backup and restore privileges in the User Manager's User Rights Policy dialog box—"Backup files and directories" and "Restore files and directories."

Like many of NT's components, Backup can be modified by third parties, and programs are available that take the basic Backup structure and add features. Even before NT was released, for instance, Conner Software had finished their Backup Exec program, which improves upon NT's Backup. It has a simplified scheduling utility, allows file sorting, creates a list of files modified since the last backup, lets you rename files as you restore them, and lets you set a password on archived data. Conner Software had a head start on other software companies— they created NT's Backup program for Microsoft—but other companies will catch up, so if you find Backup to be lacking, you can replace it with a more advanced system.

Preparing the Hardware

Most small-capacity tape drives are not SCSI devices—they run off a floppy-disk drive controller (large-capacity drives, typically over 700 MB, are usually SCSI devices) or a special adapter board. Yet NT uses a SCSI interface to work with tape drives. However, that doesn't mean it only runs with the large SCSI tape drives—your non-SCSI drive may work also.

Most SCSI adapter cards have a connector to which you can attach the cable that runs to your floppy disks—this isn't a SCSI port, it's a normal floppy-disk port that happens to be on the SCSI board. This connector may also be used to connect to a tape drive. All three of these devices—drive A:, drive B:, and the tape drive—attach to the same connector on the adapter card, using a special cable. For instance, a ribbon cable may run from the adapter to the tape drive, then another cable may attach to a connector in the middle of the first cable, and run to the two disk drives.

If you have a non-SCSI tape drive you should start by finding out if it can connect to the SCSI adapter's floppy-disk port. Then find out if you can run it along with two floppy-disk drives. Some early Colorado Memory Jumbo tape drives, for instance, will connect to a SCSI card, but only with *one* disk drive. If you want to use two floppy-disk drives you have to upgrade the tape drive. (Of course if you only have one floppy-disk drive, this doesn't matter.)

Then find out if NT has a driver that will run the tape drive. If you have a Colorado Memory Jumbo drive, there is an NT driver that you can use—the QIC-40/QIC-80 floppy tape drive driver. Call your drive's manufacturer to see which driver you need.

Installing the Driver

Windows NT Setup

Before you can use your tape-backup drive, you must install the driver. This is done through the Windows NT Setup dialog box, not through the Control Panel's Drivers dialog box. Double-click on the icon in the Main program group. When the Windows NT Setup dialog box opens, select **Options|Add/Remove Tape Devices**. When the Tape Device Setup dialog box opens, click on the **Add** button, and you'll see the Select Tape Device Option dialog box. Select the correct driver from the drop-down list box and click on **Install**. Setup will ask for the path to the installation files. Enter the CD-ROM or disk drive you are using and click on Continue. If you are using floppies, Setup won't be able to find the files, so it will then tell you which floppy to place in the drive.

After the driver has been installed, you will have to shut down Windows NT for the changes to take effect. The first time you boot after installing the driver, make sure that the tape drive doesn't have a tape in it—the first time you boot and start Backup can be *very* slow for some tape drives if there's a tape installed.

When you boot NT you might see a message telling you to look at the Event Log. If so, you need to open the Event Viewer (see Chapter 13) and look at the messages in the System Log that were created during boot. You might see a message such as "Could not find the tape drive. Please verify connections to the drive and restart the system." Make sure you have the drive installed correctly. You might see "Format of tape is unknown. You must format this tape before it can be used." Make sure the tape is inserted correctly, or try another tape. You could also see something like "There is no cartridge detected in the drive." Although you don't have to have a tape in the drive during boot, if you do, and you receive this message, make sure the tape is fully inserted. The tape should "snap" into place, and the light on the drive will turn on for a while.

Initializing Backup

If you plan to back up data from a network drive, connect to that drive—in File Manager—*before* you open Backup. The application looks for connected drives while it is opening, and there's no way to connect to a drive from inside the application.

Backup

Double-click on the Backup icon in the Administrative Tools dialog box to see the Tape Backup window, as shown in Figure 19.1. It may take a few minutes for the utility to initialize the hardware. In fact, if there's a tape in the drive it might take as long as 20 minutes. When the message in the status bar says Ready, the initialization is over, and you can begin. As you've run this first initialization without a tape in the drive, you won't yet be able to back up anything, even if you now insert a tape, because Backup won't know the tape is there. When you first open the backup window it has two "document" windows—Drives and Tapes—though one may be minimized at first. The Drives window shows all the hard drives on your system, and is where you will start selecting the files and directories that you want to back up to tape. The Tapes window will later show a listing of the tape *catalogs*, and is where you will select the tapes and data that you want to restore to your hard drives.

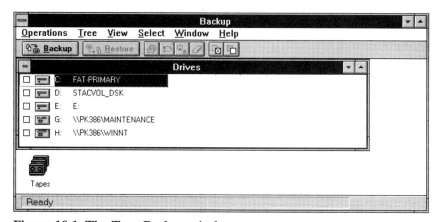

Figure 19.1 The Tape Backup window

Note After the first time you start Backup you will probably want to insert a tape before double-clicking on the program icon. That way, Backup will automatically confirm the presence of the tape when it starts.

Insert the tape into the drive and then choose the **Operations|Hardware Setup** command. You'll see a dialog box with a drop-down list box, listing all the tape drives on your system. If you only have one tape drive, that one should already be selected. Select the correct one, if necessary, and click on OK. Backup will again initialize the hardware, and will read the tape. When the initialization is finished, the Tapes document window will show a tape icon and a message—it may say Blank Tape or perhaps show the date it was created. You may also see "The tape drive is busy" for a moment while the tape drive reads the tape.

Backing Up a Hard Drive

 When you're ready to back up data, begin at the Drives window. Each hard-drive volume on your system is listed, including network drives that were connected in File Manager when you started Backup. You won't see removable drives (such as Bernoulli drives) or CD-ROM drives, though. If you want to back up an entire drive you must place a check mark in the check box before the drive icon—**click once** on the check box, or select it and press **Spacebar**, or select it and click on the **Check** button in the toolbar, or select it and choose **Select|Check**. When you press Spacebar the check box is checked, and the highlight moves to the next drive—so you can quickly select several drives by pressing Spacebar several times.

Note Before backing up, make sure none of the files you want to back up are in use, and that you have access to the files and directories. If you are an Administrator or Backup Operator you automatically have Backup access for all files.

If you don't want to back up the entire drive, but want to select specific directories or files, **double-click** on a drive, or select it and press **Enter**. A directory window will appear. Of course you're already familiar with this window, because it's the same as the File Manager directory window. The commands in the Tree menu work in the same manner as those in File Manager, expanding and collapsing branches on the directory tree, as do the commands in the View menu (though the Status Bar, Toolbar, and Font commands are found in File Manager's Options menu). Of particular interest in this menu is the **All File Details** command. You may want to use this so you can back up files of a particular date, or check the size of files, or select those with the A (Archive) attribute set. The Archive attribute indicates a file which has not been backed up—backup programs turn the bit off when they back up files, and the bit is turned back on when the file is modified the next time. Unfortunately, there's no way to display *only* files which have not been backed up. However, there's another way to do a "modified files only" backup, using options in the Backup Information dialog box. To use this method you would select the drive or directories containing the files, then select the appropriate Backup Type in the Backup Information dialog box. (We'll look at that in a moment.)

You can select and check several files at once. Drag the mouse pointer across the filenames to highlight several at once, or press Shift and use the arrow keys. You can select several blocks by dragging the mouse pointer across the names, holding down Ctrl, then dragging across the next series of names. Or hold down Ctrl while you click on the ones you want to select. You can also click on one and then hold while you click on another, to select all the files between the two. Once you've selected the ones you want, click on the toolbar button or select **Select|Check**.

Figure 19.2 shows the Backup window with a single disk and several files and directories selected for backup. Note that when you click on a directory name or directory icon, the contents of the directory are shown in the panel to the right. If you want to actually select that directory you must click on the check box to the left of the icon. Likewise, you must click on a file's check box to select it—clicking on the filename or file icon will not select it.

You can use these methods to select entire drives and directories, or individual files. You can also *remove* files and directories from directories and disks that you have selected to back up. For instance, if you want to back up most of a disk, excluding one or two directories, you would select that drive and then find the

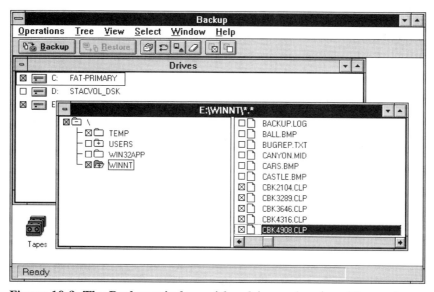

**Figure 19.2 The Backup window, with a drive and various files and
directories selected**

directory you don't want. This time you'd click on the **Uncheck** toolbar button, or select **Select|Uncheck**. Pressing Spacebar works in the same way also, removing a check mark from an already filled check box. Notice the check boxes next to the directory icons. If the check box is clear, no files in that directory have been selected. If the check box is white with a black X in it, all the files in the directory have been selected. And if the box is *gray* with a black X in it, some—but not all—of the files have been selected.

Note   There's a significant weakness in this directory and file listing. It won't show you the amount of storage it's going to take to back up all the data you have selected. Nor can you automatically *exclude* files. For instance, you can't tell Backup to exclude all files that end with .TMP, or automatically exclude PAGEFILE.SYS (the paging file, which you don't need to back up). You'll have to select those individually.

Once you've selected all the data you plan to back up, click on the toolbar's Backup button, or select **Operations|Backup**. The first line in the Backup Information dialog box shows the name of the **Current Tape**. This is automatically assigned to a tape the first time you record data on it, though you can enter a different name in the **Tape Name** text box. If this is the first time you've used the tape, the Current Tape entry will be empty.

The **Creation Date** is the date you first used the tape, or the date that the backup set on the tape was replaced. The **Owner** is the first user of this tape—the computer name and the account name. The **Tape Name** field is one which you can modify, *if* you have selected the **Replace** option button in the **Operation** area. Replacing will remove the data already on the tape and replace it with the new data. **Append** will add the new data to the tape—in which case the tape will retain its original name and creation date.

The **Verify After Backup** check box tells NT to compare the data on the tape with the data on the disk, once the backup has been completed, to confirm that all the data has been copied correctly. The **Backup Local Registry** check box tells NT to copy the configuration registry data onto the tape, in addition to the files and directories you selected. This option is only enabled if you have selected the disk volume drive that contains the NT system files.

You can also choose to **Restrict Access to Owner or Administrator**. This tells NT not to let another user take data off this tape, unless that user is an Administrator or a member of the Backup Operator's group. Nor will another user be allowed to delete the tape or write onto it. And if the tape is taken to another computer, only Backup Operator's or Administrators will be able to use it, even if you log on with the same account name. You won't be able to change this option if you selected **Append**—it will retain its original setting.

The **Backup Set Information** area displays information about each disk volume you selected in the Drives document window. There's also a scroll bar—click on the scroll bar and, if there is a second set, its information appears. NT Backup regards the data from each disk volume as a separate set. The **Drive Name** shows the drive letter and volume name. You can enter a **Description**—you might want to type a short explanation of what the data is. There's no need to include a date, because that will be reported automatically.

Now you can select the **Type** of backup. You have five options:

Normal	Copies the selected files and directories to the tape, and resets each file's archive bit to show that it has been archived. This type of backup is similar to a "Full" backup (although a Full backup often implies that everything on the selected disk is backed up, in an NT Normal backup you must select the data you want backed up). The files' archive bits are reset.
Copy	Copies the selected files and directories to the tape, but doesn't reset the files' archive bits.
Differential	Checks the selected files to see if the archive bit has been set *on.* (If the archive bit is on, the file has changed since the last time it was backed up.) It copies only those files that have been changed. After copying the files to tape it does *not* change the archive bits— the bits are left on.
Incremental	Checks the selected files to see if the archive bit has been set *on.* It copies only those files that have been changed. After copying the files to tape it changes the archive bits, turning them off.
Daily	Checks the selected files to see which ones have been changed during the current day. It copies only those files that have been changed during the day. After copying the files to tape it changes the archive bit, turning it off.

The last three options are very useful. Differential lets you simply select a disk drive, and tells NT to find which files have been changed. You would use this in combination with a Normal backup. First, you do a normal backup, and back up all the data on the disk drive. Then each subsequent day you will do a Differential backup, automatically copying only those files that have changed since the last time you did the Normal backup. Because Differential doesn't change the archive bit, each time it's used it copies all files changed since the Normal backup, not since the last Differential backup. If you ever need to restore an entire hard disk you only need to do two restores—the Normal set followed by the *last* Differential set.

Note The major problem with these forms of backup is that there's no way to tell Backup to *exclude* files such as .TMP and the NT paging file or Windows 3.1 swap-file. If you use Differential, Incremental, or Daily, remember to *deselect* those files after selecting a disk drive, or expect to eat through tapes quickly.

The Incremental backup is similar to the Differential, but each time it copies files it sets the archive bit *off*. The next time you use Incremental it only backs up files that have changed since the last Incremental backup, not since the last Normal backup. This gives you a complete record of all the changes made to your files. However, it also means that if you ever want to restore an entire hard disk you would have to restore all the backup sets—the Normal set followed by each Incremental set, in the order in which you recorded them. You will want to use Incremental if you need a copy of previous versions of each file, rather than just the most recent version. The drawback is that you need to keep all the Incremental backup sets. With Differential you only need to keep the most recent set. Incremental backups are quicker than Differential backups, though, as you are only copying recent changes, not all the changes since the last Normal backup.

The Daily backup is a quick and simple way to back up only changes made during that day, and may be used for transferring the day's work to another computer—perhaps a computer at home. You could use Daily to ensure that both computer's have exactly the same files. Daily is different from Incremental in that it doesn't change the archive bit, and from Differential in that it ignores all changes that occurred on previous days.

Your final options are in the **Log Information** area. Backup can provide a **Log File** that will tell you how the backup operation went. By default the file is called BACKUP.LOG, but you can click on the button at the end of the text box and enter a new name, or select another existing file. If you select an existing file it will be overwritten with the new data.

You now have three options. You can select a **Full Detail** log—you'll not only get progress and error messages, but a list of all the files that were backed up. This can make the file quite long, of course. You can also select **Summary Only** to omit the list of backed-up files. Or you can turn off logging entirely using the **Don't Log** option.

Tip   Create an icon in the Administrative Tools program group that will automatically open the log file for you. For example, enter NOTEPAD E:\WINNT\BACKUP.LOG in the Program Item Properties' Command Line text box.

Click on OK and your backup begins. You'll see the Backup Status dialog box (Figure 19.3). If you selected the Replace option in the Backup Information dialog box you'll also see the Replace Information dialog box, warning you that you are going to destroy the existing data on the tape. You can click on Yes to continue, replacing the existing data, or click on No, in which case you'll see another dialog box asking if you want to *append* the data onto the tape. Click on Yes to continue with the backup, or No to see *another* box asking if you want to continue. Click on No to cancel the operation, or Yes to insert a new tape and continue.

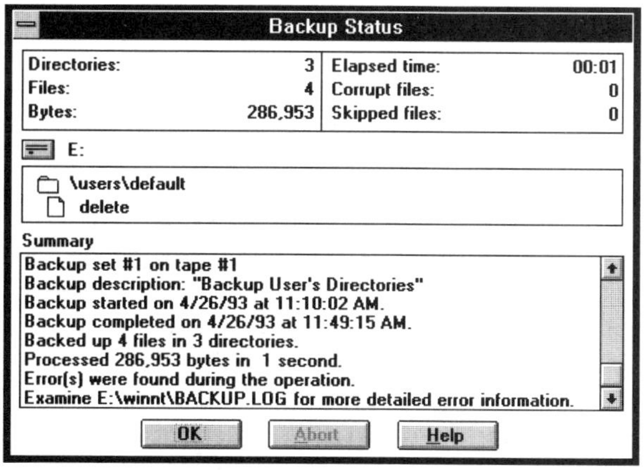

Figure 19.3 The Backup Status dialog box

During the backup you can watch the progress in the Backup Status dialog box. You'll see the number of **Directories**, **Files**, and **Bytes** that have already been backed up. You can also see the **Elapsed Time**, the number of **Corrupt Files** (files that couldn't be read for some reason) and **Skipped Files** (files that Backup didn't back up because they were in use or locked). If Backup finds files that are in use it will display a dialog box while it waits 30 seconds before trying to back the file up one more time. If you can get to the application using that file and close the file in time, it will be backed up. Or you can click on the Cancel button to continue the backup without waiting for that file to become available.

Below this information is a drive icon—during the backup you'll see the drive letter and volume label of the drive currently being backed up. In the box below the icon you'll see the directories and filenames flash by as they are backed up.

The **Summary** area shows you the progress of the backup procedure. You'll see messages telling you that the tape is being rewound, the name, date, and time of the backup, the backup set number, and the description. If any errors occur you'll also see a message, perhaps telling you to view the backup log. Notice also that there's an **Abort** button at the bottom of the dialog box. You can use this to end the backup at any time. (When aborting a backup, you may be asked to decide whether to finish backing up the current file, or log it as a corrupted file.)

If any errors occur you may also see a message box pop up. You might see a message such as "Fatal tape format inconsistency on Drive 1. Do not append to this tape" or "Tape drive error." And if you come to the end of the tape before all the selected data is backed up, you will be prompted to insert another tape.

If everything goes well, you'll eventually see a message telling you that the backup is complete. Close the dialog box and Backup will write the data to the log file, if you specified that one should be created.

Restoring Data

When you need to restore data, first consider what and why you are restoring. If you need to completely restore all the data to a hard disk, you will begin by restoring the most recent Normal backup. If you keep Differential backups, you can then restore the most recent Differential backup, and ignore all earlier Differential backups. This will restore all the modified files, and include all the changes to those files that have occurred since the most recent Normal backup.

If you keep Incremental backups you will restore the most recent Normal backup, followed by *all* the incremental backups, starting with the oldest and finishing with the most recent. It's important to restore in this order, or old files may be copied onto newer versions.

 When you want to restore, begin by displaying the Tapes window. This will show the tape currently in the tape drive and, in the panel to the right of the tape, the first backup set—it won't show all the backup sets until you've retrieved the tape's *catalog*. **Double-click** on the tape, or select **Operations|Catalog**, or click on the third toolbar icon. Backup will search the tape—you'll see a dialog box while it's doing so—and then add the additional sets to the right panel in the Tapes window. (If the tape is part of a multitape set, you may be prompted to insert another tape.)

Now you will decide what you want to restore, in much the same way that you decided what you wanted to back up. If you want to restore an entire set, you can click on the check box next to the set's icon. Notice that each icon has a **question mark** inside—this means that Backup does not have that set's catalog. (You just loaded the catalog of sets, not each set's catalog.) If you want to selectively restore, double-click on the icon or set name, and Backup then loads the individual catalog for that set, and displays another directory window. The icon in the Tapes window now shows a + sign, meaning the catalog has been retrieved. You can now select the individual directories and files that you want to restore. Files with a red icon containing an X are damaged files.

Note   If you are trying to restore from a tape without complete on-tape cataloging information—perhaps because you are missing one tape in a multitape set—you may be given the option of stopping or continuing the cataloging. If you continue, NT Backup will try to reconstruct the backup-sets information. This may take some time.

 When you're ready to restore the data, click on the second toolbar icon or select **Operations|Restore**. You'll see the Restore Information dialog box. Much of this information is the same as in the Backup Information dialog box. You'll see the **Tape Name** and the name of the **Backup Set** that you selected. You can also see the **Creation Date** and the **Owner**. If you want to be even more specific, you can select the directory to which you want to restore the files. Click on the button at the end of the **Alternate Path** text box to see a Browse dialog box.

The check boxes below the text box are similar to those you've seen before. You can **Verify After Restore**, to confirm that the restored data is exactly the same as the data on the tape. If you are restoring NTFS data, you can **Restore File Permissions**, so the same people will have access to the files and directories as before. (If you don't select this option, the files automatically take the permissions of the directory into which you are restoring the data.) If the tape has system configuration data, you can **Restore Local Registry**.

Note File Permissions are only valid on the computer on which they were created, so don't select Restore File Permissions when transferring data between computers.

The **Log Information** is the same as in the Backup Information dialog box, except that the default filename is different, of course (RESTORE.LOG). You can select a **Full Detail** log, a **Summary** log, or no log at all.

When you click on OK you'll see the Restore Status dialog box, which is similar to the Backup Status dialog box. If Backup finds a file in the restore location that matches one you selected to restore—but with the same or a more recent date— you'll see a dialog box asking if you want to restore. You can choose Yes to restore it, Yes to All to restore all such files with no changes, No to skip that file, or Cancel to end the restore operation.

Tape Utilities

 There are a few more tape operations. You can **erase** a tape, preparing it for use, by selecting **Operations|Erase Tape**, or by clicking on the sixth button on the toolbar. You'll see a dialog box warning you that you are going to lose all your data, and, to make sure you know exactly which tape you are erasing, the box shows the tape name, owner, and creation date. You have up to three erase options, depending on the type of tape drive. You can **Quick Erase**—which rewrites the tape's header information but leaves the rest of the tape unchanged—or **Security Erase**—which rewrites the entire tape, so no data can ever be recovered. The Security Erase takes longer, of course—as much as several hours in some cases—but it is completely secure. The Quick Erase makes it difficult to read data from the tape, but not impossible. In most cases a Quick Erase is fine, but for high-security applications—such as some government work—the Security Erase may be required.

There's also a **Format** option, though this option is not available for all tape drives. (It's only available for mini-cartridge tapes.) If it is enabled you can select this option to format the tape, preparing it for use in the tape drive—which, of course, also erases all the data on the tape. Some tape drives can use the **Operations|Format** menu option to format a tape.

 You can also retension the tape and eject the tape. Select **Operations|Retension** or click on the fourth toolbar button. The tape is rewound its full length at high speed, tightening the tape and removing loose spots so that it moves across the drive's tape heads more evenly. Some manufacturers recommend that you retension the tapes regularly, every 20 uses or so. The procedure is not available for 8 mm and 4 mm tapes.

 Select **Operations|Eject** or click on the fifth toolbar button. The tape is **rewound**, and if your tape drive has an eject mechanism, ejected from the drive.

Unattended and Automated Backups

NT's Backup program is by no means the most sophisticated program around. Many users will replace it with a more advanced tape backup program. However, its command line does provide an important feature that the graphical user interface doesn't have, the ability to perform a preconfigured backup at a regular interval. You can create a batch file containing NTBACKUP instructions that is run by the AT command at a time and interval that you set.

Open Notepad and enter the NTBACKUP command on the first line. It will look like this:

```
NTBACKUP BACKUP pathnames [options]
```

The **pathnames** may be single drives or actual paths, and may specify several different drives or paths, each separated by a space. Subdirectories will automatically be included. For instance:

```
NTBACKUP BACKUP C: D:\DATA\NEW\*.DOC [options]
```

As you can see, the pathnames should include the file types, if necessary—you can use * and ? wildcards.

The options specify the type of backup that will occur. (See the earlier description of the Backup Information dialog box for more information about these options.)

Mode	By default the mode is Replace—enter **/A** if you want to Append.
Verify	By default Verify is off—enter **/V** if you want to turn it on.
Restrict Access	By default access is not restricted—enter **/R** if you want to restrict access.
Description	By default Backup will enter the date and time as the description—to use your own description enter **/D** "*description*" on the command line.
Backup Local Registry	By default the local registry information is not backed up—enter **/B** if you want to do so.

Backup Type   By default the backup will be Normal. Enter /**T** followed by the backup type (**Normal**, **Copy**, **Differential**, **Incremental**, or **Daily**).

Log Filename   By default no log file will be created. Enter /**L** "*filename*" to create a Full Detail log.

Type of Log   If you entered a log filename Backup will create a Full Detail log. If you'd prefer a Summary log, you must also enter /**E**.

Here's an example:

```
NTBACKUP BACKUP C: D: /A /D "Daily Diff. Backup, C: & D:"
/D /L "E:\WINNT\BACKUP.LOG" /E
```

This will do a differential backup on drives C: and D:, appending the data to the tape. It will enter a description, and will create a summary log file called BACKUP.LOG.

When you've entered the backup command, save the batch file. Call it something like RUNBACK.BAT. When you run this batch file the Backup window will open and begin backing up automatically. When it has finished it will automatically close itself. You don't need to take any action—the backup can be carried out while you work in another application, or even while you are not present.

If you are an Administrator, you can run the batch file using the AT command. This command will run the backup at a predetermined time, or even at a regular interval. At the Command Prompt, enter this command:

```
AT TIME /EVERY:DATE BATCHFILE
```

For instance,

```
AT 17:00 /EVERY:M,T,W,TH,F RUNBACK
```

This tells NT to run the RUNBACK batch file at 17:00 hours (5:00 PM) every weekday. All times are set in 24-hour notation, and days of the week are M, T, W, TH, F, S, and SU. You can also use days of the month (1–31) instead of days of the week. You can check to see if this command was entered correctly by typing AT and pressing Enter. You'll see a summary of the AT commands. AT commands are saved in the configuration registry, and constantly monitored by the Schedule service, so the AT command will only run if the Schedule service is running. Open the Control Panel's Services dialog box, then find Schedule in the list and change its Startup option to Automatic.

Note   If you change the system date, the AT schedule will be incorrect. Type AT at the command prompt and press Enter to resynchronize the schedule. For more information about AT, open the Windows NT Help from the Main program group, then click on Command Reference Help.

The Menu Options

Here's a quick summary of the menu options:

Operations|Backup	Begins backing up the selected files and directories to the tape. This command is disabled until the Drives document window is active.
Operations|Restore	Begins restoring the selected files and directories from the tape. This command is disabled until the Tapes document window is active.
Operations|Catalog	Loads catalogs from the tape. If you select the tape in the Tapes window, the catalog will show the name of each set on the tape. If you select a set, a directory window will open, showing all the data in that set.
Operations|Erase Tape	Lets you erase or format the tape.
Operations|Retension Tape	Retensions the tape by rewinding it at high speed.
Operations|Eject Tape	Rewinds the tape and, if the tape drive has an eject mechanism, ejects the tape from the drive.
Operations|Format Tape	Lets you format a tape.
Operations|Hardware Setup	Lets you select the tape drive onto which you want to back up data, or from which you want to restore data.
Operations|Exit (Alt-F4)	Closes Tape Backup.
Tree|Expand One Level (+)	Displays a directory's first-level subdirectories.
Tree|Expand Branch (*)	Displays all the subdirectories—at all levels—of the selected directory.
Tree|Expand All (Ctrl-*)	Expands the entire directory tree, displaying all directories and subdirectories on the tree.
Tree|Collapse Branch (–)	Collapses the tree below the selected directory, so its subdirectories are not displayed.
View|Tree and Directory	Places two panels in the current document window. The one on the left shows the directory tree, the one on the right shows the files in the selected directory
View|Tree Only	Displays only one panel in the current document window, showing the directory tree (no files).

View|Directory Only	Shows only one panel in the current document window, showing the contents of a single directory.
View|Split	Adds a split bar to the document window—between the tree and directory panels of the document window—or lets you use the keyboard to move the split.
View|All File Details	Displays each file and directory's size, time and date, and attributes in the Tapes and directory windows.
View|Status Bar	Displays and removes the status bar at the bottom of the window.
View|Toolbar	Displays and removes the toolbar.
View|Font	Lets you select the font to be used in the Drives, Tapes, and directory windows.
Select|Check	Places a check mark in the check box next to the highlighted drive, directory, or file, selecting that item for backup or restore.
Select|Uncheck	Removes the check mark from the check box next to the highlighted drive, directory, or file, removing that item from the backup or restore operation.
Window|Cascade	Places the open Drives, Tapes, and directory windows one on top of each other, such that each title bar is visible.
Window|Tile	Places the open Drives, Tapes, and directory windows within the Tape Backup window such that each is fully visible and each has equal space.
Window|Arrange Icons	Arranges the Drives, Tapes, and directory window icons at the bottom of the Tape Backup window.
Window|Refresh	Updates the file and directory listing in the selected document window.
Window|Close All	Closes the directory windows, and minimizes the Drives and Tapes windows.
Window|1. Drives	Displays the Drives window.
Window|2. Tapes	Displays the Tapes window.
Window|*pathname*	Displays the named directory window, opened by double-clicking on a drive in the Drives window or a tape in the Tapes window.

The Toolbar Buttons

These are the commands carried out by the toolbar buttons:

Button	Command
Backup	Operations|Backup
Restore	Operations|Restore
	Operations|Catalog
	Operations|Retension Tape
	Operations|Eject Tape
	Operations|Erase Tape
	Select|Check
	Select|Uncheck

20

Neat Stuff— Multimedia and Games

Windows NT has a few multimedia and "fun" applications that Windows 3.1 doesn't. In addition to Minesweeper and Solitaire—games with which you may be familiar from Windows 3.1—NT also has FreeCell (in the Games program group), a Solitaire-like card game. There are also a couple of "hidden" games— QBASIC games intended more as examples of QBASIC programs than anything else, but fun nonetheless (at least, the fighting gorillas might amuse you for a few minutes).

NT also adds CD Player, which lets you play audio CDs on your computer's CD-ROM player, Volume Control—a system-wide control for your sound board—and some important changes to Media Player and Sound Recorder.

CD Player

NT's CD Player lets you play audio CDs on your computer's CD player. It's more than just a start and stop button. You can create playlists, defining how each of your CDs should be played—what order to play the tracks and which tracks to skip, for instance. You can find out how long the current track has been playing, and how long that track—and the playlist you defined—has left. You can even tell CD Player to play the first 10 seconds of each track, one after another.

CD Player

If you have an NT-compatible CD Player connected to your computer you can start the CD Player by double-clicking on the icon in the Accessories program group. You'll see the box shown in Figure 20.1.

Insert an audio CD into your player and click on the **Play** button. CD Player starts playing the first track on the CD (unless you've loaded a *playlist* for that CD, which we'll explain in a moment.) You'll notice that there's also a **Pause** button

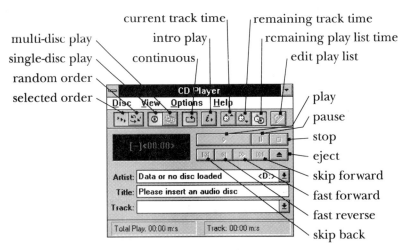

Figure 20.1 The CD Player

which pauses and resumes playing, and a **Stop** button, which stops playing and returns to the first track in the playlist (or the first track on the CD, if there's no playlist).

There's also a **Skip Back** button, which starts playing at the beginning of the current track, and a **Skip Forward** button, which starts the next track. And you can move through the current track using the **Fast Reverse** and **Fast Forward** buttons. You may also be able to use the **Eject** button to eject the CD from the player, depending on the type of player you are using. Notice also the **Track** drop-down list box—you can select another track to play from this list, and then click on the Play button.

If you have a multi-disc player, or have two or more CD drives attached, you can also select another CD from the **Artist** drop-down list box. Find the CD and select the drive, if necessary, then select the track from the Track drop-down list box.

You can also tell CD Player to play continuously. Select **Options|Continuous** or click on the Continuous toolbar button to play the same disk over and over, until you tell it to stop. Or use **Options|Multidisc Play** to play all the CDs in a multidisc player, or all the CDs in two or more CD-ROM drives. To return to playing a single CD you must select **Options|Single-Disc Play** or click on the Single-Disc toolbar button.

There's also a neat feature that helps you search for a track you want to hear. Select **Options|Intro Play**, or click on the **Intro Play** toolbar button, to hear the first 10 seconds of all the tracks on a CD. You may also choose to let CD Player select tracks for you. Select **Options|Random Order** or click on the **Random Order** toolbar button to make CD Player pick tracks at random—if you are using Multidisc Play at the same time, it will select randomly from all available CDs. Selecting **Options|Selected Order** or clicking on the **Selected Order** toolbar button returns you to the normal play order—playing tracks in the order defined in the playlist, or in the sequence in which they appear on the CD.

Playlists

For each CD in your collection you can create a playlist. Select **Edit|Playlist** or click on the **Edit Playlist** toolbar button to see the Disc Settings dialog box (Figure 20.2). Enter the name of the CD in the **Title** box, and the name of the performer in the **Artist** box. Then select a track from the **Available Tracks** list, type the title of the track in the **Track** box, and click on the **Add** button to place the track in the playlist. You can, of course, enter the tracks into the playlist in any order you want. This is the order used when you play using the Selected Order option. You can also use the **Remove** button to remove a track, and the **Clear** button to clear the list and start again. When you've finished, click on **OK**.

Having created a playlist, CD Player will automatically use the list when you click on the Play button, playing the tracks in the order in which you entered them, unless you choose some other option (such as Random Play or select another track).

Viewing Information

CD Player displays several pieces of information about your CD. You can see how long the current track has been playing by clicking on the **Current Track Time** toolbar button. To see how much time is left on the current track, click on the **Remaining Track Time** toolbar button. And to see how much time is left for the entire playlist, click on the **Remaining Playlist Time** toolbar button. All three of these statistics can also be seen by clicking on the **Time Display** window.

The status bar shows track and CD time information also. You can turn the status bar on and off using the **View|Status Bar** command. And disc and track information can be hidden or displayed using the **View|Disc and Track Info** command.

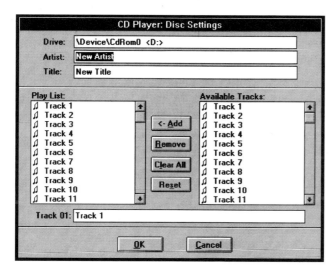

Figure 20.2 The Disc Settings dialog box

Volume Control

Volume Control

If you installed a sound driver, you can use Volume Control to control several sound functions. Double-click on the icon in the Accessories program group to open Volume Control. It may appear in its standard or expanded format (as in Figure 20.3). You can change the view by selecting **Control menu|Expanded View**, or by pressing **Alt-E**. Volume Control also has an "always on top" option. When **Control menu|Always on Top** is selected, the dialog box is visible even when another application is active. You could use this option, along with the smaller, standard format, and push the dialog box into an unused corner somewhere, so it doesn't get in the way. You can also minimize it, and the icon will remain on top.

You can move the slider bars in this dialog box by dragging them with the mouse, or by pressing Tab to move the black bar onto the slider you want to move and then pressing the arrow keys. The vertical slider immediately above the Mute button—the **Master** slider—controls overall volume. Above that slider is a horizontal, L-R slider—if you have a stereo sound board you can control the balance, the left- and right-components of the sound.

Next to the Master sliders you'll see other controls, the number of which depends on the types of sound devices you have installed. For each type of sound you'll see the same controls. You can control the overall volume and balance of **Wave** (.WAV) sounds, sounds coming from the **Line-In** socket on your sound board (tape recorder, CD-ROM player, or radio, for instance), sounds produced by your **CD** player, sounds played through your sound board's **AUX** input, and **Synth**esizer (**MIDI**) music.

The **Mute** button provides a quick way to turn the volume down without adjusting the settings. Click on it and the volume drops and the button label changes to **Un-Mute**. Click again to return to the original volume.

If you use sound applications often, you might want to add the Volume Control to your Startup program group.

Media Player

Windows NT has an expanded Media Player. It's similar to the one in Windows 3.1, but contains more features. Media Player can be used to play video sequences,

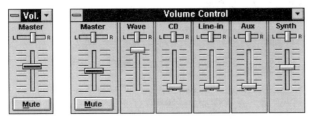

Figure 20.3 Volume Controls standard (left) and expanded (right) formats

animation files, MIDI (Musical Instrument Digital Interface) files, .WAV sound files, and any MCI (Media Control Interface) device such as an audio CD player or a video-disk player. Media Player lets you play files, but not edit them. You will have to edit them in their source applications.

Media Player

Double-click on the Media Player icon in the Accessories dialog box. The Media Player is shown in Figure 20.4.

There are two ways to "open" a media device or file depending on the type of device. To play a *simple* device—an external device such as a video-disk player or CD player—select the device from the top of the **Device** menu. Only devices for which you have installed drivers will appear here. (Drivers are installed in the Control Panel's Drivers dialog box.) Of course Media Player doesn't know—or care—what is in a simple device. Once you've selected the device you will simply play whatever you have loaded into the device (you'll see how to play it shortly).

To open a *compound* device, you have a couple of choices. A compound device is one which requires both hardware and software—a .WAV sound file or .MID MIDI (Musical Instrument Digital Interface) file, for instance, being played on a sound or MIDI board. You can select the device from the top of the **Device** menu. A device with an ellipsis (. . .) after its name is a compound device—such as Sound, Video for Windows, and MIDI Sequencer. Or you can use the **File|Open** command. Either way, you'll see a File Open dialog box. Select the file you want to play. Of course, you still need the correct device drivers to play these compound devices, just as you do with simple devices.

Playing the Device

You can see Media Player's controls in Figure 20.4. Once you have loaded the file you want to play, click on the **Play** button to start. The Play button then turns into a **Pause** button. You can use the **Page Right** and **Page Left** buttons to move through the file quickly, and the **Previous Mark** and **Next Mark** buttons to move directly to the beginning or end of the file (or the selection, if you've marked a selection—you'll see how in a moment). The two small **Back** and **Forward** arrows to the right of the slider move through the file slowly. You can also use the mouse

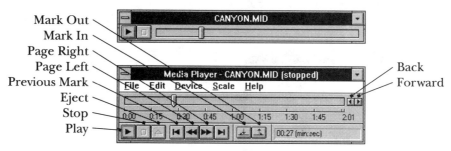

Figure 20.4 The Media Player in its reduced size (top) and normal size (bottom)

to drag the slider along the bar, or use the keyboard—press the **arrow keys** to move the slider slowly, **Home** to move the slider to the beginning, **End** to move it to the end, and **PgUp** and **PgDn** to move it quickly.

By the way, when you use the Fast Forward, Rewind, Back, and Forward buttons, the slider moves, but the file continues playing at the original position until you release the button, at which point it continues from the new position. Media Player also has a **Stop** button, and—for some devices—an **Eject** button, to eject the CD, for instance, on a CD player.

Modifying the Scale

Depending on the type of file or device that you've loaded, you may be able to change the scale. Sound files use a time scale, and this can't be changed. CDs can use a time scale or tracks—each track on the CD being indicated on the scale. You can change the scale using the **Scale** menu. The options are Time, Tracks, and Frames (as in video frames).

Marking Selections

You can mark a particular piece of a file that you want to play. The easiest way is to position the slider at the beginning of the selection and click on the **Mark In** button, then move the slider to the end of the selection and click on the **Mark Out** button.

You can also select using a dialog box. Select **Edit|Selection** or **double-click** on the scale immediately below the slider. You'll see the **Set Selection** dialog box (Figure 20.5). The **None** option button is selected (meaning none of the file is selected). You can click on **All** to select the entire file, or you can enter the **From** and **To** values in the incrementers. These values are the positions on the scale. As you enter these values, the **Size** value is automatically calculated. Or you can enter a From value, then enter a Size value and let Media Player calculate the To value for you. (For example, if you want to select a 20-second portion of the file, enter the From value, enter 20 into the Size box, and Media Player will add that value to the From and place the result in To.) Remember to click on the **From** option button before closing the dialog box—unlike in many dialog boxes, entering values in these incrementers will not automatically select the option button.

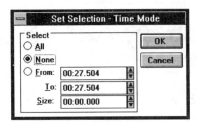

Figure 20.5 The Set Selection dialog box

Once you've selected part of the file, the controls operate a little differently. You can now start Media Player at the beginning of the selection by holding **Alt** and clicking on the **Play** button. (There's actually no difference between the way Media Player acts if you selected the None option and if you selected the All option. Selecting an entire piece is the same as not selecting any section at all, at least in the current version of NT.) The **Next Mark** and **Previous Mark** now move the slider to the section marks. For instance, if the slider is at the beginning of the file, click on Next Mark to move to the first marker, click again to move to the second marker, and again to move to the end. (Clicking on Previous Mark while the file is playing sends the slider back to the last mark, but no further.)

Media Player and OLE

Media Player is an Object Linking and Embedding (OLE) *server*. In other words, it provides data that can be placed into OLE *clients*, such as word processors. A Media Player object will appear as an icon in the client—double-clicking on the icon will play the media file.

Before creating a Media Player object, select **Edit|Options** (**Ctrl-O**). You'll see the dialog box in Figure 20.6. The **OLE Object** options are related to the object you are about to create. You can enter a different **Caption** if you want, replacing the filename. Or you can turn the caption off altogether, so the icon in the client application won't have a caption.

If you want to place the icon in the client application inside a box, make sure the **Border around object** check box is selected. The **Play in client document** option is a little confusing. If you select this option while the **Control Bar on playback** option is turned *off,* when the user plays the media clip, it will play without any controls being displayed—the sound or video will play automatically when the user double-clicks on the object, but Media Player itself won't appear, and the user will have no control over the playback. However, if you select both the Play in client document *and* the Control Bar on playback options, a short slider control bar will be displayed, so the user can stop and restart the media clip, and select a starting position.

Figure 20.6 The Options dialog box

If the Play in client document check box is *not* selected, but the Control Bar on playback check box *is* selected, you'll still see a control bar, but it will be a much longer bar. The user will be able to double-click on the Control Bar's title bar to open up the full version of Media Player, providing complete control. Finally, if neither of these options is selected, you won't see either control bar—the same as if Play in client document were on and Control Bar on playback were off.

You can also select the **Auto Rewind** option—so that after playing the file the slider returns to the beginning—or the **Auto Repeat** option—so that when the user double-clicks on the icon the file will play over and over again (until the user clicks on the Stop button). There's also an option that is available if you are using video, **Dither picture to VGA colors**. The object in the client application will be indicated by a frame from the video, not an icon. This option converts the image from that video frame to the standard VGA palette of colors. If you *don't* use this option, the image will use the video clip's palette of colors—it may not be possible for the application to display some of these colors, in which case the colors will be distorted.

Now select **Edit|Copy Object**, or press **Ctrl-O**. Swap to the application into which you want to paste the object, position the cursor, and select **Edit|Paste**. You'll see the Media Player icon appear in the document. You can now play this object at any time by double-clicking on it. Or press Alt while you double-click to open Media Player so you can change the object's settings. If you selected the Control Bar in playback option, you'll see a slider bar that you can use to control playback—you can also double-click on the title bar or press Ctrl-W to expand the Control Bar to a full-size Media Player.

Note   If you mark a selection before copying and pasting the object, that selection will automatically play when the user double-clicks on the Media Player object. If the user wants to hear the entire file, he or she can use the controls to start from the beginning.

Configuring Media Player

You've seen how to set up OLE options, but here, there are a few other configuration options. You've seen how the two check boxes at the top of the Options dialog box control the playing of compound devices pasted as OLE objects. But these are not only for OLE. You can set these as Media Player's defaults also. Turning on **Auto Rewind** makes Media Player automatically return to the beginning of any file when it finishes playing it. And **Auto Repeat** will make Media Player repeat files over and over, continuing until you click on the stop button.

You can also remove most of the controls from Media Player. Double-click on the title bar, or press **Ctrl-W**, and all the controls but the slider and the Start and Stop buttons are removed. (You can't do this until you've loaded a device or file, because the menu is also removed when you reduce the size.) You can drag the side borders in or out to shrink or enlarge the dialog box. You can get the box down to about an inch or so wide, then tuck it away in an unused corner on your screen. (This is the same control Bar that appears in an OLE client when running a media clip, if you selected **Control Bar on playback** in the Options dialog box, as we explained earlier.)

Configuring the Device

You can also configure the device you are playing. Select a device first (using the Device|*name* command or by loading a file with File|Open) and then select **Device|Configure**. You'll see the same configuration dialog box that is shown when you double-click on the device in the Control Panel's Drivers dialog box. Figure 20.7, for instance, shows the Video Playback Options dialog box, the one shown when you configure a Microsoft Video device. You can select **Zoom by 2** (to double the video frame size); **Play only if waveform device available** (tells the system not to play the video unless the audio can also be played on the sound device at the same time); **Always seek to nearest key frame** (making the system display the nearest full frame when jumping to a nonconsecutive frame); **Skip video frames if behind** (tells Media Player to make the video keep up with the audio, skipping video frames if necessary, rather than pausing the audio track); and **Don't buffer offscreen** (speeds up playback slightly, though it might also distort the image).

The actual options dialog box will depend on the type of device you are configuring. The waveform-driver options box, for instance, only lets you modify the amount of memory used for buffering the audio playback.

The Menu Options

Here's a quick summary of Media Player's menu options:

File|Open	Opens a multimedia file and assigns a device—such as a sound board or MIDI board—to play the file.
File|Close	Closes the file or releases control of the simple device (a CD or video-disk player, for instance). Simple devices continue playing even after "closing" them.

Figure 20.7 The Video Playback Options dialog box

File|Exit (Alt-F4)	Closes Media Player.
Edit|Copy Object (Ctrl-C)	Copies the file in the Media Player so it can be pasted into another OLE application as an object.
Edit|Options (Ctrl-O)	Lets you specify the manner in which a Media Object will be embedded with OLE, and lets you control auto-rewind and auto-repeat.
Edit|Selection	Selects a portion of the file to play.
Device|name	The type of device you want to work with. A compound device—one which plays a file—has an ellipsis (. . .) after its name.
Device|Configure	Lets you enter configuration information for the selected device.
Scale|Time	Sets Media Player's scale to a time scale.
Scale|Frames	Sets Media Player's scale to a video-frame scale.
Scale|Tracks	Sets Media Player's scale to a track scale (tracks on a CD, for instance).

Sound Recorder

Sound Recorder

At first glance NT's Sound Recorder (see Figure 20.8) looks much the same as the one that comes with Windows 3.1, but there are some significant differences. First, the **File\|New** command has changed. As in Windows 3.1, File\|New clears the Sound Recorder, unloading the file. But now you have two options: **Mono 11.025 kHz, 8-bit** and **Mono 22.050 kHz, 8-bit**. These control the sampling rate of the file you are about to record. The higher the kHz number, the more samples a sound program takes. So recording at 22.050 kHz takes twice as many sound samples as the 11.025 kHz. And the more sound samples crammed into every second, the higher the quality of the recorded sound—and the larger the file. For instance, a 4½-second sound file recorded at 11.025 kHz takes up almost 50 KB. At 22.050 kHz it takes up almost 100 KB.

Sound Recorder also has two new Edit options, which let you insert and mix sound files more quickly than using the Edit\|Insert File and Edit\|Mix with File. Start by using the **Edit\|Copy** command to copy a sound file to the Clipboard.

Figure 20.8 The Sound Recorder

Then open the file in which you want to mix or insert the first file. Position the slider at the mixing or insertion point, and then select **Edit|Paste Insert** (**Ctrl-V**) or **Edit|Paste Mix**. Remember that inserting a sound places it at the slider point, pushing the existing sounds further along. Mixing a sound places the sound at the slider point, but mixes it in with the existing sound.

The Sound Recorder is the same as that found in Windows 3.1 in one other way: You are still limited to a 60-second record time, though you can restart at the end of 60 seconds.

FreeCell

Freecell

When you first open FreeCell and select **Game|New Game** (**F2**), you'll see a window like that shown in Figure 20.9. There are three areas of play. The cards are initially laid, face up, in eight card stacks. The aim of the game is to move all the cards into the four home cells in the top right of the window. You will place the cards face up, beginning with the ace, in four stacks, each suit separately and in the correct order (ace, 2, 3, 4, 5, 6, 7, 8, 9, 10, jack, queen, king). To the left of the home cells are the four free cells. These are used as temporary storage spaces for the cards, and each cell can only hold one card at a time.

Each card in the eight stacks can only be moved to three different places:

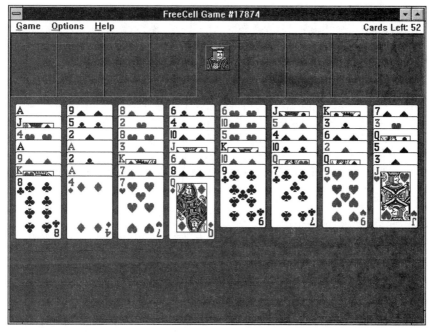

Figure 20.9 The FreeCell window

To an empty free cell.

To the card immediately preceding it in its own suit, on the home cells. Thus you can only place a 5 of diamonds on a 4 of diamonds in the home cell area.

To any card immediately following it but of a different color. Thus you can move a 4 of diamonds onto a 5 of spades or clubs anywhere in the eight stacks.

Cards in the free cells can be moved back down to the stacks or onto the home cells, following the same rules. You can move a card by clicking on it and then clicking on the position in which you want to place it. When an ace is uncovered, FreeCell automatically moves it to the home cells, and if a 2 is uncovered after the ace from the same suit has been placed on the home cells, FreeCell moves it automatically onto the ace. After that, it's usually up to you to move the cards onto the home cells when you can. But placing cards onto the home cells is not always a good idea, because once there you can't get them back. If both black 7s are on the home cells and you have a couple of red 6s, where are you going to put them? And how are you going to build stacks for all the lower numbers of both suits? In fact, it's not a good idea to move lots of cards from both suits of one color, but not the other. If you start shifting lots of diamonds and hearts up to the home cells, but few spades or clubs, you will get "unbalanced" and be unable to move cards around on the stacks. Ideally, you should shift cards to the home cells at an equal rate for all the suits, or avoid moving to the home cells at all, if possible, until later in the game.

FreeCell will shift other cards up to the home cells automatically if they are no longer needed, though. If moving a card exposes a red 4, for instance, and there are no more black 3s, FreeCell assumes that the card is not needed anymore and shifts it for you.

If you want to see a message each time you attempt an invalid move, select the **Options|Messages** command. You probably won't want to do that, though, as it's rather redundant. You can quickly tell if a move is invalid—it won't work. A quick way to see if the move is valid before making it is to look at the mouse pointer. When you move the pointer over a card or space to which you can move the card, the pointer turns into a fat, vertical arrow, pointing down (if over the card stacks) or up (if over the free or home cells). If you change your mind, and don't want to move the selected card, simply click on it again, then click on the card you do want to move.

You can move several cards at once—up to five—if you have spare free cells. If, for example, you want to move a small stack containing a red 6, black 5, and red 4, across to a black 7 on another stack. Click on the red 6, then click on the black 7, and—if you have at least two spaces in the free cells—FreeCell will move the cards for you. In fact, you will see the red 4 and black 5 move to the free cells, the red 6 move across to the black 7, and then the red 4 and black 5 move down onto the red 6. Remember, you need one less cell space than the number of cards you want to move. Now and then when you try this method, FreeCell will display a box asking if you want to move the column or a single card. By column, it means the few cards you selected, from the one you clicked on, up to the top of the stack (not necessarily the entire column), and it's asking if you want to move just one card, because it figured out that you may have accidentally clicked lower in the stack, but only want to move the top card. This dialog box appears when you are trying to move several cards onto an empty stack. Just click on the appropriate button and FreeCell continues.

You can also use blank areas in the stacks—areas left when you emptied a stack—to hold cards temporarily while moving cards between stacks. You won't be able to move more than one card at a time using this method.

There are a couple of shortcuts. To move a card directly from the stacks to a free cell, double-click on it. To see a card lower down in a stack, point at it and press the right mouse button.

It's easy to get stuck in this game—to play it well you have to be able to see several plays down the road. You'll find that cards you really need end up on the bottom of the stack, and there's no way to get to them. A few critical cards down near the bottom of the stacks and you are lost. FreeCell's Help file says that "it is believed (but not proven), that every game is winnable." That's hard to imagine, as the luck of the draw may put so many important cards in impossible-to-reach places that recovery seems virtually impossible.

Take a good look at each stack before you rush into the game. Aces stuck near the bottom of stacks, and kings stuck in the middle are a problem. Try to empty some of the stacks to leave room for kings to be placed—ideally you don't want to create stacks on kings when there are other cards below those kings, because you will have problems getting to them later on. Empty stacks can also serve as temporary storage places, in addition to the free cells. Try to keep free cells empty whenever possible. Frequently look at all the cards in the free cells and on the tops of the stacks, checking to see if you've missed a possible move. Look at the cards two and three positions down in the stacks, and figure out where they could go if you shifted the top card out of the way.

If you get yourself into a position in which you can make no more moves, FreeCell displays a dialog box telling you that you've lost the game. If there's only one possible move, FreeCell's border flashes. That doesn't mean the game is hopeless; that one move may open up other possibilities. By the way, you can lose a game without FreeCell ever telling you. FreeCell only tells you when you have no possible moves. But there are also situations where you might have only one, utterly worthless move. FreeCell will keep you guessing. For instance, you have a red queen on top of a black king, and the only other place you can move it is another black king. You've lost the game, but FreeCell will never tell you, because you will always have a possible move—you can move the queen back and forth between the kings forever.

When you get close to the end, FreeCell will take over for you. At the point that there's no strategy left, when it's simply a matter of moving cards from the card stacks to the home cells in the correct sequence, FreeCell will do it for you. Because it moves unneeded cards up to the home cells automatically, each time it moves a card the ones immediately higher and in the opposite suite are no longer needed, so they, too, get moved, and so on.

When you've finished a game—or if you lose a game—you have a few options. Select **Game|New Game** or press **F2** to let FreeCell set up a new game for you. You can also select **Game|Restart Game** to make FreeCell deal the cards in exactly the same way as the last time, to give you another shot at winning. Finally, you can select **Game|Select Game** or press **F3** to see a dialog box into which you can type a game number, any number up to 32,000. This won't mean much to you until you've played a few games and noted down the numbers of the games you want to retry. (You'll notice that once you've selected the game its number is displayed in the title bar.) If you've just lost a game that you want to retry, but need to stop playing (perhaps you've actually got work to do!), you could note the number and replay the game later using the Select Game command.

There's one more command we haven't covered: **Options|Statistics** (**F4**) displays a dialog box that shows information about your playing—the number of games you've won and lost since you opened FreeCell (and the percentage of wins). Because this information is stored when you close FreeCell, the Statistics dialog box can also show you the number of games won and lost, and the percentage won, since the last time you cleared the statistics using the Clear button. It also shows you your winning and losing streaks, and the result of the last game.

FreeCell is an intriguing, addictive game, like many computer games. My advice is to leave it alone and get on with your work.

QBASIC Games—Gorilla and Nibbles

NT has a couple of QBASIC sample games you might want to try, Gorilla and Nibbles. To run **Gorilla**, use the Program Manager File|Run command to run E:\WINNT\SYSTEM32\QBASIC.EXE GORILLA.BAS (or create an icon with this in the Command Line). QBASIC—the Basic programming-language editor—opens and loads the GORILLA.BAS file. Press **Shift-F5** and the game begins.

You can enter the names of the two players (there are always two gorillas, though you can control both), the number of points to play to in each game, and the strength of gravity that you want to use (for all these options you can just press Enter to accept the defaults). Then press **P** and you'll see a "cityscape" with two gorillas standing on tall buildings. Your job? To lob exploding bananas between the gorillas. Starting with Player 1 you'll type an angle, the angle at which the gorilla will throw the banana into the air. Then press Enter and type the velocity with which the gorilla will throw the banana. Press Enter again, and the gorilla throws the banana up, hopefully with a trajectory that will land it on the other gorilla. When the banana lands, it takes out lumps of building (and of gorilla, if it's on target—see Figure 20.10).

When selecting the angle and velocity you have to take into account gravity, wind speed (shown by the arrow at the bottom of the screen), and the buildings. After a while you'll get the feel for which angle and which speed does what.

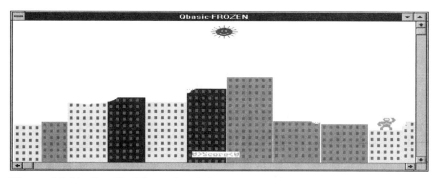

Figure 20.10 Gorilla Player 2 celebrating victory.

Nibbles (NIBBLES.BAS) is a simple game in which a snake—depicted by a line of block characters—winds its way around the screen. You can change the snake's direction with the arrow keys, and your job is to get the snake to eat numbers that appear on the screen, without letting the snake run off the screen or run into another snake—if it does, it dies. The more numbers you eat, the higher your score and the longer your snake. You can adjust the skill level and the speed—at the highest levels the game is virtually unusable, as the game is over before you have a chance to figure out where your snake is. Two players can play at the same time (the second player uses the W, A, D, and S keys to move the snake).

21

Finding More Information

Windows NT is a huge program, and there's a lot of detail that most users simply never need to know. If you *do* need more information, though, there are a number of places you can go.

What's Inside NT?

If you are interested in the internal workings of Windows NT—how the program does what it does—get a copy of Helen Custer's *Inside Windows NT* ($24.95, Microsoft Press). This is by no means a layman's guide to Windows NT, so if talk of environment subsystems, asynchronous operations, mapped file I/O and file caching, and virtual address descriptors spooks you, this isn't the book for you. Most buyers are probably programmers who want a detailed overview of the program for which they are writing code. Helen Custer worked with the NT development team, so she has an inside view of what it's all about, and how it works.

CompuServe

CompuServe is a large computer bulletin board or information system that you can dial up from your computer. It has *forums*, areas of the bulletin board in which you can find information about particular subjects—everything from Abacus Software to the Zagat Restaurant Survey. Microsoft maintains a number of forums on CompuServe that are related to Windows NT. You can enter these forums and use the menus to find a subject in which you are interested, and then leave messages for other users or for Microsoft personnel. You can also enter the "libraries" and download documents, shareware, drivers, and bug fixes.

At the time of this writing, Microsoft had two Windows NT forums: MSWIN32 (the WIN32 Software Development Kit forum, with support for application developers) and WINNT (the prerelease forum, with information about using NT). The WINNT forum had these areas:

1. Non-tech service
2. General Discussion
3. Setup & Install
4. MS-DOS/Win3.x Apps
5. 32-bit Windows Apps
6. OS/2, POSIX Apps
7. Utilities/Applets
8. H/W Compatibility
9. FT & File System
10. Device Drivers
11. Network services
12. Printing
13. Admin & Security
14. Documentation
15. Connectivity
16. WinNT RAS
17. MSMail (32-bit)

The forum also has these libraries, from which you can download software and documents:

1. General Information
2. Fixes & Updates
3. Problem Reports
4. Support Tools
5. WINNT Archives
6. Windows NT Surveys

It seems likely that these forums will stay, although names may change, as may the names of the areas and libraries. These forums are an excellent source for information about NT. For instance, at the time of writing you could find a file called DOSNT.OS2, an ASCII file explaining how to install DOS, NT, and OS/2 2.0 on the same machine. It's a nonofficial procedure, but is provided by Arthur Knowles, a Windows NT "guru" who is well respected within Microsoft. This file was in WINNT's library 1. Or how about MBOOT.ZIP, a file that explains how to set up Windows NT, OS/2, DOS, *and* Coherent (a UNIX clone) on a single hard disk.

There's also BOOTNT.TXT, a file explaining how to boot NT from OS/2's Boot Manager by editing the hard disk's partition table to allow NT to boot from OS/2's Boot Manager menu. Again, this is a nonofficial procedure, and one that you definitely shouldn't try unless you are quite comfortable with working on the partition table. You can also find this file in WINNT's library 1.

You can also find RASINF.ZIP which explains how to get started working with Windows NT Remote Access Service, TOOLWR.ZIP (describes development tools for Windows NT—MSWIN32 forum, library 16), and MFTPD.ZIP (allows a Windows NT machine to run as a TCP/IP server—MSWIN32, library 1). You will find hundreds of useful documents and programs in these forums (you can see examples of some of the programs in Chapter 22). If your job is to maintain or configure NT computers, you need to at least take a look and see what is available.

Microsoft has a number of other forums on CompuServe, several of which may be helpful to NT users. You may want to try these forums:

MSKB	The Microsoft Knowledge Base, the data base used by Microsoft's technical support people. You can use this when technical support is closed, or during the day to save money: You'll pay connect charges, but you won't pay long distance charges or be put on hold. And because you'll have control over how to search and what to search for, you may get a more complete answer than going through technical support.
MSL	MS Software Library, a library containing Windows-related files such as device drivers. You can use this to get the latest versions of drivers, or newly released drivers.
WINAPA	Windows 3rd Party forum A. Try also WINAPB and WINAPC. These are forums for third-party software developers.
WINFUN	Fun applications for Windows—icons, sounds, wallpaper, amusing utilities, and so on.
WINSHARE	Windows shareware.

CompuServe Navigators

If you are going to use CompuServe for more than just a few minutes a month, you need to find a program that will help you, a *navigator*. CompuServe is not a simple system to use. It has all sorts of twists and turns, and hidden commands, and can be quite expensive to use if you spend a lot of time online. Programs such as OZCIS and TAPCIS (DOS programs) and John Dvorak's NavCIS (with Windows 3.1 and DOS versions) can help you save more money by letting you do most of your work offline. Before you log onto CompuServe, you write any messages you want to post, determine what files you want to search for, select the forums you want to check for messages, and so on. Then you tell the program to do the work. It goes online, does it all as quickly as it can—using CompuServe's shortcut commands—and logs off. If you had mail or messages waiting for you, you can read them when the program has finished.

There's simply no way you could work as quickly as one of these programs, and the savings can be considerable. For instance, instead of looking at a list of forum messages and selecting the ones you want to read, or even reading all of them in case you find some that interest you, you can use one of these programs to save a list of all the recent message subjects. Then, offline, you can select the ones that interest you, send the program online to collect them, and read them offline.

Microsoft Seminars and Training

Microsoft has a large organization dedicated to nothing but training end users and getting the word out about new products. They hold seminars and conferences in large cities throughout the country. A three-month "Business Solutions Conference & Expo," dedicated mainly to familiarizing people with NT, toured 21 cities early in 1993, and other tours are planned. If you would like more information about these conferences, call (800) 942-1185.

There's also Microsoft University, an organization that puts on training courses for many of Microsoft's products. A five-day course, Supporting Microsoft Windows NT, was being planned at the time of writing. It will cover such subjects as troubleshooting, performance optimization and tuning, administering Mail and Schedule+, configuring hard disks for fault tolerance, and setting up security. If you would like more information about Microsoft University, call (206) 828-1507.

Microsoft TechNet

Microsoft's Technical Information Network charges an annual fee of $295. For that you'll get a special forum on CompuServe, and a copy of WINCIM, a Windows-based "front end" to access the forum; a Services Directory, which tells you who to contact for information about any Microsoft product or service; invitations to conferences, seminars, and trade shows; and, most importantly, a TechNet CD each month.

The CD contains the latest Microsoft KnowledgeBase, the database used by Microsoft Technical Support. It contains a huge library of documents about all of Microsoft's products, including NT. It also has the Resource Kits, which contain information and utilities for several products (see earlier in this chapter); training materials; conference session notes; "customer solution profiles" explaining how some customers use Microsoft products; and downloadable libraries of DLLs, drivers, and utilities. For more information about the TechNet, call (800) 344-2121, extension 017.

Installation Questions

For installation questions, Microsoft is currently offering warranty support without charge.

22

Improving Windows NT

Windows NT may be brand new, but there are many 32-bit programs available already. Microsoft shipped 55,000 copies of NT's beta release, and many of those copies went to programmers busy trying to get an early start on NT applications.

For a list of companies creating 32-bit applications and their programs, take a look at the file named W32CA2 or W32CAT. These are available on CompuServe (see Chapter 21), and list literally hundreds of firms and programs.

There are also plenty of free or low-cost utilities around that will help you work—or play—with Windows NT. In this chapter we're going to take a look at the freeware and shareware utilities that are already available. Some of them can help you work with NT—like Desktop+, which can effectively "turn off" the logon procedure, so you don't have to enter an account name and password. Others help you work in File Manager, or simply use 32-bit technology to goof off a little.

Of course these utilities are constantly changing. The following descriptions will give you an idea of whether you will find the utilities useful, but when you obtain one you may find it has more features, or has changed in some other way.

Microsoft Windows NT Shareware Contest

Microsoft held a shareware contest, and announced the winners at the Fall 1992 COMDEX exhibition in Las Vegas (actually some of the winners are *freeware* as opposed to shareware). Microsoft selected three winners in each of five categories: Business, Tools, Utility, Widget, and Games. These programs were regarded as the best of the first 32-bit Windows shareware applications at that time.

The CIS numbers in the listings below refer to the CompuServe email addresses. And take a look at the price of the product. If it's FREE, then don't expect the author to spend much time providing support. You may be able to find these programs on CompuServe (perhaps in the WINFUN or WINSHARE forums, or maybe somewhere in the WINNT forum), or on other bulletin boards. The shareware catalogs will probably also offer NT shareware soon.

Business

While You Were Out	A "message pad." Caliente Software, (203) 667-2159, CIS: 70324,2055. Price: $99.95 for five users.
MortCalc	A mortgage calculator. Robert J. Paul, CIS: 72550, 3021. Price: FREE.
Time and Money Tracker	A timer for tracking time spent on projects. Wintronix, (801) 532-4865, CIS: 70054,1007. Price: $25.

Tools

MicroEMACS	A configurable text editor that runs on various platforms (VAX, UNIX, MS-DOS, Amiga, etc.) Pierre Perrett, CIS: 73757,2337. Price: FREE.
Kermit	A Kermit data-transmission program. Wayne Warthen, CIS: 73457,2401. Price: FREE.
Nutmeg-32	A circuit simulator. Robert Zeff, (209) 521-1448, CIS: 70323,1251. Price: $275.

Utility

WinBatch	A batch-program language for Windows NT. Wilson WindowWare, (206) 938-1743, CIS: 73260,2535. Price: $69.95.
4DOS	Adds functions to the Command Prompt. JP Software, (617) 646-3975, CIS: 75300,210.
TrashMan	A File Manager Trashcan. Trigon Software GmbH, +49 30 661 2986, CIS: 100021,2706. Price: $25.

Widget

Icon Manager	An icon utility, for organizing Program Manager icons. Leonard Grey, CIS: 71630,1703. Price: $19.95.
WinMod	Plays Amiga MOD sound files. Norbert Unterberg, CIS: 100112, 2740. Price: $15.
Prime32	Calculates 32-bit prime numbers. Dick Jarrett, (207) 637-2879. Price: FREE.

Games

Klotz	A Tapcis-like game. Wolfgang Strobl, +49 228 213 463, Internet: strobl@gmd.de. Price: FREE.
Mah Jong	The Chinese tile game. Ron Balewski, (717) 735-3736, BIX: RBALEWSKI. Price: $20.
Thieves and Kings	A card game. Paul DeWolf, CIS: 72250,3067. Price: $20.

Some of these programs—and others not included in this list—are described below. We've included the name of the author and the price of the program. We've also included the filename of the archive file in which the program is stored in CompuServe. This filename may change, of course, or the program may be available on other bulletin boards under a different name.

Note Software stored on bulletin boards is often saved in a compressed .ZIP archive file, as are all of the files mentioned below. To extract the program file you will need PKUNZIP V. 2.04 or later. This is available on most bulletin boards.

Control Panel Upgrade—Desktop+

Desktop+ is a neat little utility that installs in the Control Panel and lets you modify several settings that are normally modified through the configuration registry (see Figure 22.1). Double-click on the Desktop+ icon in Control Panel to see the Desktop Settings dialog box. The Menu Settings area lets you change the alignment of windows menus. By default, menus are left aligned, so the menu is lined up with the first character of each option below the first character of the menu name. But you can select right aligned, so the last character of each option is below the last character of the menu name. You can also modify the delay used by a cascading menu—how long the application waits after the highlight lands on an option before opening the associated drop-down menu.

The Icons area lets you modify the spacing between icons in Program Manager, and the font used in the icon names. If you'd like to modify the colors used in Windows help screens, you can click on the color bars and select from 48 options.

The four buttons in the lower right corner lead to more options. Click on the Program Manager button if you'd like to limit access to various options for the current user (see Chapter 4 for more information on limiting Program Manager

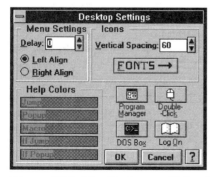

Figure 22.1 The Desktop+ dialog box

access). The DOS button lets you change the background color of the Command Prompt window, and the screen columns, rows, and buffer size (though these options can be changed from the Command Prompt's Control menu—see Chapter 9). The Mouse button lets you change the double-click width and height—the distance the mouse cursor can move between double-clicks and still have NT recognize the clicks as a double-click. Most importantly, the LogOn settings button lets you change startup features. You can make NT boot to a different "shell" instead of Program Manager. You can define a default user and computer name—usually the Logon dialog box shows you the last entries used. And you can even disable the Logon procedure entirely, so that NT boots directly into Program Manager, without asking for a username or password.

This free utility can be very useful—in particular, the ability to disable Logon will be helpful to people who don't need the security of a password. But be careful, as one false step can disable NT. (You can recover, though, using the Last Known Good Configuration procedure, as explained in Chapter 3.) (Desktop+, NTDESK.ZIP, Babarsoft, Mark Gamber. Free.)

Open a Command Prompt Window—FM Shell

File Manager Shell provides a quick way to open a Command Prompt window with the command prompt in exactly the directory you need it. Select the directory in File Manager, then select Command|Shell At and the Command Prompt window opens. It's a very simple utility, which takes about 10 seconds to install or uninstall, and can be very handy if you find yourself going to the Command Prompt often. (FMShell, SHELL.ZIP, P.M. Dickerson. Free.)

File Manager Utilities—FExtend

FExtend is a File Manager Extension that uses "drag and drop" to make File Manager easier to use. When you install the program an extra menu appears on File Manager's menu bar. The menu lets you display four icons: Trash Can, Information, Attributes, and Date/Time.

The Trash Can lets you delete files, of course. Just drag them onto the icon, then click on OK or Yes to All in the Delete Files dialog box that appears. The Information icon displays a dialog box showing the filename, size, attributes, time, and date of each file that you drag onto the icon. If you'd like to see Windows file information—the file version number, publisher's name, internal program name, programmer's comments, and so on, you can also click on the Version button (this information isn't available for all Windows files). If you want to see technical information—the file's operating system, the size of the code, and other programming data, click on the Info button. Again, this information is not available for all files.

The last two icons modify the file. Click on the Attributes icon with the right mouse button and a dialog box pops up. Select the attributes you want to set for certain files, close the dialog box, then drag those files onto the icon. For instance, if you want to make files read only, click on the Read Only check box, close the dialog box, then drop the files onto the icon. The Time/Date icon works in a similar way. Click the right button on the icon to see a dialog box. Select a time and date, or simply click on the Use System Time check box. Now, when you drop files onto the icon, the files' modification time and dates are changed.

This is a very simple utility to use. You can set it up so that the icons open automatically, so you never need to use the menu. Icons are removed by double-clicking on them. The help files are clear and easy to understand. (FExtend, FEXTEN.ZIP, Babarsoft. Free.)

Drag 'n' Drop Utilities—clySmic Software

The programmers at clySmic Software have created several drag-and-drop utilities for Windows NT. Each one runs as an icon, not a window, and each can be set "always on top," so it's always visible and ready to use. (See Figure 22.2.)

EXE Type tells you information about an executable file. Just drag a file (an .EXE, .DLL, .DRV, .386, and some others) onto the icon and you'll see the program name, the type, its signature, machine type, and subsystem. In a few cases, you may even see a description of what the file does.

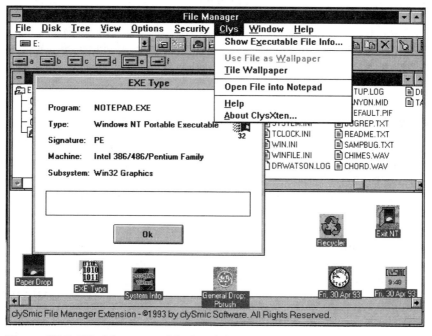

Figure 22.2 File Manager with the clySmic Drag 'n' Drop Utilities

Exit Windows NT provides a quick way to get out of NT. You can make the icon "always on top," then, when you want to exit, select Logoff, Shutdown, or Reboot from the Control menu (you can also double-click on the icon to Shutdown). You can turn confirmation messages off, too, so you can close NT very quickly.

General Drop automatically associates any file you drop onto it with a chosen application. For instance, by default the chosen application is Notepad. You can drop *any* file onto it—not just .TXT, but also .DOC, .ASC, .EXE, .DLL, whatever you want—and Notepad will open and display the contents of the file. You can select any other application in Notepad's place, though in most cases only appropriate file types can be opened, of course (you couldn't open a .EXE file in Paintbrush, for instance).

Paper Drop provides a quick way to change NT's selected wallpaper. Instead of opening Control Panel and selecting a new paper from the Desktop dialog box, just drag a .BMP file onto the Paper Drop icon.

System Info displays four types of information on its icon—the NT version number, the amount of real and virtual memory available, the number of screen colors, the resolution, and the number and type of CPUs installed in the computer. Double-clicking on the icon changes the data that is displayed. (The numbers can be a little difficult to view on some monitors.)

Recycler is simply a drag-and-drop "trashcan." Drag files onto it to delete them. The utilities also come with two clocks, one analog and one digital. Both run as icons (not as windows), showing both time and date. The analog clock has over 20 different faces to choose from and an optional second hand—both have an "always on top" feature and the ability to display Greenwich Mean Time. And you can add Paper Drop, EXE Type, and General Drop to File Manager's menus and toolbar—though the General Drop menu command only works with Notepad, as there's no way to select another "drop" application. (Drag 'n' Drop Utilities, NTUTIL.ZIP, clySmic Software. $14.95.)

Drag-and-Drop Viewing—File Viewer and LI

File Viewer is a useful utility for viewing the contents of files. It uses Windows' drag-and-drop capabilities to let you drag a file from File Manager, drop it onto the application or icon, and view the contents of the file. It has an "always on top" feature that's a great help. Enable "always on top," then minimize File Viewer. Find the file you want to view, and drag the file icon on top of the File Viewer icon. File Viewer automatically restores to its previous size so you can view the contents. When you've finished, minimize and find the next file.

You can mark text in the file you are viewing and copy it to the Clipboard. You can view the file as text, raw text, or hexadecimal data. You can also turn word wrap on and off and select a font type. (File Viewer for Windows NT, NTFVIE.ZIP, Maze Computer Communications. $9.95.)

Another utility—more complicated but also more capable than File Viewer—is LI 32, a file viewer that comes with a lot of extras (see Figure 22.3). You can

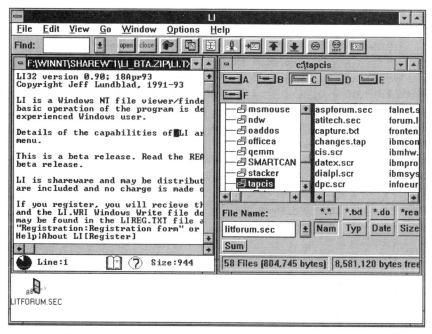

Figure 22.3 LI 32 file-viewing utility

view files as text or hexadecimal, and have several document windows open at once. You can drag files from File Manager and drop them onto the window or icon. There's no "always on top" feature though, a feature that makes File Viewer for Windows NT very easy to use.

You can print a file or just a part of it, and specify your own headers or footers. You can also copy to the Clipboard or another file. LI also has a relatively sophisticated search function—it can search for files that matching a file specification, a file size range, a file date range, and contain specified text, including regular expressions, and use Boolean expressions (AND, OR, NOT) in the search statement. You can even delete files, create directories, and launch other applications. (LI 32, LI_BTA.ZIP, Third Millennium Technologies, Jeff Lundblad. $20.)

Exiting Windows NT—WinEXIT

WinEXIT provides a quick and easy way to close NT. It places an icon on your desktop, and when you double-click on the icon it carries out an exit operation: Logoff, Shutdown, or Shutdown and Reboot. Your configuration choice defines which operation should be carried out on the double-click, but you can also use the Control menu to select any of the operations. You can also make WinEXIT display a shutdown-delay dialog box, so that the system is not shutd own immediately. And several command-line switches let you create different WinEXIT icons for different types of shutdown. (WinEXIT, WINXNT.ZIP, Silverware Consulting. Free.)

Improved Command Prompt—4DOS

You may have worked with 4DOS in MS-DOS. It enhances the command prompt, providing extra commands, online help, speeding up directory switching, and so on. Well, there's already a version of 4DOS for Windows NT. It works in the same way as the DOS version, providing about 80 commands, mostly new but also enhanced from the DOS commands. You'll find commands such as SELECT (which lets you use the cursor keys to select files), ALIAS (to create new commands that run combined commands, or assign commands to a key), CANCEL (to terminate batch-file processing), a CD command that lets you change drives at the same time you change directories, IFF (to allow IF/THEN/ELSE processing of commands), and INKEY (to store a user's single keystroke in an environment variable). (4DOS, 4DOSNT.ZIP, JP Software. $79.)

Organizing Program Manager Icons— Icon Manager

Icon Manager is a neat little utility for organizing, editing, and creating Program Manager icons. You can load .ICO, .ICL, .IL, .NIL, .ICA, .EXE, and .DLL icons into *sheets*, document windows which look like Program Manager's program groups. To edit an icon you simply double-click on it, and Icon Manager asks you what "transparent" color should be used—the area "below" the icon (see Figure 22.4). Select a color and click on OK, and the icon is loaded into Paintbrush.

Icon Manager also has a simple way to replace any Program Manager program-group icon with one you select in Icon Manager. You'll see a dialog box listing

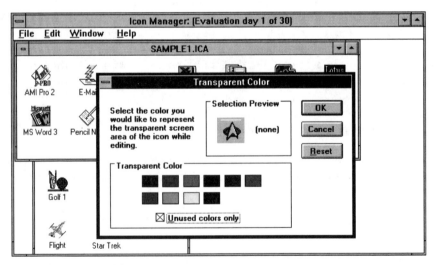

Figure 22.4 Icon Manager

the program groups—select a group and you'll see a list box containing all the icons. Select the icon and click on OK and the icon is replaced with the new one. (Icon Manager, IMN10.ZIP, Impact Software. $24.95.)

Add Applications To Program Manager

The unusually—but aptly—named Add Applications To Program Manager is a simple application that searches a disk or directory and finds all the files of the type you specify (see Figure 22.5). They might be executable files, bitmaps, icon files (.ICO), cursor files (.CUR) or whatever you want. You can use this to quickly search CDs, which Windows NT Setup's Setup Applications command won't let you do. Once it's found all the files, you can then select the ones you want to add to a program group—you can select which program group, or name a new one. (Add Applications To Program Manager, ADDAPP.ZIP, TDAC Software, Timothy D. A. Cox.)

Animated Cursors—ANI Make

ANIMake

The new Cursors dialog box in the Control Panel lets you select animated cursors. But how do you create them? You could use ANI Make. This program installs itself as an extra icon in the Control Panel, immediately before the Cursors icon. It lets you select several .CUR files, and combine them into an .ANI file which can then be selected in the Cursors dialog box. (Each .CUR file will be one part of the motion, in the same way each frame in a film provides one moment of the motion.)

You can get .CUR files from the Windows SDK (Software Development Kit) and they can be created in some other utilities—ANI Make can't create them, though an Image Editor is planned for a future release. (ANI Make, ANIMAK.ZIP, Babarsoft, Mark Gamber. Free.)

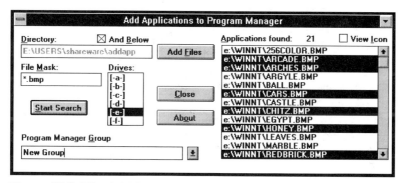

Figure 22.5 The Add Applications To Program Manager dialog box

A Software Observatory—Astronomy Lab

Astronomy Lab is a shareware astronomy program that generates graphs, reports, and "movies." (See Figure 22.6.) You can use the program to predict when and where astronomical events will occur, and to view animated reconstructions of events such as eclipses, lunar and planetary occultations, and the motions of the planets. It has extensive online help, including a user's guide and tutorial. (Astronomy Lab, ALW_NT.ZIP, Personal MicroCosms. $15.)

A Programmer's Editor—M-Edit

M-Edit is a programmer's editor designed for Windows NT (see Figure 22.7). It has a toolbar that can be converted to a toolbox, and all the usual Windows features—cut, copy, paste, undo, a search function, user-configurable colors, fonts, and tab stops. You can customize the environment, and the Build menu lets you compile, build, debug, and so on. (M-Edit, MEDIT2.ZIP, Babarsoft, Mark Gamber.)

If you are interested in a programmer's editor, you might also look at Winner, a joint effort by a variety of NT programmers. The source code is provided, so anyone can make changes. It's a simple editor with a toolbar, search functions, and compile, build, and execute commands. You can have two documents open at once, and select a typeface. (Winner, WINNER.ZIP. Free.)

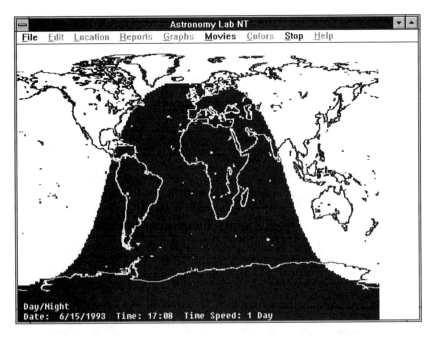

Figure 22.6 Astronomy Lab, showing the Day/Night chart

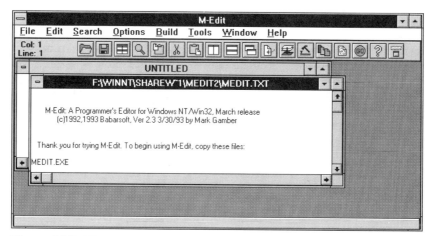

Figure 22.7 The M-Edit Programmer's Editor

ASCII Files—Notebook

Notebook is an excellent replacement for Windows NT Notepad (see Figure 22.8). It looks much the same, but it has many more features. You can merge text files, print selected text, and select a different font and font size. You can carry out find-and-replace operations, select text and modify its case, set bookmarks, and define a starting window size and position. You can even edit nonprinting ASCII printer-control codes. The File menu also has a History command, showing the last four files opened by Notebook. There's even a utility that lets you delete files and run other applications without leaving Notebook. (Notebook, NOTENT.ZIP, Mark Berlinger. $10.)

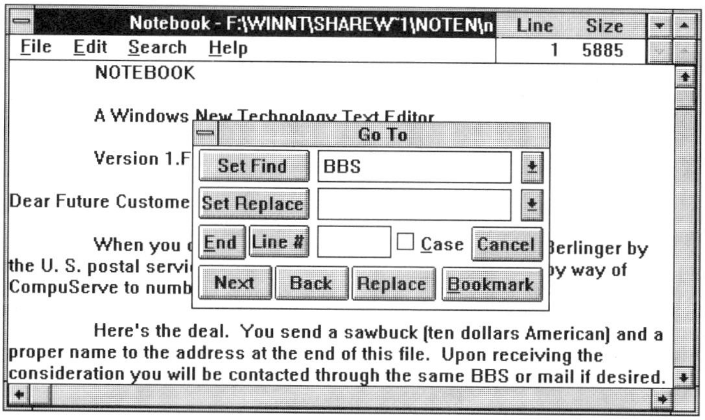

Figure 22.8 The Notebook window, showing the GoTo dialog box

Talking Calculator—RCALC NT

RCALC NT is a Reverse Polish Notation calculator—one which requires that all the numbers are entered *before* the operation is carried out—and it talks to you (see Figure 22.9). It's very easy to use (if you use Reverse Polish Notation, that is), and comes with an excellent help file. If you have a sound board attached, you can also turn on sounds, so that each time you click on a button or press a key, the name of the key is spoken. This can be useful when entering lots of numbers—it acts as a verbal check as you type the figures. (RCALC NT, NT_RCA.ZIP, Pocket-Sized Software, Eric Bermann-Terrell. Free, $5 if you really like it.)

Stopwatch, Talking Clock, and Astronomy Clock

As you've already seen, Pocket-Sized Software has been busy. In addition to the programs we've already mentioned, they have also created three 32-bit clocks. Stopwatch NT is a small application with a clock that measures time down to 1/100th of a second and up to several days. You can also record many separate events. Click on the program's Save button and the current elapsed time is entered into a list box and given a sequence number. (Stopwatch NT, NT_SW.ZIP, Pocket-Sized Software, Eric Bermann-Terrell. Free, $5 if you really like it.)

Talking Clock NT is a very simple digital clock (no analog option) with an "always on top" option. Most importantly, if you have a sound board it will tell you the time—literally—every 15 minutes. (Talking Clock NT, NT_TCL.ZIP, Pocket-Sized Software, Eric Bermann-Terrell. Free, $5 if you really like it.)

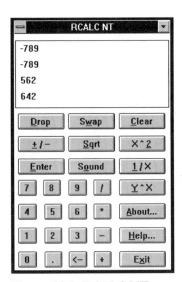

Figure 22.9 RCALC NT

Astronomy Clock is a digital clock that displays several different times. You enter your location by selecting from a list of dozens of US cities and a few international cities, or by entering the Longitude. Astronomy Clock then figures out your time zone. You can then select to view Local Mean Time (the time in your time zone); Universal Time (the local mean time in Greenwich, England, which is not adjusted by daylight savings time—this time is often used when describing astronomical events); Local Sidereal Time (a time system based on the motion of stars); and Greenwich Sidereal Time (the local sidereal time for Greenwich, England). You can also make the clock chime every hour. (Astronomy Clock NT, NT_ACL.ZIP, Pocket-Sized Software, Eric Bermann-Terrell. Free, $5 if you really like it.)

System Tests—WinTach

Texas Instruments has created a free system-testing program called WinTach (see Figure 22.10). It tests the speed at which your Windows 3.1 applications run by simulating four types of application—word processors, CAD and draw, spreadsheets, and paint programs. You'll actually see these four types of application running as WinTach carries out its tests. There's also a cursor stability test, which checks to see how your video board handles displaying a mouse cursor on top of a constantly updating area of the screen, an indication of how your system will respond to applications with a lot of video output.

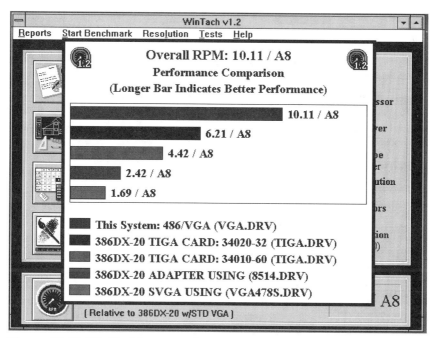

Figure 22.10 WinTach's report sheet

For each program type it provides a system rating, comparing your machine to a 386DX-20 as a guideline. There's also an overall rating, and you can print a report or copy it to the Clipboard. This utility is useful for testing the comparative speeds of different video modes, and for comparing different machines. (WinTach, WINTAC.ZIP. Texas Instruments. Free.)

Messages—While You Were Out

While You Were Out is a messaging system based on the familiar phone-message pad—the sort of pad used by secretaries, with check boxes for Called To See You, Will Call Again, Please Call, and so on. Each user is assigned a directory in which his messages will be kept. When the secretary receives a call for that person, he selects the person's name from a list (see Figure 22.11), enters the caller's name, company name, and phone number, selects one of the call types—Urgent, Telephoned, Wants To See You, and so on, types a short message (up to about eight lines), and clicks on Send. The message is sent to the "WYWO Message Rack," from which the recipient can retrieve it. It's a simple program, but gets the job done. It's much easier than using Mail, for instance, though of course it's purpose and capabilities are more limited. The shareware version is a three-person utility. You can purchase systems for 5 to 100 people, ranging from $20 to $12.50 per person. (While You Were Out, WYWONT.ZIP, Caliente Intl. $99.95 for 5 users.)

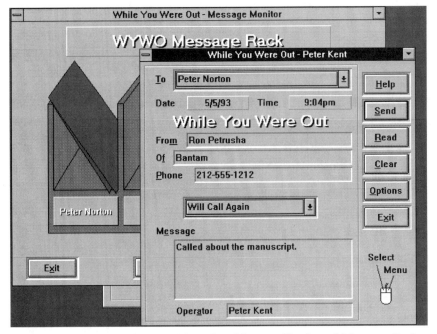

Figure 22.11 The While You Were Out Message Rack and Message Pad

Screen Savers—Spooks and Melt

Windows NT comes with several of its own screen savers. Unfortunately Windows 3.1 screen savers are not compatible, though they use the same file extension (.SCR)—you can't just copy them to the WINNT directory and expect that they'll work. So here are a couple of free screen savers you may want to try.

Spooks gradually fills your screen with a colorful array of ghosts and skulls (Figure 22.12). Melt works very slowly. It gradually moves pixels from random positions around the screen, so the picture slowly grows fuzzy. Melt only works well over long periods of time, which may be a drawback. An extremely fuzzy screen is an indication that the screen saver has been running for hours, a message that you may not want to leave for your boss or supervisor. (Melt, MELT.ZIP, and Spooks, SPOOKS.ZIP, Babarsoft, Mark Gamber. Free.)

Note Screen savers cost money—they require electricity to run, which in turn requires nonrenewable resources to be wasted and pollution to be generated. If you are leaving your computer for a long time (such as overnight), Shutdown and turn off. If you are leaving for a short time, use NT's Lock Workstation feature (press Ctrl-Alt-Del) and then turn off the monitor. It's a myth that computers must be run continuously for the sake of reliability.

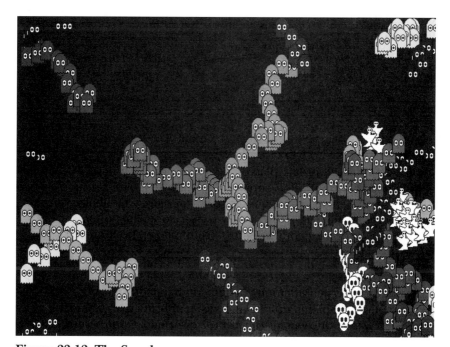

Figure 22.12 The Spooks screen saver

Klotz—A Tapcis-Like Game

Klotz is a Tapcis-like game from Germany. (Klotz is short for Klotzchenspiel, meaning a game with blocks.) Blocks fall down inside a "window," and it's your job to stack the blocks such that no spaces are left free (see Figure 22.13). You can control the speed at which the blocks drop, rotate them, and even "park" them in one position. The game has a number of special features, such as the ability to change the keys that control the block movement, add a grid to the window to make it easier to see the path the blocks will take, display a statistics chart, and so on. (Klotz, KLOTNT.ZIP, Wolfgang Strobl. Free.)

Card Games—Thieves and Kings

Thieves and Kings is a program containing two card games, Forty Thieves and Kings Corners (see Figure 22.14). Forty Thieves starts by dealing seven stacks of five cards, face up. Another card is placed face up at the bottom. This single card can "take" any of the cards at the top of the seven stacks, as long as the card is immediately above or below it in sequence, regardless of suit. A 7 can take a 6 or 8 from any suit, for instance. If there are no cards that you can take, you must deal another card. The aim is to remove all the cards, and you score for each card removed, depending on the type. The game ends when you either remove all the cards or use the last card in the stack.

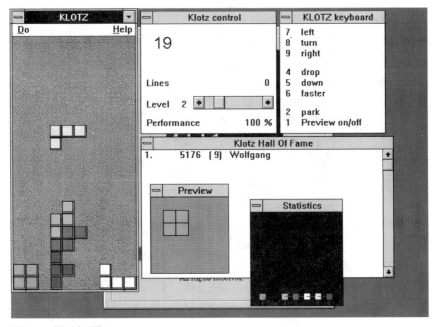

Figure 22.13 Klotz

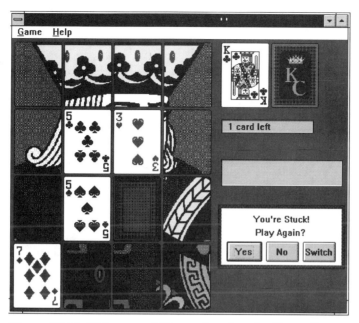

Figure 22.14 Thieves and Kings, showing the Kings Corners window

In Kings Corners, you are given a grid of four cards square. Each card that is dealt must be placed on this grid—the kings must go on the corners, the queens must go on the four side middle places, between the kings' corners, and the jacks must go on the four top and bottom middle spaces, between the kings' corners. Other cards go wherever you want. Once you've filled the grid with the first 16 cards, you can remove the numbered and ace cards, leaving the kings, queens, and jacks. You can remove any 10, or any two cards that add up to 10. Once you've removed all the cards you can, you deal more and place them onto the grid.

The difficulty, of course, is that you sometimes are forced to block the outside ones—if you are ever dealt a king, queen, or jack and its grid space is filled with another card, you've lost.

Both games are quite enjoyable and, as usual, addictive. As the author notes in his Help file, "you really should be doing something else." (Thieves and Kings, THINGS.ZIP, Paul DeWolf. $20.)

Word Games—Bog NT and Hangman NT

Bog NT (see Figure 22.15) is a word game in which you create as many words as possible from 16 letters selected by the computer and displayed in the Bog window on cubes (actually buttons). You can only choose letters that are on selected cubes. You enter words by typing and pressing Enter, or by clicking on the cubes and clicking on Enter. There is one way to cheat—by telling Bog that a non-word you have just entered is actually a real word.

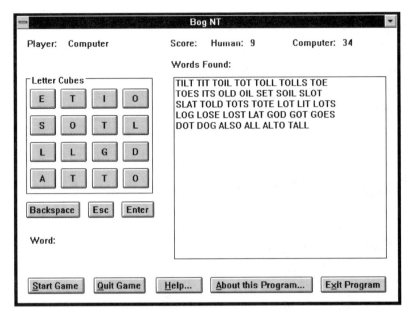

Figure 22.15 The Bog NT window

When you've finished the game the computer will find as many matching words as it can, completely humiliating you. It's an interesting game, and may be of interest to users who are tired of Minesweeper and NT's card games. (Bog NT, NT_BOG.ZIP, Pocket-Sized Software, Eric Bermann-Terrell. Free, $5 if you really like it.)

Hangman NT is a version of the popular kid's word game. Actually it's more like Wheel of Fortune. You have to select letters to create a word, and you are allowed only 10 incorrect guesses—and there's no one on a gallows. (Hangman NT, NT_HAN.ZIP, Pocket-Sized Software, Eric Bermann-Terrell. Free, $5 if you really like it.)

Fractals—FracView NT

FracView is a very simple program which displays a Mandelbrot fractal image— the same image each time, unfortunately. (See Figure 22.16.) You can zoom in on an area, and even copy the image to the Clipboard so you can paste it into another application. FracView NT also has a neat Program Manager icon that you may want to use even if you rarely use the program itself. (FracView NT, NT_FRA.ZIP, Pocket-Sized Software, Eric Bermann-Terrell. Free, $5 if you really like it.)

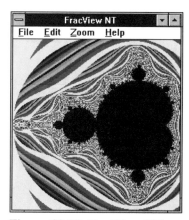

Figure 22.16 FracView NT

A Number Puzzle—Puzzle-8 NT

Puzzle-8 NT is a computerized version of the familiar eight-tile puzzle, in which eight tiles are placed on a nine-space grid, and the aim is to move the tiles around until the numbers are arranged in the correct order (see Figure 22.17). If it's been a while since you played this, you may not remember that it's a lot more difficult than it at first appears. (Puzzle-8 NT, NT_PZL.ZIP, Pocket-Sized Software, Eric Bermann-Terrell. Free, $5 if you really like it.)

Desktop Music—MIDI JukeBox NT

MIDI JukeBox NT is a simple program for playing .MID and .WAV files through a compatible MIDI or sound board. You enter the files you want to play in a list, in the order in which you want to hear them, then click on Play. You can also play the files in a continuous loop, and use the Next, Prev, and Pause buttons to control playback.(MIDI JukeBox NT, NT_MJB.ZIP, Pocket-Sized Software, Eric Bermann-Terrell. Free, $5 if you really like it.)

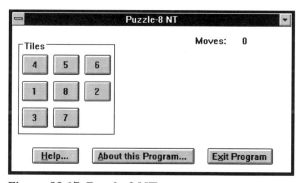

Figure 22.17 Puzzle-8 NT

Appendix

Applet Updates

Much of Windows NT has been taken straight from Windows 3.1, with few or no changes. We have described the major changes elsewhere in the book—for instance, Multimedia Player has changed so much that we described the new one in Chapter 20. In this appendix we are going to summarize some other, less significant, changes to Windows "applets."

These applications are the same as in Windows 3.1:

> **Calculator**
> **Cardfile**
> **Character Map**
> **Terminal**
> **Write**

The following describes the changes in applications since Windows 3.1.

Calendar

Calendar is not available in Windows NT. If you have the Windows 3.1 version you can run it, of course, and the About dialog box will say it's the "Windows NT Calendar," but it's not.

You don't need Calendar anymore, because NT has Schedule+ instead, a much more powerful calendar and scheduling application. Your old .CAL files can be imported by Schedule+. See Chapter 17.

ClipBook Viewer (Clipboard in Windows 3.1)

NT's ClipBook Viewer is an update of the one found in Windows for Workgroups. It incorporates the Clipboard, and allows you to share Clipboard data across the network, or to save Clipboard data for future use. See Chapter 18.

Clock

The Clock has undergone one minor change. There's now a **Settings|GMT** option. This makes the clock display Greenwich Mean Time, the time at the Royal Observatory in Greenwich, near London, England. GMT is used in many disciplines, including astronomy and navigation.

Command Prompt (MS-DOS Prompt in Windows 3.1)

The MS-DOS Prompt is, in effect, incorporated into the NT Command Prompt. It looks the same as the MS-DOS Prompt (and the Program Manager icon is even the same), but strictly speaking, it's not a DOS prompt—you can use it to launch DOS, NT, POSIX, and OS/2 applications, and run DOS and NT commands. See Chapter 9 for more information.

Control Panel

The Control Panel looks the same as in Windows 3.1, and works in the same manner. It has more icons, though, and some of the ones that are also in Windows 3.1 have been modified for NT. See Chapter 6 for more information.

File Manager

There are lots of changes to File Manager. NT's File Manager is closer to the one in Windows for Workgroups than Windows 3.1. See Chapter 7 for more information.

Help

Windows NT
Help

The Windows NT Help system has a couple of modifications. The first difference you'll notice is the format of the Contents pages. You can now click on an Expand button to expand the contents, and add subheadings. NT has also added a "system-wide" search feature. In Program Manager, double-click on the Windows NT Help icon. You'll see a windows with several options (see Figure A.1):

Figure A.1 The Windows NT Help window

Search Windows NT Help Files	Lets you search for information through up to 14 different help files at the same time.
Command Reference Help	Displays a listing of all the Command Prompt commands, and detailed information about each one.
Windows NT Glossary	A glossary of Windows NT-related terms.
Microsoft Support Services	Displays information about NT support services.
Microsoft Access and Disability Support	Displays information about Microsoft's Access and Disability Support services.
Instructions	Displays instructions on using the full-text search feature.

You can click on the first button in this window, or on the **Find** button on the buttonbar, to see the Find dialog box (Figure A.2). Type the text you want to search for. You can carry out Boolean searches; click on the **Hints** button to see an explanation of how to do this. In Figure A.2, for instance, `Replicator NEAR Directory` would search the help files for an area in which the word *Replicator* was found within eight words of *Directory*—though in the bottom of the Hints dialog box you can select another **NEAR means within** value. You can also use `AND` to find both words, `OR` to find either word, `NOT` to find a topic containing the first word but not the second, `"  "` to find the exact phrase within the quotation marks, parentheses to combine searches, such as `(" Replicator") AND`

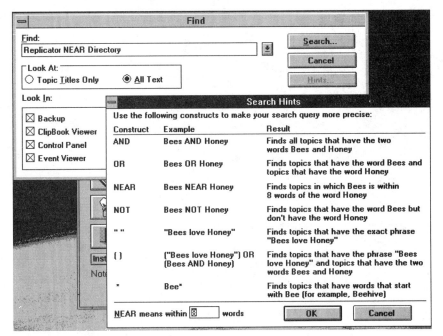

Figure A.2 The Find dialog box, with the Search Hints box on top

(Replicator AND Directory), and the wildcard, * to define a word starting with several characters, such as *replic**. If you want to search for a specific word, without any Boolean modifiers, make sure you place the text in quotation marks.

Note Not all the words in a help file are indexed—you couldn't search for "and," for instance. If you enter a word that isn't indexed, you'll see a message when you click on the Search button.

Next, decide whether you want to search the full text of an article (**All Text**), or only the topic titles (**Topic Titles Only**). Finally, select which help files you want to search from the **Look In** list box. By default all the help files are selected, but you can change this.

When you click on **Search**, NT looks through all the selected help files for the information. If it finds matching entries you'll see a Topics Found dialog box, similar to the History dialog box, with the first entry displayed in the help window. You can click on the **Next** and **Previous** buttons to work your way through the entries. You can also double-click on an entry, or click once and click **Go To**.

The **Command Reference** help displays information about all the Command Prompt commands, and even includes many examples (see Chapter 9). The **Glossary** is similar to that in Windows 3.1, with an improved indexing method. You can click on a button at the top of the window to move directly to the entries beginning with the letter on the button. Click on P to move to the P entries, for instance.

NT's help system now lets you have more than one help window open at a time, returning to the pre-Windows 3.1 state. In 3.1, each time you open an application's help window, any currently open help window is closed.

Media Player

Though similar to Windows 3.1 applications, NT's Media Player has a few important changes. It has more OLE options, more "front panel" controls, and the ability to mark a section of the media clip. See Chapter 20 for more information.

Notepad

Notepad appears exactly the same as in Windows 3.1. However, there's an important difference. You can now load much larger files into Notepad. If you are used to seeing the Windows 3.1 Notepad message saying that it can't open a file, try NT's Notepad. You're unlikely to see that message again.

Object Packager

NT's Object Packager remains the same as in Windows 3.1. Microsoft is not bothering much with Object Packager, as the plan is to get rid of it in the next major OLE update.

Paintbrush

Paintbrush has the same commands as in Windows 3.1, but there's an important change. In Windows 3.1, everything you did offscreen was lost. For instance, if you selected an area of the picture and "pushed" it offscreen, the offscreen part would be lost. If you used the Paint Roller tool to fill an area, the filling would stop at the scroll bars—it wouldn't fill any part of the picture that was offscreen.

In Windows NT, this limitation has gone. Paintbrush no longer regards the edge of the screen as its working limit. This is important in one area in particular—it makes taking screen "snapshots" much easier. Press Print Screen to take a snapshot—a picture of everything on your screen. Go to Paintbrush and press Ctrl-V to paste the image into the picture. When you use the scroll bars to move around the picture, you'll find that the entire screen was placed in the window; it wasn't cropped at the edge of the windows. (In Windows 3.1 you have to select View|Zoom Out, press Ctrl-V, then click on the toolbox to fix the picture in position, then select View|Zoom In.)

PIF Editor

Most of a PIF file's settings have no effect on NT, though the PIF Editor retains the settings so that you can create PIF files that will work in both NT and Windows 3.1. You can also now specify the AUTOEXEC and CONFIG files that will be run before the application itself. See Chapter 10.

Print Manager

Print Manager has changed dramatically: It's a whole new animal. See Chapter 8.

Recorder

Recorder is no longer available in NT. If you need such an application you will have to find a third-party product. The Windows 3.1 version of Recorder won't work in NT. (If you open the application, however, and look in the About dialog box it will tell you that it's the "Microsoft Windows NT Recorder." It isn't, the About box is just using a generic template.)

Sound Recorder

NT's Sound Recorder is much the same as the one in Windows 3.1, though you can now use the File|New command to define the sampling rate for recording a new file. You can also paste sounds from the Clipboard, mixing or inserting the sound into the original file. See Chapter 20 for more information.

Windows Setup

NT's Windows Setup application is very similar to that in 3.1. When you open it you'll see the Display, Mouse, and Keyboard, and you can use this application to change those settings. You won't see the Network, though—to change the network, you'll go to the Networks icon in the Control Panel. You can also use Setup to Set Up Applications and Remove Windows Components, just as you would in Windows 3.1.

There are three more options: You can use the Setup menu to Add/Remove SCSI Adapters, Add/Remove Tape Devices, and Delete User Profiles. See Chapter 3 for more information.

Index

A

Abilities, built-in ability, 71
Access control lists, 9
Accountability, 9
Accounts
administrator account, 66
assignment to Directory Replicator, 98
Guest account, 66
initial account, 66
ACLCONV, 179
Adapter cards, networks, installation of, 261–262
Add Applications to Program Manager utility, 385
Address Book, 280–281
adding addresses to phone book, 281
removing addresses, 281
viewing personal address book, 280–281
Administrative Tools group, program icons of, 54–55
Administrator
Administrative Account Setup, 37
designation of, 23
functions of, 13, 70
and network configuration, 260
overruling of owner, 112
password of, 23
and tape backup, 341
and use of commands, 159
Administrator account, 66
Advanced Server, capabilities of, 12–13
Alerts, 221–224
adding alert item, 221
customization of, 223–224
editing items, 223
and networks, 273
pasting in application, 231
running program on, 221–222
using data of log file, 228–229
Alt-Enter, 197
Alt-Esc, 197
Alt-PrtSc, 197
Alt-Space, 197
Alt-Tab, 197
ANI, 94
ANI Make, 385
APPEND, 179

Application programs
compatible timer hardware emulation, 199
cutting and pasting between, 202
non-NT programs
custom startup files, definition of, 198–199
MS-DOS applications, 192–193
program information files, 194–198
Windows 3.1 programs, 192
OS/2 programs, 200–201
start-up for, 201–202
ARP, 188
ARP TCP/IP, 179
Astronomy Clock, 389
Astronomy Lab, 386
AT, 179
ATTRIB, 179
Auditing
of events, 239
of file and directory, 120–121
printing, 148–149
Authentication, 9
AUTOADMIN.EXE, 45
AUTOEXEC.BAT, 56, 90, 192–193
AUTOEXEC.NT, 192, 193

B

BACKUP, 179
Backup
hard drive, 344–349
See also Tape backup
Backup operators, functions of, 70
Batch files, 194
Binding, network, 264–265
Block-character mode, 145
Bog NT, 393–394
Bookmarks, in log file, 227
Boot files, creation of, 45
BOOT.INI, 44, 45, 49
Boot loader, 17, 89
BOOTSECT.DOS, 45, 47, 49
BREAK, 179
BUFFERS, 179
Built-in abilities, 71–72
functions of, 71
types of, 71–72

C

Calculator, RCALT NT, 388
Calendar, 55, 397
CALL, 179
Case sensitivity, passwords, 24
CD Player, 55, 179, 357–360
  features of, 358
  Playlists, 359
  viewing information, 359
  volume control, 360
CD-ROM
  incompatibilities with NT, 18
  and installation
    non SCSI CD-ROM drives, 31
    SCSI CD-ROM drives, 31
Charts, 216–220
  creation of chart, 216–219
  intervals displayed by, 219–220
  modification of chart, 219–220
  options for, 216–217
  using data of log file, 228–229
Chat, 55, 331–334
  bug related to, 334
  color, changing of, 333
  fonts, 333
  opening of, 331–332
  special characters, sending of, 332
  use of, 332–333
CHCP, 179
CHDIR, 180
Checkpoints, 8
CHKDSK, 180
C language, and NT, 9
Clipboard event logging, 239–240
ClipBook Viewer, 55, 334–340, 398
  connecting to another ClipBook, 337
  copying to/from ClipBook, 335–336
  data sharing, 336–337
  embedding, 338
  linking images, 338
  menu options, 338–340
  opening of, 334
  security, 338
  viewing contents, 334
Clock, 398
CLS, 180
CMD, 180
CODEPAGE, 180, 188, 201
Colors
  Chat, 333
  Disk Administrator, 255
  printing, 139, 141
  Schedule+, 323
  screen, selection of, 174–175
Command buffers, of Doskey, 166
Command prompt, 55, 398
  capabilities of, 158

characteristics of, 157
  terminate, 173
Command prompt window, 165–172
  coping data between windows, 176–177
  cutting and pasting between applications, 202
  different command prompt windows, creation
    of, 176
  File Manager Shell, to open window, 380
  home directory, creation of, 176
  modification of
    display mode, 175
    display options, 173
    fonts, 172–173
    screen colors, 175
    screen size and position, 174
  opening of, 165
  saved settings, 176
Commands
  and Administrator, 159
  command symbols, 189–190
  configuration commands, 158
  from DOS 5.0, 159–161
  from LAN Manager 2.1, 162–164
  listing of NT commands, 179–189
  MS-DOS commands, running of, 157
  native commands, 158
  network commands, 158
  and NTFS file names, 165–166
  OS/2 CONFIG.SYS commands, 188
  special purpose commands, 158
  subsystem commands, 158
  TCP/IP utility commands, 159, 188–189
  unavailable commands, 161–162, 164–165
  to view help, 177
Common program groups, 56
COMP, 180
Compatible timer hardware emulation, 199
CompuServe, 373–376
  navigators, 375–376
  Windows NT forums, 374
CONFIG.NT, 192, 193
  MS-DOS configuration commands used in, 194
CONFIG.SYS, 56
CONFIG.SYS commands, OS/2, 200–201
Configuration commands, 158, 194
Configuration of disk
  extended partition, 251–252
  logical drives, 250, 252
  primary partition, 250, 251
  saving and restoring configurations, 254–255
Configuration Registry, 26, 203
Control panel, 398
  cursor, 94
  date/time, 93–94
Control Panel
  Desktop+, 379–380
  devices, 99–100
  fast access to dialog boxes, 103

fonts, 88
icons in, 87–88
mouse, 89
multitasking, 92–93
services, 95–97
sound, 95
startup options, 97–98
system, 89–90
uninterruptible power supply, 100–103
virtual memory, 91–92
CONVERT, 47–48, 180
COPY, 180
COUNTRY, 180, 194, 201
CREATOR OWNERS, 112, 119
Ctrl-Esc, 197
Cursor
animated cursors utility, 385
dialog box, 94
Custer, Helen, 373

D

DATE, 180
Date/time
dialog box, 93–94
setting, 38
DEBUG, 180
Dedicated-server network, 259
DEL, 180
Deleting information, from User Manager, 78–79
Desktop+, 379–380
Desynchronized input queues, 8
DEVICE, 180, 194
DEVICEHIGH, 180
DEVICENAME, 200
Devices, dialog box, 99–100
DEVINFO, 180, 188
DEVINFO-KBD, 201
DIR, 180
Directories
auditing of, 120–121
directory replication, 271–272
group for, 70
home directory, 76, 176
individual permissions for, 115
ownership of, 112–113
sharing on network, 121–123
standard permissions for, 114–115
startup directory for programs, 195–196
working directory, 76, 176
Discretionary access control, 9
Disk Administrator, 13, 54
configuration of disk, 250–252
extended partition, 251–252
logical drives, 252
primary partition, 250, 251
customization of, 255–256
deleting disk partition, 250

drive letters, assignment of, 254
formatting new partitions, 253–254
marking volume as active, 254
menu options, 257
opening of, 249
restoring configurations, 254
saving changes, 253
saving configurations, 254–255
stripe sets, creation of, 252–253
volume sets, creating and extending, 252
of Windows NT Advanced Server, 256
DISKCOMP, 181
Disk compression, MS-DOS incompatibility and
NT, 19
DISKCOPY, 181
Disk drives, drive letters, assignment of, 254
Disk duplexing, 13
Disk mirroring, 12
characteristics of, 256
meaning of, 20
Disk partition
creation of, 22
and installation, 33
reformatting of, 33–34
DISKPERF, 181
Disk stripping with parity, 13
meaning of, 20
Display. See Screen
Distributed networking, 259
Dr. Watson, 57–58
Domain, 259, 260–261
characteristics of, 260
joining domain, 263–264
DOS, 181, 194
Doskey, 166–172, 181
command buffers of, 166
command template, 169
functions of, 166
keystrokes for recalling/editing commands,
167–168
macros with, 169–171
modification of, 171–172
simple method for use of, 168–169
DOS names, 108–109
Drag-and-drop utilities, types of, 381–382
Drivers
for adapter card, installation of, 262
printer driver, loading of, 143
tape backup, 342–343
DRIVPARM, 181
DRWATSON.EXE, 57
Dynamic data exchange (DDE), 6, 127

E

ECHO, 181
ECHOCONFIG, 181, 194
EDIT, 181

Editor, M-Edit, 386
EDLIN, 181
80–86 based computers, and installation, 30
Email. See Mail
Emergency Recovery Disk, 50–52
Emergency Repair Disk, creation of, 38
EMM, 181
EMS memory, 196
ENDLOCAL, 181
Environment subsystem, 5
ERASE, 181
Error messages, 43
   characteristics of system for, 178
Escape character, 144, 146
Escape codes, 144
Event logging, 43, 121, 235
   auditing of events, 239
   Clipboard event logging, 239–240
   control of file-security event logging, 238–239
   printer event logging, 239
   of Registry Editor events, 240
   setting up logging, 236–237
   types of events for logging, 237
Events
   application events, 237
   printer events, 239
   security events, 237
   system events, 237
Event Viewer, 43, 54, 240–248
   clearing logs, 247
   logging events on network computer, 247
   menu options, 247–248
   modification of data, 244–245
   preferences, setting of, 245
   saving data, 246
   start-up of, 241
   viewing event, 243
   window, columns of data in, 241–242
EXE2BIN, 181
EXE Type, 381
EXIT, 181
Exiting NT, 41–42
   Exit Windows NT utility, 382
Exporting data, 230–231
   steps in, 231
Extended characters, 166
   use in Chat, 332
Extended partition, 251–252
   creation of, 251–252
Extensions, associating document files, 126–128

F

FASTOPEN, 181
Fault tolerance, 20, 33
FC, 181
FCBS, 181, 194
FExtend, File Manager utility, 380–381

File allocation table (FAT), 5
   converting FAT to NTFS, 47–48
   converting NTFS to, 48
   and installation of NT, 19–20
   and security system, 112
File Manager, 12, 26, 398
   accessing data on network, 124–126
      disconnecting network drive, 126
   associating document files, 126–128
   auditing file and directory, 120–121
   data sharing on network, 121–124
      checking on file use, 123–124
      ending network sharing, 124
      sharing directories, 121–123
   DOS names, 108–109
   FExtend utility, 380–381
   file properties, 110–111
   function of, 66
   icons in, 105–106
   menu options, 129–131
   multitasking in, 128
   security options, 111–120
      access permissions, defining, 113–117
      assignment of permissions, 117–118
      deactivation of file security, 121
      guidelines related to permissions, 119
      and ownership of files/directories,
         112–113
   toolbar, customization of, 106–108
File Manager Shell, opening command
      prompt window, 380
File names
   display of, 109
   DOS file names, use of, 108–109
   long filenames, 20
      viewing of, 109–110
   and NTFS commands, 165–166
   rules for, 108
File properties, 110–111
   dialog box, 110
      viewing of, 110–111
File replication, 12
FILES, 182
Files
   auditing of, 120–121
   checking on file use, 123–124
   creating new file type, 126–127
   individual permissions for, 116
   ownership of, 112–113
   of Performance Monitor, 215–216
   standard permissions for, 115
File system. See NTFS (NT File System)
File Viewer, 382–383
FIND, 182
FINDSTR, 182
FINGER, 182, 189
Flexboot, 17, 22, 89
   modification to, 44–45

Fonts
  Chat, 333
  dialog box, 88, 128
  modification from command prompt
      window, 172–173
  Schedule+, 324
FOR, 182
FORCEDOS, 182
FORMAT, 182
Formatting, disk formatting, 253–254
Forms, printing of, 146–147
4DOS, 378, 384
FracView NT, 394
FreeCell, 55, 367–370
  playing procedure, 368–370
FTP, 182, 189

G

Games
  Bog NT, 393–394
  FreeCell, 367–370
  Gorilla, 370
  Hangman NT, 394
  Klotz, 392
  Nibbles, 371
  Thieves and Kings, 392–393
General Drop, 382
Global groups, functions of, 66
Gorilla, 57, 370
GOTO, 182
GRAFTABL, 182
Graph, pasting in application, 231
Graphical user interface, 4–5
  demands on hardware, 4–5
  example of use, 4
GRAPHICS, 182
Graphics resolution, and printing, 139
Groups, 65–66, 68–72
  creation of, 68–70
  global groups, 66
  groups automatically created, 70
  local groups, 65
  special groups, 71
  types of, 70–71
  user groups, 65
Guest account, 43, 66
Guest group, 70

H

Halftones, 140–142
  nature of, 140
  printing options, 140–142
Hangman NT, 394
Hard drive
  backup of, 344–349
  restoring data to, 350–351

Hardware
  and graphical user interface, 4–5
  incompatibility and NT, 18–19
  and installation, 32
  requirements for Windows NT, 14–15, 27
Hardware abstraction level, 10
HELP, 54, 182, 398–401
Help
  commands for viewing of, 177
  modifications to, 398–401
High performance file system (HPFS), 5
  converting to NTFS, 47–48
  converting from NTFS, 48
  and installation of NT, 20
  and security system, 112
HKEY_CLASSES_ROOT, 205, 207
HKEY_CURRENT_USER, 205, 206
HKEY_LOCAL_MACHINE, 205, 206
HKEY_USERS, 205, 206
Home directory, creation of, 176
HOSTNAME, 182, 189

I

Icon Manager, 378
  Icon Manager utility, 384–385
IF, 182
Importing data, from Schedule+, 322–323
Individual permissions, 114, 115–116
  for directories, 115
  for files, 116
Initial account, 66
Inside Windows NT (Custer), 373
INSTALL, 182
Installation of NT
  Administrator, designation of, 23
  beginning installation
    on 80–86 based computer, 30
    from floppies, 31
    from network drive, 31
    from non-SCSI CD-ROM drive, 31
    on RISC-based computer, 30
    from SCSI CD-ROM drive, 31
  boot files, creation of, 45
  boot loader, 17
  configuration problems, recovery from, 49–52
  Custom Setup, 32
  and disk partition, 22, 33
  Express Setup, 32
  file system selection, 19–21
    decision making about, 21
    file allocation table, 20
    NTFS, 20–21
  hardware incompatibility, 18–19
  hardware requirements, 27
  installation from network, 38–39
  and keeping second operating system, 17–18, 26
    with MS-DOS and OS/2, 22–23

Installation of NT (*cont'd*)
  location of NT, 21–22, 34
  network-adapter configuration, 36
  passwords, 23–25
  phase one of, 32–34
  of printer, 36
  reinstallation of, 52
  setup phase, 34–38
  software incompatibility, 19

K

Kermit, 378
KEYB, 182
Klotz, 378, 392

L

LABEL, 182
LAN Manager 2.1
  commands of, 162–164
  unavailable commands, 164–165
LASTDRIVE, 182
LH, 182
LI 32, 382–383
LIBPATH, 183, 188, 201
Lighting, printing in halftones, 141–142
LOADFIX, 183
LOADHIGH, 183
Local groups, functions of, 65
Local procedure call system, 11
Lock Workstation, 59
Logging on, 39–41
  bypassing logon procedure, 45
Logical disk drives, 250
  creation of, 252
Logs, 225–230
  bookmarks in log file, 227
  clearing logs, 247
  recording data, 225–227
  relogging, 229–230
  using data of log file, 228–229

M

Macros, and Doskey, 169–171
  creation of, 170
  removing macros, 170
  use at Command Prompt, 171
Mah Jong, 378
Mail, 55, 274–298
  accounts, adding of, 278
  Address Book, 280–281
  administration of Post Office, 294
  attaching data, 284
  automatic opening of, 279–280
  closing Mail, 295
  and common post office, 275

deleting messages, 286
embedding objects, 284
exporting folders, 290–291
folders for, 286–288
mailing lists, 291
menu options, 295–298
modification of operations, 293–294
moving messages, 286
moving Post Office, 294–295
opening Mail, 278–279
password, 278
printing messages, 292
reading mail, 284–285
renaming Post Office, 294–295
replying to messages, 285–286
saving messages, 288–289
searching for messages, 291–292
sending messages, 281–283
setting up, 275–277
terminals, adding of, 277–278
text files, creating from message, 288–289
undeliverable mail, 283
upgrading to Mail 3.2, 277
MD, 183
MD-DOS applications, running programs with
    Windows NT, 192–193
Media Player, 360–366
  changes to, 401
  configuration of
    device, 365
    Media Player, 364–365
  features of, 360–361
  marking selections, 362–363
  menu options, 365–366
  modification of scale, 362
  and Object Linking and Embedding, 363-364
  start up of, 361–362
M-Edit, 386
Melt, 391
MEM, 183
MicroEMACS, 378
Microsoft
  seminars/training, 376
  Technical Information Network, 376
MIDI JukeBox NT, 395
MIDI Mapper, 103
MKDIR, 183
MODE, 183
MONEY.BAS, 57
Money Manager, 57
MORE, 183
MortCalc, 378
MOVE, 183
MS-DOS
  commands available, 159–161
  commands not available, 161–162, 164–165
  configuration commands used in
    CONFIG.NT, 194

disk compression and NT, 19
DOS extender, 193
Doskey, 166–172
limitations of, 2
removing from system, 47
using with Windows NT, 18, 22–23
MSRMND32, 57, 307, 325
Multiprocessing
    symmetric multiprocessing, 7
    Windows NT, 7–8
Multitasking
    advantages of, 60–61
    dialog box, 92–93
    and File Manager, 128
    nonpreemptive multitasking, 7
    preemptive multitasking, 7
    Windows NT, 7–8

N

Native commands, 158
NBTSTAT, 183, 189
NET ACCOUNTS, 183
NET COMPUTER, 183
NET CONFIG, 183
NET CONFIG SERVER, 183
NET CONFIG WORKSTATION, 183
NET CONTINUE, 183
NET FILE, 184
NET GROUP, 184
NET HELP, 184
NET HELPMSG, 184
NET LOCALGROUP, 184
NET NAME, 184
NET PAUSE, 184
NET PRINT, 184
NET SEND, 184
NET SESS, 184
NET SESSION, 184
NET SHARE, 184
NET SHARE ALERTER, 184
NET START BROWSER, 184
NET START "COMPUTER BROWSER", 184
NET START "DIRECTORY REPLICATOR", 184
NET START EVENTLOG, 184
NET START LOCATOR, 184
NET START MESSENGER, 185
NET START NBT, 185
NET START NETLOGON, 185
NET START REPLICATOR, 185
NET START RPCSS, 185
NET START SCHEDULE, 185
NET START SERVER, 185
NET START SNMP, 185
NET START TCPIP, 185
NET START "TCPIP NET BIOS PROTOCOL", 185

NET START TELNET, 185
NET START WORK, 185
NET START WORKSTATION, 185
NETSTAT, 183, 189
NET STATISTICS, 185
NET STATS, 185
NET STOP, 185
NET TIME, 185
NET USE, 186
NET USER, 186
NET VIEW, 186
Network commands, 158
Network drive
    disconnecting, 126
    as home directory, 76
Networks
    accessing data on network, 124–126
    alerts, 273
    data sharing on, 121–124
        checking on file use, 123–124
        ending network sharing, 124
        sharing directories, 121–123
    dedicated-server network, 259
    directory replication, 271–272
    disconnecting network drive, 126
    distributed networking, 259
    domains
        characteristics of, 260
        domain-administered networking, 259
        domain controllers, 259
        installation of settings, 36–37
        joining domain, 264
    features of Windows NT, 11–12
    installation of NT from, 38–39
    installation of, 260–265
        configuration of software components, 262–263
        joining domain, 264
        joining workgroup, 263–264
        modification of network search order, 262
        network bindings, 264–265
        Network settings options, 260–261
        network software, 261–262
    log events on network computer, 247
    network-adapter configuration, 36
    printers, 149–150
        connecting to printer, 149
        selection of printers, 136–137
        sharing printers, 149–150
        using server viewer, 150
    server, 124, 259, 265–266
        making computer a server, 265–266
        memory requirements and auto start, 266
        server connections, control of, 266–270
        system resources, 266
        viewing resources in use, 268–270
    utilities
        Chat, 331–334

Networks (*cont'd*)
    ClipBook Viewer, 334–340
    Mail, 274–298
    Schedule+, 299–329
    workgroups
        characteristics of, 260
        installation of settings, 36–37
        joining workgroup, 263–264
    workstation, 124, 259, 273–274
        management of, 273–274
Nibbles, 57, 371
NLSFUNC, 186
Nonpreemptive multitasking, 7
Notebook utility, 387
Notepad, changes to, 401
NTBOOTDD.SYS, 45, 49
NTDETECT.COM, 45, 49
NTFS (NT File System), 5, 8, 11
    advantages and disadvantages of, 20
    converting from to FAT or HPFS, 48
    converting FAT and HPFS disk partitions to,
        47–48
    functions of, 11
    removal of, 48–49
NTLDR, 45, 49
NT native services, 5
Nutmeg-32, 378

O

Object Linking and Embedding, 6
    ClipBook Viewer, 338
    Media Player, 363–364
Object manager, 9
Object Packager, changes to, 401
OEMSETUP.INF, 262
Offline line, 317–318
Online files, 317–318
Operating systems
    and installation, keeping non-NT system,
        17–18, 22–23, 26
    removing non-NT systems, 47
Orientation, printing, 139
OS/2
    CONFIG.SYS commands, 200–201
    CONFIG.SYS file, commands of, 188
    removing from system, 47
    running programs with NT, 200–201
    using with Windows NT, 18, 22–23
Ownership
    of files and directories, 112–113
    of printer, 148

P

PAGEFILE.SYS, 45, 49
Page frame, 91
Paging, nature of, 91

Paging file, 37, 91–92
Paintbrush, changes to, 401
Paper Drop, 382
Parity striping, 256
Passwords, 13, 23–25
    of Administrator, 23
    case sensitivity, 24
    change password button, 59
    and creating user accounts, 73–74
    expiration of, 74
    forgetting passwords, solutions to, 79
    and installation, 37
    length of, 73
    Mail, 278
    password policies, changing of, 82–83
    tips for use of, 24–25
PATH, 186
PAUSE, 186
Performance Monitor, 54
    alerts, 221–224
    charts, 216–220
    customizing window of, 231
    exporting data from, 230–231
    logs, 225–230
    menu options of, 232–233
    reports, 224–225
    saving/reusing settings, 230
    setting parameters of, 216
    start-up of, 214–216
    toolbar buttons, 233
    types of files of, 215–216
    windows of, 214–215
Permissions
    assignment of, 117–118
    defining access permissions, 113–117
    guidelines related to, 119
    individual permissions, 114, 115–116
    nature of, 65, 77
    restriction of, 85
    setting up entire disk drive with, 120
    standard permissions, 114–115
Personal program groups, 56
PING, 186, 189
Planner, 309–310
Playlists, 359
POPD, 186
Portability, of Windows NT, 9–10
PORTUAS, 186
POSIX, 5, 19
Post office, Mail
    administration of, 294
    moving of, 294–295
    renaming of, 294–295
    See also Mail
Power failure, and uninterruptible power
        supply feature, 100–103
Power Users, 67, 71
    functions of, 70

Preemptive multitasking, 7
Primary partition, 250, 251
 creation of, 251
Prime 32, 378
PRINT, 186
Printer
 installation of, 36
 types of, 135
Print file, creation of, 136
Printing
 information about print job, 152–153
 messages, 292
 operations of printer window, 151
 printer profiles, modification of, 154
 from Schedule+, 319–321
 steps in, 150–151
Print Manager, 14
 forms, 146–147
 halftones, 140–142
 job defaults, changing of, 139
 menu options, 154–155
 networking printers, 149–150
  connecting to printer, 149
  selection of printer, 136–137
  sharing printers, 149–150
  using server viewer, 150
 opening of, 133
 printer details, 137–139
 printer driver, loading of, 143
 printers, creation of, 135–137
 printer settings, 142
 printer setup information, entering, 143–144
 printer window, use of, 133–134
 security, 147–149
  auditing printing, 148–149
  setting permissions, 147–148
  taking ownership, 148
 separator files, creation of, 144–146
 toolbar buttons, 134–135
Program groups
 common program groups, 56
 creating groups, 56
 personal program groups, 56
Program information files, 194–198, 402
 custom startup files, 198–199
 options used by Windows NT
  application shortcut keys, 198
  display usage, 196–197
  EMS memory/XMS memory, 196
  optional parameters, 195
  program filename, 194
  reserve shortcut keys, 197–198
  startup directory, 195–196
  window title, 194–195
PROGRAM.INI, 61
Program Manager, 13, 26
 Add Applications to Program Manager utility, 385
 Administrative Tools group, 54–55

getting to from other applications, 63
hidden applications for, 56–58
 DRWATSON.EXE, 57
 MSRMND32.EXE, 57
 QBASIC.EXE, 57
 REGEDIT, 56–57
 REGEDT32.EXE, 57
 SYSEDIT, 56
limiting access to features, 61–63
menu options, 63–64
new menu options, 53
program groups
 creating groups, 56
 personal program groups, 56
starting applications from, 60–61
Projects, 312
PROMPT, 186
Protected subsystems, 10
PROTOSHELL, 186, 188, 200
PrtSc, 197
PUSHD, 186
Puzzle-8 NT, 395

Q

QBASIC, 57, 186
QuickEdit, 177
 for cutting and pasting, 202

R

RAID5, 13, 256
RCALC NT, 388
RCP, 186, 189
RD, 186
Recorder, 55, 402
RECOVER, 186
Recycler, 382
REGEDIT/V, 56–57
REGEDT32.EXE, 44, 57, 61, 204
Registry Editor, 204–212
 advanced operations, 209–210
 configuration trees of, 205–207
 event logging, 240
 functions of, 204–205
 menu options, 210–212
 modification of entries of, 207–209
 opening of, 57
 running of, 204
 stopping access to, 43–44, 204
 structure of, 203
Relogging, 229–230
REM, 186
Reminder, Schedule+, 307–308
REMLINE.BAS, 57
REN, 186
RENAME, 187
REPLACE, 187

Replicators, functions of, 70
Reports, 224–225
    adding items to, 224–225
    deleting items, 225
    modification of sample interval option, 225
    pasting in application, 231
    using data of log file, 228–229
Resource account, Schedule+, 316–317
RESTORE, 187
REXEC, 187, 189
Rights
    advanced user rights, 81–82
    assignment to users, 79–82
    function of, 71, 77
    types of rights, 80–81
RISC-based computers, and installation, 26, 30
RMDIR, 187
ROUTE, 187, 189
RSH, 187, 189

S

Saving
    in Disk Administrator, 253
    in Event Viewer, 246
    in Performance Monitor, 230
Schedule+, 55, 299–329
    adding features to appointments, 306
    Appointments, dialog box, 301–304
    archiving data, 321–322
    closing, 325
    colors, modification of, 323
    defaults, setting defaults, 324–325
    deleting appointments, 308
    entering appointments, 305–306
    fonts, 324
    group-scheduling system, 314–316
        advantages of assistant, 316
        assigning assistant, 315
        types of access, 315
    importing data, 322–323
    menu options, 326–329
    messages, 304–304
    moving file to another computer, 318–319
    Notes box, 300
    offline and online files, 317–318
    Planner, 309–310
    printing reports, 319–321
    recurring appointments, creation of, 308–309
    reminder, 307–308
    resource account, 316–317
    sorting entries, 313
    start-up, 299–300
    Task List, 311–314
        assignment of time to tasks, 314
        editing tasks, 313–314
        missing tasks, 314
        projects, 312
        recurring tasks, 312–313
        removing tasks from list, 313
        viewing tasks, 313
    tasks, assignment of time to, 314
    use of another's data, 316
Screen
    colors, selection of, 175
    display mode, modification of, 175
    modification from command prompt window, 174–175
    running DOS applications, 196–197
Screen savers, 391
SCSI
    and CD-ROM drives, 18
    and interface with devices, 18
    SCSI adapters, and installation, 32
    and tape drives, 19, 342
Search order, network, 262
Security
    auditing security events, 84
    bypassing logon procedure, 45
    Change Password, 59
    ClipBook Viewer, 338
    deactivation of file access security, 121
    features of, 9
    File Manager, 111–120
    Lock Workstation, 59
    and NTFS (NT File System), 20
    printers, 147–149
        auditing printing, 148–149
        setting permissions, 147–148
        taking ownership, 148
    security log, creation of, 84
    and use of second operating system, 17
    viewing dialog box for, 58
Security events, defining types of, 237
Security identifier, 78
Separator files, creation of, 144–146
Serial ports, specifying for printer, 142
Server, 259
    See also Networks
Server Viewer, 150
Services, dialog box, 95–97
SET, 187, 201
SETLOCAL, 187
SETVER, 187
SHARE, 187
Shareware, listing of, 378–379, 386
SHELL, 187
SHIFT, 187
Shortcut key combinations
    application shortcut key, 198
    and DOS applications, 197
    types used by Windows NT, 197
Small computer standard interface. See entries under SCSI
Software, incompatibility and NT, 19
SORT, 187

Sorting, appointments, 313
Sound
    CD Player, 357–360
    dialog box, 95
    Media Player, 360–366
    MIDI JukeBox NT, 395
    Sound Recorder, 366–367
    volume control, 360
Sound Recorder, 366–367, 402
    features of, 366–367
    mixing sounds, 366–367
Spooks, 391
Stacker, 19
STACKS, 187
Standard permissions, 114–115
    for directories, 114–115
    for files, 115
START, 187
    starting application programs, 201–202
Starting NT, 42–43
    dialog box, 97–98
Startup files, defining custom files, 198–199
Stopwatch NT, 388
Stripe sets, creation of, 252–253
Structured exception handling, 8
SUBST, 187
Subsystem commands, 158
SWITCHES, 187
Switches, of programs, 195
Symmetric multiprocessing, 7
Synchronized queues, 8
SYSEDIT, 56
System, dialog box, 89–90
System configuration
    configuration structure, 204
    Registry Editor, 204–212
System Infor utility, 382
SYSTEM.INI, 56, 192

T

Talking Clock NT, 388
Tape backup
    and Administrators, 341
    automated backups, 352–353
    erasing tape, 351
    formatting tape, 351–352
    hard drive backup, 344–349
    initializing backup, 343–344
    installation
        hardware preparation, 342
        installation of driver, 342–343
    menu options, 354–355
    restoring data, 350–351
    toolbar buttons, 356
    utilities, 351–352
Tape drives
    non SCSI-drives, 19

and SCSI, 19, 342
Task List, 311–312
    creating new task, 311–312
    projects, 312
    starting applications from, 61
TCP/IP, 179
    utility commands, 159, 188–189
Technical Information Network, 376
TELNET, 188, 189
Template, of Doskey, 166, 169
Termination handlers, 8
TFTP, 188, 189
Thieves and Kings, 378, 392–393
TIME, 188
Time, setting, 38
Time and Money Tracker, 378
TITLE, 188
Toolbar, customization of, 106–108
Transaction logging, 8, 20
TrashMan, 378
TREE, 188
TYPE, 188

U

Unicode, 11
Uninterruptible power supply
    dialog box, 100–102
    functions of, 100–102
    testing of, 103
UPS interface, 14
User accounts, 72–77
User groups, 26
    functions of, 65, 70
User Manager, 9, 54
    assignment of rights to users, 79–82
    deleting information, 78–79
    dialog box options, 238
    disabling of, 85
    function of, 66
    groups, 65–66, 68–72
    menu for, 85–86
    modifying information, 77–78
    opening of, 237
    password policies, changing of, 82–83
    permissions to files/directories, restriction of,
        85
    security events, auditing of, 84
    user accounts, 72–77
Usernames
    changing, 77
    in creation of user accounts, 72
    examples of, 37
User profiles, removal of, 47
Utilities
    Add Applications to Program Manager, 385
    ANI Make, 385
    Astronomy Clock, 389

Utilities (*cont'd*)
  Astronomy Lab, 386
  Desktop+, 379–380
  Exit Windows NT, 382
  EXT Type, 381
  FExtend, 380–381
  File Viewer, 382
  FM Shell, 380
  4DOS, 384
  FracView NT, 394
  games, 392–393
  General Drop, 382
  Icon Manager, 384
  LI 32, 382–383
  M-Edit, 386
  MIDI JukeBox NT, 395
  networks
    Chat, 331–334
    ClipBook Viewer, 334–340
    Mail, 274–298
    Schedule+, 299–329
  Notebook, 387
  Paper Drop, 382
  Puzzle-8 NT, 395
  RECALC NT, 388
  Recycler, 382
  screen savers, 391
  shareware, listing of, 378–379, 386
  Stopwatch NT, 388
  System Info, 382
  Talking Clock, 388
  While You Were Out, 390
  WinExit, 383
  WinTach, 389–390

V

VER, 188
VERIFY, 188
Virtual DOS machine (VDM) Subsystem, 5
Virtual memory
  dialog box, 91–92
  set up of, 37–38
Virtual Memory Manager, 8
VOL, 188
Volume, marking as active, 254
Volume control, 55, 360
Volume sets
  creation of, 252
  extending of, 252

W

While You Were Out, 378, 390
Win32 Subsystem, 5
WinBatch, 378
Windows 3.1, 5, 6, 11

and placement of NT, 21
running programs with Windows NT, 192
Windows NT
  compatibility with other operating systems,
    5–6
  CompuServe forums, 373–376
  exiting NT, 41–42
  extensibility of, 10
  file system of, 11
  graphical user interface, 4–5
  hardware for, 14–15
  installation. See Installation of NT
  internal workings of, 373
  logging on, 39–41
  Microsoft seminars/training on, 376
  modification of, 46
  multiprocessing, 7–8
  multitasking, 7–8
  networking features, 11–12
  NTFS (NT File System), 5, 8, 11
  as operating system, 1–3
  performance of, 11
  portability of, 9–10
  reliability of, 8
  removal of, 48–49
  security system, 9
  shareware/software related for, 378–379
  startup of, 42–43
Windows NT Advanced Server, 12–13
  disk mirroring in, 256
  parity striping, 256
Windows NT Diagnostics, 57
Windows NT-J, 10
Windows NT Setup, 67, 402
  and future modifications, 46
  installation procedure, 34–38
WinEXIT, 383
WIN.INI, 56, 192
WinMod, 378
WINMSD.EXE, 57
WINNT, 34
WINNT/SYSTEM32, 44, 45, 103
WinTach, 389–390
WINVER, 188
Workgroup, 12, 260–261
  characteristics of, 260
  installation of settings/domain, 36–37
  joining of, 263–264
Working directory, 76, 176
Workstation, 259
  See also Networks
WOW (Windows on Windows NT), 6

X

XCOPY, 188
XMS memory, 196